the Illinois Story

"Illinois' Enterprises"
by Irene Macauley

Photo Research by William Recktenwald
and Kenan Heise

Sponsored by the State of Illinois
Illinois Department of Commerce and Community Affairs
Pam McDonough, Director
Brian Reardon, Manager of Communications, Information and Marketing

Illinois Publishing Group
Zion, Illinois

the Illinois Story

The State's History and Competitive Edge Today

By Kenan Heise, William Recktenwald, and David M. Young

In memory of

Myrtle Sullivan Toohey

1900-1985

Special thanks to the Illinois State Historical Library
for their generous support of this project.

Illinois Publishing Group
Publisher Don Toohey
Director of Sales C. David Turner

Editor Karen Story
Photo Editor Doug O'Rourke
Editorial Assistant Kathy B. Peyser
Indexer Teri Davis Greenberg
Designer Ellen Ifrah

Library of Congress Control Number: 2001132830
ISBN: 0-9711780-0-3

Right: Photo © Mark Segal/Index Stock Imagery

Page 2/3: Photo © Mark Segal/Index Stock Imagery

Page 12: © 2000 *Chicago: As It Was,* published by Currier and Ives/The Bridgeman Art Library

Page 116: Photo © Paula Bronstein/Stone

Page 238: Photo © Vic Bider/Index Stock Imagery

Endsheets: Photo © Tim Bieber/The Image Bank

 228

Contents

Governor's Message · **9**

Introduction ·**10**

PART ONE **Illinois' Historical Heritage**
by Kenan Heise and William Recktenwald

CHAPTER ONE
From the South Up · **15**

Louis Jolliet and Father Jacques Marquette, the first European explorers to visit Illinois, traveled by canoe down through Wisconsin rivers to the Mississippi and returned north on the Illinois River toward Chicago. In 1818, when Illinois gained statehood, its capital was Kaskaskia. Two years later the seat of government was moved north to Vandalia, then the western terminus of the National Road. Abraham Lincoln, who came to Central Illinois from Southern Indiana, was seen as a "Westerner" when he assumed the presidency in 1860 and led the country and tens of thousands of Illinois volunteers in the effort to save the Union.

CHAPTER TWO
Chicago and the Prairies Find a Port · **51**

Indians, explorers, and fur-traders used the portage at Chicago by paddling, pushing, or pulling their canoes and bateaux down the Chicago River and through Mud Lake to establish a link between the Great Lakes and the Mississippi Valley. During the nineteenth century this connection would create the fastest-growing city and one of the great urban areas of the world. Through the succeeding decades, Chicago would continue to change by its incredible resources and adapting to technological opportunities.

CHAPTER THREE
Northern Illinois Comes Into Its Own · **89**

The state's first rail line was started at Meredosia in 1838 and reached Springfield 59 miles away in 1842. Within the next few generations railroads were built that crisscrossed Illinois, making Chicago and the state the crossroads of the nation for rail travel. The Illinois Industrial University, one of the country's first land grant colleges, was established at Urbana in 1867. It is now known as the University of Illinois. During World War I more than 350,000 Illinoisians served in the armed forces. In World War II that number was almost double at 670,000.

PART TWO **Illinois' Robust Economy Today**
by David M. Young

CHAPTER FOUR
From Hog Butcher to Pork Bellies Trader · **119**

Carl Sandburg's "city of big shoulders" developed deft hands and a quick mind as it adapted to meet the challenges of the telecommunications and computer age. The old smokestack industries are still around; they're just not as big as they used to be. The surviving companies—as well as the new ones—have tended to become national or global in scope in order to survive and prosper.

This page, top to bottom:
Photo © Bruce Leighty/Index Stock Imagery;
Photo © Scott Berner/Index Stock Imagery

Facing page, top to bottom:
Photo © Terri Froelich/Index Stock Imagery;
Photo © 2000 Mark Segal/Stone;
Photo © Omni Photo/Index Stock Imagery

CHAPTER FIVE

Outgrowing the City · **169**

Two hundred years ago the region's principal industry was beaver pelts. Then it became lead, and finally agriculture. Today agriculture remains important, and there is also a tremendous amount of manufacturing in the more than 250 communities that encircle Chicago. By the 1990s the suburbs could claim that collectively they housed more corporate headquarters of major companies than did Chicago.

CHAPTER SIX

Land of Lincoln and Soybeans · **197**

The state has changed dramatically since Charles Dickens visited in the 1840s and complained about the heat, mud, and mosquitoes. Illinois has a world-class symphony orchestra, highly respected universities, an expanded park system, and eclectic museums with collections that rival all others.

Epilogue · **230**

PART THREE **Illinois' Enterprises**
by Irene Macauley

CHAPTER SEVEN

Manufacturing and High Technology · **241**

Illinois' central location and qualified work force attract global manufacturers and high-technology industries to the state.

Archer Daniels Midland, 242-245; Motorola, Inc., 246-249; Deere & Company, 250-251; FMC Corporation, 252-253; Sara Lee Corporation, 254-255; A. M. Castle & Co., 256-257; The Boeing Company, 258; Caterpillar Inc., 259

CHAPTER EIGHT

Business and Finance · **261**

Business and financial institutions, accounting firms, and computer technology combine to put some impressive numbers on Illinois' ledgers.

Heller Financial, Inc., 262-263; Bank One, N.A, 264-265; Carr Futures, 266-267; CNA Financial Corporation, 268; Safeway Insurance Group, 269

CHAPTER NINE

Networks and Professions · **271**

An integral part of the state's infrastructure, the communications, transportation, and professional communities provide a wealth of vital services, expertise, and insight.

Graycor, 272-273; International Profit Associates, Inc., 274-275; Suburban Chicago Newspapers, 276-277; Accenture, 278; Chicago Defender, 279; Daniel J. Edelman, Inc., 280; Jordan Industries, Inc., 281; Amtrak, 282-283

CHAPTER TEN

Labor Unions and Contractors' Associations · 285

Historically the champions of workers' rights, the state's labor unions continue to help improve the quality of life and work for their members.

IBEW Local 134 and Electrical Contractors' Association, 286-289; Chicago Journeymen Plumbers' Local Union 130 UA, 290-291; Plumbing Contractors Association of Chicago and Cook County, 292; Plumbing Council of Chicagoland, 293; United Brotherhood of Carpenters and Joiners of America, 294-295; Chicago and Northeast Illinois District Council of Carpenters, 296-297; International Union of Operating Engineers, Local 399, 298-299; Architectural and Ornamental Iron Workers Local 63, 300-301; International Brotherhood of Teamsters Joint Council 25, 302-303; United Union of Roofers, Waterproofers and Allied Workers Local 11, 304-305; Painters' District Council #14, 306-307; International Association of Heat and Frost Insulators and Asbestos Workers Union Local 17 and the Illinois Regional Contractors Association, 308

CHAPTER ELEVEN

Quality of Life · 311

Medical and educational institutions contribute to the exceptional quality of life enjoyed by Illinois residents and visitors.

Abbott Laboratories, 312-315; Loyola University Chicago, 316-317; Illinois Institute of Technology, 318-319; Robert Morris College, 320-321; Blue Cross and Blue Shield of Illinois, 322-323; DeVry Inc., 324-325; Museums In the Park, 326-330; Hots Michels Enterprises for Organ Donor Awareness, 331; Children's Memorial Hospital, 332

CHAPTER TWELVE

The Modern Marketplace · 335

The state's retail and dining establishments, service industries, products, and convention facilities offer an impressive variety of choices for Illinoisians and visitors alike.

Illinois Department of Commerce and Community Affairs, 336-339; Sears, Roebuck and Co., 340-343; Ace Hardware Corporation, 344-345; Jewel-Osco, 346; Galileo International, 347; The Spiegel Group, 348-349; Chicago Convention and Tourism Bureau/Metropolitan Pier and Exposition Authority, 350-351; Corporate Travel Management Group, 352-353; Cardwell and Randall Enterprises, LLC, 354-355; Gibsons Bar and Steakhouse, 356; J&B Signs, 357

About Illinois Publishing Group · 358

Notes on Sources · 359

Acknowledgments · 359

County Map of Illinois · 360

Directory of Corporate Sponsors · 361

Index · 363

This page, top to bottom:
Photo © Kathleen Kliskey-Geraghty/Index Stock
Imagery; Photo © 2000 Doris De Witt/Stone

OFFICE OF THE GOVERNOR
JRTC, 100 West Randolph, Suite 16
Chicago, Illinois 60601

GEORGE H. RYAN
GOVERNOR

Dear Reader:

On behalf of the residents of Illinois, I am pleased to introduce the *Illinois Story*.

The story of Illinois is a reflection of the story of America. Founded by pioneers and built by immigrants, our great state has evolved into a global center for commerce and has become the crossroads of North America. Illinois is a rich tapestry of culture and geography, where skyscrapers soar to the clouds and where some of the Earth's most fertile soil provides nourishment for the world.

The history of Illinois includes the courageous leadership of Abraham Lincoln, the vision of Frank Lloyd Wright and the insight of Carl Sandburg. In our state, ideas were born that changed the world. It's where nuclear fission and the Web browser were created. Today, the people of Illinois are developing new innovations that will change how we work and live.

I'm proud to present the *Illinois Story* as a record of the accomplishments and contributions the people of Illinois have made to mankind. I'm confident you'll enjoy learning about our great state in the following pages and hope the discoveries you make will lead you to explore in person all that Illinois has to offer... *Right Here. Right Now.*

Sincerely yours,

GEORGE H. RYAN
Governor

Introduction

Long before humankind recorded history on paper or with symbols etched in rock, a series of events profoundly changed the nearly 57,000 square miles that comprise the state of Illinois. More than 60 million years ago glaciers started molding the land into its unique configuration.

Today Illinois is a rich tapestry of the nation's midsection. While Chicago, Southern Illinois, and Northern Illinois—its three major regions—have distinct characteristics and crucial differences, the state has time and again provided leadership and influence to the nation and the world.

It was here that atomic power was harnessed, that free public education for all was launched. Its vast prairies were broken, plowed, and then harvested with the tools of its inventors. Illinois is home to the companies that produce farming and earth-moving equipment used around the world.

The state is a nucleus of commerce by rail, road, air, and river. From its earliest history it has been a leader in each of these modes of transportation. Its largest public works project of the nineteenth century was the building of a rail system, while statewide roads were constructed early in the twentieth century and major airports during the rest of the century.

Illinoisians were key to the development of the Wright brothers' first powered aircraft, and tens of thousands of airmen trained at its airfields during the world wars. A complex system of canals and locks on the Illinois river system provides a water highway for bulk items, from corn to coal and from sand to soybeans.

The state set an example for the nation by enacting laws to assure safe working conditions. It spearheaded civil service, occupational disease laws, workmen's compensation insurance, minimum wages, and child labor laws. Illinois established separate courts for juveniles in the early 1900s.

Illinois pioneered women's rights, allowing the vote in some elections as early as 1891, and tied with two other states to be first in ratifying the nineteenth amendment affording women the right to vote. It also elected the third woman to serve in the U.S. House of Representatives and the only African-American woman to serve in the U.S. Senate.

The land of Abraham Lincoln, Illinois provided leadership at the nation's most precarious time, when its Civil War was waged, not against a common enemy, but between its own states.

Illinois was the first to ratify the 13th Amendment prohibiting slavery, and the first to vote in favor of the 24th Amendment prohibiting poll taxes, enabling more citizens a voice in elections.

Illinois has given us modern architecture, *Poetry Magazine*, improvisational theater, and such writers as Vachel Lindsay, Ernest Hemingway, Gwendolyn Brooks, Mike Royko, Studs Terkel, Carl Sandburg, Edgar Lee Masters, and Saul Bellow.

In the following chapters we will explore each of the three regions of Illinois from the earliest times to the twenty-first century.

PART ONE

Illinois' Historical Heritage

by Kenan Heise and William Recktenwald

CHAPTER ONE

From the South Up

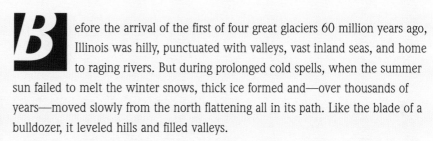

Before the arrival of the first of four great glaciers 60 million years ago, Illinois was hilly, punctuated with valleys, vast inland seas, and home to raging rivers. But during prolonged cold spells, when the summer sun failed to melt the winter snows, thick ice formed and—over thousands of years—moved slowly from the north flattening all in its path. Like the blade of a bulldozer, it leveled hills and filled valleys.

The Kansan and Nebraskan glaciers were the first to push through parts of the state and during their slow retreat left deposits of rich soils carried from farther north. The surface materials left by the glaciers, called drift, vary from a few feet to 500 feet in thickness. The massive meltwater generated as the glaciers retreated helped to carve great rivers—the Mississippi, Illinois, and Ohio.

The Illinois Glacier arrived, geologists estimate, 300,000 years ago. It covered 90 percent of what is now the state for which it was named, extending south to a line roughly marked by Illinois Highway 13. The southernmost seven counties of Illinois, an area of gentle hills, rock outcroppings, high bluffs, and unique rock formations, were not covered. The area that escaped the ravages of the Illinois Glacier is today called the Shawnee Hills. The far northwest corner of the state, Jo Daviess County, is also unglaciated, as is Calhoun County at the confluence of the Illinois and Mississippi rivers.

Left: This artist's rendering of Father Jacques Marquette and Louis Jolliet traveling down the Mississippi in 1673 is somewhat fanciful, considering the dangers of standing in a canoe. Courtesy, Illinois State Historical Library

The final icy visitor, which arrived a mere 50,000 to 15,000 years ago, almost yesterday in geological terms, was the Wisconsin Glacier. It extended about halfway down the state, as far as Mattoon and Peoria. It left behind the rich fertile lands of the Illinois River Valley and Lake Michigan, a 23,000-square-mile inland sea carved by the melting ice.

Once the glaciers receded, the region became a vast prairie. While Illinois is 378 miles in length and 212 miles wide, its elevation varies by barely less than 1,000 feet. Its drainage system is 275 rivers, all of which flow gently, devoid of waterfalls, white water, or thundering rapids. These waterways connect to form an extensive network used by early settlers and later for commerce.

During dry periods after the retreat of the Wisconsin Glacier, a thick fertile layer of topsoil was carried by the wind and covered much of the state. Many areas are covered with five to 10 feet of the fertile loess. In some areas it is more than 20 feet in depth.

The promise of Illinois also lies beneath its surface. Sedimentary bedrock layers, primarily limestone and

The distributions of the major Illinois tribes in 1800 are shown in this map. Courtesy, Illinois State Historical Library

sandstone, are relatively flat and contain multiple layers of valuable minerals. Bituminous coal underlays more than half the state. Lead ore is found near Galena in the northwest and the nation's largest deposits of fluorite are in Hardin County in the southeast corner of the state.

Oil and gas deposits are found throughout Central and Eastern Illinois, and the earliest settlers used evaporation to produce salt along the Saline River in Gallatin County.

Illinois is bordered mainly by water. On its west is the Mississippi River, to the south and east the Ohio and Wabash rivers, and Lake Michigan on the northeast. Of Illinois' 1,160 miles of border just 305 miles are not naviga-

ble waters. Its river system is a keystone in the drainage of North America. Rainfall on any of 23 states will pass through Illinois as it travels to the sea.

The Arrival of Humankind

The first human inhabitants of Illinois likely came from Asia, crossing from Siberia to Alaska and traveling through Canada more than 10,000 years ago.

These prehistoric peoples, known as Paleo-Indians, gathered edible plants and hunted the mastodonic animals they lived among. Evidence of their culture has been found in many places along streams and rivers, but one of the most significant discoveries was the Modoc site, under an overhanging rock ledge above the Mississippi River in Randolph County. It is believed to be the oldest continuous site of human habitation in North America. In 1932 students from the University of Chicago found artifacts that were scientifically determined, using a radioactive dating process, to be about 8,000 years old.

After about 2000 B.C. a new epoch began. Known as the Woodland period, it included the making of ceramics and the cultivation of plants. Eastern Woodland period Indians lived in villages that were orderly and included elaborate burial rituals. This culture, called Hopewellian, reached its peak in the millennium after 500 B.C., but by A.D. 500 the society had faded. Scientists theorize that the Hopewellian people began to live in larger groups and discontinued construction of the burial mounds that so clearly defined their culture.

By A.D. 900 the highly sophisticated Mississippian culture flourished near the Wabash, Ohio, Illinois, and Mississippi rivers.

The Cahokia Mounds

The Hopewellian and Mississippian

This artist's conception illustrates what a native village looked like in the 1700s. Courtesy, Illinois State Historical Library

peoples buried their dead in large earthen mounds. Monks Mound, near Cahokia just outside East St. Louis, is the largest prehistoric earthwork in North America. It is 100 feet high, 1,080 feet long, and more than 700 feet wide. The truncated pyramid covers 16 acres. It is estimated that 20,000 individuals lived at Cahokia at its peak. The area has been designated by the United Nations as a historic site and is maintained by the Illinois Historic Preservation Agency.

Other traces of the Mississippian culture can be found in such places as Rim Rock in Gallatin County, where a rock escarpment thrusts nearly 100 feet from the surrounding countryside. At one end of this plug of earth are the remains of a stone wall that clearly served as a fortification for those who lived on top of Rim Rock. Southern Illinois has more of these mysterious Indian walls than any other state.

Thousands of small burial mounds that line the Illinois River come from the Woodland and Middle Mississippian eras.

The Illinois Tribes

Among historic Indians, the Illinois Confederation, also called Illiniwek, consisted of six tribes: the Cahokia, Kaskaskia, Michigamea, Moingwena, Peoria, and Tamoroa. Also closely related to the Illiniwek were the Miami, who for a time inhabited an area just south of Chicago. The Illiniwek often battled the Iroquois and later local tribes such as the Potawatomi. There were other tribes as well: the Algonquian, Chippewa, Ottawa, Sauk, Fox, Winnebago, Kickapoo, Piankashaw, and the Shawnee.

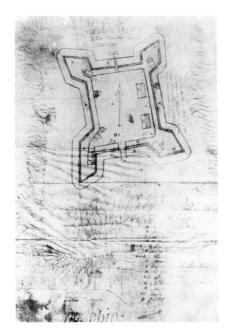

Above: The French built Fort Massac on the Ohio River opposite the mouth of the Tennessee River. In 1745 plans were made for a large stone fortification, but a smaller wooden fort was constructed in 1747. This photograph of the original plan for the fort was used when the state built a replica in what became Illinois' first state park, dedicated in 1908. Courtesy, Illinois State Historical Library

Right: George Rogers Clark and a small group of soldiers crossed Illinois in the winter to surprise British troops at Fort Sackville in Indiana in 1779. Believing that Clark's force was much larger than it was, the British surrendered. Courtesy, Illinois State Historical Library

Modern Illinois has frequent reminders of its historic Indian tribes. The state itself, as well as six counties—Iroquois, Kankakee, Macoupin, Peoria, Wabash, and Winnebago—all carry Indian names. Literally scores of towns and villages throughout the state bear names derived from these tribes.

The size of the native population is chronicled by French explorer René-Robert Cavelier, sieur de La Salle, who wrote in 1680 that a village of the Kaskaskia on the Illinois River near Lake Peoria had 460 lodges, each housing several families. He reported that annual tribal assemblies were attended by 6,000 to 8,000 people.

The First Europeans

The first European explorers to visit Illinois came by canoe across Wisconsin rivers to the Mississippi. Louis Jolliet, a young Canadian who had studied in France, and Father Jacques Marquette, a Jesuit priest who came from France in 1666, left St. Ignace at the Mackinac Straits on May 17, 1673.

Jolliet, 27, was an excellent mapmaker, and the gentle priest, Marquette, 35, had mastered several Algonquian tongues. Jolliet and Marquette, along with five boatmen and a supply of food, set out on Lake Michigan, down Green Bay to the Fox River. Friendly natives showed them a

portage to the Wisconsin River and the explorers were soon passing the bluffs of Jo Daviess County as they headed south on the Mississippi River.

Once past the unglaciated area, the men marveled at the great expanse of flat land as they continued south. The party continued on past the Ohio River, far enough to determine that the Mississippi continued to the Gulf of Mexico and was not a route to the Orient.

Catholic Missionaries Arrive

In 1699 Catholic priests from the Seminary of Foreign Missions established the Mission of the Holy Family at Cahokia. Four years later the Jesuits moved their Mission of the Immaculate Conception, which had been founded in 1675 near what is now Peoria, to Kaskaskia 60 miles south of Cahokia.

The Mississippi River villages began to boom about 1720, at the same time that New Orleans did. The French built Fort de Chartres 15 miles upstream from Kaskaskia and it soon became the seat of French military power in Illinois.

Illinois and the French

In 1727 the fort was destroyed by a flood but then rebuilt in stone, with three-foot-thick and 15-foot-high walls enclosing an area of about four acres. It was said to be one of the strongest fortifications in the New World. Today Fort de Chartres is maintained by the Illinois Historic Preservation Agency as a historic site, and during the first full weekend in June it comes alive with visitors celebrating the fur-trading era.

Nearby the pastoral village of Prairie du Rocher became Illinois' third most important early settlement. Along the Ohio River opposite the mouth of the Tennessee River, the French constructed Fort Massac in 1747. These settlements and traders

George Rogers Clark, 1752-1818, stood six feet tall, had red hair, and wore a rugged look. At age 22 he served as a militia captain fighting the Shawnee. Later he led settlers to Kentucky and then formed a militia to defend the frontier. His bold military actions during the Revolutionary War won claims to the area west of the Alleghenies for the colonies. He led a small contingent that seized Fort Kaskaskia from the British without firing a shot and captured Fort Sackville in 1779. He retired to a cabin near Clarksville, Indiana, and suffered a stroke that required amputation of a leg, which was done without anesthetic. His brother, William, was the noted explorer of the Lewis and Clark team. In 1936 President Franklin Roosevelt dedicated a monument to commemorate the battle of Fort Sackville, saying of Clark, "With a flash of genius the 26-year-old leader conceived a campaign that was a brilliant masterpiece of military strategy."

Illustration courtesy, Illinois State Historical Library

were spread very thinly over a vast area of the Midwest.

When the British declared war on France in 1756, the Mississippi Valley French played practically no role in what was called the French and Indian War. Battles were centered in Ohio and to the east. The British captured Quebec and Montreal in 1763, and all French territory east of the Mississippi except New Orleans was ceded to Great Britain.

Battles with the Indian leader Pontiac, chief of the Ottawa, started the same year the war ended and delayed British occupation of Illinois. Pontiac and his warriors fought vigorously, if unsuccessfully, against white encroachment.

The Coming of the British

It took Captain Thomas Stirling until October 10, 1765, to make his way with 100 men of the 42nd Highlanders Regiment, the Black Watch, to Fort de Chartres. The following day the French garrison was relieved, the fleur-de-lis lowered, and the soldiers crossed to Mississippi headed to a new post, Fort St. Louis 60 miles to the north. France had secretly ceded the area west of the Mississippi to Spain in the Treaty of Fontainebleau in 1762. It would be re-ceded to France in 1800 and then sold to the United States by Napoleon three years later.

At Fort Kaskaskia, the townspeople burned their fort rather than have it occupied by the British. French power in the Americas had for all practical purposes come to an end.

Although the British proclaimed in 1763 that no white settlers would live west of the crest of the Allegheny Mountains, the order was widely ignored as Tennessee, Kentucky, and far Southern Illinois began to see more settlers arrive.

The American Revolution and Illinois

Meanwhile, the British manned a small garrison at Kaskaskia, but at the outbreak of the American Revolution Captain Hugh Lord and his British troops were ordered to move from Kaskaskia to Detroit.

When white settlers moved on to Indian hunting grounds, violence became commonplace as natives and the new arrivals inevitably clashed. By the end of 1776 many settlers had retreated back to the East while others took refuge in a few stockaded forts.

American Forces Arrive in Illinois

In 1777 a Virginian named George Rogers Clark was authorized by Patrick Henry, first governor of the Commonwealth of Virginia, to form seven companies of 50 men each to protect the new frontier west of the Alleghenies. Clark believed the British at Detroit were instigating the Indian attacks. But first Clark wanted to capture Fort Kaskaskia.

The immediate difficulty Clark encountered was that he could only enlist 175 men, half the number authorized. He went by keelboat on the Ohio River from Louisville to Fort Massac. Anticipating that Philippe de Rocheblave, the British agent now in charge at Kaskaskia, would expect an attack by water, Clark and his men made a difficult six-day march from Fort Massac to Kaskaskia.

On July 4, 1778, Clark and his men arrived at Kaskaskia and took control from its meager defenders without firing a shot. On December 9, 1778,

James P. McFarlan, 1776-1837, was an early

Illinois settler who came from North Carolina to Elizabethtown in 1808. He took over operations of a ferry that transported people across the Ohio River from Kentucky in 1812 and constructed a 24- by 24-foot brick tavern overlooking the river. McFarlan was a captain in the local Big Creek militia and served as the postmaster of McFarlan's Ferry when it opened in 1830. The town was renamed for McFarlan's wife, Elizabeth. A meal at McFarlan's Tavern was 25 cents, a half pint of whiskey or a quart of beer cost 12 cents, and lodging was also 12 cents a night.

the Virginia government created the County of Illinois.

A Bold March, a Great Bluff, and a British Defeat

Late in 1778 additional British troops from Detroit came to Fort Sackville at Vincennes, Indiana, just across the Wabash from Illinois. With winter approaching, the British at Vincennes discharged their Indian allies, as they did not anticipate any attack by Clark until spring.

When Clark heard this news he marched out of Kaskaskia on February 5, 1779, for a dangerous and very difficult march across Illinois. Much of the 160-mile area was flooded and the troops suffered greatly during their journey.

On February 24 Clark and his men opened fire on the British post. The stunned British, seeing half a dozen of the new United States flags flying in the distance, thought Clark's force was much larger than it actually was. The British surrendered the following day. Clark, almost single-handedly, had won the western phase of the Revolutionary War.

In May 1779 John Todd, newly named as county lieutenant, arrived at Kaskaskia. He had been appointed by the governor of Virginia to establish courts in the area.

The area became known as the American Bottom, to distinguish it from the Spanish Territory west of the Mississippi. In 1780 the British came down the Mississippi for a final attack on Cahokia but were repelled. The County of Illinois lasted just three years before the Virginia government realized it could not support an area so far removed. For the next eight years Illinois struggled in near anarchy.

The Northwest Territory

On July 13, 1787, an ordinance organizing "a territory of the United States

northwest of the river Ohio" was adopted. It provided a system of government that included a governor, a secretary, and three judges. This Northwest Ordinance provided that when the population of free men of full age reached 5,000 they could elect a House of Representatives and that owners of 50 or more acres could vote.

General Arthur St. Clair, commander of the army after the American Revolution, was named the territorial governor and arrived in Kaskaskia on March 5, 1790. His arrival ended the period of anarchy. St. Clair County, covering about a quarter of the state and encompassing all or part of 31 modern counties, was established. To facilitate the administration of the courts, St. Clair County was divided in October 1795 with its southern third becoming Randolph County.

The Cavern of Crime

Settlers heading to the new territory faced dangers from Indians as well as from gangs of bandits. Among the most notorious was a group who inhabited a large cave in a bluff on the Ohio River. In 1797 a man named Samuel Mason advertised "A Liquor Vault and House of Entertainment" to pioneers coming down the Ohio near Cave-in-Rock. He

Above: Shadrach Bond, a native of Maryland, became the Illinois Territory's representative to Congress in 1812. He settled near Kaskaskia and when Illinois became a state in 1818, Bond was named its first governor. He later became the keeper of the land office in Kaskaskia, Illinois' first capital. Courtesy, Illinois State Historical Library

Right: This artist's drawing depicts the swearing in of Shadrach Bond as the first governor of Illinois at the state capitol in Kaskaskia. Courtesy, Illinois State Historical Library

robbed many before he moved on, only to be replaced by the Harpe Brothers, Micajah and Wiley, who came from North Carolina and were known for their wanton cruelty that often ended in the execution of unwary travelers.

Several ferries began operating on the Ohio in the mid-1790s at Cave-in-Rock, Elizabethtown, Golconda, and Massac. Those using James Ford's ferry at Cave-in-Rock often were robbed, or worse. Soon settlers heading west on the Ohio were warned to stay midstream from Shawneetown to Fort Massac. The only remaining Ohio River ferry still operates at Cave-in-Rock but it is known today for its congenial operators.

Protestant Clergy Arrive

The end of the 1700s saw the arrival of Protestant clergy in the territory. Elder Daniel Badgley, a Baptist, established a 28-member church in 1796. A Baptist association was formed by 1807 with five churches, four ministers, and 111 members. The first Methodist minister, the Reverend Joseph Lillard, arrived in 1793.

In 1800 the Northwest Territory was divided and Illinois became part of the Territory of Indiana, which at the time covered the modern states of Illinois, Indiana, Wisconsin, and most of Michigan as well as part of Minnesota.

The 1800 census showed that

Illinois had 2,458 residents. These were clustered in a few villages along the Mississippi, with 90 people in the area of Fort Massac and about 100 Frenchmen carrying on a fur trade at Peoria. Roads were little more than trails. Each settlement of consequence was along a navigable stream.

The Territory of Illinois

On February 3, 1809, Congress created the Territory of Illinois with its capital designated as Kaskaskia. It included all of modern Illinois, Wisconsin, and a portion of Minnesota.

Overland trails were beginning to be used in the far southern part of Illinois. Some of these were the paths used by buffalo as they migrated. George Rogers Clark had blazed a trail from Fort Massac to Kaskaskia in the 1770s. Later Stephen Miles led a group of settlers who arrived on flatboats on the Ohio River. Miles and his group carefully marked a trail from Elizabethtown to Kaskaskia.

The route, called Miles Trace, was designated for a time as a boundary between early counties. It ran northwest about where today's Highway 34

Shawneetown is shown in this postcard with streets filled and business thriving. The city was devastated so often by the spring floods along the Ohio River that most of its residents moved after the 1937 flood to higher ground a few miles west. Courtesy, Gordon Pruett

Above: Before Illinois became a state, Shawneetown was one of the first places that settlers traveling on the Ohio River would encounter. Courtesy, Gordon Pruett

Below: Once a thriving Ohio River town, Shawneetown was home to this impressive structure that housed the City National Bank. The Illinois Historic Preservation Agency now owns the building. Courtesy, Gordon Pruett

is located, then west near Marion to Kaskaskia. Clark's trail, Miles Trace, and a path from Shawneetown converged west of Marion at Bainbridge's Tavern.

In 1803, when the United States obtained the vast area west of the Mississippi from France in the Louisiana Purchase, it meant that Illinois was no longer the western border of the fledgling United States of America.

In 1812 Illinois was granted status as a territory of the second class, which meant that free white males who were landowners, paid their taxes, and were over 21 had the right to vote. In October 1812 Shadrach Bond was elected as the Illinois delegate to Congress.

First Government Land Offices

U.S. land offices were established at Kaskaskia and Vincennes in 1804. With a minimum down payment of $160, a man could purchase a section of land (640 acres) for two dollars an acre. At first the minimum purchase was half a section, but later it was changed to a quarter section.

The basic method used in dividing the land was the township and range

system. It had begun where Pennsylvania, Ohio, and West Virginia meet at the Ohio River when the Land Ordinance of 1785 was passed. The system was simple and worked particularly well on the vast prairies of Illinois. Each township was six miles square, and contained 36 one-mile-square numbered sections.

The third primary meridian ran north and south at approximately 89 degrees 10 minutes west and, serving as a base line, virtually split the state in two. An east-to-west divider crossed the state just south of Centralia. Using the township and range system it was possible for surveyors to write a precise description of a piece of property so that it could not be confused with any other.

The War of 1812

The War of 1812 pitted the new United States against Britain, affecting Illinois primarily through the Indians who were allied with the British. Tecumseh, the leader of the Shawnee, died on October 5, 1813, in the battle of the Thames River near Moraviantown, Ontario. The war ended on December 24, 1814. But the threat of marauding Indians was so great in Illinois that a $50 bounty was offered for the death of any Indian "who entered a settlement with murderous intent."

In 1808 James McFarlan had arrived in Elizabethtown and took over an Ohio River ferry that had been operating for more than a decade. In 1812 he built a tavern and hotel high on a rocky point with a commanding view of the river.

In time, two additions were completed to McFarlan's 24- by 24-foot tavern and hotel. In 1830 a post office was opened at McFarlan's Ferry and a few years later it was renamed after McFarlan's wife, Elizabeth. In the late

Tecumseh, **1768-1813,** a chief of the Shawnee, devoted himself to uniting various tribes to resist the advance of the American frontier. He had allied himself with the British, who promised to support Indian claims for land. Tecumseh died during a battle of the War of 1812 in Canada just a few miles east of Detroit. Tecumseh, who nearly always dressed in simple deerskin, was the leader of many tribes, not just the Shawnee. He met with Indiana territorial Governor William Henry Harrison in 1810 and told him, "It is true I am Shawnee. My forefathers were warriors. Their son is a warrior. From my tribe I take nothing. I am the maker of my own fortune. Once (we) were a happy race. Now (we) are made miserable by the white people who are never contented but always encroaching…the only way to stop this evil is for all the red men to unite…" Harrison yielded nothing to Tecumseh, who soon joined with the British.

Illustration courtesy, Illinois State Historical Library

1800s Sara Rose bought it and changed the name to hers. When the Rose Hotel closed for a time in the late twentieth century it had been the state's longest-operating hotel.

In 1998-1999 the Illinois Historic Preservation Agency restored the

---

Daniel Pope Cook, 1794-1827, had been a frail child who was often sickly but never failed to muster a smile. He moved to Kaskaskia at age 20. With the help of his uncle, Nathaniel Pope, with whom he studied law, Cook became auditor of public accounts for the Illinois Territory. In 1817 he purchased the *Illinois Herald* and later moved to Washington, D.C., where he was a courier. On a voyage back from England he befriended John Quincy Adams. Cook returned to Illinois to agitate for statehood through his newspaper and as the clerk of the territorial assembly. He was the second man elected to Congress from Illinois, serving as the chairman of the ways and means committee. He was reelected three times. After a defeat in 1826 he served a brief stint in Cuba as a diplomat. As his health deteriorated he returned to Illinois and later to Kentucky. Cook County, which he apparently never visited, is named for him.

---

hotel, which had been added to the National Register of Historic Places in 1972. Before proceeding with the restoration, the Center of Archaeological Investigations at Southern Illinois University examined the site. Prehistoric artifacts, including pots and crude cooking utensils from 2,000 years ago, were found in the area, along with food storage pits and other evidence of a substantial Woodland Indian settlement.

Today the restored Rose Hotel is in business again, with a concessionaire running the five-room bed and breakfast for the state.

Statehood, After a Questionable Count

Illinois statehood came in 1818. It was urged by two men, a youthful and precocious Daniel Pope Cook, who found work in federal service, and his uncle Nathaniel Pope, the newly elected delegate to Congress from the territory.

Young Cook was a part owner of the *Illinois Herald*, founded in 1814 by Matthew Duncan. Cook changed the paper's name to the *Illinois Intelligencer* and crusaded for statehood. When he became clerk of the territorial assembly in Kaskaskia he found himself in a position to influence the legislation needed.

A census of the proposed state was short of the required 40,000 residents. Some manipulation of the numbers by Cook and other officials was made and the enabling legislation was passed. Appropriately, Cook County is named for Cook, who was the state's first attorney general and served in Congress from 1819 until 1827. Pope County is named for Cook's uncle.

The first Illinois constitution was signed on August 26, 1818, at Kaskaskia. Shadrach Bond was inaugurated the first governor on October 6, 1818.

Shawneetown, Center of Commerce and Home to Legend

Immediately after statehood, Shawneetown, just below the confluence of the Wabash and Ohio rivers, became a center of commerce and an arrival point for a tide of immigrants from the east. At peak times there would be 50 to 60 wagons waiting to cross the Ohio River. It was a base for the multitudes who would cultivate a new civilization in Illinois.

The federal government in 1812 had plotted the city. Salt was harvested from springs 12 miles west near the

Saline River. In 1814 the federal government had opened a land office in the town. By 1824 it was a meeting point for stagecoaches that ran to Vincennes, Golconda, and McLeansboro.

John Marshall established a private bank in his Shawneetown home in 1812. It was the first in Illinois. In 1839 a state bank that had opened in 1816 moved to an impressive building erected on the main street. Legend has it that a group of businessmen came to the bank in the early 1800s hoping for a loan to support their new settlement. The men were turned down because the settlement, called Chicago, was deemed too far from Shawneetown to amount to anything.

While the legend makes for a delightful story, there is little historic basis for it. The first phase of banking in Shawneetown took place from 1817 to 1823, when Chicago was home to just a handful of fur traders who would have gone to several other more conveniently located places if indeed they were looking for a loan. Chicago was beginning to boom by the time the Shawneetown Bank reopened in 1834, but there was no reason to apply for a loan in a place so remote to Chicago as Shawneetown, especially because Chicago's economic roots were in the East. But some researchers continue to search for documentation of the denied loan that will prove the folklore is fact.

So many Ohio River floods had ravaged Shawneetown that after the great 1937 flood the town was relocated three miles west. It is now the seat of Gallatin County. Old Shawneetown remains a village with fewer than 350 residents and virtually no business base. Vestiges of the pioneer era are the big bank building with its impressive Grecian architecture and Doric columns, John Marshall's home, and a

Elijah Lovejoy, 1802-1837, was a graduate of Waterville (now Colby) College, and then studied theology at Princeton. In 1833 he became editor of the *Observer*, a Presbyterian weekly in St. Louis. Lovejoy advocated gradual emancipation of slaves and his views became extremely unpopular. He moved to Alton in 1836 and advocated immediate abolition in his *Alton Observer*. Outraged mobs had destroyed his presses three times, and on November 7, 1837, while guarding a new press, he was shot to death by members of a mob attacking it.

Illustration courtesy, Illinois State Historical Library

handful of lesser historic sites.

Morris Birkbeck wrote of Shawneetown in 1817 in his *Notes on a Journey in America:*

"This place I account as a phenomenon, evincing the pertinacious adhesion of the human animal to the spot where it has once fixed itself. As the lava of Mount Etna cannot dislodge this strange being from the cities which have been repeatedly ravished by its eruptions, the Ohio, with its annual overflowings, is unable to wash away the inhabitants of Shawneetown."

In 1820 a road was cut from Shawneetown west to Kaskaskia, Edwardsville, and Alton, replacing the rough trail that had been used for some years. That same year Illinois' capital was moved north to Vandalia. All of the

Abraham Lincoln, 1809-1865, who had been born in Kentucky and raised in Indiana, came to Illinois in 1830. He worked in a grocery store, volunteered in the Black Hawk War, but saw no fighting in his 80 days of service. He returned to the area and operated a store that went bankrupt. He became an assistant surveyor and then a postmaster before being elected to the Illinois General Assembly in 1834. He was a floor leader, and was reelected three times. Lincoln was instrumental in moving the capitol to Springfield. His efforts to repay debts from his bankruptcy earned him the moniker of "Honest Abe." He received his law license in

1836 and practiced in a circuit covering 12,000 square miles of Southern Illinois. The six-foot four-inch Lincoln served one term in the U.S. House of Representatives before returning to Springfield in 1848. Disenchanted with politics, Lincoln practiced law until he became active with the new Republican Party. In 1856 he was one of several men nominated, but not selected, to be the party's vice presidential candidate. He lost the race for U.S. Senate to Stephen A. Douglas in 1858 but received national attention from a series of debates during the race. In 1860 he was elected president. Months later the Civil War was under way. In 1863 Lincoln signed the Emancipation Proclamation freeing slaves, but only in the rebellious states. In 1865 the Civil War ended. A few days later Lincoln was assassinated while watching a play at Ford's Theater in Washington.

Photo courtesy, Illinois State Historical Library

state records were placed into two wagons and trundled 111 miles northeast to the city that would be their home for the next 20 years.

Ironically, Illinois' capitol would have been destroyed if it had not been moved. Kaskaskia was severely damaged in Mississippi River floods in 1844 and 1881 and the final remains washed away in 1910. The flooding turned Kaskaskia into an island, its 20,000 acres remaining as the only portion of Illinois west of the Mississippi River.

In one of the state memorials at Kaskaskia is a bell retrieved after the flooding. It had been cast in 1741 and was used in a Catholic Church. It is called the Liberty Bell of the West because joyful townspeople rang it after George Rogers Clark's arrival in 1778.

Vandalia would, in 1838, become the western terminus of the National Road, the brainchild of President Thomas Jefferson. Also called the Cumberland Road, it wound through the Cumberland Gap. Connecting Columbus, Ohio, with Indianapolis, it ended at Vandalia. Its construction was the federal government's first major road-building project and was eventually replaced by U.S. Highway 40 and later Interstate 70.

The Winter of Great Snow

The winter of 1830-1831 was particularly harsh in Illinois and the following year's corn crop was nearly nonexistent in the northern three-quarters of the state. Only the extreme southern tip of the state produced an acceptable crop.

That area near the confluence of the Ohio and Mississippi rivers is one of the world's major river junctions. It was often compared to the land of the Nile, and in 1818 a St. Louis merchant obtained an act from the territorial legislature incorporating the city of Cairo.

Farmers from the north regularly

traveled south and many of them, deeply rooted Bible readers, allowed that they were like "the sons of Jacob traveling to Egypt for corn." These are the likely reasons that Southern Illinois is known even today as "Egypt" or "Little Egypt." That regional nickname was subsequently buttressed with towns named Goshen, Karnak, and Thebes.

Lincoln in the General Assembly

Abraham Lincoln, a youthful lawyer from New Salem, took his seat in 1834 as a member of the Illinois General Assembly meeting in Vandalia.

In 1837 the legislature agreed to move the capital north again, from Vandalia to Springfield. Lincoln was an instigator of the move. Construction began on the new capitol

Above: From his humble beginnings, Abraham Lincoln eventually lived in this frame home in Springfield. This engraving was made for a book on Lincoln. Courtesy, Illinois State Historical Library

Left: President Lincoln is shown in this rare photograph talking with a Union officer inside a tent at a field headquarters. Courtesy, Illinois State Historical Library

This painting by George Parrish, Jr., depicts the fever pitch of the construction of the Illinois Central Railroad. From the chartering of the company in 1851, some 705 miles of track were completed in just five years. Courtesy, Illinois State Historical Library

and in 1839 the government moved to yet another home.

Editor Slain

Illinois was a free state but slavery existed in it. Although it was not as prevalent as in the South, both African-Americans and some Indians were indentured servants. There was a rising movement to outlaw slavery but there was also opposition. Nothing exemplified and focused this more than the 1837 murder of Elijah P. Lovejoy, editor of the abolitionist newspaper the *Alton Observer*, who was slain by a mob that attacked his paper and for a fourth time destroyed his press.

Lovejoy was an advocate and martyr

for abolition and for a free press. Just before his death, he had been ordered by a group to stop publishing his newspaper and to leave Alton. Lovejoy told his critics:

"I know that I have the right freely to speak and publish my sentiments, subject only to the laws of the land for the abuse of that right...You can crush me if you will; but I shall die at my post, for I cannot and will not forsake it..."

His death converted many religious and conscientious people to the abolition cause in Illinois and elsewhere throughout the northern states.

Abraham Lincoln was elected as a

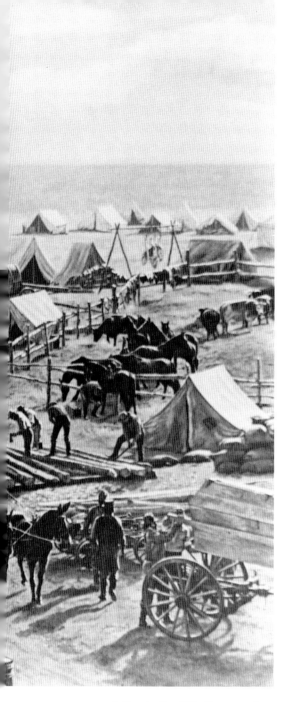

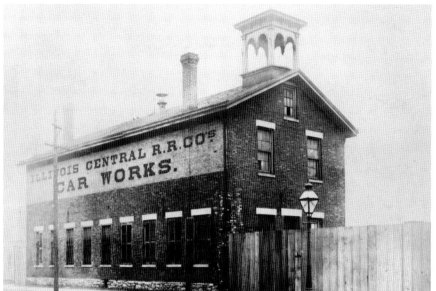

representative to the U.S. Congress in 1846. Over the next two years Illinois supplied six regiments of men to fight in the Mexican-American War. In 1848 the state's second constitution was adopted, giving more power to the governor and requiring popular election for state and county offices.

A Trail of Tears

In 1838 Illinois soil was stained by an Indian tragedy. The Cherokee Nation was being forcibly relocated from Georgia to Oklahoma on a route now called the Trail of Tears. It crossed the Ohio River near Golconda. The proud southern Indian nation was not acclimated to the North's harsh winters and many died while moving through Illinois during those months.

The First Railroads

The Northern Cross Railroad, the state's earliest rail line, was short-lived. The laying of rail began in 1838 at Meredosia and ran east and west through Jacksonville, reaching Springfield in 1842.

The state-owned steam line had many problems, not the least of which were the rails themselves. They consisted of metal strips nailed to oak stringers. The metal had the bad habit of breaking loose, popping up, and puncturing the rail cars. Within two years the single old steam engine had broken down and mules were substituted for the 59-mile journey. The Northern Cross was sold at auction in 1847 for $21,100, one-fortieth of its original cost.

What would become Illinois' largest private railroad was chartered in 1851 and in just four years the state boasted 2,005 miles of track. By 1857 some 11 main lines operated with seven radiating from Chicago on 3,953 miles of track. Illinois now had a first-rate transportation system.

The grand railroad of Illinois was the Illinois Central. Congress, after consid-

Jonathan Baldwin Turner, who taught Latin and Greek at Illinois College in Jacksonville, was an early supporter of the conservation of wildlife and natural resources. He helped develop techniques to assist farmers and fruit growers. Courtesy, University of Illinois Archives

In 1900 these members of the French Club at Southern Illinois Normal College, a training ground for teachers, gathered for a picnic. Courtesy, Southern Illinois University Library Special Collections

erable lobbying by Senator Stephen A. Douglas, granted public lands to the railroad. The swath of land reached the length of the state, from the northwest corner to Cairo. It formed a large "Y" where it branched at Centralia with one branch heading to Chicago.

The township and range system was used in granting land to the railroad. All even-numbered sections for six miles on both sides of the right-of-way were assigned to pay for the work.

The railroad did a great deal for growth in Illinois. A string of railroad towns was created and finally settlements were not limited to the proximity of navigable waterways. For purposes of commerce the trains, particularly on the northbound runs, would be faster than river steamers and not limited during winter months.

The mainline of the IC ran from Galena to Cairo bypassing St. Louis, which was an economic rival. The grant of 2.5 million acres to the railroad was done in tandem with the government holding an equal amount (the odd-numbered sections) that would be sold for twice the usual amount. To

avoid forfeiture the railroad needed to be completed in 10 years.

There was competitive bidding for the rights to build the line and they were awarded to an eastern firm that pledged 7 percent of the gross profits to the state. The 705.5-mile Illinois Central railroad would be the largest public works project ever attempted up until then in Illinois. The work began and by September 1856 was completed, making the Illinois Central the wonder of the world.

Dozens of cities like Carbondale, Centralia, Effingham, Mattoon, Champaign, Rantoul, Bloomington, Galesburg, Rockford, and Mendota were born or boomed because of the railroads. From 1850 to 1860 Illinois sustained tremendous growth, more than doubling its population and surpassing the one-million mark to 1,711,951. Today Illinois has 7,500 miles of active railroads serving all areas of the state.

Education Leadership

The 1850s brought many milestones for education. In 1854 the first superin-

tendent of the Office of Public
Instruction, Ninian W. Edwards,
the son of a former governor, was
appointed. A year later legislation was
approved to provide for a free public
school system, making Illinois a leader
in education.

A tax was imposed to support
public schools, and by 1860 some
472,247 children were attending
9,162 public schools maintained by
8,958 school districts. Most schools,
however, went only to the eighth-
grade level and were predominantly
one-room settings. There were just
a few high schools, with the West
Jacksonville district chartering the
first public high school in 1851.

In 1847 Illinois established the
Illinois State Hospital for the Insane at
Jacksonville. It was "a well established
and skillfully conducted hospital," said
Dorothea Dix, who was one of its
prime motivators. A school for the blind
opened in Jacksonville in 1848.

At an 1851 farmers' convention in
Granville, Jonathan Baldwin Turner, a
Yale-educated professor who taught at
Jacksonville's Illinois College until 1847,
proposed the establishment of institutions
for scientific industrial learning. This laid
the groundwork for the establishment of
all land grant colleges. It was a decade
later that the federal government gave
480,000 acres of land in western states
to Illinois. Their sale financed the con-

At Southern Illinois Normal College in
Carbondale this class of 38 posed in 1903 for a
photograph while wearing their finest clothing.
These students were apprentice teachers. Today
more than 22,000 students are enrolled at SIU's
Carbondale campus. Courtesy, Southern Illinois
University Library Special Collections

Stephen Arnold Douglas, 1813-1861, was a

lawyer, judge, state representative, member of Congress, and presidential candidate. He was elected to the Illinois general assembly in 1836 and appointed in 1840 by the governor as secretary of state. The following year the legislature appointed him as a Supreme Court

justice, where he served before his election to the U.S. House of Representatives in 1843. In the House he was chair of the committee on territories. In the U.S. Senate he served as chair of its committee on territories. In his run for the presidency, Douglas was second in popular vote but fourth in a field of four in electoral

votes. Douglas contracted typhoid fever and died while traveling to muster support for the Union in the early months of the Civil War.

Illustration courtesy, Illinois State Historical Library

struction of the University of Illinois at Champaign-Urbana.

The Universities

In 1856 Presbyterians chartered Carbondale College as a teachers' school. Ten years later, when it was sold to the Christian Church and its name was changed to Southern Illinois College, it counted 300 students. But there was still a dire need for better-educated teachers, and in June 1868 more than 1,000 Southern Illinois educators met in Carbondale to voice support for a public normal school to serve that part of the state.

In 1869 Southern Illinois Normal College was chartered, construction began, and in July 1874 its first classes were held. Southern's first building was a spectacular Roman Gothic-style four-story structure that contained nearly 100,000 square feet of space, including an auditorium that could hold 1,200. The facility was destroyed by fire on Thanksgiving weekend in 1883 and classes were moved to temporary buildings until a new structure was completed four years later.

Lincoln and Douglas Debate

The political event of the decade was the series of debates by two candidates for U.S. senator from Illinois. The debates focused attention on the increasing tensions surrounding the issue of slavery. Until the 17th Amendment was ratified in 1913, senators were elected by their respective state legislatures, not by popular vote.

The two candidates, a tall slim Springfield lawyer named Abraham Lincoln and Stephen A. Douglas, a short man called "The Little Giant," agreed to a series of debates in each of Illinois' seven congressional districts. The popular vote was advisory, not binding.

Douglas was appointed to the U.S. Senate in 1847 and served until 1861. He had already attained national status when he began his debates with Lincoln. Some eastern Republicans urged Illinois Republicans to allow him to stand for reelection without opposition. But Lincoln and his supporters felt strongly that Douglas was wrong on the issue of slavery.

The two men began their campaign debates starting on August 21, 1858, in Ottawa followed by others in Freeport, Jonesboro, Charleston, Galesburg, Quincy, and a final debate at Alton on October 15.

In a speech before the Illinois Republican convention in Springfield, Lincoln had made clear his feelings about slavery:

"I believe that this government cannot endure permanently half slave and half free. I do not expect the Union to be dissolved. I do not expect this house to fall, but I do expect it will cease to be divided."

The debates were not much more than a political sparring match, but Douglas was forced into a position that would make him unacceptable to the South when he sought the presidency two years later. They also provided the unknown Lincoln with extraordinary exposure.

The popular vote was Lincoln 125,430 to Douglas' 121,609 but when the legislature voted, Douglas was chosen for a third term as senator, 54 to 46.

Just two years later the men were rivals again, but this time it was for the office of president of the United States. Douglas ran as a Democrat and Lincoln represented a new party on the political scene, the Republicans. Douglas carried Missouri and New Jersey but with the vote split by Whigs and Southern Democrats, Lincoln went to Washington as president without a majority of the popular vote.

The Civil War Begins

The attack on Fort Sumter on April 12, 1861, marked the start of the Civil War. Douglas promptly went to the White House to assure President Lincoln of his loyalty to the Union. The two former rivals conferred often over the next weeks. The articulate Douglas died of typhoid fever on June 3, 1861, at a time when the country most needed his oratory and good counsel.

Eventually 11 contiguous southern states seceded from the Union and went to war with the remaining 22 states of the Union. The war was total and devastating, leaving 620,000 dead, a staggering figure that touched nearly every family in America, north and south.

During the Civil War 259,092 Illinois men went to battle on behalf of the Union. General officers of the Union army included John Pope, Stephen

Left: Brigadier General Benjamin Prentiss served with Ulysses S. Grant at Vicksburg. Courtesy, Illinois State Historical Library

Dorothea Lynde Dix, 1802-1897, the daughter

of a Massachusetts physician, took up the cause of care for the mentally ill. At the time their custody was poorly regulated and often the patients were restrained by cuffs, anklets, straitjackets, and iron collars. Dix began a campaign in Massachusetts to improve conditions in poorhouses, prisons, and insane asylums. In the 1840s she expanded her efforts to other states and reached Illinois in 1846. She addressed the general assembly and convinced them that a "well-established, skillfully conducted hospital" was required for the care of the mentally ill. This led to the establishment of the Illinois State Hospital for the Insane at Jacksonville, which opened in 1847. Dix urged prison reform and supported establishing the penitentiary at Joliet in 1858 as a far more humane facility than then existed. Commissioned during the Civil War as superintendent of United States Army nurses, she helped care for the wounded in many of the war's major battles.

Right: John M. Palmer was one of the more successful political generals of the Civil War. Major General Palmer fought gallantly in Tennessee and was named to command an army corps, but he turned down the honor because he refused to take orders from a West Point graduate he considered his junior. Palmer was elected governor in 1868, and U.S. senator in 1891. Courtesy, Illinois State Historical Library

Far right: Major General John A. Logan, who served in the Civil War, was the first commander of the Grand Army of the Republic, a group of Civil War veterans. He created Memorial Day as a time to decorate the graves of soldiers. Later in his career he served as a U.S. senator from Illinois. Courtesy, Illinois State Historical Library

In 1838 John A. McClernand was appointed as secretary of state by Governor Thomas Carlin, but the Supreme Court rejected the appointment because no vacancy existed. He served in Congress but resigned to become a major general during the Civil War. McClernand was known as a political general who kept one eye on political fences while plotting for advancement. Courtesy, Illinois State Historical Library

Hurlbut, I.N. Haynie, Benjamin Prentiss, John McClernand, Michael Lawler, John Palmer, John A. Logan, and Ulysses S. Grant. Grant went to service from his home in Galena. Early in the conflict, he commanded the troops in the district of Cairo.

There was little hesitation by the men of Illinois to serve in the Union army. By May 3, 1861, about 200 completed companies had volunteered, enough for 20 regiments. According to the census there were just over 342,000 men of military age in Illinois. Some 259,092 served and only 3,538 of those were drafted to service.

Illinois troops served in every theater of battle and it was the flag of the 13th Illinois that was first raised in the capture of Richmond, capital of the Confederacy. The battles brought enormous cost in injury and loss of life. The 82nd Illinois was mauled at Chancellorsville, where the 155 casualties included 47 dead. Illinois units were the backbone of the Army of Tennessee and were butchered at Shiloh, where at least 638 Illinoisians lost their lives.

Historian William Fox compiled a list of the 300 federal regiments with the highest casualties of the war: 23 were from Illinois, and only New York with 59, Pennsylvania with 53, and Ohio with 24 suffered greater losses.

The far southern tip of Illinois was less supportive of the effort than the northern part of the state. The reasons were obvious. With much of the area south of Richmond and many residents with relatives and roots in the South, it provided scant support for Lincoln in his run for the presidency.

Some in Southern Illinois sympathized with the South, and indeed a few left to join the Confederate army. Southern sympathizers in the North were called Copperheads, after the snake that strikes without warning. But with rare exception the area held steadfast with the Union and its men fought bravely.

In July 1861 Captain Charles M. Ferrell organized Company A of the 29th Infantry with men from Hardin County. They marched the 200 miles to Camp Butler near Springfield, where they were mustered to service four days later. A wagon driver with the unit was John Ferrell, brother of the commander. Before the war he had been a riverboat pilot on the Ohio.

The younger Ferrell was transferred to the navy and assigned to the USS *Neosho*, an ironclad gunboat that patrolled the Ohio, Tennessee, and Cumberland rivers. Eight of the Cairo-class gunboats were built at Mound City in Pulaski County. They were 175 feet long, and each carried 13 cannons protected by two-inch-thick metal plating. Each carried a crew of 250.

house and, taking the flag from where it lay, tied it up to the stump of the main signal staff, which was the highest mast we had remaining..."

For their actions both men were awarded the Medal of Honor. Ferrell was one of 98 Illinois men to receive the award during the Civil War. He returned to ply the river after the war and died in 1900. He is buried in a small cemetery at the edge of Elizabethtown along with his brother, who eventually rose to the rank of colonel.

Illinois saw no major battles, but there were skirmishes in the far southern part of the state. On August 14, 1864, the *Chicago Daily Tribune* reported on its front page that "a rebel force of 1,800 cavalry had crossed the Ohio River at Saline Bar." Confederate Colonel Adam R. Johnson had taken

The heroic Cumberland River battle involving the monitor USS *Neosho* is depicted in this sketch by Adam Rohe. Two men earned medals of honor for their actions in the engagement. U.S. Navy photograph

On December 6, 1864, the *Neosho* engaged a Confederate battery on the Cumberland just north of Nashville. Lieutenant Commander Leroy Fitch of the Mississippi squadron reported just days after the battle:

"During the engagement of the 6th, all our flag and signal staffs were shot away and the flag lay drooping over the wheelhouse... while still under fire of the enemy artillery and musketry, pilot John Ferrell and John Ditzenback, a quartermaster, went out of the pilot

advantage of the low water levels of mid-summer to stage the daring raid on Illinois where the Saline River enters the Ohio.

The Emancipation Proclamation freeing all slaves in the southern states went into effect on January 1, 1864. The following March Ulysses S. Grant became supreme commander of the Union forces and began hammering the troops of Confederate General Robert E. Lee in Virginia.

Lincoln was reelected president in November 1864. On February 1, 1865,

Ulysses S. Grant, 1822-1885, was an 1843 graduate

of West Point who first saw action in the Mexican-American War. In 1854, disenchanted with the army, he resigned and went to Missouri to farm. In 1860 he moved to Galena and worked in his father's leather shop. When the Civil War broke out he was placed in command of the 21st Illinois Regiment. He quickly was promoted to brigadier general in charge of the District of Cairo. In February 1862 he led Union troops in capturing Forts Henry and Donelson in Tennessee. It was the Union army's first significant victory. After leading troops at the battles that climaxed with the taking of Vicksburg he was promoted to lieutenant general (the highest rank then used) and became supreme commander of the Union army. On April 9, 1865, Confederate General Robert E. Lee surrendered to him at Appomattox Court House. The following year he was promoted to the new rank of full general. In 1868 he was elected president of the United States and was reelected in 1872.

Photo courtesy, Illinois State Historical Library

Illinois became the first state to ratify the 13th Amendment to the Constitution, outlawing slavery and involuntary servitude in the United States and its territories.

The South Surrenders and Lincoln is Killed

On April 9, 1865, Lee surrendered at Appomattox Court House, Virginia, and the Civil War came to an end. Just five days later Lincoln was assassinated in Washington. A funeral procession carried his body by train to Springfield, Illinois, making frequent stops during its emotional 12-day journey. On the morning of May 4 Lincoln was interred at Oak Ridge Cemetery.

Illinois, through its martyred president and the sacrifice of its soldiers, had contributed far more than its fair share to the preservation of the Union. As the wave of admiration and grief engulfed the country, Oak Ridge Cemetery where Lincoln was buried became a national shrine. As lesser men assumed leadership in the Republican Party, Illinois relied on its natural resources to sustain its economic engine.

Coal is King

Commercial mining of coal started in Jackson County as early as 1810, when coal was loaded on a barge on the Big Muddy River and floated down the Mississippi to New Orleans. As trees were cut and depleted, coal became an even more welcome source of energy.

As was the case with most settlements, the first coal mines bordered rivers. They were drift or slope mines cut into the exposed seams of coal on bluff sides. Soon it was determined that coal was less expensive than wood to fuel locomotives and the coal industry boomed.

At places like Du Quoin and

De Soto in Southern Illinois, and in Grundy, Bureau, Rock Island, Stark, and Knox counties in the northern half of the state, most of the mines were near Illinois Central rail lines.

As coal mining grew, so did the labor unions that represented the miners. Even surface, or strip, mining was perilous and working underground in the deep-shaft mines was among the most dangerous jobs available.

In 1909 a calamitous mine fire at the little town of Cherry in Bureau County left 259 men dead. This disaster gave new urgency to efforts

Williamson." In subsequent decades labor wars, gang wars, race riots, and Ku Klux Klan activity supported the moniker.

During a strike by members of the United Mine Workers at a strip mine there on June 22, 1922, an armed mob captured about 50 strikebreakers who had been brought from Chicago to work at the mine. The mob ordered the men to run, then opened fire, killing 19 of them. Some 214 local men were indicted in the killings. All were acquitted.

At about this same time Klan

to provide workmen's compensation and to implement reforms in mine safety. Mine rescue and firefighting stations were established throughout the state in coal-mining areas beginning the following year.

Violence in the South

Violence became commonplace in coal-mining labor disputes, and no place is better remembered for this than the town of Herrin in Williamson County. A 10-year-long vendetta begun in 1868 earned it the title of "Bloody

members took charge of enforcing local laws, and tried to stop liquor sales and gambling. The Klan brought a man named S. Glenn Young to the county. Young had been fired from his job as a federal Prohibition agent because of his propensity for violence.

Just over a year later, after a series of raids, Young, two of his guards, and a deputy sheriff were shot to death in a cigar store gunfight in Herrin. National Guardsmen were sent to the town to restore order, an effort that kept them on duty for nearly four years. During

After the assassination of Abraham Lincoln, his body was carried on an ornately decorated funeral train that slowly wound its way from Washington, D.C., to Chicago and then on to Springfield. Along the route tens of thousands stood by in an emotional outpouring. Courtesy, Illinois State Historical Library

this time 20 more people were gunned down.

Following the suppression of the Klan, a war between the Shelton brothers and the Charlie Birger gang began. Most of the violence occurred in Williamson and Franklin counties, where 14 people were killed, including two mayors and a state highway policeman. Birger was hanged in 1928 and the Shelton brothers continued to operate downstate for decades.

Carl Shelton met an unceremonious end when he was murdered on the family farm near Fairfield in 1947. Bernie Shelton was gunned down in front of his Peoria tavern in 1948. Earl Shelton was shot in the Farmers Club in Fairfield in 1949. Roy Shelton was

killed while driving a tractor on his Wayne County farm in 1950; their sister, Lulu Shelton Pennington, was machine gunned in Fairfield in June 1951, but survived.

Although the reputation of Fairfield was besmirched by the Sheltons' gangster image, its earlier history includes the claim that its Republican organization on March 31, 1860, became the first to endorse Lincoln for president. The name of the town purportedly came from the attestation of early settlers who stopped their wagons and proclaimed there was "no fairer field." When the settlement was finally named in 1819 it was called Fairfield.

Racial Turmoil

Labor troubles left deep marks on relations between blacks and whites in Southern Illinois, and in May and again

Left: Concerned townspeople, many of them relatives of those who worked in the coal mine at Cherry, stream to the entrance of the mine as workers begin to remove the victims of a tragic fire in 1909. Courtesy, Illinois State Historical Library

Left, bottom: On November 13, 1909, some 259 coal miners died in a fire near the small village of Cherry in North Central Illinois. This photograph shows some of the bodies wrapped in tarpaulins after being removed from the mine. Courtesy, Illinois State Historical Library

in July 1917 the National Guard was dispatched to East St. Louis to quell race riots.

Some factory operators had encouraged as many as 10,000 blacks to migrate from the South. They filled already-crowded slums and took over work previously done by whites because they could be hired for lower pay. Troops restored order for a while but after they left, groups of whites opened fire on the homes of blacks. In retaliation, two white policemen were slain. At least 39 blacks and nine whites died in one 24-hour period.

Some 250 buildings burned during the rioting and 144 men were eventually indicted for crimes ranging from murder to arson, but no convictions were ever obtained.

A Statewide Road System

In 1918 Illinois approved its first bond issue of $60 million to build a system of hard roads statewide. The 1920s saw an explosion of their construction during the term of Governor Len Small. While earliest roads followed the routes used by buffalo and Indians, later country roads were often at one-mile intervals following the section lines used to survey the state.

As automobiles became more popular and taxes were imposed on them in 1914, roadways began to be constructed of brick and concrete, aptly called hard roads. By the mid-1920s there was a network of paved roadways serving nearly every part of Illinois.

The earliest included Illinois Highway 1, running from Chicago south near the Indiana border; Illinois Highway 2 along the Rock River; Illinois 3, running near the Mississippi in the southwest corner of the state; and east-west roads such as Illinois 13, 14, 9, and U.S. Route 66 from Chicago to St. Louis. Over the decades the numeric designations of some roads changed as the interstate highway system evolved in the last half of the twentieth century.

A second major bond issue was passed for $100 million in 1924, and helped to make Governor Small the most prolific road builder in the nation. In 1929 a gasoline tax was instituted to help maintain the roadways.

Today Illinois has 17,000 miles of state highways, including 2,050 miles as part of the interstate highway system, and there are tens of thousands of

On June 22, 1922, a group of 50 strikebreakers brought to Herrin from Chicago were fired on by a group of striking miners. Nineteen of the strikebreakers were killed in what became known as the Herrin Massacre. After the bloody incident locals moved quickly to bury the victims. While some local men were charged in the killings, they were eventually acquitted by Williamson County juries. Courtesy, Gordon Pruett

miles of county roads and municipal streets.

Transportation

In the early nineteenth century stage-coaches operated along major Illinois roads near the Ohio River. These routes expanded during the next century and were replaced with bus and interurban rail lines in the early twentieth century. Today some of those roads have been designated as "Scenic Byways" by the U.S. Department of Transportation: The 188-mile-long Ohio River Scenic Byway runs through seven southeastern counties and the Meetings of the Great Rivers Scenic Byway, a 50-mile route, is near the confluence of the Illinois and Mississippi rivers.

In 1855 the hot-air balloon *Eclipse*

was flown at a Chicago exhibition, and soon such balloons became common sights at carnivals. Octave Chanute, a railroad engineer who moved to Chicago in 1889, was conducting experiments in powered flights and corresponded often with the Wright brothers, encouraging them before their 1903 flight at Kitty Hawk.

By 1911 Chicago was home to its own aircraft-manufacturing company. When the U.S. entered World War I, flying schools opened at Scott Field near Belleville and at Chanute Field in Rantoul.

Chicago's municipal airport opened in 1927. It would later be renamed for the World War II battle of Midway. A second Chicago area airport was established at Orchard Place, northwest of

Charlie Birger and his gang became something of folk heroes in far Southern Illinois during Prohibition. The boyish Birger is shown here, sitting atop the car in the center. He was later hanged for the murder of a state policeman. Courtesy, Illinois State Historical Library

Above: During World War II Army Air Corps mechanics received their training at Chanute Field north of Champaign. Octave Chanute, a French-born and American-educated engineer who settled in Chicago, showed the Wright brothers that it was theoretically possible to fly a plane with the power of an internal-combustion engine. One of Chanute's gliders was used as a model for the Wright brothers' plane that made the first powered flight at Kitty Hawk. Courtesy, Illinois State Historical Library

Right: After labor disturbances and the Haymarket Riot of 1886 that killed many people, including seven Chicago police officers, officials lobbied for a military post to be built nearby so federal troops would be available if needed. Fort Sheridan, with a 10-story tower as its headquarters building, was constructed 27 miles north of the city on the shore of Lake Michigan. Courtesy, Illinois State Historical Library

the city, in 1942. Although it was renamed for a World War II navy flying hero, Edward "Butch" O'Hare, its identifier, seen on the luggage tags of millions, remains ORD.

New Labor Laws

In 1867 Illinois lawmakers passed legislation stating that with the exception of farms, eight hours would be considered the official work day. While the law helped to placate some workers it was widely ignored by employers. The first workplace safety laws were enacted in 1869. These governed the operations of threshing machines and corn shellers.

John Peter Altgeld became governor in 1893. Born in Germany, he was the first foreign-born governor and the first Democrat from Cook County. The liberal former judge was an advocate of progressive labor laws.

In 1893 the General Assembly

passed the Sweatshop Act, which provided for the inspection of factories and the regulation of child labor. The first team of inspectors began to check on conditions in Illinois factories and found that many of the workers were under the age of 13. In 1903 an improved

Above: Airships were maintained at Scott Field during World War I. This interesting picture shows a fixed-wing aircraft that is taken aloft with the airship. Courtesy, Illinois State Historical Library

Left: Great Lakes Naval Training Station was a major training facility during World War I. In this photograph airplanes fly over a parade of recruits. Courtesy, Illinois State Historical Library

Right: No Illinois governor had a more difficult administration than Henry Horner, who was elected at the height of the Great Depression. The state's first Jewish governor and the first native of Cook County literally worked himself to death. He became ill and died a few months before the end of his second term. Courtesy, Illinois State Historical Library

Facing page, top: During World War I so many recruits underwent training at Great Lakes Naval Training Station in North Chicago that most were housed in tents. Courtesy, Illinois State Historical Library

Facing page, bottom: During the Great Depression thousands of men were employed on public works projects through the federal government's Civilian Conservation Corps. During the summer many lived in camps such as Camp Saline near Eldorado. This company of CCC members posed for their photograph, which would be turned into a picture postcard the men could buy and mail for just a penny. Meals were eaten outside. Each member had his own metal mess kit. This family-type photo included the camp dog (front). Courtesy, Gordon Pruett

law was enacted, making Illinois the first state to establish the eight-hour day and 48-hour work week for children.

Altgeld, the first Democrat in four decades, discharged many officials appointed by his Republican predecessors. One of his appointments backfired when a treasurer for the University of Illinois was convicted of misusing endowment funds and was sentenced to the penitentiary.

Free employment service offices were established in 1899 for all cities with a population of more than 50,000. A state employee civil service code was established in 1905 and administered by an appointed commission.

John Peter Altgeld, 1847-1902, was Illinois' first

foreign-born governor. After serving five years as a Cook County judge, the German-born Altgeld ran for governor in 1892 as a Democrat. His administration rigidly enforced labor laws requiring factory inspections. In 1893 he pardoned three Anarchists in the Haymarket bombing of 1886. An 18,000-word justification supported his action but few read it. Led by newspapers including the *Chicago Tribune*, his opponents called him John "Pardon" Altgeld. The poet Vachel Lindsay created a name by which he is remembered today, "The Eagle Forgotten." He clashed with President Grover Cleveland, who sent federal troops during a railroad strike although Illinois had not requested them. Altgeld rebuffed Cleveland at the 1896 Democratic convention and helped nominate William Jennings Bryan. He lost his reelection bid. In 1899 he ran for mayor of Chicago and lost. In private life Altgeld joined the law firm of his friend Clarence Darrow.

Photo courtesy, Illinois State Historical Library

During World War II thousands of Army Air Corps troops received training at Scott Field. This photo, taken from the ceiling of a hangar, shows students studying at their desks. Courtesy, Illinois State Historical Library

World War I

At the time the United States entered World War I, Illinois had the curious distinction of having more citizens of German and Austrian ancestry than any other state. Indeed, Chicago was the sixth-largest German city in the world. Just before hostilities broke out, 25 German-American leaders from Chicago traveled to Washington to urge President Woodrow Wilson not to enter the war.

When the Declaration of War was presented, Illinois congressmen cast five of the 50 votes against it. All the congressmen who opposed the war were reelected. But despite their Teutonic bloodlines, Illinoisians served with distinction in "The War to End All Wars."

The Illinois National Guard was mustered as the 33rd—or Prairie—

Division, the 16th American division to reach France. It counted 1,274 killed and 6,266 wounded. All told, some 350,000 Illinoisians served in the military during World War I and 4,266 of them died.

Illinois was a major training location for the war, with thousands stationed at Camp Grant near Rockford, the Great Lakes Naval Center, and Fort Sheridan north of Chicago. In 1917 two aviation bases opened: one near Belleville, called Scott Field, and at Rantoul, which became Chanute Field, a major air force training center.

The Great Depression

There was general prosperity in the 1920s, until "Black Friday," when the bottom fell out of the stock market on October 24, 1929. The Great

Depression had begun. The following year payrolls dropped by 30 percent, many mines closed, and more than 700,000 were unemployed, a figure that doubled by January 1933.

Chicago was hard hit, as were Williamson and Franklin counties, and banks were failing regularly. Franklin D. Roosevelt was elected president in 1932 and Illinois Governor Henry Horner, the state's first Jewish chief executive, acting with New York Governor Herbert H. Lehman, closed all the banks in their states on the eve of Roosevelt's inauguration. In two days the "Bank Holiday" had spread across the nation.

Within three months the bulk of Illinois' 704 state banks were operating again. Emergency relief was paid to many families, but it was so little that it barely could feed a family. In Southern Illinois payments were significantly lower than in the north. Cook County families averaged monthly payments of $29, while downstate families averaged just under $13, and in Alexander County the average jobless family received just $1.83 a month.

Thousands of men worked at public projects run by the Civilian Conservation Corps and the Works Progress Administration. They lived in large camps and their public service projects are still in evidence today throughout Illinois, from the great lodge at Giant City State Park to lakes such as Pounds Hollow in Gallatin County, formed by a levee built by CCC teams who lived in tents at nearby Camp Cadiz.

In 1937 oil was discovered in a field near Salem. Within two years the state had become the fourth-largest producer of oil in the nation, pumping nearly 94 million barrels of oil a year from fields around Salem and along the east side of the state.

World War II

The clouds of war filled the air in Europe and Asia by the end of the 1930s and Illinois' 33rd Division was quietly mustered to federal service and sent to Camp Forrest, Tennessee, nine months before the Japanese surprise attack on Pearl Harbor on December 7, 1941.

At least 670,000 men and 19,000 women from Illinois served in the military in World War II. The army reported 18,527 killed in action; the navy, 3,665.

Scott Field near Belleville became the chief communications school for the Army Air Corps, and George Field near Lawrenceville provided advance flight training. With the Illinois National Guard already in federal service the state formed what was called a reserve militia, something equivalent to a second-string National Guard to be used in emergencies. At East Alton the Western Cartridge plant produced three billion bullets during the war years.

When the war ended in 1945 veterans returning to Illinois received a soldier's bonus of about $500, adding $300 million to the state's bonded debt.

Roland W. Burris, 1937- , was born in Centralia to a four-generation Southern Illinois family. Burris received a degree in political science from Southern Illinois University in Carbondale and his law degree from Howard University. After working as a bank examiner, Burris was employed by Continental Illinois National Bank, the state's largest, rising to second vice president in eight years. Burris served in the cabinet of Governor Dan Walker and in 1978 became the first African-American elected to a statewide constitutional office when he was elected state comptroller, a post to which he was reelected twice. In 1990 he was elected attorney general. Burris waged an unsuccessful campaign for the Democratic nomination for governor in 1998.

THE FORKS
1. Mark Beaubien's Sauganash Hotel
2. The First Post Office 1833
3. Wolf Tavern
4. Sam Miller's Public House

SOUTH BRANCH

SOUTH WATER STREET 1834

LAND

TRAIL TO DANVILLE

Latitude 41°53'
Longitude 87°38'
Elevation 584 ft.

SITE OF DEARBORN MASSACRE
at foot of 18th Street

ROAD TO DETROIT

Sand Hills

Mail Service
over this Road once a
week from Niles, Mich.

The TOWN OF CH...
Population 350

WELLS

LASALLE

CLARK

DEARBORN

STATE

Wm. Jones
Farm

1st Public
School

Calhoun's House

Sauganash
Tavern

Second
b...

U.S. GOVE...
RESER...

Fort Cemetery

CHIC...

LAKE MICHIGAN

A
MAP
of
CHICAGO
Incorporated as a Town
August 5
1833

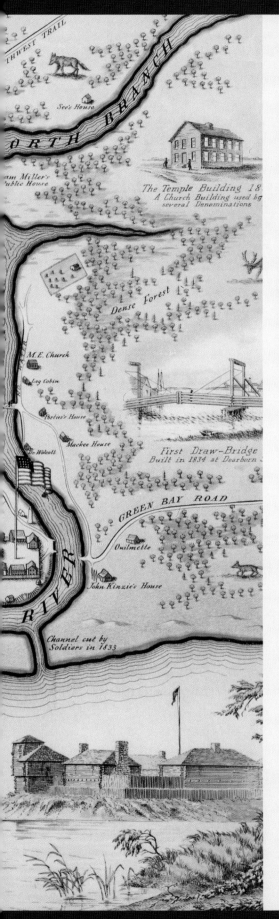

See's House

RTH BRANCH

in Miller's
ublic House

The Temple Building 18
A Church Building used by
several Denominations

Dense Forest

M.E. Church

Log Cabin

Beaubien's House

Mackee House

Dr. Wolcott

First Draw-Bridge
Built in 1834 at Dearborn

GREEN BAY ROAD

Ouilmette

John Kinzie's House

RIVER

Channel cut by
Soldiers in 1835

CHAPTER TWO

Chicago and the Prairies Find a Port

The Administration of President Thomas Jefferson in 1803, the same year it purchased the Louisiana Territory from France, chose the mouth of the Chicago River for a new military outpost, Fort Dearborn.

The site, already marked by a small trading center for fur traders and Indians, represented to the far-seeing U.S. president the heart of the then-wilderness and a key opportunity for both American settlement and future commercial expansion.

It was a tiny part of his grand vision for America's future.

The small mansion and farm compound that already stood on the opposite bank from the fort, on the other hand, represented the area's immediate past. These had been the home and trading post of Jean Baptiste Pointe DuSable's family. He was black, a farmer, and a trader. His wife, Catherine, was Potawatomi. They had two children, Jean and Suzanne.

The DuSables had sold this property three years earlier and moved on, as soon would the French and British and then their Indian fur-trading partners.

Left: Recreated 100 years after the 1830 plat of Chicago, this map features roads to Detroit and Danville as well as a cut made through the sandbar to unblock the river. Courtesy, Chicago Public Library

First, however, there would be a cataclysm, a military engagement of the War of 1812 that would soak the soil with the blood of American settlers and Indians. The latter had aligned with the British and massacred the residents of the fort. For generations, the land had contained for them abundant wildlife, excellent trade routes, and the graves of their ancestors. They had no desire to let the region be taken from them.

For American settlers, the place held promise.

The Chicago River emptied east into Lake Michigan and reached west almost to the Des Plaines, which flowed southwest and emptied into the Illinois and ultimately into the Mississippi. This connection would make Chicago the gate between the East and West in much the same manner as if it were a mountain path between a highly populated industrial region and a verdant, lush valley.

Initially, the small fort had remained hundreds of miles from any other settlement or seat of civilization. Still, the outpost was seen as holding the key to

In this artist's depiction, U.S. Army Lieutenant James S. Swearingen supervises the construction of Fort Dearborn in 1803. Courtesy, Chicago Public Library

A depiction of the DuSable residence as it looked when it was owned by the Kinzie family in 1832. Constructed 50 years earlier by Jean Baptiste Pointe DuSable (contemporaries spelled it "Point de Sable"), it would later house two generations of Kinzies. From *History of Chicago* by A.T. Andreas. Courtesy, Chicago Public Library

unlocking the region that had been chartered by the Continental Congress as the Northwest Territory.

Chicago then was not so much a place as a river with a portage used by Indians, fur traders, and an occasional adventurer. On the French maps, the small stream had been called "Chicagou," after a local Indian word for the wild garlic plants that grew along its banks.

By the end of the nineteenth century, what had been an outpost 100 years earlier would become an exciting, mature, world-renowned metropolis populated by more than two million people. It would be recognized, by then, as a special place, the heart of the heartland, the most American of cities.

Something had exploded. Actually, a place had.

Chicago, with its own brand of culture, would in that century start creating a new architecture that would be imitated much the way Athens and Rome had been. It would become known for a genuine literature that was producing such original works as Frank Baum's *The Wonderful Wizard of Oz*, Henry B. Fuller's *The Cliff Dwellers*, and Theodore Dreiser's *Sister Carrie*.

When the village was laid out in 1830, only a few dozen settlers populated the swampy area at the mouth of the Chicago River. At the time, New York had a population of 400,000; London, two million; and Paris, more than one million. Chicago would, within an individual's lifetime, join the ranks of these world-class cities.

The German leader, Otto von Bismarck, would say in 1870, "I wish I could go to America, if only to see that Chicago."

Chicago was married to Lake Michigan and connected to the Mississippi River Valley by a tenuous, mud-filled river and then by a canal and railroads. It continued to grow by leaps and bounds throughout the nineteenth century. For the farmers of the

Midwest, Chicago proved to be their port on the prairie and their gate to the East. It would, as a result, become an exchange center, a depository, and a disburser for the enormous natural wealth of the entire surrounding area.

People proceeded to come in the way they might rush to a discovery of gold, only they hurried to Chicago in much greater numbers. More than a million of them would arrive in the city from so many varied places around the world that one commentator projected there eventually might be found in Chicago "the composite photograph of mankind." World observers saw Chicago's explosive growth as a phenomenon unrivaled in history.

In the early years of the twenty-first century—200 years after soldiers and workers had cut trees and erected a fort at the mouth of the Chicago River—a multi-ethnic metropolis could take stock of itself. It could pride itself not only on the height of its buildings, the size and diversity of its population, its many economic accomplishments, and world recognition, but also on its preserved natural beauty and frequently earned respect.

A city known throughout its growing spurts for its boasts, Chicago would no longer need the voice of its boosters to proclaim its greatness. Chicago would be a city much discussed, described, and defined around the world and locally embraced, enjoyed, and appreciated.

Questions and Their Answers

How and why did this extraordinary success of Chicago come about? The answers seemed simple: There was money to be made in Chicago, lots of it, and there were jobs to be had, generations of them.

Such answers, however, had their explanations. They went back not just

Jean Baptiste Pointe DuSable, 1745-1818,

a fur trader and farmer at the site of present-day Chicago from 1784 to 1800, was the first settler there and its first black resident. An account of the sale of the property when he left included a "mansion," two barns, a horsemill, a poultry house, a workshop, a dairy, a smokehouse, and a bakehouse. Historian John Swenson points out in *Early Chicago* that contemporary records spelled his name Jean Baptiste Point de Sable.

100 or 200 years, but to events that had been happening over a multitude of millennia. These had programmed Chicago with phenomenal possibilities. Much of this voice of fate could be heard not only of the past, but also in the present and for the future.

To the farmer—pioneering in the early 1800s—the areas that Chicago served were comprised of vast prairies that held soil, rich beyond belief. Equally important, they had river and canal waterways and railroad lines that could ship their produce from this port on Lake Michigan to eastern markets via the Great Lakes and the Erie Canal.

To those who would build a city or a simple farmhouse, there was an abundance of means to do so: an almost unlimited supply of stone for foundations, clay for bricks, trees for lumber, as well as iron ore and coal for producing steel.

Through its long pre-history the area surrounding Chicago had served as a special depository for and cornucopia of all of these resources and more.

Treasures Deposited Here

To the north of Chicago, in an area centered in Northern Minnesota, time immemorial had placed the phenomenal iron deposits of the Mesabi and other ranges. It had stored copper beneath the ground of the Upper Peninsula of Michigan and lead and zinc throughout the Galena area of Northwestern Illinois and Southwestern Wisconsin.

These ores with their incredible potential awaited a time when man could transform them.

Over a period that lasted for hundreds of millions of years, the sea would cover the Chicago area at least three times. The life forms in those waters lived, died, and accumulated on the vast lake bottoms. Such remnants, formed today into limestone, constitute deposits hundreds of feet thick that serve as the city's bedrock. After being quarried, they would become stone and cement building materials used to construct the city's buildings and highways.

Lengthy eras, in which lush ferns and trees grew and multiplied, lasted millions of years, eventually creating the enormous coal deposits in South and Central Illinois. These would help heat Chicago and stoke the region's steel plants as their ovens processed iron into steel.

The Glaciers Come and Go

The area after the seas had resided remained flat and featureless, until the glaciers, great fields of ice moving down from the north, shaved and reshaped it.

The glaciers came, receded, and returned again. The greatest of these measured more than a mile thick and their weights were inestimable as they compacted the earth beneath them. They scraped and pushed the soil and rocks in front of them, as they grew larger and relentlessly spread over more land.

Nature, in one last enormously generous gesture to the area, used the most recent glacier, 50,000 to 15,000 years ago, to set the table for the Chicago area.

Called the Wisconsin Glacier, its handprint is still strong upon the land. It formed Lake Michigan, gave the Chicago area a continental divide, and created its river system. The ice sheet also left a unique treasure in the form of some of the richest soil deposits in the world.

As it started to melt and recede, the glacier's runoff filled with water a vast, gouged-out area that geologists refer to as Lake Chicago. This consisted of the present-day Lake Michigan and more. The additional area it covered included what is now the city of Chicago along with many of its immediate suburbs.

This lake was lipped on the southwest shore by a swath of small hills formed by the glacier and called by geologists the Valpariso Moraine. This lengthy, semicircular formation is basically the route now followed by the Tri-State Tollway, I-294. It was, several thousand years ago, the rim of Lake Chicago. The waters found a major breakthrough where Summit, Illinois, now is and then rushed downward toward the valley systems of the Illinois and Mississippi rivers.

As the waters started to ebb, two areas rose above the surface of this great lake. These bear names that recall their pasts. One, Blue Island, is a suburb of Chicago; the other, a ridge and

Right: This artistic face, etched 500 years ago on a marine shell, was found on the chest of skeletal remains uncovered in 1958 at the Anker site along the Calumet River. Courtesy, Field Museum

street in the city, is Stony Island.

The Valpariso Moraine today is seen as a continental divide. The area east of it, the immediate Chicago region, is shaped like half a bathtub, drains into Lake Michigan, and shares a soil that has characteristics quite different from those to the west of it. There, the deep rich soil is dark loam and the run-off water flows toward the Mississippi River and the Gulf of Mexico instead of to Lake Michigan.

The glaciers pushed rich topsoil from the north and left it 18 inches deep throughout Northern and Central

Sieur Louis Joliet

The 1673 visitor to Chicago used two "L"s in his name. This bronze of the explorer and cartographer spelled it with only one, as does the city southwest of Chicago. The alternative spelling arose from the fact that the town was formerly called "Juliet," as in Shakespeare's *Romeo and Juliet.* Courtesy, Chicago Public Library

A depiction of Father Jacques Marquette's stay in the winter of 1674-1675 along the south branch of the Chicago River. If the illustrator of this fanciful drawing had read the Jesuit's account, he would have known that the area Indians did not live in teepees but in "cabins." Courtesy, Kenan Heise collection

Illinois, helping to produce some of the richest farmland in the world. Prairie grasses formed a tangled sward to protect it from erosion.

Here could be grown crops to produce wheat, corn, and soybeans as well as farm animals to supply chicken, beef, and pork.

In those places throughout Wisconsin and Michigan, where the soil was not endowed quite as richly by the moving glaciers, there still was enough good earth to nourish vast forests of hardwoods such as oak, hickory, maple, and basswood as well as enormous needle-leaf stands of fir, pine, and spruce to afford a growing America an enormous supply of wood.

These would be cut and milled to create in Chicago the lumber mart of the

continent in the twentieth century. It would supply construction materials for the homes, stores, and office buildings first for the city and then for the country. The wood would also go into making ships, paper, furniture, and boxes.

Routes through the Valpariso Moraine to and from the immediate Chicago area served as paths for Indians and early settlers. Today they are roads and highways.

The major route through Summit, making use of the Chicago and Des Plaines rivers, used a short, rugged canoe portage to create a trade route for Indians and fur traders. This same way would be followed in carving out the two waterways, first the Illinois and Michigan Canal and, later, the Sanitary and Ship Canal. It would also serve

Above: Fort Dearborn (rebuilt in 1816) and the Kinzie (DuSable) house remained local landmarks for decades. In 1823 visitor William Keating commented: "The appearance of the country near Chicago offers few features upon which the traveler can dwell with pleasure." Courtesy, Kenan Heise collection

Right: Fort Dearborn was reconstructed for the "Century of Progress" Chicago World's Fair of 1933. Courtesy, Kenan Heise collection

Facing page, bottom: The junction of the north and south branches of the Chicago River can be seen in this 1830 illustration. The small building on the left is Wolf Point Tavern, whose crossbar flies a flag with a wolf depicted on it. From *History of Chicago* by A.T. Andreas. Courtesy, Kenan Heise collection

those laying out Ogden Avenue and I-55, the Stevenson Expressway.

Time awaited man and his inventiveness to find new ways to utilize all this potential to produce an indigenous and, seemingly at times, unlimited wealth for the people who lived or invested in the region.

Prehistoric Indians

Indigenous peoples lived in the area for 10,000 to 15,000 years before the white man arrived. The first humans of whom we have traces hunted mammoths and other large animals on the tundra that edged the ice sheets covering the region. Called today Paleo-Indians, they were nomadic and lived

in family groups or bands.

The historic era started when the first European explorers reached the Chicago River and its surrounding area in 1673. Among the local residents they encountered were the Illinois and Illiniwek Indians. These hunted bison and raised crops.

The early European-descended settlers at Chicago would tap into the potential of the area and be astounded by it. They would describe their fate as "manifest destiny," a belief that God had chosen them and this region to prosper and grow exceedingly wealthy.

Today we can look back and see with more detail what it was that gave Chicago its impetus, promise, and prosperity. It was and continues to be a unique and, so far, abundant storehouse from the past.

The Explorers Arrive

The first descendants of Europeans known to have visited the Chicago area were the Jesuit priest, Jacques Marquette; the explorer-cartographer, Louis Jolliet; and five *voyageur* companions.

After a trip of exploration down the Mississippi River, they followed the advice of Indians they had encountered and returned to Lake Michigan via the Illinois and Des Plaines rivers and then the Chicago portage and river, reaching the lake in September 1673.

Marquette had made notes about the fertility of the soil and the abundance of game in what is now Northern Illinois. Jolliet suggested a canal could be built at Chicago to link Lake Michigan to the Mississippi River system.

A decade later, another *voyageur*, René-Robert Cavelier, sieur de La Salle, built a stockade and cabin at the site he

called "Checagou" or "Chicagou."

When fur-trader-turned-farmer Jean Baptiste Pointe DuSable established a farm and trading post at the mouth of the Chicago River in the mid-1780s, the Potawatomi and the allied tribes of the Ottawa and Kickapoo resided in the area. Through the 1783 Treaty of Paris, which ended the Revolutionary War,

This survey map was prepared by Frederick Harrison, Jr., assistant to William Howard, who was appointed by the U.S. Army Corps of Engineers to supervise the survey for a port of Chicago and a canal linking Lake Michigan and the Illinois River. From *History of Chicago* by A.T. Andreas. Courtesy, Kenan Heise collection

Built in 1834, the Dearborn Street drawbridge was the city's third bridge and first drawbridge. It replaced a free ferry but became such a point of contention between North and South Side residents that a mob of citizens gathered and chopped it down with axes in 1839. From *History of Chicago* by A.T. Andreas. Courtesy, Kenan Heise collection

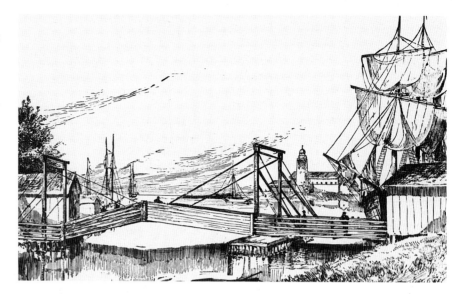

the United States acquired claim to the lands of the Northwest Territory.

The United States, in 1795, forced the Indians to sign the Treaty of Greenville. A provision in it ceded a strip of land six miles square "at or near the mouth of the Chicago River."

In 1800 DuSable sold his home and farm to Jean La Lime, who subsequently resold it to John Kinzie, a fur trader and silversmith. Kinzie later killed La Lime in a fight and was forced by the soldiers at the fort to bury him in the yard of his home, where he cared for his victim's grave until his own death.

Fort Dearborn

Although the area was now part of the United States, the dominant influence remained the British. The U.S. government established Fort Dearborn on the land ceded in the Treaty of Greenville. Today the fort's exact location and outline are recalled with metal markers in the pavement around the south end of the Michigan Avenue Bridge.

For the military stationed there, the fort proved a dull, wilderness assignment until the possibility of war with the British and trouble with their Indian allies started to create tensions in 1812.

The murder by a band of Indians of

two settlers at Hardscrabble a mile or so up the Chicago River indicated even worse problems ahead for the garrison and settlers at Fort Dearborn.

The United States declared war against Great Britain over the latter's policies on the high seas. The regional military commander at Detroit ordered Fort Dearborn abandoned as impossible to hold against attack by the British and Indians.

As the Fort Dearborn soldiers and civilians exited the fort and traveled along the lakefront two miles south of the river, a force of 600 Indians attacked them. Captain William Wells, a white man who had been raised among the Miami, led a valiant defense of the Americans, but was killed. According to research by Allan Eckert in *Gateway to Empire*, the dead included 53 soldiers, 12 members of the Chicago militia, six women, two men, and 12 children. The rest were taken prisoner, although French settlers remained "neutral" and Kinzie's family was allowed to escape.

The massacre did not, however, cause hesitation for those with the American dream of expansion. The Kinzies and other Chicagoans were examples. The fort, which had been burned, was rebuilt four years later after the War of 1812 ended. The fam-

The Sauganash Hotel as it appeared in 1837. It was built in 1831 by settler Mark Beaubien and was used until 1851, when it burned to the ground. Courtesy, Chicago Public Library

ily returned to their home along with a new garrison and a handful of settlers, farmers, and fur traders.

On October 1, 1818, a homesick 16-year-old apprentice fur trader, Gurdon S. Hubbard, arrived at the small settlement with a crew of veteran American Fur Company *voyageurs*. He was feted by the Kinzie family, who had a son his own age. The son, John H. Kinzie, would later run for mayor, losing in the first city election. Hubbard would live to become one of Chicago's preeminent entrepreneurs and see its population rise to include almost half a million people.

Others who arrived in the following decade at the Fort Dearborn site saw little future for the location, despite the fact that Illinois had become a state in 1818. Surveyor Stephen M. Long commented that "the dangers attending the navigation of the lake, and the scarcity of harbors along the shore, must ever prove a

serious obstacle to the increase of the commercial importance of Chicago."

Critical comments listing reasons why the location could never amount to much would be reinforced by the comments of many who visited it. They cited obstacles that ranged from major problems with mud to isolation and the lack of a harbor. Still, Chicago would move past these limitations and surge forward faster and further than even its most optimistic visionaries foresaw.

The major decision that would make it all possible was the one to build a canal linking the Chicago and Illinois rivers and, thereby, the Great Lakes and the Mississippi River. In 1816 the U.S. government had negotiated a treaty to purchase from the Indians a 90-mile-long strip of land 20 miles wide from Chicago to Ottawa on the Illinois River.

The canal would not be started before 1836 and would not be completed until 1848, but the future of Chicago as the

Above: J. Young Scammon (1812-1876) was a lawyer, alderman, and president of the Galena and Chicago Union Railroad. He was also founder of the Merchants Bank and an advocate for public schools. Courtesy, Kenan Heise collection

Right: This daguerreotype of the Chicago River flood of March 12, 1849, was the city's first "news" photo. It shows the results of a massive build-up of ice in the south branch followed by heavy rains. The resulting flood took a half-dozen lives, destroyed three bridges, and damaged or annihilated 57 canal boats, 24 brigs, four steamers, and two sloops. From *History of Chicago* by A.T. Andreas. Courtesy, Kenan Heise collection

gateway for the produce and wealth of the heart of America was fated.

On August 4, 1830, civil engineer James Thompson filed his plat and survey of the Chicago site, giving it a legal geographic designation. He also did the same for Ottawa. Chicago became a village in 1833 by a vote of 12-1. The lone dissenter, Russell E. Heacock, actually lived outside the proposed corporate limits.

The key need was for a harbor. Lake Michigan offered no natural one anywhere along its western shores. The mouth of the sluggish Chicago River

recognized harbor and port. The rush to wealth was on. Newcomers started to pour in by covered wagon, on Great Lakes schooners, and by foot. Investors in the East began to understand the future of the awakening port on Lake Michigan. People who purchased sections or "blocks" from the government at $1.25 an acre broke them into lots and offered them at auction.

An article in the *Philadelphia Commercial Herald* in 1835 listed the "manufactories" of Chicago as "one foundry, a steam gristmill, a steam sawmill, a brewery and a soap and

was frequently clogged. A sand bar formed so that its stream of water hooked lazily southward rather than straight out into Lake Michigan. All ships had to anchor offshore while passengers and cargo were transported into the city by lighters.

A lighthouse had been erected in 1832 and the next year U.S. military engineers cut a channel through the sandbar that had blocked access to the river. One of those who worked on it was West Point graduate Lieutenant Jefferson Davis, who would later serve as president of the Confederate States of America.

In July 1834 the 100-ton schooner *Illinois* entered the Chicago River and raised the village's status to that of a

candle factory."

The principal business, however, was land speculation. The auction prices of lots could double or triple within days. Usually, they were purchased not with cash, but on credit. What had sold for tens of dollars now went for ten of thousands. It was not only Chicago that was up for sale but also the prairies of Illinois, the forests of Wisconsin, and the sand hills of Michigan, along with what historian J. Seymour Currey described as "an almost unbroken chain of supposititious villages and cities."

The Bubble Bursts

Chicago was incorporated as a city on March 3, 1837, with a promise of con-

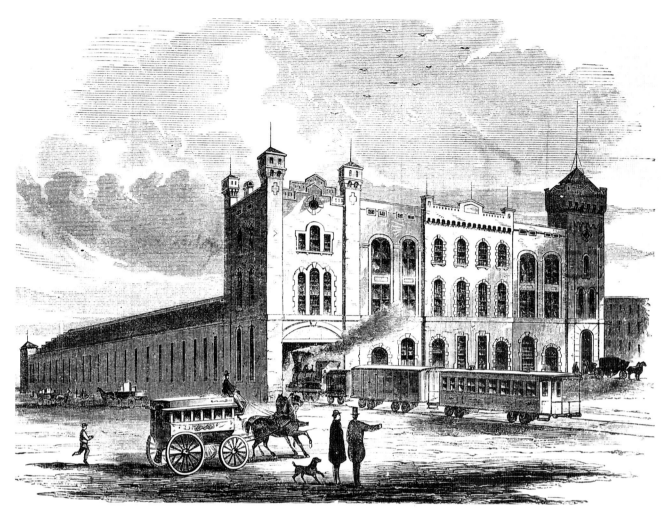

tinued growth and development that was beyond imagining. The non-Indian population had jumped from 30 in 1830 to 300 in 1833 to 4,000 by 1836.

The promise, however, was only for its new arrivals. The Indians, who had held the land in a communal trust, had been cheated out of it in the 1833 Treaty of Chicago. The negotiations had begun with U.S. Commissioner George Porter stating, "As their great father in Washington had heard they wished to sell their land, he had sent commissioners to treat with them."

The Indians replied, "The great father in Washington must have seen a bad bird which told him a lie, for that far from wishing to sell their land, they wished to keep it."

The commissioners had their way, however, and the Indians signed their Xs, selling Northern Illinois for two cents an acre and reluctantly agreeing

to be moved west of the Mississippi.

Chicago's promise included first a proposed canal and subsequently a railroad. Work on each was begun with great fanfare in 1836.

The realization of a promise is almost always further ahead than the dreamers think. The nation, and especially Chicago, found itself deflated in 1837 when the bubble of economic speculation burst. The Depression that followed found most scrip money worthless. As a result, neither canal nor railroad would become reality for another 12 long years.

The city's economy and finances remained in deep trouble. The early 1840s in Chicago offered a sharp contrast with the exciting 1830s that had been so full of promise and had seen a population boom.

Reflecting on Chicago in 1841, Joseph Balestier 35 years later wrote:

The depot of the Illinois and the Michigan Central Railroad, 1857. Chicago became connected to the East, to the South, and to the Mississippi River in the 1850s. The mileage of railroads leading out of the city grew from 10 to 4,000 between 1848 and 1857. Courtesy, Chicago Historical Society

Below: Colonel Elmer Ellsworth, a former clerk in Abraham Lincoln's law offices, became one of the first Union officers killed in the war. Courtesy, Kenan Heise collection

"At that day, all that remained to support life in Chicago was hope. The poverty of the place was visible and unfeigned. The more land a man had, the worse off he apparently was. Money and the people had long been strangers. But there were few who despaired for the Genius of the place forbade. To the dullest eye it was evident that a great destiny awaited our muddy little town, squatted upon the low banks of its sluggish bayou."

Changes were beginning to happen, however, ones that would count. Irish immigrants had come to the Chicago area and were working to dig the canal. Ogden, having served but one term as mayor, was wearing a different hat. He visited with farmers

to raise funds to build the railroad.

The new West desperately needed doctors. Rush Medical College was organized in 1843 to serve that need. The small city could now boast hotels (including a temperance one), a variety of stores, a number of newspapers, and several printers.

Gurdon Hubbard and then Archibald Clybourn went into the slaughtering business and Cyrus McCormick erected a plant along the north bank of the Chicago River to manufacture reapers that could do the work of several field hands. A national River and Harbor Convention in 1847 brought to Chicago such speakers as New York journalist Horace Greeley and Illinois politician Abraham Lincoln.

Year of Destiny: 1848

In 1848 everything seemed to come together for the city. Like a seed popping out of its encasement, Chicago broke through its isolation. It was that same year that the Chicago Board of Trade opened with 83 members. A plank road was extended southwest through the swamps to help bring produce and livestock to market, and a telegraph line was strung to connect Chicago and Milwaukee. The Illinois and Michigan Canal was opened to the Illinois River and *The Pioneer,* the first train out of Chicago, chugged its way west to the Des Plaines River on the tracks of the Galena and Chicago Union Railroad.

Suddenly Chicago was the fastest-growing city in the country. In 1848 its population was 20,023. By 1860 it had increased fivefold to 102,906.

The immediate reasons for this dramatic success were the canal, the railroads, the new plank roads, and an improved harbor. By 1854 Chicago had 10 railroads serving the city. It was shipping processed goods that had come from the East by boat through the Great Lakes and Erie Canal and then southwest via the Illinois and Michigan Canal, reaching as far south as New Orleans.

Noted Chicago historian Bessie Louise Pierce elaborated on this phenomenal development:

"The extension of the transportation system made Chicago the commercial center of the great Middle Valley. Dealers and commission men who sent eastward abundant stores of produce gathered from neighboring plains and fields amassed large fortunes and became the potentates of the far-flung back country. Speculators won and lost on the exchanges. Wholesalers who sent finished products commodities to the farms became prosperous. By 1851, the volume of grain coursing through Chicago became so swollen that the city came to be the greatest corn market in the country; in 1856, it attained preeminence as the foremost lumber mart in the United States; and during the Civil War it emerged as the greatest packing point."

And it grew on a parallel scale as the shopping mart for the farmers of the Midwest and West.

Lincoln is Nominated for President

Chicago achieved national political prominence in 1860, when the forces

Above: The Illinois Central Railroad as it appeared in 1860. The railroad purchased the unoccupied portion of the Fort Dearborn Reservation. Grant Park was eventually developed on land created by filling in Lake Michigan along the railroad tracks. Courtesy, Illinois Central Railroad

Below: In the 1860s trading in commodities and livestock started with cattle and pigs being driven to the Union Stock Yards, while wheat and oats were measured and stored in the city's grain elevators. Courtesy, Kenan Heise collection

Marshall Field, 1834-1906, embodied the modern merchant, balancing the roles of servant and lord in his establishment. In running the firm named for him, he demanded that his employees "Give the Lady What She Wants," whether that was quality merchandise, liberal credit and return policies, or the first department restaurant anywhere. To those around him, he was known for saying little but acting decisively. They called him "Silent Marsh," as he accumulated through his store and investments the largest fortune in the city.

Levi Z. Leiter (above) and Marshall Field took over Potter Palmer's store on Lake Street. Courtesy, Kenan Heise collection

Right: The Field, Leiter & Co. department store moved in 1868 to State and Washington streets. Courtesy, Kenan Heise collection

of the city came together to help Illinois' favorite son and political underdog Abraham Lincoln win the presidential nomination of the Republican Party. The convention was held in a wigwam built for the occasion in Chicago.

Ironically, the man with whom he would compete for the presidency, Senator Stephen A. Douglas, was not only an Illinoisian but a Chicagoan as well.

Civil War

When the Civil War erupted in 1861, it found Chicago in many regards out of harm's way. To be sure, some of its sons would be killed in the conflict, including one of the first officers to die for the Union cause, Colonel Elmer Ellsworth. Also, *Tribune* executive Major William Medill would fall at Gettysburg. Compared to other cities, however, Chicago did not lose as many men. One reason was that its residents frequently had enough money to pay bounties to hire substitutes from the farms, small cities, and the flow of immigrants to take their places. The city, as a result, met its quotas and saw no one drafted until the final months of the war.

Chicago prospered. It was the second-largest supplier of war materiel behind New York. Many purchasers,

government and otherwise, chose it over rival St. Louis because it was farther away from the beaten paths of war. The national manpower shortage caused by recruitment made the McCormick reaper vital to the Northern cause and piled the company's desk high with orders.

Chicago's meatpacking industry supplied the Union army, as did its wheat and grain elevators. It provided an entire line of products for the war effort, even including such songs as "Rally 'Round the Flag, Boys" from the Chicago firm of Root & Cady's long list of patriotic sheet music.

Senator Douglas' former estate at 33rd Street and the lakefront served first as a staging center for new recruits and later as the tragic prisoner-of-war facility, Camp Douglas.

The city staggered under Lincoln's assassination, which followed within days of Robert E. Lee's surrender. On May 1, 1865, Lincoln's funeral train arrived in Chicago, where he had left many personal friends when he went east to serve as President.

The Stockyards

On December 25 of that same year, Chicago consolidated its stockyards on the Southwest Side. The Union Stock Yards and Transit Company covered a mile square with slaughterhouses, pens, and railroad tracks. It was awesome both in production and odor. By the 1890s fully 20 percent of Chicago's workers were employed in the meatpacking trade and that figure was much higher among immigrants. It was the ultimate end of the line for the Chisholm and the Santa Fe trails and the cowboys who brought the cattle to market.

The industry was immensely productive not only because of the available transportation and Chicago's ideal loca-

tion, but also because its meatpackers were extraordinarily inventive. They not only improved ways to salt and can beef and pork, they also developed the refrigerated boxcar to preserve the meat for distribution to more distant markets.

Men such as Philip D. Armour and Gustavus F. Swift found ways "to use everything from the hog but the squeal." They were equally economical with cattle and sheep. They utilized hides, hair, bones, horns, dung, fat, and blood to create products such as medi-

cine, strings for musical instruments, glue, gelatin, soap, sporting goods, chess pieces, souvenirs, and fertilizer. Last, but not least, they used the stockyards themselves as a leading Chicago tourist attraction.

Upton Sinclair's 1906 novel, *The Jungle*, would paint the inhumane downside of the industry. Ultimately, refrigerated trucks and the country's expressways would lead to Chicago losing the industry to other locations through decentralization.

Merchandising—Retail and Wholesale

Another industry that began to burst onto the national scene from Chicago at this time was merchandising—retail

Above: This building on State Street, next to the Field, Leiter & Co. store, housed new and used book dealers and was known as Bookseller's Row. From *Harper's Weekly.* Courtesy, Kenan Heise collection

Top: Ira Couch (1806-1857) and his brother James, considered the city's first millionaires, owned the Tremont House Hotel. Ira's mausoleum still stands in Lincoln Park, east of the Chicago Historical Society. Courtesy, Kenan Heise collection

The famous castle of Potter and Bertha Palmer stood at 1350 North Lake Shore Drive. The mansion was the focal point of society in Chicago. There the couple entertained three presidents and innumerable princes and princesses. Courtesy, Kenan Heise collection

and wholesale. The city's merchants had started by selling off the backs of the wagons that had brought their products to the city and then by opening small grocery, hardware, or clothing stores.

By the 1850s these establishments, especially the dry goods shops, found themselves selling to more particular and wealthier customers. Such firms, mostly located on Lake Street, included John V. Farwell and Co., where

Marshall Field and Levi Leiter worked their way up to partnerships. The two men purchased Potter Palmer's store in the 1860s to form Field, Leiter & Co. The latter today is known as Marshall Field & Co.

These men were not only ingenious retailers, they were also in the right place at the right time. Their markets and customers multiplied and entrepreneurs, real estate and grain speculators, as well as all manner of business own-

Philip Danforth Armour, 1823-1901, founder of the meatpacking firm of Armour & Co., was a noted philanthropist who funded the Armour Institute, later known as the Illinois Institute of Technology. His highly successful company earned a reputation for using by-products to create gourmet foods, medicines, soaps, and leather goods.

ers, began to accumulate untold wealth. The top firms managed to survive the periodic downturns such as those in 1857, 1866, and 1873 that weeded out many over-stretched businesses. They also began to see the benefits of extending credit in a careful manner and expanding into the wholesale trade to small-town stores. Most of all, they realized that customers wanted to be treated well. Marshall Field's motto of "Give the Lady What She Wants" still makes good business sense today.

Palmer got out of the dry goods business, bought and developed State Street real estate, and then founded the Palmer House hotel. The city's sumptuous hotels such as the Grand Pacific, The Briggs House, the fire-plagued Tremont House, the Drake, and the Sherman House rivaled some of the best from around the world, but always retained a touch of the common to fit in with the city's style.

Leiter eventually was bought out by Field, but his own careful investments had made him one of the wealthiest men in the country. Field garnered it all. His firm prospered and reached out far into the hinterlands with wholesale as well as retail establishments. His other investments in real estate, mining, traction, and banking saw him become one of the wealthiest men in the nation before his death in 1906.

Chicago, like these men, was finding itself well situated for the future by 1871—and then something bigger than all their efforts combined happened.

The Chicago Fire

It is known in American history simply as the Chicago Fire. Sometimes, it has been called "The Great Chicago Fire," but the word "Great" is generally considered superfluous.

The Chicago Fire is still recognized, according to a recent commentary, as

Bertha (1849-1918) and **Potter** (1826-1902) **Palmer** set the pace for Chicago's newly wealthy families. He founded the department store that became Marshall Field & Co. and established the city's top hotel, the Palmer House. She was the undisputed queen of local society from the Chicago Fire through World War I. Together, they built a Lake Shore mansion in 1882 that started the exodus of well-to-do families from Prairie Avenue on the Near South Side to the Gold Coast on the North Side.

"the single most important event in the history of Chicago and one of the most spectacular of the nineteenth century."

Mere statistics alone do not at first seem to merit such a label. On the same days in 1871, October 8 to 10, for example, a small town, Peshtigo, Wisconsin, suffered a worse conflagration in terms of lives lost and area burned.

In Peshtigo, 1,200 people died; but in Chicago, the total number of dead was estimated at 300. Only a portion of the city, principally the business district, was destroyed. Still, it was this fire that received the world's attention and that still blazes in its memory.

The drama of the fire arose as much out of the situation as from the facts. The story of the *Titanic* had added drama, for example, because it had been a ship "that not even God could sink." The deity was also involved in the Chicago story in some people's minds. The city's luck and enormous prosperity showed that the hand of the Almighty was favoring and supposedly protecting it, to their way of thinking. Chicagoans and other believers called it "manifest destiny," and saw it as a place chosen by nature and therefore God to represent abundance, unlimited opportunity, and the ingenuity of man.

To disparage Chicago was to criticize

This painting of society doyenne Bertha Palmer is by Anders Leonard Zorn. Courtesy, The Art Institute of Chicago

Above: Those fighting the Chicago Fire hoped the river would stop the flames. It did not. Courtesy, Chicago Public Library

Right: The story of the Chicago Fire is a combination of the personal tales of its more than 330,000 survivors. This newspaper depiction of a scene on Dearborn Street tells of the efforts of firefighters to save victims. Courtesy, Kenan Heise collection

God's extraordinarily benevolent plan for His favorite country and seemingly select city. Such a view was not publicly espoused but remained in the back of many minds with a "good Presbyterian" belief that prosperity was a sign of God's favor.

This city existed. It could be visited and wondered at. Blocks of tall, elegant buildings stood where 20 years earlier cattle had roamed; yards stacked high with lumber lined the Chicago River; grain elevators, many stories high, were filled with wheat; and bank storage vaults, with money.

A spark that many say was caused by a cow kicking over a lantern, seemed at first to put an end to all of it.

Chicago and the entire Midwest had been parched from a long stretch without rain. The city's buildings were predominantly wood and their builders had no fire codes to follow in constructing them. Voices warning of disaster that had been loud and clear were ignored.

On Sunday night, October 8, it came, starting in Mrs. Kate O'Leary's barn on DeKoven Street. The city's fire department was exhausted from fighting a major fire the previous day and there were complications in determining which alarm had sounded and where the fire was.

The conflagration roared northeast toward the river and the downtown area, strengthened by strong winds and the heat-created gales that added to and fanned the flames. They did not stop at the river but rather leaped it in two places. The city hall bell rang to warn people, but most had already heard the commotion of the approaching fire and those rushing by their doors to escape the devastation.

The lumber and coal yards along the river fueled the flames, as did the gasworks and the homes of the poor Irish who lived in the area known as "The

Patch." The fire moved swiftly and inevitably toward the hotels, office buildings, and stores in the crowded commercial heart of Chicago. It voraciously devoured Field, Leiter & Co., Potter Palmer's brand-new hotel, the Crosby Opera House, the *Tribune*'s recently constructed building, wharves and elevators, factories and mansions.

People fled, a number of them escaping into the cold waters of Lake Michigan, while others ducked into the open graves in the City Cemetery (now Lincoln Park), from which bodies had recently been removed.

The fire finally burned out on Tuesday morning, October 10, near Fullerton Avenue and the lake. A Chicago journalist reported:

"The great, dazzling, mounting light, the crash and the roar of the conflagration, and the desperate flight of the crowd combined to make a scene of which no intelligent idea can be conveyed in words."

Soot and Ash

The burgeoning glory of Chicago had turned to black soot and ash. An estimated 90,000 people had been made homeless and 7,450 buildings,

Kate O'Leary, 1835-?, is blamed for owning the cow that allegedly kicked over a lantern and started the Chicago Fire on October 8, 1871. She was an Irish immigrant businesswoman who owned a home, a barn, five cows, a calf, and a horse. She had a milk route on the city's Near Southwest Side. The fire apparently did start in her barn, sparing her home as it burned toward downtown. Some writers have argued that it was rather a neighbor, Peg Leg Pete, who was the cause, while one author has speculated that the fragment of a comet hit the barn.

Although the city had many commercial photographers, apparently not one of them took a single shot of the Chicago Fire while it was burning. Courtesy, Kenan Heise collection

Myra Bradwell, 1831-1894, although trained and qualified to be a lawyer, was stopped from becoming one by the Illinois and U.S. supreme courts in the early 1870s. As a married woman, they said, she incurred "a legal disability." They argued that as a wife she had to tell her husband everything, thus incurring a conflict of confidentiality. She subsequently founded and edited the *Chicago Legal News*, the most widely circulated legal newspaper in the country. Bradwell also helped her friend, Alta Hulett, become the first woman allowed to practice law in Illinois.

destroyed. How many disconsolate Chicagoans left the city for good cannot even be imagined.

Still, the story of the Chicago Fire is inevitably told in terms of the city's recovery from it. Both buildings and lives were reconstructed. Fortunes were remade. The Palmer House, Field, Leiter & Co., and the *Tribune* soon had grander buildings than before. A fire district ordinance was enacted requiring that all structures within its limits be built with stone or brick rather than wood.

The late Robert Cromie, Chicago reporter, author, and expert on the fire, wrote of the world's reaction:

The population—334,000 at the time of the fire—had almost doubled to 503,298 by the end of the decade. Around the world, Chicago became known as "The Phoenix City" for its image of having risen out of its own ashes.

While few of the Sunday sermons given within thousands of miles of Chicago failed to make a reference to God's hand in the fire, people started speaking less of "manifest destiny." Such a predetermined concept did not adequately take into account the fragile nature of what man had constructed. The focus became more on human accomplishment. While some slight lesson may have been learned, other preachers confidently attributed the conflagration to such specific causes as the city failing to close saloons on Sunday.

The Chicago Fire was followed by several years of Depression, during which many Chicagoans went hungry and some starved. It represented a national economic downturn in which the insurance and business losses sustained as a result of the Chicago Fire

Joseph Medill, 1823-1899, was the editor and publisher of the *Chicago Tribune* during the last 25 years of the nineteenth century. He also served as mayor of Chicago immediately following the Chicago Fire in 1871. He and Dr. Charles Ray purchased the newspaper in 1855 from owners who had been identified with the Know-Nothing Movement. They made it into a publication respected nationally, were early supporters of Abraham Lincoln for president, and earned respect and attention for their effective Civil War coverage.

had played at least a minor part.

The economic downturn led to strikes and riots, which gripped the city in 1877 and would result in social and political unrest that continued through the 1880s with mass protest rallies, the Haymarket trial, and subsequent hangings of the leading dissidents.

The Art of Architecture Takes a Dramatic Turn

Another true revolution that was happening in Chicago occurred in architecture and construction. The city, with its need for new buildings, attracted architects and engineers who began to work through some of the age-old problems entailed in creating more functional and cost-effective commercial and residential structures.

The invention of the mechanical elevator in the 1850s had made much taller buildings feasible but it would take three decades to work through the many construction problems this new opportunity afforded.

The list of innovative Chicago architects of the period is long and exciting. It includes John Van Osdel, who designed ships, homes, the iron-front five-story buildings of pre-fire Chicago,

William Le Baron Jenney, 1832-1907, one of

the most inventive architects in history, had served in the Civil War as
an engineer under Generals Ulysses S. Grant and William Tecumseh
Sherman before settling in Chicago. He trained a number of young
architects who included Louis Sullivan, Daniel Burnham, William
Holabird, and Martin Roche. Together they constituted the nucleus
of the "Chicago School." In the mid-1880s he developed the steel
skeletal construction that made true skyscrapers possible. The first,
which he designed, was the Home Insurance Building (1885-1931)
on the northeast corner of LaSalle and Adams.

Right: One has only to count the smokestacks to determine exactly how prosperous the artist wanted the city to appear in this depiction of the Chicago lakefront in 1855. Courtesy, Kenan Heise collection

Facing page, bottom: The careers of architect Frank Lloyd Wright (left) and poet Carl Sandburg were closely associated with Chicago. Their parallel careers illustrated the city's ability to attract genius and support it. Courtesy, Archie Lieberman

and many of those that replaced them. Also on the list are William Le Baron Jenney; Daniel Burnham and John Wellborn Root, whose Rookery and other Loop office buildings still memorialize them; Louis Sullivan and Dankmar Adler, represented by the Auditorium and some of the great pieces of architecture in modern history; and Frank Lloyd Wright, whose works helped culminate the efforts of other Chicago architects.

Louis Sullivan, 1856-1924, considered by many to be

the father of modern architecture, created such buildings that still
adorn Chicago as the Auditorium and the Carson Pirie Scott and
Company store. These and his Transportation Building at the World's
Columbian Exposition, Chicago Stock Exchange, and Garrick Theatre
each represented a dramatic break with the past. Through admiration
for his work and by his writings, his "form follows function" approach
replaced a classical tradition with a more useful and serviceable
concept of architecture.

Frank Lloyd Wright, 1869-1959, was viewed throughout his long life as an architectural genius who was always creating something different. Since his death, there have been hundreds of books written about him and his work. He is now recognized as an innovator who saw possibilities others did not. Among his creations were the "Prairie Style" house, the earthquake-proof Imperial Hotel in Tokyo, the spectacularly environment-integrated Fallingwater near Pittsburgh, and the Guggenheim Museum in New York City. His own home and studio in Oak Park, just outside of Chicago, are still preserved for visitors.

Mother Francis Xavier Cabrini,

1850-1917, who founded Columbus Hospital in 1905, died there in 1917. In 1946 she became the first American citizen to be canonized a saint by the Catholic Church. Her work among the poor Italian immigrants in the city resulted in the Cabrini Homes on the Near North Side being named for her.

Photo courtesy, Kenan Heise collection

The Splendid Chaos of Chicago

Chicago grew more and more exciting and confusing to the people of the world. It was unquestionably a place of creative, new ideas, but it also was indubitably chaotic. In the 1880s English journalist G.W. Steevens described Chicago as:

"Queen and guttersnipe of cities, cynosure and cesspool of the world: Not if I had a hundred tongues, everyone shouting a different language in a different key, could I do justice to such splendid chaos. The most beautiful and the most squalid, girdled with a twofold zone of parks and slums; where the keen air from the lake and prairie is ever in the nostrils and the stench of foul smoke is never out of the throat; the great port, a thousand miles from the sea; the great mart which gathers up with one hand the corn and the cattle of the West and deals out with the other the merchandise of the East; widely and generously planned, where it is not safe to walk at night; the chosen seat of cutthroat commerce and munificent patronage of art; the most American of cities and

yet the most mongrel; the second American city of the globe, the fifth German city, the third Swedish, the second Polish, the first and only Babel of the age. Where in all the world can words be found for this miracle of paradox and incongruity?"

It was in the freedom afforded by this chaos that Chicagoans found a source and chance for creativity. In Chicago, artists, musicians, and writers did not have to follow the same rigid rules as elsewhere. This gave them greater opportunities for invention and originality.

But change and challenge are not always acceptable. The capitalist system was working in Chicago, at least for those on top. They had become frightened by the riots of labor unrest in 1877 and by the speeches and writing of the city's Socialists and, especially, Anarchists.

The Haymarket Tragedy

Communists, Socialists, and Anarchists all preached revolution. Some prepared for it coming about through violence, if necessary. These, with little exception, merely talked about it. Most worked toward more immediate goals such as unionization and the eight-hour work day. On May 3, 1886, six protestors were killed in volleys of police fire against strikers outside the McCormick Reaper Works.

The next day a mass protest rally was scheduled for the Haymarket Square, west of the Loop, to protest their deaths. Mayor Carter Harrison was there and later termed it "tame." A contingent of police under the excitable and corrupt Inspector John Bonfield, however, attempted to break it up after the mayor and chief of police had left.

An individual, undetermined to this day, threw a bomb at the police. Bonfield replied by ordering his men to fire at the crowd. Some of them shot back. Seven policemen were killed and more than 50 others were wounded. Crowd members carried their dead and wounded away.

The state's attorney and police Captain Michael Schaack went after the city's radicals, charging conspiracy and arguing that they had incited the "riot." The jury was hand-selected by a bailiff who wanted to see them hang. The judge, Joseph Gary, handed down heavy-handed rulings against any rights for the defendants.

Four of them—Albert Parsons, August Spies, Adolph Fischer, and George Engel—were hanged. A fifth, Louis Lingg, bit a dynamite cap on the morning of the execution and died hours later. The other three served prison terms but were later unconditionally pardoned by Governor John Peter Altgeld. Judge Gary, he wrote, had conducted the trial with "malicious ferocity."

Jane Addams

On September 14, 1889, Jane Addams and Ellen Gates Starr moved into a rickety old mansion in the Harrison-Halsted streets neighborhood. The structure was called Hull House after its former owner, Charles J. Hull.

Of Chicago in that year, Henry Justin Smith later wrote:

"It had money and power. Both of these it wasted as it chose. It pulsed with complex human energies; it was quick to adopt new inventions and apply new ideas."

The five men sentenced to die as a result of the Haymarket affair had been convicted for conspiracy in one of the most controversial trials of the nineteenth century. Courtesy, Kenan Heise collection

Albert Parsons, 1848-1887, the gentle, thoughtful editor of *The Socialist* and co-editor of *The Alarm*, was hanged as a result of the Haymarket tragedy. A native of Texas and a Confederate veteran, he nevertheless wanted to achieve justice and racial equality through eliminating capitalism. In a letter he left for his young children, he wrote: "I leave you the legacy of an honest name and duty done."

James Weber Linn, Jane Addams' nephew, repeated Smith's words in describing the opening era of Hull House and added that it was:

"True of most northern American cities in the '80s and '90s, but truest of Chicago."

Hull House became a fresh, innovative catalyst for efforts to include the poor and the immigrant in the vibrant life of Chicago both by the personal efforts of the women associated with it and through such institutional changes as organizing unions, holding rallies, and offering a full range of caring, community service programs.

The World's Columbian Exposition

Four years later the 1893 World's Columbian Exposition became one of the major events in Chicago's history, a world's fair still commemorated today by one of the four stars in the city's

flag. Held in the South Side's Jackson Park along the lake, it brought people from around the globe to "that Chicago," which Bismarck 23 years earlier had wanted to visit.

The architecture of "The White City," as the exposition was nicknamed, was in the classical style in imitation of Greece and Rome. This contrasted sharply with Chicago itself, where skyscrapers were being erected with a new, American, and far more functional design and beauty.

The 1893 event proved a draw for inventors, writers, theologians, artists, reformers, arms manufacturers, hucksters, and farm families out to see the big city. Some of each group would stay to become part of Chicago.

The world's fair helped stave off for a short time the effects of a depression that hit the country. It struck Chicago full by the end of 1893, with people

who had worked at the exposition now living on the streets or in the jail cells that were opened to them for sleeping.

The Pullman Strike

In the summer of 1894 this economic downturn exploded into the Pullman

William Rainey Harper, 1856-1906, was

the inspirational co-founder and first president of the University of Chicago, which opened on October 1, 1892. He convinced Marshall Field to donate the Hyde Park neighborhood land and John D. Rockefeller and steel magnate William Ryerson much of the start-up money. His vision and foresight set the standard for the university that would see the founding of the science of sociology, the first sustained nuclear reaction, and more Nobel Prize winners than any other institution in the world.

Above: The Columbian half dollar, designed by Olin Lewis Warner, was the first U.S. commemorative coin. Minted in 1892 and 1893, it sold for one dollar at the World's Columbian Exposition in 1893, but was later released into circulation at face value. The obverse shows a bust of Christopher Columbus; the reverse depicts his flagship, the *Santa Maria.* Courtesy, C.D. Hayden

Right: The Transportation Building at the World's Columbian Exposition was the work of Louis Sullivan. In designing this structure with its golden door, Sullivan broke with classical style and helped establish modern architecture. Courtesy, Kenan Heise collection

Ida B. Wells-Barnett, 1862–1931, a daughter

of slaves and a fighter for human and civil rights, gave the United States a clarion call against the lynching of blacks in the South by publishing the first statistical study of it. She came to Chicago in 1893 to protest a lack of involvement by blacks in the World's Columbian Exposition. Mrs. Wells-Barnett headed the Negro Fellowship League to help newly arrived African-Americans and was a founder in 1909 of the National Association for the Advancement of Colored People (NAACP).

Photo courtesy, Kenan Heise collection

A view of State Street on October 21, 1892, looking north from Monroe Street, as the city prepared for the World's Columbian Exposition. Courtesy, Kenan Heise collection

Strike. In the early 1880s George Pullman, manufacturer of luxurious sleeping cars, had created south of the city a company town for his workers. To his great disappointment and displeasure, however, his employees subsequently voted to become part of Chicago.

In 1894, with business slow, he cut his workers' wages, but not their rents or utility charges. They tried to work it out with him, but he stated, "There is nothing to negotiate." They struck, and then pleaded with Socialist Eugene V. Debs to allow them to join his American Railway Union. He acceded. The union called a sympathy strike that included a manned boycott to stop all trains to which Pullman cars were attached.

Normally, federal troops could be sent into a state to quell disorder when its governor or mayor requested them. Neither Governor Altgeld nor Chicago

Mayor John Hopkins, both of whom sympathized with the strikers, did so. President Grover Cleveland, whose attorney general had been general counsel for the railroads, sent them into Chicago on the Fourth of July anyway. The troops broke the strike and Debs was imprisoned for six months on a charge of contempt of court for refusing to tell union members to stop the strike.

Theodore Dreiser, 1871-1945, Chicago reporter turned novelist, was an eminent American realist. His *Sister Carrie* (1900) helped change the direction of American fiction. In the book, Carrie Meeber's "sin" of living with a married man goes unpunished, thus breaking the accepted tenet that art must serve established morality.

Mary McDowell, 1854-1936, founder and director for two generations of the University of Chicago Settlement House in the Back of the Yards neighborhood, earned such nicknames as "Fighting Mary," "The Garbage Lady," and "Duchess of Bubbly Creek." The area was described, at the time, as "an ugly, dirty neighborhood separated from the rest of Chicago by a square mile of packing plants and stockyards." She ran an innovative, multi-program settlement and fought to get the city's open garbage closed and Bubbly Creek, which served as the stockyard's sewer, cleaned up.

Above: In the 1890s thousands of laborers, using the most modern equipment available at the time, blasted, dug, shoveled, and cut their way through 43 million cubic yards of dirt and rock to construct the 32-mile-long, 20-foot-deep, Sanitary and Ship Canal linking the Chicago River with the Des Plaines and Illinois River systems. The district constructed this channel to complete the reversal of the flow of the Chicago River away from Lake Michigan, source of the area's drinking water supply. Courtesy, Barbara Rumsey

Right: Chicago's Hudson Avenue 36th Precinct police force is depicted in this 1907 photograph. Courtesy, Kenan Heise collection

If Christ Came to Chicago

Also in 1894, William T. Stead, a British reformer and journalist, published a book titled *If Christ Came to Chicago.* It would prove one of the most powerful and interesting exposés of an American city ever compiled. It gave details and named names. It excoriated the three leading business figures in the city—Marshall Field, Philip D. Armour, and George Pullman—calling them "The Chicago Trinity" and criticizing them more for sins of omission than commission.

The book also dug into political corruption in Chicago and quoted a source saying that all but two members of the city council accepted bribes.

The man most identified with corruption in the 1890s in Chicago was traction magnate Charles T. Yerkes. He routinely paid bribes to obtain street franchises from the city for extending his elevated and streetcar lines. His ultimate downfall in Chicago was made possible by an unlikely duo, First Ward Aldermen Michael "Hinky Dink" Kenna and "Bathhouse" John Coughlin. These two, noted for their reign over the wild and woolly Levee District, refused to accept a bribe in this case to give Yerkes an almost lifetime control of the city's traction lines.

Creativity and Originality

If there were indications of chaos, corruption, and borderline anarchy in Chicago at this time, there was also a unique force for creativity and originality. Chicago was the cauldron in which

The *Chicago Defender* donated holiday food baskets to the hungry in 1913, an annual tradition. Courtesy, *Chicago Defender*

American and thereby modern ideas broke loose from the bones of Greece and Rome. It was also the progenitor of new ways of doing business, such as the giant catalog houses of Sears, Roebuck and Co. and Montgomery Ward and Co. In 1912 Chicagoan Harriet Monroe founded *Poetry: A Magazine of Verse*. It continues today to introduce the city's top poets to America.

Writers—among them Theodore Dreiser, Edgar Lee Masters, Carl Sandburg, Sherwood Anderson, Finley Peter Dunne, Willa Cather, Margaret Anderson, and Hamlin Garland—were making such a mark that in 1917 H.L. Mencken dared to call Chicago "The Literary Capital of America."

It was an era when Chicago could claim educator John Dewey; Maurice and Ellen Browne, founders of the Little Theater Movement; *Tarzan* creator Edgar Rice Burroughs; poets Carl Sandburg, Vachel Lindsay, and Edgar Lee Masters; and the ingenious journalism of Ring Lardner, Ben Hecht, and Finley Peter Dunne.

Disasters

Meanwhile, the burgeoning metropolis of Chicago found itself stunned by a series of devastating disasters:

- The Iroquois Theater fire, December 30, 1903. A drape caught fire by touching an arc lamp. Flames engulfed the so-called "fireproof" theater and claimed the lives of 603 victims, including 212 children.

- The *Eastland* disaster, July 24, 1915. A passenger ship, sitting in the Chicago River with 2,000 Western

Above: Lieutenant William Leo Sullivan of the Chicago Fire Department was one of the leaders in the movement to organize the firefighter's union in the city. He was also honored for his valiant rescue efforts during the Iroquois Theater fire of 1903. That blaze, which occurred during a children's matinee performance of *Mr. Bluebeard* starring Eddie Foy, Sr., claimed the lives of 603 people, including many children. Courtesy, Don Toohey

Facing page: Street scenes, such as this 1898 depiction of Randolph Street looking east, were popularly used for postcards, souvenir booklets, and stereoscope collections. Courtesy, Kenan Heise collection

Electric employees aboard, capsized. Many of them had gone to one side of the vessel to watch a boat pass by. The ship had given up some of her ballast so she could carry more passengers. The tragedy resulted in 812 deaths, including many entire families.

- The *Wingfoot Express* crash, July 21, 1919. A blimp caught fire while crossing the Loop and crashed into the skylight of the Illinois Trust and Savings Bank. Three aboard the craft and 10 on the ground were killed. The pilot and a mechanic parachuted to safety.

World War I

According to polls in the early days of World War I, Chicagoans were recorded as being especially reluctant to have the United States become involved. These included such idealistic progressive individuals and groups as Jane Addams, Clarence Darrow, Eugene V. Debs, the Industrial Workers of the World, and a number of Socialists. Their numbers also embraced much of the large German-American population and the city's flamboyant mayor, William "Big Bill" Thompson, who hated the British.

Later, the war fervor brought the city and all but a few objectors into its frenzy.

The aftermath of the war was devastating to Chicago. The availability of jobs during the conflict brought thousands of African-Americans to the city from the South. When it ended, they found resentment rather than employment and a race riot exploded in July 1919. The death toll was 22 blacks and 14 whites. A commission was appointed to study causes and solutions. It added fuel, however, to the flames of future racial prejudice and discrimination by calling for stricter segregation practices.

The Gangster Era

Chicago's reputation took a serious, hard blow from events that flowed from the onset of Prohibition on January 17, 1920. The date also happened to be the 21st birthday

Above: A defense attorney, writer, and orator, Clarence Darrow loved to speak and fight for the underdog and unpopular positions. In 1924 he saved young thrill-killers Richard Loeb and Nathan Leopold from a sentence of death. They were given "life plus 99 years." Courtesy, Kenan Heise collection

Right: "Scarface" Al Capone used such ruthless methods as the St. Valentine's Day Massacre to control bootlegging and other rackets in Chicago. Courtesy, Kenan Heise collection

of a young New York thug who would later come to Chicago and make quite a reputation for himself. That man was Al Capone.

"Scarface" Al Capone—along with other bootleggers such as Johnny Torrio, Dion O'Banion, "Little Hymie" Weiss, "Machine Gun" McGurn, and "Bugs" Moran—helped give the city an international reputation as the crime capital of the world.

What Else?

Not credited to Chicago was the fact that during Capone's years, 1924-1931, three women who wrote in and about the city (Willa Cather, Edna Ferber, and Margaret Ayer Barnes) won Pulitzer Prizes for literature. A fourth, Janet Ayer Fairbanks, was announced as

second in 1927, when Sinclair Lewis refused the prize for *Arrowsmith*.

At the same time, the University of Chicago was establishing its reputation for scholarship under its new young chancellor, Robert Maynard Hutchins.

The American music scene was undergoing a major revitalization from happenings in Chicago that included the founding of Gospel music here; the urbanization of blues and jazz to the point where Chicago styles of both were recognized; the nationalization of country and western music through the WLS Barn Dance radio program; the creation of swing by Benny Goodman;

the Chicago Symphony Orchestra being the only one regularly playing American composers; and the promotion of folk music through the publication of Carl Sandburg's *The American Songbag*.

In 1933 the mayor of Chicago, Anton Cermak, was assassinated. He was shot in Miami by a bullet apparently aimed at President-elect Franklin Roosevelt. He had gone to meet with the president to ask his help in paying the salaries of Chicago teachers who had been given scrip in place of money because the city was so hard hit by the Depression.

Another World's Fair

Chicago's bright spot in the 1930s,

The Chicago World's Fair, called "A Century of Progress," was held along the lakefront in 1934. It included exhibits and structures from around the world. Courtesy, Kenan Heise collection

sometimes called "The Dismal Decade," was the "Century of Progress" exhibition along the lakefront. The world's fair was held in 1934 in conjunction with the 100th anniversary of Chicago's incorporation as a village.

The architecture and design of this event, in contrast to the World's Columbian Exposition 40 years earlier, was distinctly contemporary and, at times, even futuristic. Chicagoans and people from around the world enjoyed it as a respite from the Depression and it was a resounding financial success. Corporate America showed off its latest wares and accomplishments and so did Chicago. Local talent included Sally Rand, a fan dancer who reminded older

residents of Little Egypt, who had danced the hoochie coochie on the Midway of the White City in 1893.

No matter how depressed the city grew in the following years, Chicago did not lose its reputation for a unique élan. Its burgeoning advertising industry was responsible for developing and writing the scripts for a new form of popular theater, the radio soap opera. The city's African-American community was caught up in a cultural renaissance that paralleled and outlasted the one in Harlem.

In 1935 noted American writer Christopher Morley authored a book titled *Old Loopy: A Love Letter for Chicago*. In it, he wrote:

Louis "Satchmo" Armstrong, 1901-1971,

came to Chicago from New Orleans in the summer of 1922 and started playing trumpet on the South Side with Joe "King" Oliver's band. His experimentation, paraphrasing, and originality quickly made him the voice and ambassador of jazz. Musically, his style helped emphasize the African-American contribution to an era that broke away from tradition and proclaimed individual freedom.

Photo courtesy, Kenan Heise collection

"It is not my wish nor ability to offer a philosophical essay on Chicago. I simply want to tell her I love her. She is one of the few big towns that can be loved as an integer; a subtle unity holds her together, makes her apprehensible...

"She is unruly at heart; more than a little goofy; she will be the last to be tamed by the slow frost of correctness...She spikes the small beer of living with the pure alcohol of the impossible."

Chicago Goes to War

One of the impossible things some Chicagoans believed was that it would be possible to keep the United States out of World War II. A handful of these were members of the German *Bund* organization that supported

Right: One of the most discussed features of Chicago's fair was the famous dancer, Sally Rand. Her fans are preserved in the Chicago Historical Society. Courtesy, Kenan Heise collection

the Nazi regime. A greater number were active in the isolationist America First Movement. Among these was Sears, Roebuck president General Robert E. Wood.

Once the United States entered the war after the attack on Pearl Harbor, Chicagoans began to serve the war effort enthusiastically. There were a sizable number of conscientious objectors who accepted jail or ambulance service in combat zones over joining the army, but the vast numbers served in various win-the-war capacities, from military enlistment or conscription to serving as air raid wardens or working in war plants.

Chicago was especially positioned to help through its capable and extensive transportation facilities and systems. Its radio-manufacturing and burgeoning electronic industries also uniquely aided the war effort by producing radar equipment and walkie-talkies.

Probably Chicago's greatest contribution, other than supplying volunteers and draftees, was that made by the men and women who operated its steel furnaces, which industry helped outflank the enemy.

To Chicago's great credit, it proved possibly the most hospitable of any major city to the interned Japanese-Americans attempting to find jobs and leave the concentration camps. Older members of the community still have memories of themselves or their parents being able to come to the city and find jobs and housing rather than rank prejudice and discrimination.

The city was such a harbor that

Iva Ikuko Toguri D'Aquino settled here. The UCLA graduate had been convicted in 1949 (on rather tenuous grounds, as there were no records) for broadcasting in Japan during World War II as "Tokyo Rose." Before coming to Chicago, she had served six and a half years of a 10-year sentence.

Long before the arrival of Japanese-Americans, Chicago earned a reputation not only as the city "of the big shoulders" but also of the open arms to those persecuted and discriminated against elsewhere. The statistics of the 2000 census indicating significant growth in the numbers of Asian-Americans and Hispanic-Americans shows it continues to be so.

This traffic jam at Randolph and Dearborn streets was, according to some sources, staged to test what would happen without supervision. Nevertheless, this often-reprinted image has become a symbol of deep chaos, considered a source of Chicago's creativity. Courtesy, Kenan Heise collection

Mary Garden, 1877-1967, was Chicago's diva, the toast of its operatic scene from 1910 through 1931. A millionaire friend paid for her voice training in Paris and she performed such noted roles as Thais, Louise, and Salome. In the latter, the city's police chief compared her to "a cat wallowing in catnip." In 1921 she was made general director of the Chicago Opera Association, the first woman ever to head an opera company.

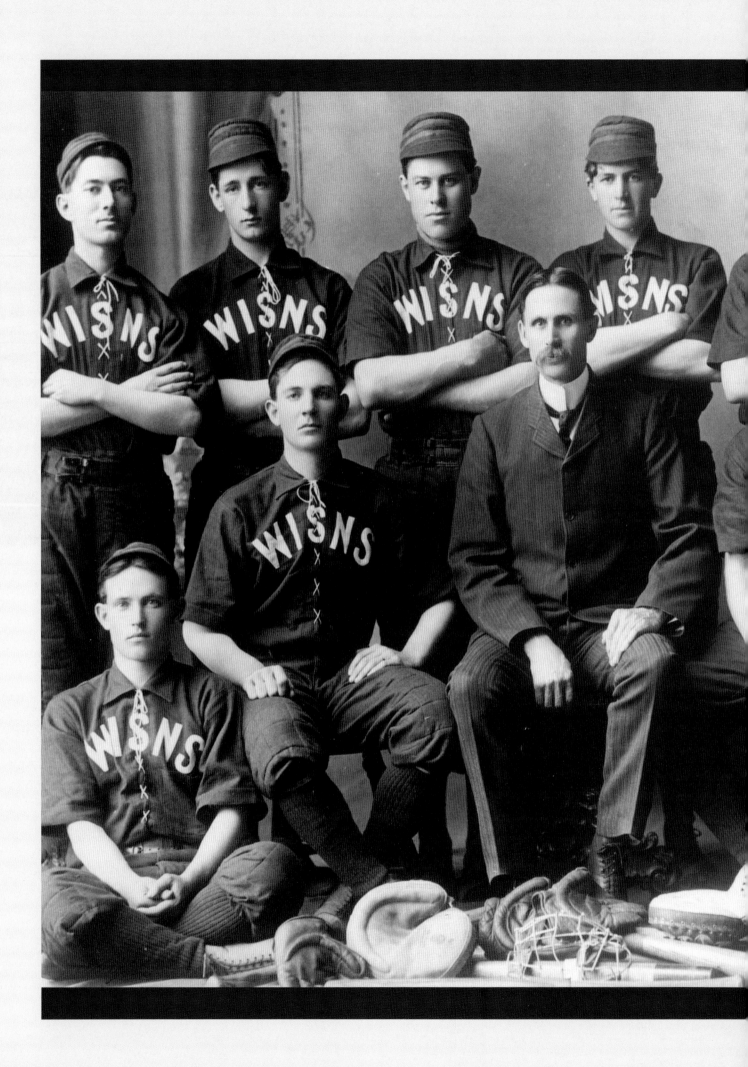

CHAPTER THREE

Northern Illinois Comes Into Its Own

It would have been interesting to eavesdrop on Louis Jolliet and Father Jacques Marquette, the first Europeans to visit Illinois, as they traveled by canoe down the Mississippi River in 1673.

Did the high palisades near Savanna fascinate them? Did the vast treeless prairie cause discussion? We can only imagine what the cartographer spoke about with the Jesuit. The men headed down the Mississippi to a point where they were certain that the river was not a route to the west. Then the party headed north again.

On the return voyage, following the advice of natives, the explorers crossed the future state of Illinois, proceeding up the Illinois and Des Plaines rivers, stopping to visit the village of Peoria and the Kaskaskia Indians near the site of the present city of Ottawa. The expedition portaged at Chicago and returned to Lake Michigan, where they went north in late July 1673.

Left: The 1904 baseball team of Western Illinois State Normal School at Macomb and their well-dressed coach pose for a photograph. Founded in 1899 as a teachers' college, today Western Illinois University has an enrollment of more than 11,000 students. Courtesy, Illinois State Historical Library

At Green Bay the two men parted company. Marquette was ill and convalesced at the De Pere Mission near the tip of Green Bay while Jolliet pressed on to Montreal. As the result of an accident while he was negotiating rapids, most of Jolliet's maps and journals of the expedition were lost along with two of his men.

In 1674 Marquette returned to Illinois and founded the Mission of the Immaculate Conception of the Blessed Virgin at the Kaskaskia village he had visited the year before. Father Marquette never regained his health and the following year he started a return trip to St. Ignace near the straits of Mackinac. Marquette died on May 18, 1675, on the east side of Lake Michigan near the mouth of the river now named for him.

More Jesuits came to Illinois to follow in the footsteps of Father Marquette and to baptize Indians into the Catholic faith. According to Jesuit records some 32 priests served in the Illinois country from 1673 to 1763, converting tens of thousands to Catholicism.

In 1673 Jacques Marquette, a Jesuit priest and missionary, traveled by canoe with six others to what would become Illinois. This drawing shows him holding an Indian peace pipe. Courtesy, Illinois State Historical Library

Arrival by Another Route

René-Robert Cavelier, sieur de La Salle, and a party of 14 men including three Franciscan priests made the journey to Illinois by heading up the St. Joseph River on the east side of Lake Michigan. They portaged to the Kankakee River in Indiana and then headed down it to the Illinois River. The voyage was made in the dead of winter of 1679-1680.

Along the Illinois where the river is wide enough to be called a lake,

La Salle and his lieutenant Henri de Tonti erected Fort Crevecoerur. Tonti had lost a hand in a naval battle and his iron hook made him quite a curiosity to natives. While La Salle traveled east again on a perilous 65-day journey of 1,000 miles across land to Fort Frontenac on the north shore of Lake Ontario, there was a mutiny at Fort Crevecoerur. The fort was destroyed, and never rebuilt.

When La Salle returned to Illinois he traveled with Tonti and others to the mouth of the Mississippi, where he laid claim on behalf of France to all the area watered by the great river. He named the area Louisiana.

La Salle, Tonti, and their men returned upstream and built a second fort in 1682 high on the top of a sand-stone promontory 125 feet above the Illinois River. At the time it was called simply "the Rock." Sometime in the next century Indian legend has it that some Illinois tribesmen would be starved there while under siege by Potawatomi.

If this did occur, it was after French

In 1682 explorer La Salle built a fort atop this 125-foot promontory overlooking the Illinois River. Legend has it that after the French left, a group of Illinois tribesmen were starved there by Potawatomi who lay siege. From this folklore springs the name Starved Rock State Park. Courtesy, Illinois State Historical Library

missionaries had moved on. There is no documentation of the event, but the tale has been handed down from generation to generation. It is from this folklore that Starved Rock State Park earned its name and fame.

La Salle Dies

La Salle returned to France after 1682. During his attempt to return to Illinois, he was shot to death in an ambush. La Salle was 43 in 1687 when he was killed somewhere along the Trinity River in what is now Texas.

Tonti continued to explore the central part of the continent after La Salle left, venturing as far north as Lake Superior and west to what is now Arkansas. In 1691 he left the fort on the rock and established a new fortification about 80 miles downstream on the west side of the Illinois River. He called it Fort Pimitoui.

In time Tonti placed his nephew in charge of the new fort and traveled south on the lower Mississippi. In 1702 Tonti died of yellow fever at Mobile, Alabama. He was 54.

The Bounty Land

After the War of 1812 a huge portion of the Illinois Territory was set aside for the soldiers and sailors who had served in the war. It was called the Military Tract, or the Bounty Area.

Each veteran was to receive 160 acres for his service. The area set aside was between the Illinois and Mississippi rivers from their confluence north to Kewanee. This giant triangle of land comprised more than 3.5 million acres.

A group from Connecticut founded Kewanee, at the northern edge of the Military Tract, in 1836. They urged the promotion of education and piety for Illinois. The New Englanders paid $250 for land that included a lot in town, 160 acres of prairie, and some

René-Robert Cavelier, sieur de La Salle, 1643-1687, studied briefly to become a priest as a boy in France, but left the seminary. In 1666 he sailed to Canada. Seven years later the governor of New France made him commandant of Fort Frontenac in Ontario and granted him a patent of nobility. In August 1679 La Salle and Henri de Tonti set out on the Great Lakes in the sailing vessel, the *Griffon*, to travel to Green Bay. In time La Salle went along Lake Michigan to the site of present-day St. Joseph, Michigan. They then continued on the St. Joseph River to the Illinois River, where they constructed a fort. In 1683 La Salle and a small party descended the Mississippi to its mouth where he took possession of the whole valley for France, calling the region Louisiana. La Salle returned to France and received authority to colonize parts of North America. He set out by ship in 1684 for the mouth of the Mississippi. He reached the Gulf of Mexico, but because of the sandy sameness of the coastline he was unable to determine the main channel of the Mississippi. He and his men landed on what is now Texas when they made attempts to reach the Mississippi overland. On the third attempt his own men murdered him.

Illustration courtesy, Illinois State Historical Library

woodland. The construction of the Military Tract Railroad began in 1854. It later would become the Burlington Santa Fe Railroad.

The Northern Addition

In April 1818 Congress acted on the Illinois statehood proposal. Congressional delegate Daniel Pope Cook had offered an amendment to move the northern boundary of the state to 42

degrees 30 minutes north. The measure passed and the new Illinois gained a coastline of more than 40 miles along Lake Michigan. The addition is the most economically important 8,000 square miles of Illinois. Without it, Chicago, Rockford, and 14 counties would not be part of the state.

A census of the proposed state was considerably short of the required 40,000 residents but the enabling legislation was approved after some skillful manipulation of the population figures by the young legislator Cook.

The first Illinois Constitution was signed on August 26, 1818, at Kaskaskia. Shadrach Bond was inaugurated as the first governor of the state on October 6, 1818.

A Lead Discovery

In 1823 settlers forced the local Fox and Sauk Indians to tell them where their secret lead mines were in the region now called Galena (Latin for "lead sulfite") in the far northwest corner of Illinois. There were physical threats and instances of torture. A rush began to the area, and by 1827 more than 13 million pounds of lead were being produced there. The Irish, French, Cornish, and Southerners who

flooded the area turned Galena to a bustling boom town. Initially slaves were also used to work in the mines.

During the early years of Illinois' statehood, the Erie Canal in the East stirred an increase in trade to Northern Illinois. The importance of the canal is demonstrated by the fact that New York Governor DeWitt Clinton, the primary force in the building of the canal, is the only individual to have two Illinois counties named for him.

By 1827 Congress gave land to a project that would allow Illinois to build its own canal, linking the Illinois

River and Lake Michigan. It would be 10 years before the canal would be started. Its 96-mile route included a series of locks and was not finished for 12 more years.

Illinois' Final Indian War

The Sauk and the Fox Indians were ordered to leave their lands in the northwest part of the state in 1829. They complied, crossing the Mississippi River, but in 1831 an elderly Sauk leader named Black Hawk returned with a group of followers. In short order a large force of regular soldiers and volunteers drove Black Hawk from

Black Hawk, **1767-1838,** whose Native American name was Makataemishkiakiak, was chief of the Sauk. In 1804 the Sauk and Fox Indians ceded their lands east of the Mississippi River for a payment of $1,000. Black Hawk immediately repudiated the deal, contending the whites had persuaded the Indians to sign after getting them drunk. He had fought with the British against the United States in the War of 1812. By 1823 most Sauk and Fox had settled west of the Mississippi, but in 1832 he led 500 warriors and their families back east of the river into Illinois. This precipitated the Black Hawk War, which ended on August 3, 1832, when many Native Americans died in the Battle of Bad Axe in Wisconsin. Black Hawk, then 65, surrendered several weeks later and was settled on a reservation near Des Moines. There he wrote *The Autobiography of Black Hawk*, which has become an American classic.

his village near the Rock River.

The following year Black Hawk, 500 men, and 1,000 women and children returned to Illinois. Governor John Reynolds mobilized a militia of more than 1,900 who—along with 1,000 regular troops from Fort Armstrong on Rock Island—moved up the Rock River valley.

Soldiers in the force included Jefferson Davis, who would later become president of the Confederacy; Zachary Taylor, who would become the 12th president of the United States; and a grocery store clerk from New Salem whose family had recently arrived from Indiana. His name was Abraham Lincoln.

On May 14, 1832, Black Hawk sent several representatives carrying a flag of truce to speak with a unit of some 275 volunteer militia under the command of a Major Isaiah Stillman. Stillman's troops were undisciplined and opened fire on the Indians. During the ensuing battle 12 soldiers and several Indians died. It was the first battle of the Black Hawk War. Although the Indians were outnumbered six to one, the militia turned and ran. It led to highly exaggerated reports of the strength of the Indians. A panic spread across the area.

The military eventually chased the Indians north to Wisconsin. The end came in the Battle of Bad Axe between

LaCrosse and Prairie du Chien. Most of the Sauk tribe was driven into the Mississippi River. Soldiers opened fire as they tried to reach the west bank, killing warriors, women, and children, as well as the old in a heavy slaughter.

Black Hawk escaped but was soon captured and imprisoned. Eventually he was sent to a reservation in Iowa. The Black Hawk War was the last war waged in Illinois. The Treaty of Chicago in 1833 gave white men absolute control of the state.

A Blacksmith Changes Farming

In 1837 an invention by a blacksmith

in his shop at the settlement of Grand de Tour on the Rock River would forever change how farmers would till the soil. John Deere invented the self-scouring plow, which allowed the open prairies to be farmed with relative ease. In time Deere moved his shop from Grand de Tour, a switchback on the Rock River, 120 miles downriver nearer to the Mississippi where transportation was better.

Today, across the country and around the world, the familiar green and yellow of John Deere farm machinery helps to feed the world. The Deere Foundation maintains a period museum in Grand Detour (which has now adopted the American pronunciation).

No Return to Wisconsin

In 1838 officials from Wisconsin petitioned Congress, without success, to regain the 14 counties across the top of Illinois that Cook had maneuvered to make part of Illinois some 20 years earlier. Officials from nine of the counties agreed, and the vote that followed was one-sided in favor of leaving Illinois. Illinois Governor Carlin simply ignored the claim of the Wisconsin territorial governor that the area was "accidentally and temporarily" under control of Illinois. During the squabble Cook

County officials also ignored the question. While Cook County is named for the young politician who helped add the region to the state, there is no historical evidence that he ever visited the area.

The Mormons Arrive

Two years after the crusading abolitionist newspaper publisher Elijah Lovejoy was slain in Alton, another group of persecuted people arrived in Illinois. About 5,000 Mormons, shepherded by Brigham Young and driven from Missouri, arrived at Quincy. The following spring they founded the town of Nauvoo on the Illinois side of the Mississippi 90 miles upriver. By 1845 Nauvoo had grown to become the largest city in the state with a population of at least 12,000 and possibly 20,000. The great Mormon Temple of Nauvoo set on a hill overlooking the town was 128 by 88 feet with a spire 157 feet high.

John Deere, 1804–1886, a native of Rutland, Vermont,

moved his family to a small village along the Rock River, Grand de Tour. There he opened a blacksmith shop. Deere recognized the problems of the farmer and how difficult it was to plow the open prairie because the cast-iron plowshares then in use accumulated huge quantities of mud in a short time. Deere, an inventor, produced the first self-scouring steel plowshares in the 1830s. His invention helped farmers across the nation and around the world. In time he moved his business to Moline and incorporated the now-familiar Deere & Company there in 1868.

Photo courtesy, Illinois State Historical Library

The home where John Deere lived in Grand de Tour is now part of a period museum maintained by the John Deere Foundation. The complex includes a working blacksmith shop and docents in period dress. Courtesy, Illinois State Historical Library

The city was platted into four-acre blocks each with four lots so every family could have a garden, fruit trees, and livestock. A steady stream of converts continued to arrive in the new city. Nauvoo had its own militia, the Mormon Legion, second in size only to the U.S. Army.

Religious persecution followed the Mormons. Their founder and prophet Joseph Smith and his brother Hyrum were jailed on charges that they had destroyed the press of a newspaper that had challenged their authority.

Above: Thomas Carlin was the seventh governor of Illinois. A Democrat, he was among a bipartisan group that welcomed the Mormons to Illinois. After serving a single term he returned to farming. In 1844 he waged a losing battle with Stephen A. Douglas for a seat in Congress. Courtesy, Illinois State Historical Library

Right: Ninian W. Edwards, son of the state's third governor, served as Illinois attorney general and was the state's first superintendent of public instruction. In 1855, a year after his appointment, legislation was passed to provide for free public school education to all Illinois children. Courtesy, Illinois State Historical Library

While in the jail at Carthage, 18 miles from Nauvoo, both were shot by an anti-Mormon mob that stormed the facility on June 27, 1844. For the next two years the Mormons were in disarray, and violence was frequent during what was called the Mormon War. The Mormons split into two factions, The Church of Jesus Christ of Latter-day Saints and the reorganized Church of Latter-day Saints. Most left Illinois when the groups traveled to Salt Lake City, Utah, and Independence, Missouri, respectively.

Second Constitution

Illinois' second constitution was adopted in 1848, giving more power to the governor and requiring popular election for state and county offices. Today some important ideas from it remain, including the popular election of state supreme court justices.

Also in 1848 the first boat went through the Illinois and Michigan Canal. The crafts using the 60-foot-wide canal were required to go through 17 sets of locks during their journey. The waterway would operate for 87 years.

Higher Education

By 1840 Illinois had a dozen colleges operating, but only Illinois College at Jacksonville, founded in 1828, was issuing degrees. The 1850s brought many milestones for education: In January 1851 Northwestern University was chartered, and Illinois Wesleyan University received its charter in February 1853. In 1854 the first superintendent of the Office of Public Instruction, Ninian W. Edwards, the son of a former governor, was appointed. A year later legislation was approved to provide for a free public school system.

In 1857 the first state normal (teachers') university was approved and opened in the town of Normal. Now called Illinois State University, it is near the geographic center of the state in a twin city adjacent to Bloomington, where Illinois Wesleyan is located. One of those who helped prepare the legal papers for the teachers' college was Illinois Board of Education lawyer Abraham Lincoln.

The University of Illinois at Urbana-Champaign was one of the nation's first land grant colleges, established under the Land-Grant College Act signed by President Lincoln in 1862. It opened in 1867 with 77 students, three faculty members, and a head farmer. For several decades it would be primarily an agricultural institution.

In the same year that the University of Illinois opened its doors, a small public college for teachers began on Chicago's South Side. Chicago Teachers College (today known as Chicago State University) had an initial enrollment of 13 students.

For several decades in the latter part of the 1800s, higher education was neglected in the state. But the election

Above: A student teacher in a classroom at Northern Illinois University is shown here at the turn of the twentieth century. Like most state universities of the day, NIU was a teachers' college or "normal school." Courtesy, Illinois State Historical Library

Left: What is now the administration building was the only structure at Northern Illinois University until 1911. It was renamed Altgeld Hall in 1963 in memory of Governor John P. Altgeld, who backed legislation to establish the school. Architects designed it to the wishes of Altgeld, a native of Germany, who was fond of castle-like buildings. Courtesy, Illinois State Historical Library

of John Peter Altgeld in 1892 brought a strong supporter of higher education to the governor's office.

Altgeld supported increases in funding for the University of Illinois, changing it from an agricultural school to a comprehensive university. Andrew S. Draper, who had been superintendent of public instruction in the state of New York, became president of the university. Succeeding Draper was Edmund James, a former president of Northwestern University.

In 1895 George Huff moved to the

University of Illinois from Dartmouth to coach the baseball and football teams. Along with the University of Chicago, Lake Forest College, and Northwestern, Illinois formed an athletic conference that expanded in the following years to include Wisconsin, Purdue, Minnesota, and Michigan.

A private college of medicine and a

Sherman Hall at Western Illinois University, founded in 1899, looks stark in this 1904 photograph. Courtesy, Illinois State Historical Library

college of pharmacy in Chicago became part of the University of Illinois. While the university continued to grow, the need for more teachers was evident and nearly every county wanted to be home to a new normal school modeled on the college at Normal.

Eastern Illinois University opened its

doors in 1895 at Charleston. Although just a scant 60 miles from the University of Illinois, it was felt that the two institutions were not competitors. DeKalb was chosen as the site for Northern Illinois University, largely because Joseph Glidden, the inventor of barbed wire, had donated extensive land there for the campus. Northern Illinois Normal College was chartered in 1895 and opened its doors four years later as a teachers' college with 173 students.

Western Illinois Normal College, now Western Illinois University, opened in Macomb in 1899. Macomb was chosen primarily because it was nearly the geographic center of the Military Tract. Western became the sixth public teachers' college and allowed the boast that no one in the state was more than 100 miles from a public institution of higher education.

Off to War

At the outset of the Mexican-American War in 1846 Illinois supplied six regiments of soldiers, as well as several independent companies. Lincoln, who was elected that year to Congress as a

Ely S. Parker, a Seneca, was military secretary to General Ulysses S. Grant. In this 1864 picture in front of the winter headquarters for the Army of the Potomac, Lieutenant Colonel Parker is third from left. Grant met Parker when both lived in Galena. Courtesy, Illinois State Historical Library

Whig, took a stand against the war. For this his political fortunes suffered in the short term.

During the battle of Buena Vista two Illinois regiments were among 4,500 troops commanded by Zachary Taylor. These fought a two-day defense against 20,000 Mexicans under Santa Anna. Two other Illinois regiments helped capture the Cerro Gordo mountain pass.

Grant Serves

Ulysses S. Grant, who left the army in 1854, had taken up residence in Galena. As the North mobilized for the Civil War he left his job as a clerk in his brother's leather goods store and escorted a company of volunteer infantry to Springfield.

Grant, who was familiar with military paperwork, was given a job and paid two dollars a day by the governor. In June 1861 he was made a colonel of the 21st Illinois Volunteer Infantry, a troublesome group called "Governor Yates' Hellions."

Grant brought the troops under control. In August, with the help of Galena Congressman Elihu Washburne, he was promoted to brigadier general and placed in charge of the troops of the Cairo District.

At the battles of Belmont and Fort Donelson, casualties to Illinois troops were heavy, but the Union victory was very important. Grant became a rising star in the military hierarchy.

In February 1862 Grant earned his second star as he was promoted to major general of volunteers. On July 4, 1863, that promotion was changed to a regular army major general's commission.

During the Civil War Illinois furnished 170 general officers. Grant was one of nine who came from Galena.

In February 1864, after victories at Vicksburg and Chattanooga, Grant was promoted again. He was made a lieu-

Ely Samuel Parker, 1828-1895, a Seneca born in New York State, became a chief in 1852. He attended Rensselaer Polytechnic Institute where he studied engineering. Soon he was working for the government in Galena, where he became friends with a salesman in a luggage store named Ulysses S. Grant. At the outbreak of the Civil War, Grant was instrumental in getting Parker into the army, where he served as Grant's military secretary and a trusted confidante rising to the rank of brigadier general. When Grant became president, Parker was appointed to head the Bureau of Indian Affairs. He was the first Native American to hold a major federal office. Parker helped to avert a total genocide of Native Americans, but in doing so made many enemies. He was charged with fraud by the U.S. Senate but exonerated. He resigned his post in 1871.

Photo courtesy, Illinois State Historical Library

tenant general. At the time this was the highest rank a soldier could attain. When Grant accepted General Robert E. Lee's surrender at Appomattox Court House another Illinoisian was at his side: Lieutenant Colonel Ely Parker, a Seneca Indian Grant had known from Galena. Parker was city engineer.

In the late 1850s Parker had studied engineering at Rensselaer Polytechnic Institute and began to work for the federal government, supervising public

works projects. During one such project at Galena he befriended a local clerk, Ulysses S. Grant.

Parker attempted to join the army at the outbreak of the Civil War, but could not be released from his construction duties until 1862. Due to his Indian heritage, even then he could not receive an army commission.

Parker was finally commissioned as a captain of engineers in 1863. Later that year he became a staff officer under Grant, who subsequently appointed him his military secretary. Upon Lee's surrender at Appomattox Court House on April 9, 1865, Parker took Grant's dictation of the surrender orders.

After the war ended Congress approved a rank of "General of the Armies" and Grant was immediately promoted to the four-star rank. It would be the highest military grade given until 1944.

From Soldier to President

Grant was nominated for president at the Republican Convention in Chicago in 1868. He won easily and was inaugurated in March 1869.

One of Grant's first appointments when he became president was Parker. He was named commissioner of Indian

Affairs on April 13, 1869. During his tenure in office Parker sought to work both for the United States government and the Native Americans he represented. His attempts to bring justice to various tribes over land deals and treaties, however, earned him many enemies. He was accused of defrauding the government and was tried by the House of Representatives in February 1871. Although he was exonerated of all charges, Parker resigned from office.

In 1872 Grant was reelected by an even larger margin. In many ways history has not been kind to Grant, portraying him as a hard-drinking man, but he also should be remembered as a president dedicated to Reconstruction and one whose policies toward the Indians averted a complete genocide.

As Grant was elected president, in Illinois many thought the governor should also be a soldier. John McAuley Palmer, a popular solider, was nominated but he had repeatedly indicated he did not wish to serve. One of his opponents at the nomination convention was Robert G. Ingersoll of Peoria, who had been appointed by Governor Richard Oglesby as attorney general.

Ingersoll, who had served in the Civil War as a colonel in the cavalry, was one of the finest orators of the day. He might well have won the nomination had he not been found objectionable by a number of Christian leaders. Ingersoll, known as the "Great Agnostic," could not win the nomination, and Palmer was elected.

Women in the War

It was not just the men of Illinois who were involved in the Civil War. Mary Ann Bickerdyke of Galesburg was one

Mary Ann Bickerdyke, a widowed nurse from Galesburg, stayed with the western armies during 19 major battles of the Civil War. Known as Mother Bickerdyke, she would scour battlefields after engagements searching for wounded soldiers. Courtesy, Illinois State Historical Library

Frances Elizabeth Willard, 1839-1898, was

born in New York and educated at Northwestern Female College in Evanston. She gave up her career as an educator in 1874 to become secretary of the Women's Christian Temperance Union. A leading crusader for temperance, she became president of the WCTU in 1879. In 1882 Willard helped to organize the Prohibition Party and became a leader in the struggle for woman suffrage.

Photo courtesy, Illinois State Historical Library

of the first women to arrive on the battlefield and she became a legend.

A widowed mother of two, she had been trained in botanic medicine. She volunteered at the Cairo camp just after the war began and spent four years on 19 battlefields. She commandeered what she needed, had no patience with corruption, and made clear her feelings, often with rough language.

Mother Bickerdyke, as she was known, once caught an official of a front-line hospital wearing gifts intended for the injured. She stripped him of his shirt, shoes, and socks, to

the delight of the injured soldiers who were watching.

When one officer questioned on whom her authority rested, she responded, "On the authority of the Lord God Almighty. Have you anything that outranks that?" Responding to a complaint, General William T. Sherman said, "If it was she, I can't help you. She has more power than I—she outranks me." At night after the bloody battles ended, Mother Bickerdyke would venture on to the battlefield with a lantern, searching for anyone who might still be alive.

Gertrude Fifer, the former first lady of Illinois, congratulates her daughter Florence Fifer Boher in 1925, after the latter had just been elected as the first woman to serve in the state senate. Boher was the daughter of Illinois' 19th governor, Joseph Fifer. Courtesy, Illinois State Historical Library

Some said that Bickerdyke's explosive tirades were for the benefit of the soldiers. She was just the opposite in temperament to some of her helpers, among them Mary Safford, called the Angel of Cairo, who spent untold hours tending the wounded. After the war Safford became a medical doctor and was a pioneering physician and surgeon in Chicago.

Women contributed much during the Civil War. In the words of Stella Coatsworth, a Chicago nurse who served on the battlefield, "American women no longer followed the full beaten track of example, but striking out into new and untried paths, lay their plans and execute purpose...(the War)...enabled her to rise to a measure of usefulness...undreamed of."

Other Battles for Women

In the 1870s groups of praying women began to descend upon—and to force the closure of—saloons throughout the Midwest. One early organization, called Woman's Crusade Against Alcoholism, met in convention at Bloomington in 1874 and became the Women's Christian Temperance Union.

Its first secretary was Frances Elizabeth Willard. She had graduated from Northwestern Female College in Evanston and later became its president. After the Chicago Fire the college became part of Northwestern University. Willard became dean of women but soon left after a dispute about the status of women's education with the university president, who also was Willard's former fiancé.

Willard joined the temperance crusade and in 1878 became the WCTU president. Willard viewed saloons as a symbol of separatism of the sexes. Stressing the themes of family, home, and temperance, Willard led the WCTU to support the Prohibition Party.

As an outgrowth of the WCTU, numerous women's groups organized and soon came to collaborate with men on civic events even in times of peace. The 1893 World's Fair had a "Board of Lady Managers."

In 1895 Illinois voters elected Lucy Flower as a trustee of the University of Illinois. Flower was elected shortly after Julia Holmes Smith was appointed to fill a vacancy. Smith was the first female trustee.

Lottie O'Neill of Downers Grove became the first woman elected to the Illinois General Assembly in 1922. O'Neill was reelected as representative 12 times. Her only break in service was in 1930, when she ran unsuccessfully for the U.S. Senate.

Florence Fifer Boher of Bloomington had been the first woman elected to the state senate, in 1924. Boher, a Republican, was the daughter of Joseph Wilson Fifer, who had served as Illinois governor from 1889 to 1893.

In 1922 Winnifred Mason Huck of Chicago won the race for the unexpired term as U.S. representative held by her father William E. Mason. He had died in office.

Illinois Farming

The vast prairie and fine soil of Illinois made the state ideal for farming. While most farmers arrived in family groups, a few—such as the Mormons—came in large contingents.

In 1846 Erik Jansson led a group of Swedish immigrants to an area of Illinois southeast of Rock Island. Jansson had been prosecuted in Sweden for burning hymnbooks as he preached that only the Bible could be used in religious ceremonies.

Jansson's followers, nearly 1,500 strong, lived as individual families but ate in a common dining hall and drew clothing from a common warehouse at Bishop Hill, a settlement named for Biskopskulla in Sweden. They worked together in large groups to till the ground, plant corn, and harvest wheat. With the power of many hands working together, they performed the tasks that are now completed by modern farm machinery.

A Mini-Metropolis

In 1673 Jolliet and Marquette had paddled past the big rock island where the Rock River enters the Mississippi. The region eventually became a metropolitan area of worldwide import. Commonly called the Quad Cities, today it encompasses 10 cities and towns in Illinois and Iowa.

During the War of 1812 it was near here that U.S. troops sent in keelboats from St. Louis to repulse the British advancing from the north. Fort Armstrong, built in 1816 to defend against Indians, is the site of the Rock Island Arsenal. It was opened in 1862 to manufacture weapons. The busy Mississippi River port is a key in the transport system of corn, grain, and the farm equipment manufactured at the nearby John Deere factories, which were established in 1847.

In 1857 an African-American slave named Dred Scott sued for his liberty on the basis that he was residing in Illinois, a free state. In a Supreme Court decision that inflamed abolitionists and many others in the North, the high court ruled that he was not emancipated, and he was returned to slave territory.

The Iowa city of Davenport is named for Colonel George Davenport, who arrived there soon after the War of

William E. Mason served in the U.S. Senate from 1897 to 1903, and was elected to the U.S. House of Representatives. After he died in office, his daughter was elected to fill out his term. She was the third woman to serve in Congress and the first from Illinois. Courtesy, Illinois State Historical Library

Right: During World War I the Rock Island Arsenal was an assembly line for these Mark VIII tanks. Courtesy, Illinois State Historical Library

Facing page, bottom: During the Civil War the Rock Island Arsenal in the Mississippi River was a prisoner of war camp for thousands of captured Confederate soldiers, seen here with their blue-uniformed Union army guards. Courtesy, Illinois State Historical Library

1812. In the early twentieth century W.J. Bettendorf purchased 70 acres on the Iowa side of the river and moved his rail shop there. On the Illinois side, Rock Island is named for the island but also includes a large landmass at the mouth of the Rock River. Moline and East Moline draw their names from a grist-mill built in 1829. It is a corruption of "moulin," the French word for "mill."

In about 1836 the Reverend George Washington Gale and 50 or so families moved to a 20-square-mile area in the Military Tract. Gale, a Presbyterian, saw that the deeds provided that no liquor would ever be sold on the land. The purchaser of each site was given a scholarship to the newly established Knox College. Today Galesburg, with more than 36,000 residents, is the seat of Knox County.

Galesburg grew when the Burlington Railroad, now the Burlington Santa Fe, was built in 1854. It brought to the town groups of Irish Catholics. Swedes, from Bishop Hill just to the north, also moved to the area.

Galesburg is the birthplace of the great prairie poet Carl Sandburg, and the site in 1856 of the fifth of the famed Lincoln-Douglas debates. It took place on the east side of the Old Main

building of Knox College. Not as well known, but surely as important, Galesburg was the home of George W. Brown who, by inventing the corn planter, eliminated the need to stoop and plant each kernel by hand.

The Oldest Village

To support the contention that Peoria is the oldest permanent village in Illinois, some historians point to Henri de Tonti and Francois de la Forest, who moved their fort about 1681 from Starved Rock to a place on Lake Peoria, a wide portion of the Illinois River. Just how permanent the village was can be debated, but there is no doubt it is one of the oldest in Illinois.

The town was platted in 1826 by a group of people of French heritage, and the original streets ran northwest-

southeast in orientation. Later these would be merged with streets that ran north and south. The first steamboat reached the area about 1828, but Peoria was not incorporated as a village until 1835. For more than a century before there had been Europeans living in the area.

Beautiful Land

"Kankakee" in the language of Native Americans translates to "Beautiful Land." Located 57 miles south of Chicago on the Kankakee River, a city was platted in 1835 as Bourbonnais. It was there that Francois Bourbonnais had operated a trading post. His name survives as a suburb of Kankakee. La Salle envisioned the river as a connection from the St. Lawrence and the Mississippi valleys, but the portage near South Bend, Indiana, never became practical.

Kankakee became a railroad town on the Illinois Central line, popularized in the words of the Arlo Guthrie song "The City of New Orleans." Today some consider the city, which stands on Interstate Highway 57, just a distant suburb on the southern edge of the mighty nine-county megalopolis called Chicago.

Elgin, 38 miles northwest of Chicago, was settled by Europeans in 1835. These first settlers built a dam to power a grist- and sawmill. B.W. Raymond, the third mayor of Chicago, invested in the area in 1838 and was instrumental in the construction of the Galena and Chicago Union Railroad, which passed through Elgin. In the early 1800s Elgin was a primary supplier of milk to Chicago. Gail Borden developed condensed milk in the city. A psychiatric hospital was established there by the state in 1872.

Down the Fox River a few miles, brothers Joseph and Samuel McCarty arrived from Elmira, New York, in 1834 and dammed the Fox River to power a sawmill. The area boomed in 1848 when the Burlington Railroad was built, and the city that grew there was named Aurora, after the Roman goddess of dawn.

Southeast of Aurora, a budding hamlet called Joliet received a post office in 1833. Its name is an altered spelling of the name of French explorer Louis Jolliet, who passed through the area 140 years earlier. Joliet is on the Des Plaines River upstream from where

Governor Frank Lowden traveled to Hoboken, New Jersey, to greet the Illinois National Guard's 33rd Infantry Division as they returned by ship from service in France during World War I. He is shown here with Major General George Bell. Courtesy, Illinois State Historical Library

it joins the Kankakee River to become the Illinois River. In 1848 Joliet celebrated the opening of the Illinois and Michigan Canal, which paralleled the Des Plaines River.

A more modern waterway was opened in 1938; it connects the St. Lawrence Seaway to the Mississippi River. The waterway is busy year-round carrying huge barges of oil, grain, corn, sand, and other bulk materials.

The first of its five railroad lines, the Rock Island, opened in 1852. Joliet is also known for its two huge penitentiaries, the Old Joliet Prison and Stateville.

Fencing the Range

Another agricultural milestone from Illinois is barbed wire, the now-ubiquitous fencing material that was developed and manufactured in DeKalb. In 1874 Joseph Glidden invented an improved fencing wire. About that same time another DeKalb resident, Jacob Haish, patented a process for manufacturing the new wire. Wire manufacturing left DeKalb in 1938. In 1895 Glidden donated the campus of what is now Northern Illinois University.

Cattle ranchers used the new fencing to convert open ranges into pastures. Barbed wire is credited with

doing more than the long rifle or the covered wagon to conquer the West.

The Northwest

By the mid-1830s there was a rough road that led from Galena to Chicago. Travel time was often weeks. It allowed lead to be transported by other than the Mississippi River boats. In 1838 a stagecoach began to use the route. About halfway on the route where the road crossed the Rock River, a settlement began to appear. It was called Rockford.

In the 1840s a dam was built across the Rock River to harness its power for several mills. In 1851 the rail line from Chicago reached Rockford and the area sprung to life. It was soon one of the largest metropolitan areas of the state, second in population only to Chicago.

Small Towns

If there were ever a golden age for small towns in Illinois it occurred in the half-century following 1875. Small towns generally were self-sustaining and the automobile had not yet arrived in large enough numbers to allow residents the luxury of trips to metropolitan centers. Most towns were built along railroad lines and nearly all had a siding where goods could be delivered.

Nearly every small farm-area town had churches of several denominations, a main street with a dry-goods emporium, a food market, a grain/hardware store, and a grain elevator. It could boast a nice mix of homes, simple ones near the railroad tracks and larger ones at the edge of town.

Such small towns provided inspiration to some of Illinois' greatest writers, poets, and artists.

Edgar Lee Masters was born in Kansas in 1869, but his family homesteaded in Petersburg, the seat of Menard County. When Masters was 12 his family moved a few miles north

Left: Lottie Holman O'Neill, a Republican from Downers Grove, in 1922 became the first woman elected as a state representative. She served 13 terms in the House of Representatives and was a state senator, retiring in 1964. Her only gap in service was for two years beginning in 1930, when she unsuccessfully campaigned for the U.S. Senate. Courtesy, Illinois State Historical Library

to Lewistown, the seat of Fulton County. Masters went on to attend Knox College in Galesburg and later became a lawyer, practicing for many years in Chicago. In 1914 he wrote the highly acclaimed *Spoon River Anthology*, a series of poems about residents of a graveyard who talk about their lives.

Other products of Illinois' small towns included Carl Sandburg, the first poet laureate of Illinois, from Galesburg; Owen Lovejoy, brother of slain newspaper editor Elijah Lovejoy, who settled in Princeton to write against slavery; Robert Ingersoll, who was educated in Greenville and then practiced law in Marion and Shawneetown before moving to Peoria; and Francis Snyder, a physician who wrote numerous volumes on history from his home in Virginia, Illinois.

James Jones from Robinson wrote *From Here to Eternity*. Paul Simon ran a newspaper in Troy, then was elected to the general assembly, beginning a 42-year career as an elected official. He retired from the U.S. Senate in 1996, and is the author of 19 books, the latest, *Lovejoy, Martyr to Freedom*.

Paul Angle, a Springfield historian and expert on Lincoln, also wrote *Bloody Williamson*; Marjabelle Young

Adlai Ewing Stevenson II, 1900-1965,

the grandson of a U.S. vice president of the same name, was educated at Northwestern, Princeton, and Harvard. He practiced law in Chicago from 1926 to 1931 and from 1934 until 1941. In the intervening years he was a federal government attorney. During World War II Stevenson was counsel in the Navy Department. After the war he joined the Department of State and attended the United Nations Charter conference in San Francisco. In 1948 Stevenson won election as Illinois governor. In 1952 he was drafted by the Democrats to run for president but lost to Dwight D. Eisenhower. The Illinois governor won the nomination in 1956. After John Kennedy was elected president in 1960, Stevenson was appointed as ambassador to the United Nations, a post he continued to hold under President Lyndon Johnson.

Photo courtesy, Illinois State Historical Library

Stewart, of Kewanee, is the author of 15 books on etiquette; and Arthur Geisert, a printmaker, hails from Galena where he draws his illustrations of country living.

Mail-Order Homes

Illinois was also headquarters for a special kind of home. From 1908 to 1940 approximately 100,000 homes were ordered through the Sears, Roebuck and Co. catalog. The structures would usually be shipped by rail to the purchaser, who would then have a contractor assemble the house.

Bungalows, cottages, garages, and farm buildings all were manufactured and sold by Sears. The homes ranged from modest one- and two-bedroom bungalows to the elegant eight-room Magnolia with two and a half baths, complete with fireplace, fluted columns, and a large porch across the front.

In 1918 the Magnolia was priced at $5,200, while the modest Hudson, a

four-room cottage with one bath and 520 square feet of living area, cost $495. The homebuilder would pay a similar amount to have it erected. Most of these Sears homes have stood the test of time and are still occupied. They are, in fact, often considered chic in today's housing market.

Downers Grove, a Du Page County suburb of Chicago, is the location of possibly the largest variety of Sears homes. They can be found throughout

Above: The home of Charles Gates Dawes on the lakefront in Evanston now serves as a museum and the home of the Evanston Historical Society. Courtesy, Illinois State Historical Library

Left: A general in World War I, Charles Gates Dawes served as vice president under Calvin Coolidge from 1925 to 1929. Courtesy, Illinois State Historical Library

Illinois and neighboring states, usually not far from a rail line.

Another President

In 1911, in the small town of Tampico in Whiteside County near Dixon, a boy was born who would become well known in the community for his competency as a lifeguard. Later he would gain fame as an actor. On January 20, 1981, Ronald Reagan was inaugurated as the 40th president of the United States.

In 1913 the Illinois General Assembly granted women the right

During the Great Depression these two South Chicago men took to the streets to advertise their own qualifications for jobs. Courtesy, Illinois State Historical Library

to vote in presidential elections, making Illinois the first state east of the Mississippi River to do so.

World War I

At the outbreak of World War I there were doubts and concerns about Illinois, with its large population of citizens with Teutonic heritage, and its key position in the transportation network of the country. Republican Governor

A huge contingent of unemployed meatpackers march in the stockyards neighborhood during the Great Depression. Mounted police officers in the foreground monitor the protest. Courtesy, Illinois State Historical Library

Frank Lowden, however, was quick to allay doubts about Illinois' willingness to go to war. The governor became known as "Win the War" Lowden.

The Illinois National Guard had become an experienced fighting unit during 1912, when some of its units chased Pancho Villa along the Mexican border. One cavalry major named Robert R. McCormick raised private funds to equip his unit with some of the first modern machine guns. McCormick would eventually make his mark not as a soldier but as the iron-fisted publisher of the *Chicago Tribune*. After the war he continued to insist on being called by his eventual rank of colonel.

The men of the Illinois National Guard became the 33rd Infantry (Prairie) Division, the 16th American division to reach France. By war's end the division reported 1,274 killed and 6,266 wounded. Illinois became a training ground for aviators, sailors, and foot soldiers. Draftees from Southern Illinois went to Camp Zachary Taylor near Louisville, Kentucky, and those from Northern Illinois to Camp Grant, south of Rockford.

Some 314,504 American men served in World War I. The precise number from Illinois who died is not

---

Gwendolyn Brooks, 1917-2000, was born in Topeka,

Kansas, but lived in Chicago most of her life. A shy child who became a great reader, Brooks began writing poetry at age seven and had her first poem published at age 13. At 17 she started writing for the *Chicago Defender* newspaper. After graduation from Wilson College in 1936, Brooks worked at a variety of jobs while she continued to write

poetry. In 1945 her first book of poetry for adults was published. In 1950 she became the first African-American to win the Pulitzer Prize for her volume *Annie Allen.* Most of Brooks'

writing deals with the experience of growing up and living in black Chicago. In 1968 Gwendolyn Brooks was named poet laureate of Illinois. The energetic Brooks was a masterful storyteller who often made public appearances and sponsored a yearly poetry contest for children and youth.

Photo courtesy, Southern Illinois University Photo Communications

---

known because the War Department did not maintain such records by state. During the war Illinois, with just 5.5 percent of the nation's population, purchased 7 percent ($1.3 billion worth) of U.S. Savings Stamps and Liberty Bonds.

Governor Lowden also significantly reorganized state government. He proposed a civil administrative code that had nine major departments— public health, trade and commerce, registration and education, labor, mines and minerals, agriculture, finance, public works and buildings, and public welfare.

A director was appointed to head each department and help form the governor's cabinet. While the number of departments has grown to 26, that civil administrative code still forms the framework for modern Illinois government.

Symbolism

In 1908 Illinois schoolchildren voted for an official state flower and tree. The violet was selected as the state flower and the oak as the state tree and both were so designated by the General Assembly. In 1973 the state tree was changed from the "native" oak to the white oak.

The Illinois flag was adopted in 1915, and 55 years later it was redesigned to add the word "Illinois" below the emblem portion of the state seal.

Choosing from a list of five birds, Illinois schoolchildren in 1928 selected the cardinal as the state bird. Their choice was ratified by law.

The 54th General Assembly in 1926 designated the music of Archibald Johnston and the lyrics of Charles Chamberlain in their "Illinois" as the state's official song.

Vice Presidents Too

By the turn of the twentieth century two men from Illinois, Lincoln and Grant, had served as president. Two other Illinois men would serve as the nation's vice president. Adlai E. Stevenson, of Bloomington, came to

Illinois from Kentucky and served as assistant postmaster general during the first term of President Grover Cleveland. Stevenson was well known as the man who replaced some 40,000 Republican postmasters with Democrats.

When Cleveland was elected to a second (non-consecutive) term as president in 1892, his running mate was Stevenson. Stevenson ran for vice president as the running mate of William Jennings Bryan in 1900 and was defeated. He campaigned for governor in 1908, losing by just 23,000 votes to Charles Deneen.

In 1925 another Illinois man, Charles Gates Dawes, became vice president under President Calvin Coolidge. Dawes had been comptroller of the currency under President William McKinley, had served as a brigadier general in World War I, and was director of the Federal Bureau of the Budget. Dawes received a Nobel Peace Prize for his plan to reorganize payments of German reparations.

Later, for a brief period, Dawes served as the president of the Reconstruction Finance Corporation, which helped banks during the Great Depression. Dawes, a banker, in time returned to his stately brick residence in Evanston, which he gave to Northwestern University in 1942. The Dawes House is now a museum and the home of the Evanston Historical Society.

The Crash

The Great Depression began on October 29, 1929, when the stock market crashed, plunging the nation into financial turmoil and 12 years of the worst economic times ever. In 1932 alone there were four special sessions of the General Assembly called to deal with the state's economic problems.

The Waterways

In 1933 a flotilla of barges arrived in Chicago from New Orleans to mark the completion of the Illinois Waterway, which had come about in several stages. The Illinois and Michigan Canal had opened in 1848. In 1900 the much

Edward J. Kelly, a Democratic political boss, became Chicago mayor after Anton Cermak was assassinated. Kelly shared political leadership with Patrick Nash, the Cook County Democratic chairman, in what was called the Kelly-Nash machine. Courtesy, Illinois State Historical Library

Winnifred Mason Huck became the third woman to be elected to the U.S. Congress after her father William Mason died while in office. She is shown here being presented with flowers by Representative Alice Mary Robertson of Oklahoma, the second woman to serve in the U.S. House. The first five women representatives were Republicans. Library of Congress Photograph

deeper Sanitary and Ship Canal replaced the section from Chicago to Lockport. In 1919 the western part of this canal, which runs from Lockport to Utica, opened in 1933. The Calumet Sag Channel, completed in 1922, is also an important link between Lake Michigan and the Mississippi River.

First Cook County Native Becomes Governor

Chicago Democrat Henry Horner took office as governor in January 1933, handily defeating former two-term governor Len Small in a Roosevelt-led landslide. Horner was the first Jewish governor of the state and the first Cook County native. He was called upon to

lead it during difficult economic times. Horner's legacy was a new revenue system that included a retail sales tax.

Horner split with the Chicago Democratic organization headed by Mayor Edward J. Kelly and Patrick Nash, Cook County Democratic chairman. These two machine Democrats often called Horner "High Tax Henry."

In 1936 Horner defeated the handpicked Chicago Democrat slated by the Kelly-Nash machine and went on to win the general election. Two years into his second term Horner suffered a heart attack that made him a virtual invalid. Horner, a bachelor, continued to run the state, however, often from his bed in the executive mansion.

The general assembly passed an unemployment compensation act in 1937 requiring employers to pay into a fund that would provide checks to employees who lost their jobs.

In 1939 Illinois became the first state to establish a separate governmental entity designed expressly to work toward the prevention of juvenile delinquency.

In October 1940 Henry Horner died in Winnetka, only the second Illinois governor to die in office.

At the time, Horner and Lieutenant Governor John Stelle, an ally of the Kelly-Nash machine, were at odds. Horner had blocked Stelle's attempt to be slated as a candidate for governor. Stelle had returned to his farm near McLeansboro and was in the fields when word came of the governor's death. Stelle served the remaining 99 days of Horner's term.

After World War II former Governor Stelle helped lobby for the G.I. Bill of Rights and became the national commander of the American Legion. He turned his back on Adlai Stevenson II's bid for president and gave speeches supporting Eisenhower.

Crime Fighter Becomes Governor

With the Democrats broken into segments, the 1940 election of Republican Dwight Green was easy. Green, a former federal prosecutor who had put away the notorious Al "Scarface" Capone, would lead Illinois during World War II.

With the Japanese attack on Pearl Harbor on December 7, 1941, the nation was plunged into World War II. The Illinois National Guard had already been federalized and the state moved to a war footing. The first navy vessel built during World War II was the minesweeper *YMS-84*. It was launched on March 3, 1942, on the Chicago River.

Green was a popular governor, and was elected to a second term in 1944.

It was during that term that a mine disaster at Centralia killed 111 men. It was learned that Green had accepted campaign donations from the mine operators and ignored pleas from miners about possible dangers in the mine.

Adlai Stevenson II campaigned hard against Green, focusing on the 1947 mining disaster, the proliferation of slot machines throughout the state, and the large number of newspaper reporters who were on state payrolls. When the votes were counted in 1948, Stevenson had won by the largest plurality in state history.

Green's legacy would be that he was the first of many Republican governors who would cooperate with the Democratic mayors of Chicago.

Chicago Tribune publisher Colonel Robert R. McCormick talks with U.S. Senator C. Wayland Brooks (left) and Governor Dwight Green on the steps of the governor's mansion in Springfield in 1946 before heading to the Illinois State Fair. Courtesy, Illinois State Historical Library

PART TWO

Illinois' Robust
Economy Today

by David M. Young

CHAPTER FOUR

From Hog Butcher
to Pork Bellies Trader

"Hog butcher for the world, Tool maker, stacker of wheat, Player with railroads and the nation's freight handler; Stormy, husky, brawling, City of the big shoulders."
— Carl Sandburg, Chicago, 1916

There's still some of Carl Sandburg's Chicago remaining. The steel mills and stockyards are gone, and the grain elevators sit idle along the rivers like ancient monoliths. But there still are plenty of railroads, and any given container of freight bound from Liverpool to Yokohama is likely to pass through Chicago on one of them. The grandsons of meatpackers who once butchered hogs in the slaughterhouses are now likely to be commodities brokers trading pork bellies in the exchange pits, and the descendants of drummers who fanned out from Chicago hawking their companies' wares in the West these days might work for computerized logistics firms.

Left: The banks of the Chicago River, which was once a busy port lined by warehouses, is now a canyon of steel, glass, and stone office towers. Wacker Drive (foreground) is a two-level thoroughfare that girds the Loop in two sides. Photo © 2000 Mark Segal/Stone

The typical Chicago worker at the dawn of the third millennium is more likely to sit in front of a computer terminal in an air-conditioned, steel-and-glass office tower in the Loop than to stand sweating in front of a stamping machine in some South Side foundry. On the other hand, that office worker still likes the smash-mouth type of football played by the Bears, if his wife hasn't cajoled him into attending the Chicago Symphony Orchestra concert that weekend. There are still plenty of neighborhood taverns in Chicago but many of them serve merlot as well as draft beer.

Although Chicagoland—as the metropolitan area is known—has grown continuously for 170 years, the city itself has been losing population for the past 50 as many middle-class residents have moved to the suburbs. Chicago, second largest in the nation behind New York City for most of the century, peaked in 1950 at 3.6 million residents before beginning a long population decline that dropped it into third place behind Los Angeles. The decennial census in 2000 showed Chicago had reversed its half-century population decline and once again started growing.

The city is home to a number of commercial exchanges, including the Chicago Stock Exchange. It is smaller than its cousin in New York but is still a vital engine in the Windy City's economy. Photo © Index Stock Imagery

The city as the millennium ended had 2.89 million residents, or about 112,000 more than it had in 1990.

Chicago is probably as dichotomous as any city on earth. Its politics are still a little more rough-and-tumble than those in neighboring states, although they have toned down considerably from the days of aldermen Michael "Hinky Dink" Kenna and "Bathhouse" John Coughlin when the city council was bought and sold with regularity. The city's worldwide reputation for gangsters like Al Capone and for riots like the one at the 1968 Democratic National Convention have been hard to live down, even though most of the crime syndicate went to prison and Chicago, unlike many other cities in the world, hasn't had a peaceful demonstration run amok in a quarter of a century. The nickname "Windy City" comes not from its weather but from the bragging of its nineteenth-century boosters.

It was the site of some of the world's terrible disasters—the Chicago Fire of 1871 that leveled much of the city and the capsizing of the steamship *Eastland* at its moorings in the Chicago River in 1915, which drowned 812 souls within a few feet of land. But it was also the site of the conventions that nominated Abraham Lincoln for

president, set national time standards, and established the world's civil aviation system. The atomic age was born in Chicago with the first self-sustaining nuclear chain reaction.

The Windy City, though not as well known overseas as some other American cities, is a world-class metropolis with museums, symphony, opera, and colleges that rival any on earth. The Chicago Symphony

Orchestra regularly tours Europe and the newest attraction at the Field Museum of Natural History is Sue, the largest, best preserved, and most complete skeleton of a Tyrannosaurus rex yet discovered. Though it is less than two centuries old, the city has become a Mecca for architecture: The skyscraper was developed in Chicago, as was the balloon-frame construction technique used to build houses quickly

Above: A convention center since 1847 because of its central location, Chicago has hosted 25 national political conventions of both parties. The most recent was the Democratic National Convention in 1996. Photo © 2000 Paula Bronstein/Stone

Left: Probably because of its heavy Democratic vote in the past seven decades of the twentieth century, the Democrats have picked the Windy City for their national convention seven times since 1930. Photo © 2000 Paula Bronstein/Stone

across the North American continent. Frank Lloyd Wright made his home in the Chicago area for many years and the city and suburbs are dotted with his Prairie style homes.

Chicago has done a better job of preserving its park-like waterfront than most of the nation's cities, and it is in the process of converting its river— once a polluted port clogged with ships—into a recreational waterway. Parks were built on rubble from the Chicago Fire that was dumped into the lake as the city was redeveloped.

The city remains a melting pot with a population as diverse as any on the planet. Anglo-Saxons, Germans, Scandinavians, and Irish began their migrations in the nineteenth century, followed by Italians, Poles, African-

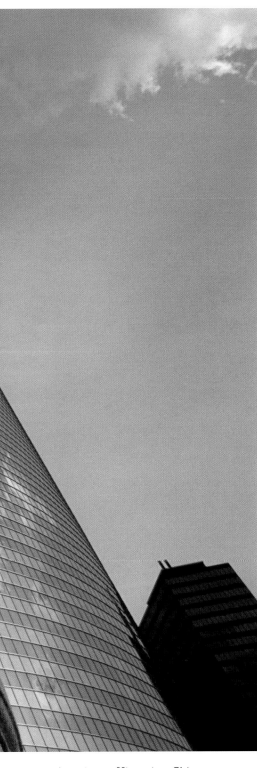

favorites are deep dish-pizza, steaks, and the all-American hot dog, but Chicago's taste in sausages also ranges to bratwurst and kielbasa.

Still a Transportation Crossroads

Chicago originated as a transportation crossroads and it continues in that role. Residents call downtown Chicago the "Loop," a nickname originating with the elevated railway system that circles the area. Frequent business travelers find it hard to avoid changing planes at either O'Hare or Midway airports, which combine to make up the nation's busiest aviation center. The city owes its existence to the fact that it was an inland maritime center more than 1,000 miles from the nearest ocean. Beginning in 1848 canals connected the St. Lawrence and Mississippi rivers systems, and Chicago remains a busy port with plenty of ship traffic from the Great Lakes and barge traffic off the rivers. The city also remains the nation's undisputed railroad center, handling by last count more than 28,000 freight cars and 15,000 intermodal containers and trailers a day. More than 675 passenger trains serve Chicago a day as well.

The public transportation system is one reason the Loop did not suffer the decline in the second half of the twentieth century experienced by the downtowns of other midwestern cities. In fact, Chicago's central business district has sprawled far beyond the original Loop, leaping the Chicago River to the north and west. North Michigan Avenue is one of the trendiest shopping areas in the nation, and the region west of the Loop, once the city's skid row home to derelicts, has undergone a renaissance in recent years. South of the Loop the sprawling railroad yards have been redeveloped in housing and public buildings.

The skyscraper was largely developed in Chicago during the second half of the nineteenth century and remains the signature of the cityscape into the twenty-first century. Some have even been built in the suburbs. Photo © 2000 Hisham F. Ibrahim/PhotoDisc

Americans, Hispanics, Chinese, Koreans, and Indo-Chinese in the twentieth. This racial and ethnic diversity has lent names to various neighborhoods, like Andersonville (Swedish), Pilsen, Ukranian Village, and Chinatown, and has provided the city with a wealth of restaurants serving everything from chimichangas to bulgogi to haute cuisine. Among the local

The first thing visitors are likely to notice even before their plane's wheels touch down at O'Hare International Airport is the city's sprawling lakefront. Chicago, more than any other Great Lakes city, was able to preserve much of its lakefront for public use as parks, yacht basins, and recreational facilities. In recent years the city has been slowly transforming its downtown river, once one of the busiest ports in the world, into a recreational waterway flanked by river walks. The commercial port long ago moved to the Calumet River on the South Side.

smaller ocean-going ships from Europe and other continents regularly call on Chicago, although international trade has never developed to the extent that proponents of the St. Lawrence Seaway hoped back in the 1950s when that waterway was built connecting the Great Lakes with the Atlantic Ocean. The locks necessary to enable ships to climb 326 feet above sea level to reach the elevation of the upper lakes were built too small (766 feet long, 80 feet wide, and 30 feet deep) at a time when ocean-going ships were increasing in size.

The illusion from an airliner window at 10,000 feet is that Chicago sits on a long ocean beach; but the body of water is actually an inland sea, a giant freshwater lake more than 300 miles long, 100 miles wide, and 900 feet deep. Lake Michigan is big enough to sustain commerce by the largest of ships, and giant ore boats 1,000 feet long—longer than the largest warship in World War II—haul iron ore, coal, and stone between ports on the four upper Great Lakes. (All vessels, regardless of size, are called "boats" on the Great Lakes. Their speed is measured in miles per hour, not knots, as is the practice on the oceans.) Somewhat

Chicago draws its drinking water from the lake and flushes its treated sewage down the canal system that connects it with the Mississippi River system. In fact, the Sanitary and Ship Canal and the Cal-Sag Channel make Chicago the only city on the continent where the St. Lawrence River watershed (into which the Great Lakes empty) connects with that of the Mississippi River. This gives Chicago access to both the Atlantic Ocean nearly 1,800 miles to the northeast and the Gulf of Mexico about 1,500 miles to the south.

No other body of water has the unique history of the Chicago River, nor

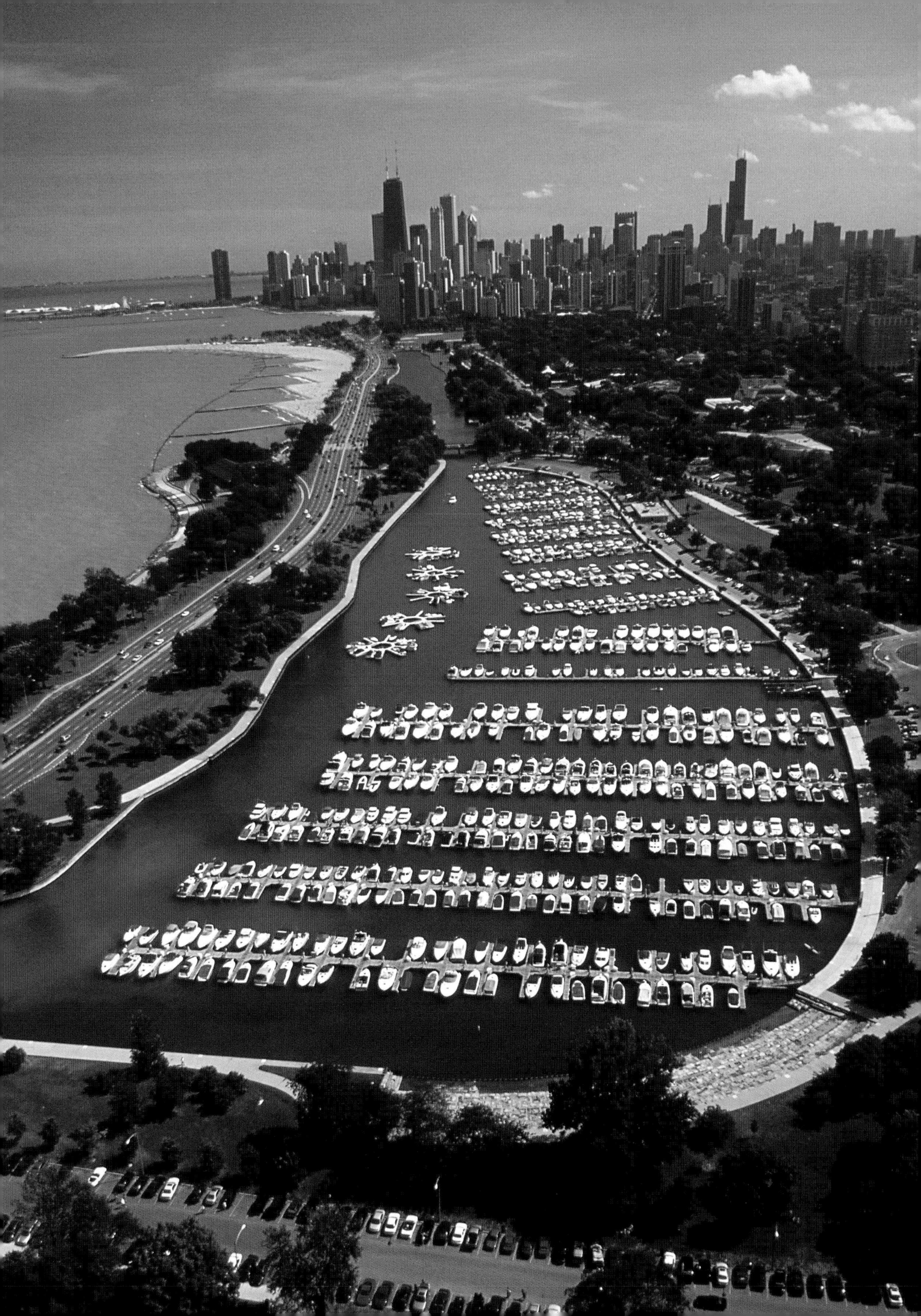

Above: The Windy City's large ethnic populations hold a number of parades and festivals throughout the year. None is more popular than the Irish St. Patrick's Day parade held each March. Photo © Mark Segal/Index Stock Imagery

Left: There is a saying in Chicago that everyone is Irish on St. Patrick's Day. Large crowds turn out to watch the parade despite the city's notoriously unpredictable March weather. Photo © Mark Segal/Index Stock Imagery

Far left: Lake Michigan is the city's eastern boundary. Too cool for swimmers during all but a couple of months in the summer and fall, the lake is popular with boaters, such as this flotilla in Burnham Harbor southeast of the Loop. Photo © Vic Bider/Index Stock Imagery

has any other river captured the imagination and fostered as many creative plans and projects for its use. The catalyst for its metamorphosis from sewer to scenic wonder has been the Metropolitan Water Reclamation District of Greater Chicago.

In the early years of the city's settlement, industrial waste and sewage was routinely emptied into Lake Michigan. In 1900 the fledgling water district completed construction of the channels and canals that redirected the flow of the Chicago River away from the lake.

The city has hundreds of restaurants serving everything from fast food burgers to haute cuisine. Although typical American fare like steaks and prime rib are popular, diners can find such exotic dishes as bulgogi and kielbasa. Courtesy, Gibsons Bar and Steakhouse

Far right: Passengers at O'Hare can use electrified and automated people mover trains to travel between terminals or to remote parking lots. Like the trains that circle Chicago's Loop, the people mover is elevated. Photo © Gary Conner/Index Stock Imagery

City dwellers take pride in having the only "river that flows backwards." During its more than 100 years of operation, the water district has constructed sewers to capture the drinking water, seven sewage plants to clean it, and a tunnel and reservoir system to store it until treatment is possible. The continued growth and prosperity of the city of Chicago depends in large part on the availability of a safe water supply.

The battle to keep the lakefront as a park was a long one and somewhat surprising in view of the city's laissez faire, "anything goes," attitudes about development. Aaron Montgomery Ward, founder of the catalog house and department store chain bearing his name, was the leader of the open lakefront movement and four times between 1890 and 1911 sued to prevent development from occurring in Grant Park. Daniel Burnham picked up the baton in his Chicago Plan of 1909 and recommended a publicly accessible lakefront. Although some commercial lakeshore development occurred on the North and South sides, the city today has 31 beaches stretching along its 22 miles of shoreline.

The Constant is Change

If there has been one constant in Chicago's economy over the past half-century, it has been change. Companies appeared, were acquired, merged, and were divested with such celerity in America's active business climate that anything written about them was liable to be obsolete even before the ink dried. "Buyouts," "breakups," and "IPOs" (initial public stock offerings) occurred with dizzying regularity not only among the older companies but the new start-ups as well.

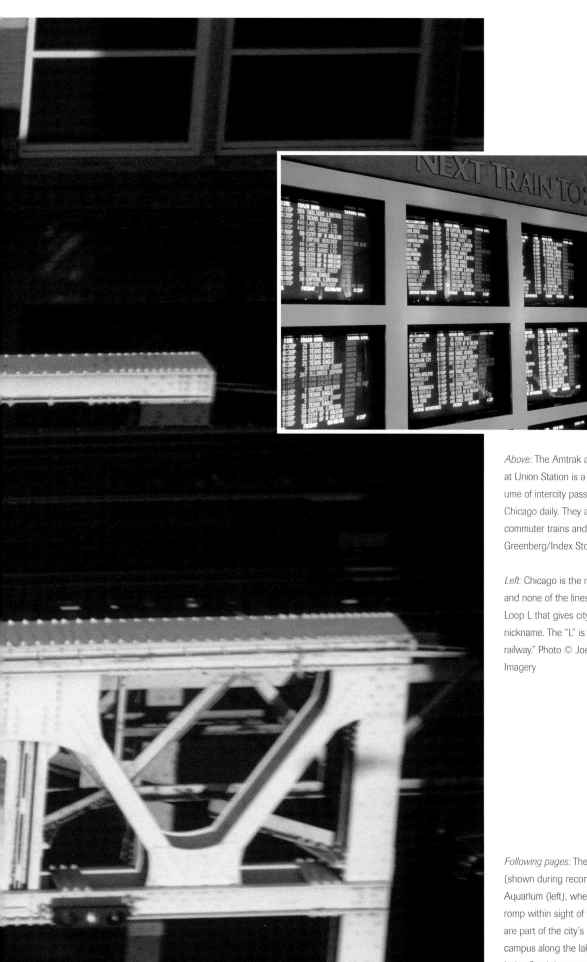

Above: The Amtrak arrival and departure board at Union Station is a clear indication of the volume of intercity passenger trains that visit Chicago daily. They are dwarfed in number by commuter trains and freights. Photo © Jeff Greenberg/Index Stock Imagery

Left: Chicago is the nation's railroad capital and none of the lines is more famous than the Loop L that gives city's downtown area its nickname. The "L" is an abbreviation of "elevated railway." Photo © Joe Mozczen/Index Stock Imagery

Following pages: The domed Adler Planetarium (shown during reconstruction) and the Shedd Aquarium (left), where a pod of Beluga whales romp within sight of the Loop (background), are part of the city's rehabilitated museum campus along the lake. Photo © Mark Segal/Index Stock Imagery

Chicago is no longer a three-industry town—agriculture, transportation, and heavy manufacturing. Many of the old-line companies—the meatpacker Armour and the Greyhound bus lines, for example—have moved elsewhere. Others, including Amoco (oil) and the Santa Fe Railroad, were merged into other companies. Some, like Continental Bank and Inland Steel, were bought out. Many firms simply went out of business: Wisconsin Steel and the Pullman rail car manufacturer are two examples.

Yet some nineteenth-century enter-

The Chicago River is used primarily by commuter boats, private pleasure craft, and sightseeing vessels. There are also occasional barge tows, some with shipments coming upriver from New Orleans and others from Great Lakes ports.
Photo © Bruce Leighty/Index Stock Imagery

prises survived by changing: The *Tribune*, dating from 1847, became a multimedia giant with radio and television stations and a stake in various Internet companies. Sears, Roebuck and Co. transformed itself from a catalog house to a venerable retail chain. Navistar, now primarily a motor truck manufacturer, was known for much of its existence as International Harvester, the farm-equipment maker founded by Cyrus McCormick.

The new companies that arose in the twentieth century were more likely to make convenience consumer products, as do Quaker Oats and Sara Lee; and electronic or communications

equipment, as with Telephone and Data Systems Inc.; or to provide services such as insurance and financing. Aon Corporation and CNA Financial Corporation are examples. In the final decades of the century, the rapidly growing computer industry resulted in a number of new companies coming into existence. By one count, one-quarter of the largest publicly held companies in the Chicago metropolitan area did not exist when World War II ended in 1945.

There has been some concern in Chicago that the wave of mergers that occurred in American business since 1980 has caused the city to lose many of its corporate headquarters, and with them its civic benefactors. For example, a global company based in London is less likely to give financial support to opera in Chicago than the local company it acquired. The *Chicago Tribune* each year publishes a survey of the 100 largest companies in Chicagoland based on market capitalization, and eight of the top 25 companies on the 1990 list did not make the list a decade later.

The surviving companies, as well as the new ones, tended to become national or global in scope in order to survive and prosper. Conglomerates were common for a while in the second half of the twentieth century, then faded in popularity as companies shed diverse acquisitions to concentrate on their core businesses and expand them into international markets. IC Industries, a railroad turned conglomerate in the 1970s, shed its acquisitions in the 1980s and in turn was acquired by the Canadian National Railroad in the 1990s. Computers became a primary tool of all enterprises, and a new business lexicon emerged. "Logistics" replaced "traffic" to describe the movement of goods from mine to machine to market. "Inventory" was replaced by "just-in-time" delivery, and "quality control" became an integral part of the mass-production process.

"Productivity" came to define not only the amount of work a given business could produce, but its cost, quality, and profitability relative to what the competition was doing. Businesses that couldn't measure up were "downsized," a process made possible by the computer and communications revolutions and painful not only to production workers on the factory floor but to office workers and executives as well. A single worker at a computer terminal could do the work of scores of bookkeepers making entries into their ledgers by hand.

The Rust Belt Renaissance

It was a hard lesson for an industrial city such as Chicago, sometimes referred to derogatorily as the "Capital of the Rust Belt." The recession of the early 1980s hit the city particularly hard, but the restructuring of its heavy industry in that decade enabled the Windy City to escape for the most part the recession a decade later that hard hit other sectors of the nation's economy.

George Pullman's railroad car-building company illustrates perhaps better than any other firm the fate of manufacturers unable to adjust to the new economy. He got his start in 1859 by converting passenger coaches into sleeping cars for overnight railway trips, and grew with the railroad industry to the point that by 1900, when railroads were the dominant form of transportation in the United States, the name "Pullman" was synonymous with sleeping cars and the company controlled 90 percent of the market. Ultimately the manufacturer ran afoul of federal antitrust laws and in the second half of the twentieth century suffered competi-

tion from the airlines and automobiles. The inability of Pullman to adapt its massive manufacturing capacity to shrunken railroad markets ultimately caused its demise.

On the other hand, Sara Lee, a chain of neighborhood bakeries in Chicago that developed into an international prepared-food giant, is an example of a business flexible enough to survive. The

Grant Park, which lies between the tall buildings in the Loop and the lake, is the result of a century-long battle to keep Chicago's waterfront open and park-like. Photo © Bruce Leighty/ Index Stock Imagery

Above: The Chicago area remains one of the country's major steel-producing centers, primarily because iron ore can be cheaply shipped in by lake boat and coal can come by boat or train. This mill is in suburban East Chicago, Indiana. Photo © Ewing Galloway/Index Stock Imagery

Facing page, top: The *Chicago Sun-Times,* the city's second-largest newspaper, has its offices along the Chicago River. The building is dwarfed by its neighbors and may be replaced by a skyscraper. Photo © Rich Remsberg/Index Stock Imagery

Facing page, bottom: Two of the city's architectural landmarks are the Wrigley Building (left) and neo-Gothic Tribune Tower (right), home of the city's largest newspaper. Lighted at night, they now share the skyline with several newer buildings. Photo © Peter J. Schulz/Index Stock Imagery

Following pages: Navy Pier in the 1990s was transformed from a vacant, dilapidated wharf into a recreational and convention complex. It is still used by tourist boats and an occasional oceanic cruise liner visiting the Great Lakes. Photo © Stephen Saks/Index Stock Imagery

company was strictly local until in 1953 it developed a way to freeze baked goods to allow them to be distributed nationally. Three years later it was acquired by Consolidated Foods Corporation and in 1964 the business moved to new headquarters in north suburban Deerfield.

By 1985 the Sara Lee brand and its advertising jingle, "Nobody Doesn't Like Sara Lee," had become so recognizable that Consolidated Foods changed its name to Sara Lee. A few years later the company bucked the trend of corporations moving to suburban office campuses and shifted its headquarters back to downtown Chicago.

Because of the city's central location and well-developed transportation system, one of its largest businesses is conventions and has been since 1847, when 20,000 delegates descended on Chicago for the National River and Harbor Convention to debate federal aid to waterway projects. The city had no convention center, so the meeting was held in a tent, and hotel space was in such short supply that delegates were billeted in homes requisitioned for the event and on ships docked in the Chicago River.

Today the city hosts 35,000 conven-

tions, trade shows, and meetings drawing 4.4 million visitors annually—everything from the international plastics show held every three years to occasional national political conventions and various annual trade shows dealing with such industries as restaurants, automobiles, hardware, and housewares. The auto show alone draws more than a million visitors a year, and the bigger trade shows that are not open to the general public vary between 40,000 and 90,000 attendees.

McCormick Place, along the lake a few miles south and east of the Loop, with 2.2 million square feet of exhibition space is the largest convention facility in North America. Because of its importance to the local economy the city and state spent nearly one billion dollars expanding and renovating the structure, a project completed in 1998. Chicago has also been promoting lakefront Navy Pier—built in 1916 to serve the Great Lakes shipping industry, later abandoned, reopened as a college in 1946, abandoned again, and reopened in 1995 as a convention and exposition center—for small and mid-size events.

To most Chicagoans, Navy Pier is a 3,000-foot-long recreational extravaganza that includes elements of an amusement park, cultural center, indoor botanical garden, theaters for movies and stage plays, and rides on tour boats, including a wind-jamming schooner. The pier's skyline is dominated by a modern version of the original Ferris wheel built for the 1893 Columbian Exposition, and nearby is a carousel. The Crystal Gardens is a one-acre, glass-enclosed botanical display. The Smith Museum of Stained Glass Windows and the Chicago Children's Museum make their homes on Navy Pier, as does a big-screen IMAX® Theater, the 1,500-seat Skyline Stage, Chicago Shakespeare Theater, and assorted restaurants.

European cruise liners occasionally dock there to pick up and discharge passengers on Great Lakes tours.

The city's convention business also sustains a substantial hotel and restaurant industry. There are nearly 28,000 hotel rooms within a three-mile radius of the Loop and hundreds of restaurants dishing up American, Korean, Chinese, Italian, Indian, French, German, Mexican, and other ethnic cooking. Chicago also has numerous legitimate theaters, movie houses, and nightclubs that provide diverse entertainment to visitors and residents alike.

The city's convention and tourism business is a direct result of its long-

held position as the nation's cross-roads—one established when Chicago became the nucleus of the nation's railroad system in the 1850s and among the busiest ports in the world by 1870. Although maritime passenger traffic dried up in the 1920s and the railroads no longer dominate land transport, Chicago's Union Station is still one of the most active facilities on the Amtrak national rail system with trains to both coasts and most midwestern cities.

The interstate highway system, originally proposed in the 1930s to bypass Chicago, now fans out in all directions from the city. Some of the city's expressways handle more than 200,000 vehicles a day.

Chicago's two airports combined are the busiest aviation complex in the nation. The older Midway Airport on the Southwest Side, the busiest aerodrome in the nation during the propeller era, in the year 2000 still handled 298,137 flights carrying nearly 15.7 million passengers, most of them domestic. On the Northwest Side, O'Hare International Airport the same year—despite federal restrictions on air traffic—was visited by more than 908,977 flights carrying 72.1 million passengers. Twenty-six international carriers operated almost 83,000 flights carrying nearly 10.5 million passengers to and from O'Hare in 2000.

World-Class Museums

Chicago is home to a number of world-class museums and scores of smaller ones. In fact, it would be possible to spend more than a month in the city and still not see all the collections. The major museums each require a couple of days of leisurely visits to see everything on display, and that would not include the collections available only to scientists. These institutions have dual roles as public exhibits and research facilities. Some

of the smaller museums are devoted to a single topic, such as Hellenic or Mexican culture or broadcasting.

Many of the major museums originated more than a century ago, some in connection with the Columbian Exposition, a world's fair held in 1893, when the city's newly wealthy merchants and industrialists began donating portions of their fortunes to culture. Marshall Field, founder of the department store chain that still bears his name, was the first major benefactor of the Columbian Museum of Chicago, which in 1905 changed its name to the Field Museum of Natural History. Julius Rosenwald, chairman of Sears, Roebuck and Co., the catalog house, a few years later visited the Deutches Museum in Munich, Germany, and returned to Chicago determined to create a museum dedicated to "industrial enlightenment." His dream in 1933 became the Museum of Science and Industry.

The first such science museum in the Western Hemisphere, the Museum of Science and Industry historically has been perhaps the city's most popular museum, attracting 1.7 million visitors annually in recent years to see the interactive exhibits, tour the coal mine, and wander through displays of Chicago's industrial past. It also has on display the U-505 German U-boat captured during World War II; Number 999, the steam locomotive that set a land speed record of more than 100 miles an hour back in 1893; and models of 50 famous ships from earliest times to the twentieth century.

Although the Field Museum has massive collections in the sciences of botany, anthropology, geology, paleontology, archaeology, and zoology, its most famous specimen is Sue, the huge *Tyrannosaurus rex* dinosaur that went on display in 2000. Also popular with the crowds is an exhibit of the two man-eating lions that killed nearly 140 railroad workers in 1898 along the Tsavo River in Uganda, Africa, and were made famous in the 1996 movie *The Ghost and the Darkness*. The museum is also home to the bones of a specimen of Brachiosaurus altithorax, a 40-foot-tall dinosaur discovered by one of its expeditions in 1900. A model of the skeleton is on display at the United Airlines terminal at O'Hare International Airport.

The Field Museum is part of the city's unique Museum Campus along the shore of Lake Michigan southeast of downtown Chicago. This park-like campus was created in 1999 when a portion of Lake Shore Drive that separated the museum from the nearby John G. Shedd Aquarium and Adler Planetarium and the Astronomy Museum was relocated. Soldier Field, where the Chicago Bears professional football team plays and where some of the World Cup soccer matches were held in 1994, is also part of the campus, and McCormick Place is just to the south.

Adjacent Grant Park to the north and west extends what urban historian Carl Condit once called "the largest, oldest, and architecturally most impressive 'cultural center' in the United States" more than a mile to downtown Chicago and such cultural institutions as The Art Institute of Chicago, the Auditorium Theater, and Orchestra Hall, home of the Chicago Symphony Orchestra. Grant Park is also home to Buckingham Fountain.

The Shedd Aquarium is best known for its collection of Beluga whales since its oceanarium housing them opened in 1991. The tropical coral reef is also a major attraction, and the aquarium has collections of seahorses, dolphins, penguins, seals, sea otters, and various species of fish as well. The Planetarium,

which sits on an artificial peninsula in the lake and also features various astronomical exhibits, has been popular among Chicago-area skywatchers since it opened in 1930.

The Art Institute of Chicago on Michigan Avenue just east of the Loop is something of a landmark because of the two bronze lions that flank its doorway, but inside are more than 225,000 works of art collected since the museum's predecessor first opened in 1879 as the Chicago Academy of Fine

Arts. The name was changed in 1882. Its masterpieces include *A Sunday Afternoon on La Grand Jatte—1884* by Georges Seurat, the oft-parodied *American Gothic* by Grant Wood, *Nighthawks* by Edward Hopper, and 33 works by Claude Monet. The institute also has a sizable research department and library, as well as a fine arts college.

Although smaller than The Art Institute, the Chicago Museum of Contemporary Art on Ontario Street on the Near North Side has more than 6,000 works of art in its collection—all created since 1945. The museum, a relative latecomer founded in 1967, has extensive collections of Surrealist art from the 1940s and 1950s and

One of the most popular Field Museum attractions is Sue. She is a 65-million-year-old *Tyrannosaurus rex*, the largest and most complete specimen of that dinosaur ever found. Photo by John Weinstein/© Field Museum

Following pages: The Great Lakes don't carry the volume of commercial boats they once did, but they're still popular with sailboating enthusiasts. The Shedd Aquarium (foreground) and Adler Planetarium (seen before its new addition) are on the lakeshore. Photo © Mark Segal/Index Stock Imagery

Minimalist art from the 1960s. It also hosts various traveling exhibits, as do the other major museums.

The still-smaller Terra Museum of American Art on Michigan Avenue north of the Loop displays such famous American artists as Whistler, Hopper, Homer, and the Wyeths. It is also home to Samuel F.B. Church's *Gallery of the Louvre*. The David and Alfred Smart Museum of Art houses the University of Chicago's primary collection of art on that campus, and the Ukranian Institute of Modern Art on the West Side features everything from folk art to modern renderings from that ethnic group. The Mexican Fine Arts Center Museum on the Southwest Side has a display on Pre-Columbian archaeology and murals by Hispanic artists.

One of the least known of Chicago's great museums is the Oriental Institute on the University of Chicago campus on the South Side. The university has been a center of ancient Near Eastern studies since its founding in 1891 and the Oriental Institute Museum exhibits antiquities from ancient Egypt, Assyria, Babylon, and Persia acquired on its many archaeological expeditions to those sites. The institute's research staff have published dictionaries of the ancient Assyrian, Sumerian, Demotic (Egyptian), and Hittite languages.

Local history is the specialty of the Chicago Historical Society about two miles north of the Loop on Clark Street. Besides a sizable museum devoted to such topics as pioneers and the Chicago Fire of 1871 that destroyed much of the city, the Historical Society maintains an impressive document and photographic archives used by scholars and researchers. Its library is open to the public.

One of the city's newest museums deals with a twentieth-century phenomenon—broadcasting. The Museum of Broadcast Communications in the Chicago Cultural Center at Michigan Avenue and Washington Boulevard features audio and video displays of radio and television broadcasting. Visitors can watch or listen to old shows in private booths.

Smaller museums scattered about the city document everything from the history of doing laundry to the stories of various ethnic communities in America. The Ridge Historical Society in the far southwest Beverly neighborhood has an interactive exhibit of wash-

ing clothes by hand, and the Hellenic Museum and Cultural Center on South Michigan Avenue records the story of Greeks in America. The Du Sable Museum of African-American History on the South Side near the University of Chicago has exhibits documenting the black experience in the United States from slavery to the present day. It also has a collection by black artists.

The Spertus Museum at the Spertus Institute of Jewish Studies on South Michigan Avenue has a permanent collection of Judaica from around the world, and the Chicago Children's Museum on Navy Pier has a building full of hands-on exhibits for youngsters, including a build-your-own airplane lab

The Art Institute houses one of the largest collections of Impressionist art outside of France. It invariably is on the itinerary of foreign tourists. Photo © C&S Chattopadhyay/Index Stock Imagery

Facing page: Bronze lions guard the Michigan Avenue entrance to The Art Institute of Chicago and have become as much a local landmark as the institution itself. A thoughtful tour of the museum's collection can take days. Photo © Jim Schwabel/Index Stock Imagery

Following pages: The Lincoln Park Conservatory is one of two indoor gardens that enable visitors to enjoy horticultural exhibits even during the city's notoriously bleak winters. The other conservatory is in Garfield Park. Photo © Bruce Leighty/Index Stock Imagery

One of the Chicago area's two major zoos is in the unlikely urban setting of Lincoln Park. The gorillas are one of Lincoln Park Zoo's most popular attractions. Photo © NATIONAL GEOGRAPHIC IMAGE COLLECTION/ Michael K. Nichols

in which kids can fabricate airplanes out of foam rubber, then test them in flight from a 50-foot-tall conveyor belt. The Chicago Academy of Sciences maintains a small museum in its Lincoln Park headquarters on the North Side. The American Police Center and Museum has numerous police and crime exhibits and has been favorably compared to Scotland Yard's Black Museum in London.

For people who like to see wildlife on the hoof, the Chicago area has two major zoos—Brookfield in the western suburbs, and Lincoln Park Zoo on the North Side. Officials of Lincoln Park Zoo like to boast that they operate one of the last admission-free cultural institutions in the United States and the last one in Chicago. The zoo began modestly in 1868 with a pair of donated swans and added a bear cub a few years later. Today its collection includes bears, birds, gorillas, lions, elephants, sea mammals, reptiles, and farm animals.

Public and Private Libraries

Besides the specialized collections in museums and universities, Chicago is home to several major libraries open to the public. In addition to the collections in 76 branch libraries scattered around the city, the Chicago Public Library's central Harold Washington Library Center on State Street in the South Loop area houses nine million books and documents in its 756,000 square feet of space. The $144-million building was opened in 1987 after the library outgrew its old quarters at Michigan Avenue and Washington Street. That facility was converted into the Chicago Cultural Center, which features galleries of contemporary art, a concert hall, and a tourist information center, as well as the Museum of Broadcast Communications.

The Newberry Library on the North Side is a privately funded, independent research library concentrating on the humanities. It was founded by a bequest by Walter Loomis Newberry, a prominent businessman who died in 1868 before Chicago had a public library. In 1896 the Chicago Public Library, which by then had come into existence; the Newberry; and the John Crerar Library, another privately funded venture, agreed to share responsibilities for research collections. The public library would concentrate on business and general topics, the Newberry on the humanities and music, and the Crerar on science and technology.

Today the Newberry has an extensive but non-circulating collection of maps, rare books, and manuscripts on the civilizations of Europe from the Middle Ages to modern times and the Americas from Pre-Columbian times to the present. Among its 1.5 million printed titles and five million manuscript pages are considerable collections dealing with genealogy and Midwest and Indian history. It also has 300,000 historic maps.

John Crerar, a railway supply company executive, willed $2.5 million in 1889 to build and maintain a free public library. It opened in 1897 with 11,000 volumes and 171 journals but in 1962, because of the difficulty of maintaining a large private library, merged with the Illinois Institute of Technology. When that arrangement failed to work out, Crerar in 1981 merged with the University of Chicago, its present home.

Arts from Opera to Improvisation

As is typical of a city its size, Chicago has a large number of organizations, professional and amateur, devoted to the performing arts. Its crown jewel is the Chicago Symphony Orchestra,

which—beginning with conductor Fritz Reiner in 1954 and continuing through Sir Georg Solti and current music director Daniel Barenboim—has gained international attention with its performances, recordings, and tours. The Lyric Opera of Chicago is one of a handful of the most important opera companies in the Western Hemisphere, and Second City has been a prolific breeding ground for American comedy performers since its founding nearly a half-century ago. The city also has small but active companies devoted to folk music and dance, ballet, and music ranging from the blues to the Baroque and Renaissance periods.

Chicago's theaters perform a wide range of plays. The city is on the Broadway touring circuit for the more popular musicals and dramas, has a house devoted to Shakespeare, and is home to smaller companies that produce important but lesser-known drama. Contemporary playwright David

Mamet (*American Buffalo and Glengarry Glen Ross*, among others) got his start in Chicago.

The Chicago Symphony, founded in 1891, performs in the recently refurbished and expanded Orchestra Hall on Michigan Avenue. The original structure, designed by architect Daniel Burnham and opened in 1904, is now on the National Register of Historic Places. Maestro Solti took the orchestra on its first European tour in 1971, and since then it has traveled back to Europe several times as well as to Japan and Australia. The 119-member orchestra's concerts are broadcast over 200 radio stations across the country, and through the years it has won 56 Grammy Awards from the National Academy of Recording Arts and Sciences.

The Chicago Civic Opera, which originally performed in the Auditorium Theater, moved into the Civic Opera House in 1929 just six days after the

Above: Chicago was an early blues center and has kept up the tradition with an annual blues festival. Jack Owens is shown at his appearance at the 1991 festival. Photo © Ellen Skye/Index Stock Imagery

Top: The Grant Park bandshell is the site of a free concert series each summer. The annual Fourth of July concert and subsequent fireworks display on barges in the lake attract huge crowds. Photo © Mark Gibson/Index Stock Imagery

The Chicago Theater was built in 1921 for live shows and silent movies. It exhibited movies for decades until it was finally restored and converted to a legitimate theater. It anchors the city's Loop theater district. Photo © Vic Bider/Index Stock Imagery

her death in 1997, continued the policy and expanded the season to include more operas. The Lyric, which sells 37,000 season tickets annually, consistently sells out its performances. The adjacent Civic Theater on Wacker Drive on the bank of the south branch of the Chicago River was used to present plays, including the premiere of Tennessee Williams' *The Glass Menagerie.*

The smaller Chicago Opera Theater on the North Side produces several operas a year, including Phillip Glass's *Akhnaten* staged in 2000. The Joffrey Ballet of Chicago presents performances around the Chicago area, and the Hubbard Street Dance is known for its contemporary and innovative presentations in its new West Loop neighborhood building and at various other venues. Each summer Chicago stages the municipally funded classical (and admission-free) Grant Park Music Festival. At the other end of the musical scale, the not-for-profit Old Town School of Folk Music promotes ethnic and folk music from America and around the world. Assorted blues and jazz festivals are held around the city, as are a number of rock-and-roll concerts.

Three theaters in the Loop—two of them converted movie houses—regularly offer Broadway shows, and various other theaters present everything from classic drama to improvisational comedy. The Chicago Theater on State Street was originally built to show films in 1920-1921 during the movie palace era, although it was also a venue for live performances by John Phillip Sousa, Duke Ellington, Jack Benny, and Benny Goodman. It was converted in 1986 at a cost of $25 million to handle stage shows. It is huge, accommodating 1,970 seats on the main floor and 1,540 in the balcony and boxes.

The Oriental Theater around the cor-

stock market crash. Utilities magnate Samuel Insull had the building and its 3,563-seat auditorium designed specifically for grand opera. The Civic Opera and its successors, after some troubled times in the Depression and during World War II, became the Lyric Opera under the direction of Carol Fox in 1956. To promote grand opera in a town better known for its factories and taverns, Fox hired some of the greatest singers of the time, including soprano Maria Callas in her American debut.

Fox's successor Ardis Krainik, who reigned over the opera from 1981 until

ner on Randolph Street was a movie house when it opened in 1926. As the movie exhibition business moved to the suburbs and neighborhoods, the Oriental stood empty for 17 years until it was refurbished and reopened as a musical theater, the Ford Center for the Performing Arts. The original Oriental decor remains, and the Ford seats 1,250. The Shubert Theater in the middle of the Loop began its existence in 1906 as a vaudeville house, the Majestic. After being shuttered for 15 years beginning in the Depression, it reopened in 1945 as the Shubert and now alternately presents Broadway shows, musicals, and solo performances.

The Goodman Theater, now on Randolph Street, has presented a variety of largely non-Broadway drama since its 1925 opening. The Auditorium Theater in the Adler-Sullivan-designed building of the same name is acoustically one of the best houses in Chicago and gives a variety of international, cultural, and community programs. Best known of the dozens of smaller theaters, many of them amateur, is the not-for-profit Steppenwolf Theatre Company on the North Side, which specializes in new and neglected plays as well as classics.

A Chicago institution is the 45-year-old Second City, a North Side theater and night club specializing in comedy in an intimate, 300-seat auditorium. Second City, which takes its name from Chicago's onetime rank as the nation's second-largest city behind New York, has had many imitators, including the "Saturday Night Live" television show. Second City's alumni include comedians Bill Murray, Alan Arkin, John Belushi, Joan Rivers, and Chris Farley.

A Professional Sports Town

The city's sports teams are popular attractions and occasionally provide good theater as well. Despite the existence of some excellent college sports programs within easy driving distance, such as Notre Dame University, Chicago is known primarily as a professional sports town.

The Cubs in baseball's National League seem to be the nation's sentimental favorites. Despite the fact that they have not appeared in a World Series since 1945 and have not won one since 1908, an average of more than 2.2 million spectators a year turn out to watch the team play in Wrigley Field, a 1914 ballpark that has lent its name to the North Side neighborhood in which its sits—Wrigleyville.

On the South Side, the Chicago White Sox playing in the American League over the years have challenged the Cubs for futility. The Sox have not played in a World Series since 1959, and have not won one since 1917. In the last half of the 1990s the team drew an average of fewer than 1.6 million fans despite the 1991 opening of their new ballpark, Comiskey Park.

Chicago was known as a graveyard for professional basketball, having two teams fold or move away between 1950 and 1963, and a third, the Bulls, dying from lack of interest in the early 1980s. Then Michael Jordan came along and the Bulls won six National Basketball Association championships in the 1990s and became the darling sports franchise of the city.

The other tenant of the West Side stadium that the Bulls call home is the Blackhawks, a National Hockey League franchise. The team in recent years has been plagued by its failure to make the playoffs and slipping attendance, although as recently as 1997 almost 950,000 fans paid to see the hockey team play.

The Chicago Bears, one of the National Football League's original

The Second City nightclub on the North Side has become famous for its improvisational comedy. Its alumni include some of the greatest names in American comedy. Photo © Bruce Leighty/Index Stock Imagery

teams and one of the most exciting in the league's first 40 years of existence, appearing in 11 championship games, have been in the doldrums for most of the past 40 years of their history. Since then, they have been in only two championship games, 1963 and 1985, winning both. The Bears, which have come to symbolize the city's tough image, draw an average of more than 56,000 fans to their games in Soldier Field.

The Chicago Fire, a Major League Soccer team, drew an average of 16,000 fans per game in its 1999 season in Soldier Field after winning the 1998 MLS championship in the team's first year of existence. Soccer is starting to gain popularity as a spectator sport in Chicago as more people become familiar with it.

The nearest college that offers a full range of top-level sports is Northwestern in the adjacent suburb of Evanston, although DePaul, Loyola, and UIC all have major basketball programs.

The Nation's Architectural Mecca

Some of Chicago's greatest artwork is free for the gazing—its architecture and public sculpture. Since the second half of the nineteenth century the city has been a Mecca for works by architects and artists from around the world, and local architect Daniel Burnham not only designed a number of buildings but gave the city its master plan as well.

The first tall buildings, or skyscrapers as they are now known, appeared in the 1880s after techniques were found to float structures on the soft sand and clay of the area using footings. The need for heavy masonry walls was eliminated by using iron and steel skeletons covered by a masonry skin. The Monadnock Building, completed in 1891 and still standing at the south end of the Loop, was designed by Burnham and John Wellborn Root using walls 72

inches thick at the base to support its 16 stories. But William Le Baron Jenney in 1885 had used a wrought-iron skeleton to build his nine-story Home Insurance Building—the world's first skyscraper.

Within a few years Louis Sullivan and Dankmar Adler were designing the Auditorium Building, the Old Stock Exchange, and the Carson, Pirie, Scott & Co. store. Although Chicago's buildings continued to grow in height as

Above: The Chicago White Sox play at Comiskey Park on the South Side. Their new stadium opened in 1991 alongside the Dan Ryan Expressway. Photo © Ellen Skye/Index Stock Imagery

Facing page: Wrigley Field, one of the oldest ballparks in the nation, is home to the Chicago Cubs. It may be best known for the vines that cling to its outfield walls and its preponderance of day games. Photo © Bruce Leighty/Index Stock Imagery

more sophisticated construction techniques were developed, one of the city's most famous architects specialized in small structures. Frank Lloyd Wright founded the "Prairie School" of architecture for private residences, and his Robie House still stands in the Hyde Park neighborhood.

Mies van der Rohe raised boxy, steel-and-glass "Bauhaus" buildings to the level of fine art. The German-born architect, who immigrated to the United States in the 1930s, designed much of the Illinois Institute of Technology campus. One of his successors as a truly international architect based in Chicago was Helmut Jahn, who added curves to Bauhaus and designed the State of Illinois' Loop offices as well as other structures.

The skyscraper-building art in Chicago culminated in the second half of the twentieth century with three structures each more than 1,000 feet

tall. The Sears Tower at 110 stories and 1,454 feet was the world's tallest building after it was completed in 1974 until the 1,483-foot Petronas Towers were built in Kuala Lumpur, Malaysia, in 1996. The John Hancock Building at 100 stories and the Aon (formerly Standard Oil) Building at 80 stories are the other thousand-footers. Both the Sears and Hancock buildings have public observation decks at the top, and

Right: Michael Jordan *was* the Chicago Bulls in the 1980s and 1990s, leading the team to six National Basketball Association championships. His statue stands in front of the United Center, where the Bulls play. Photo © Bruce Leighty/Index Stock Imagery

Below: The region's long, cold winters make basketball a well-attended sport in Chicagoland. Chicago Basketball Day attests to the sport's popularity among kids. Photo © Mark Segal/ Index Stock Imagery

each year more than a million people ascend to the Sears skydeck to catch a bird's-eye view of the city.

Far below on various streets are a number of public sculptures for which the city has also become known. The most famous and the one that has become a landmark—although it was controversial and often referred to as a baboon when it was unveiled in 1967—is Pablo Picasso's unnamed 50-foot-high steel statue in the Daley Civic Center Plaza. The venerable Spanish artist contributed its design and a model to the city he had never visited after Chicago architect William Hartmann went to Picasso's home on the French Riviera and interested him in the project.

Other well-known public sculptures include a stabile by Alexander Calder in a plaza in the federal building complex, Marc Chagall's *Four Seasons* mosaic nearby, and Claes Oldenburg's 96-foot *Batcolumn* just west of the Loop. The most recent public sculpture program dates from the Chicago Picasso, but early in the century local sculptor Lorado Taft crafted a number of works including the *Fountain of the Great Lakes* in Grant Park. The Great Depression-era Works Progress Administration commissioned murals to keep artists from starving, and per-haps the largest surviving collection in the nation was rediscovered in various Chicago school buildings, some painted over, which are in the process of being restored.

Educational Institutions

The city's public school system, like those in many big American cities, has had its problems in the second half of the twentieth century as middle-class residents fled to the suburbs to be replaced by poor immigrants from other regions and nations, but some state reforms have helped stabilize the sys-tem in recent years. Public school enrollment is more than 400,000, and another 77,000 children are enrolled in the city's excellent but shrinking Catholic school system.

The city's strength is in its higher education, however. The private University of Chicago consistently ranks near the top in surveys of the nation's best colleges. Northwestern University, another private school with its main campus in suburban Evanston and its professional schools in downtown Chicago, is also highly rated. Other major schools include Loyola and DePaul, both Catholic universities; Illinois Institute of Technology; and the University of Illinois at Chicago. The city also has a large community college system with more than 77,000 stu-dents, and North Park University, an evangelical small college in a big city.

The University of Chicago, since its 1891 founding by a collaboration of Biblical scholar William Rainey Harper's energy and oil tycoon John D. Rockefeller's money, modeled itself on a German-style graduate research institute with an English-style undergraduate col-lege grafted on. The formula worked probably beyond its founders' dreams: The university has produced 71 Nobel laureates, and its faculty over the years has included such notables as economist Milton Friedman; nuclear physicist Enrico Fermi; educator John Dewey; and meteorologist Tetsuya "Ted" Fujita, discoverer of the microburst. The uni-versity has been so influential that its research led to what are known as the "Chicago Schools" of economics, sociol-ogy, and literary criticism.

The Nuclear Age was born on a squash court beneath the university's now-demolished Stagg Field when Fermi and his colleagues on December 2, 1942, conducted the world's first

controlled, self-sustaining nuclear chain reaction—a development that later led to the atomic bomb. The same stadium was involved when then university president Robert Maynard Hutchins, who believed that undergraduate education should involve the assimilation of the "great books," declared that big-time college football had no place in the academic community and dropped the sport despite the fact that football coach Amos Alonzo Stagg was something of a national icon.

Today the university has an enroll-

ment of more than 12,000 students, only about a quarter of them undergraduates. Its faculty numbers 2,030, six of them Nobel laureates.

IIT came into existence in 1893 as a college offering education in engineering, chemistry, and architecture as the result of a sermon. Chicago meat-packer Philip D. Armour became the benefactor of what was then called Armour Institute of Technology after he heard a sermon in a South Side church given by the Reverend Frank Gunsaulus. The reverend said that for a

Above: The Wrigley Building, the southern anchor of Chicago's "Magnificent Mile," as the North Michigan Avenue shopping district is sometimes called, is clad in white terra cotta. Photo © Bruce Leighty/Index Stock Imagery

Right: The Smurfit-Stone Container Building, completed in 1984, is one of many skyscrapers with distinctive facades resulting from a desire by architects to place their individual stamps on the Chicago skyline. Photo © Mark Segal/Index Stock Imagery

Facing page: Chicago's downtown for more than a century has been a veritable museum of modern architecture. The Sears Tower (left), at 1,454 feet the tallest in the United States, dwarfs the 311 South Wacker Drive Building (right). It stands a mere 981 feet tall. Photo © Mark Segal/Index Stock Imagery

million dollars he could build a college to prepare students from all backgrounds for careers in an industrial society. The name was changed to Illinois Institute of Technology in 1940 after a merger with Lewis Institute.

Over the years other mergers have added law and business schools to the institute's technologically oriented curriculum. In 2000 IIT had more than 6,000 students, about 1,700 undergraduates, and nearly 3,000 graduates and 1,200 in law.

Loyola University, which began in

1870 as the liberal arts St. Ignatius College and was burned to the ground the next year in the Chicago Fire, today has more than 13,000 students on five campuses, including its Center of Liberal Arts near the Vatican in Rome. The main campus is near the lake about eight miles north of the Loop. In addition to the original arts and sciences school, Loyola has schools specializing in education, nursing, social work, law, medicine, and theology.

The nation's largest Catholic college is DePaul University with about 20,000 students. Founded in 1898 by the Vincentian Fathers order, DePaul was one of the first private, urban universities to try to cope with metropolitan sprawl in the second half of the twentieth century by opening five suburban campuses and to recognize the importance of the need for computer training by establishing a school for computer sciences. DePaul's main campus is in the Lincoln Park neighborhood on Chicago's North Side, and its commerce, law, and computer sciences schools are located in the Loop.

Above: Chicago has numerous examples of modern public sculpture, such as Alexander Calder's *Flamingo* in the Federal Center Plaza. Photo © 2000 Randy Wells/Stone

Facing page, top: Jean Dubuffet's *Monument with Standing Beast* in front of the John R. Thompson Center is one of the city's most enigmatic pieces of art. Photo © Mark & Audrey Gibson/Index Stock Imagery

Facing page, bottom: Pablo Picasso's world-famous sculpture is simply called *The Chicago Picasso.* Photo © Scott Berner/ Index Stock Imagery

The University of Chicago's Yerkes Observatory at Lake Geneva, Wisconsin, houses the world's largest refractor telescope. It was built at what was then a remote location so the lights of the city wouldn't interfere with stargazing. Photo © Mark Segal/Index Stock Imagery

Right: The city is dotted with summertime art fairs, murals painted on building walls, professional galleries, and outdoor classes where students polish their skills. Photo © Ralf-Finn Hestoft/Index Stock Imagery

Preceding pages: Buckingham Fountain in Grant Park is typical of European fountains and was inspired by a basin in Versailles outside of Paris. The city's largest fountain, it sprays 14,000 gallons of water a minute as high as 150 feet. Photo © Jim Schwabel/Index Stock Imagery

Preceding page, inset: Kate Buckingham donated the fountain designed by Frenchman Marcel Francois Logan to the city in 1927 as a memorial for her brother, Clarence. Photo © Jim Schwabel/ Index Stock Imagery

The University of Illinois at Chicago is a relative latecomer, having been established in 1946 as a junior college to train returning World War II veterans. Since then it has expanded to a four-year undergraduate school with graduate programs, built its own 250-acre campus on the West Side, and grown to more than 25,000 students, 16,000 of them undergraduates. The UIC also has a medical school.

City Colleges of Chicago began in 1911 as a one-campus junior college on the West Side founded as a way to educate immigrants. Although the system

had grown to 3,000 students within 20 years, it limped along for more than four decades because of lack of funding, accreditation problems, and loss of its branches to military training programs during World World II. As recently as 1976 it began offering televised courses for disadvantaged students who could not attend class. The system now has about 77,000 students enrolled on its seven campuses.

Roosevelt University was also founded following World War II but as a college specializing in urban residents and their educational needs. More recently it opened a satellite campus in northwest suburban Schaumburg and describes itself as more "metropolitan" than "urban," with curricula in liberal arts, music, business, and education. The school offers a range of courses adapted to working adults. Its main campus is in the historic Auditorium Building near the Loop.

Another downtown campus is Columbia College, which traces its roots from a woman's school specializing in oratory founded in 1890. It has grown into an institution of nearly 9,000 students offering a wide range of

programs in communications ranging from fiction writing to television. Columbia also has programs in dance, theater, music, and early childhood education.

The state university system also includes Northeastern Illinois University, a commuter college on the Northwest Side serving about 10,000 students, and Chicago State University, its counterpart on the South Side. North Park University, which began in 1891 as a school for Swedish immigrants and now offers education from an Evangelical Protestant viewpoint, is unusual among Chicago institutions in that it has a small-town college atmosphere despite its location on the Northwest Side of the nation's third-largest city.

A Metropolis of Neighborhoods

Chicago has as great a variety of housing as any city its size, from the towering apartment buildings and condominiums along the Gold Coast on the North Side to the two- and three-flats in more modest neighborhoods. The city is in the process of tearing down many of its high-rise public

The abundance of skyscrapers means that at business luncheons in the city's many clubs and restaurants, diners have spectacular views of the lake and sprawling skyline. Photo © Vcl/Spencer Rowell/FPG International LLC

The Gold Coast on the North Side has an eclectic mix of high-rise apartment buildings, a number of old mansions, and plenty of nightclubs, restaurants, and taverns. Photo © Vic Bider/Index Stock Imagery

housing projects—the "warehouses of the poor" as they are sometimes called—and replacing them with smaller structures in scattered locations. Chicago still has its slums, but it also has neighborhoods of single-family homes, like Beverly, that would be the envy of any suburb.

It also has spruced up its downtown area, once flanked by railroad yards, seedy housing, and crumbling factories. The Loop is still the financial center of Chicago with various stock and commodity exchanges, brokerage houses, and banks. It is also the site of the State Street retail district, which has declined in importance in the past quarter-century but remains home to such department stores as Marshall Field & Company and Carson, Pirie, Scott & Co. The city also has been attempting to develop portions of the Loop as the theater district.

Many of the older retail stores and

some newcomers have moved to the "Magnificent Mile," as North Michigan Avenue between the Loop and Oak Street is called. It is the site of upscale hotels, restaurants, and stores and even an in-city, vertical mall called Water Tower Place. The once-seedy River North, as the area north of the Chicago River is called, has undergone gentrification in recent years with the opening of art galleries, restaurants, nightclubs, and loft apartments.

Across the river to the west of the Loop is Greektown, the site of many of the city's best Greek restaurants, and south of it is Little Italy, where many employees of the city's West Side medical complex and UIC live alongside the obviously ethnic restaurants. Still farther south is Chinatown. The city's Korean area is Albany Park, a former Jewish neighborhood on the North Side. Still farther north is Little India. Its more than 60 restaurants, many of them family owned, serve Indian, Thai, Assyrian, and Jewish cuisine.

Albany Park and Little India aren't the only neighborhoods that have switched their ethnicity as older groups moved to the suburbs to be replaced by newer immigrants. The once Germanic Pilsen neighborhood on the Southwest Side is now Mexican. Ukranian Village,

the neighborhood northwest of the Loop, was once the epicenter of the city's huge Polish population. It has been gentrified in recent years although it is still a place to find ethnic bookstores, shops, and restaurants. Bucktown just west of Lincoln Park has been reborn as a center for young unmarrieds and has a bar scene rivaling Wrigleyville farther north. On the far Northwest and Southwest sides, neighborhoods like Jefferson Park and Ashburn are covered with modest single-family bungalows.

One of Chicago's oldest surviving ethnic neighborhoods is Chinatown, where shops catering to tourists and residents abound. The traditional Chinese herbal medicines in this shop are more likely to appeal to the locals. Photo © 2000 Don Smetzer/Stone

CHAPTER FIVE

Outgrowing the City

They're called suburbs, but they're hardly that anymore. To the ancient Romans the Latin term meant hovels clustered outside the safety of the city's walls. To the Victorians it meant a bedroom community whose residents commuted to work in the city. In early twenty-first-century Chicago those definitions no longer apply, and urbanologists are still searching for a word to describe what the more than 250 communities outside Chicago (stretching in an arc 120 miles around the southern tip of Lake Michigan) have become.

Few of them are true suburbs. Some of the biggest have giant shopping and office centers of their own to which shoppers and workers commute by car on interstate highways from rural areas as much as 100 miles from Chicago. Collectively they are now larger in area and population than the city they encircle.

"Technoburb" is a term sometimes used by urbanologists to describe such towns as Schaumburg, Naperville, and Oak Brook that have their own regional shopping malls, office campuses, and sprawling residential subdivisions. "Multi-nucleated centers" is another term sometimes applied to the 'burbs; so is "megakome," the ancient Greek word for "giant village."

Left: Suburbia grew at a record pace during the second half of the twentieth century as new subdivisions like this one in Elgin sprouted up as far as 40 miles from the Loop. In 1970 Illinois' suburbs collectively passed Chicago in population. Photo © Jim Wark/Index Stock Imagery

There are now several different types of suburbs. The old railroad suburbs born in the 1800s still exist and send many of their residents by train to the Loop each day. The cornfield suburbs—for the most part sprawling residential subdivisions dotted by commercial strips and industrial parks—were built from scratch after World War II and are wholly a creature of the Automobile Age. Many were built without sidewalks. The expressway suburbs are characterized by a corridor of high-rise office campuses along the highway, as well as subdivisions and commercial strip centers. The mall towns are just that—regional shopping complexes surrounded by offices and subdivisions. There are also some predominantly industrial suburbs dominated by factories and warehouses.

The detached single-family home is still the residence of choice in most suburbs,

One of the attractions of the suburbs is that there is plenty of open space, giving children ample room to play outdoors. Photo © Christopher Marona/Index Stock Imagery

where the term "public housing" conjures up images of the high-rise projects that had been built half a century earlier and were being razed as the twentieth century ended—a dramatic admission of the failure of earlier social engineering. In suburbia, the term "affordable housing" was being used in place of "public housing" to soften its impact on public opinion.

There are mansions as fine as any on earth in Chicago's suburbs, and there are some dismal slums. There are entire subdivisions of seemingly identical tract houses, split levels, and bungalows, and there are charming middle-class neighborhoods of what a century earlier would have been called cottages. There are treeless subdivisions of faux Victorian homes only a few years old selling for half a million dollars apiece, and a few blocks away down near the railroad station there are real Victorian homes with gaily painted gingerbread and fretwork as well as stately maples in their front yards. The elms that used to define suburban Chicago are long gone, victims of the plague of Dutch elm disease.

It is not a coincidence that when Hollywood wants to capture a nostalgic scene of America in a bygone era it fre-

Quiet, tree-shaded streets and sidewalks in suburbia have been an attraction for couples with young children. Kids need a safe environment to learn how to ride tricycles. Photo © Mark Segal/Index Stock Imagery

quently hauls its cameras to Chicago and the suburbs.

The first suburbs of Chicago began in the 1850s as summer resorts and were wholly creatures of the railroads then being built in all directions from the city. Developer Paul Cornell built his Hyde Park resort on 300 acres along Lake Michigan about seven miles south of Chicago. In 1856 he talked the Illinois Central Railroad into building a station there and then agreed to subsidize daily shuttle trains. About this same time other railroads began operating "accommodation" trains to serve the farm towns outside Chicago.

The term "commuter" originated with the practice of discounting, or "commuting," fares for daily riders. Today it describes the ordeal of getting to and from work, whether it be by foot, train, or car. The auto is the choice of the vast majority of suburbanites—more than 90 percent—although the region's extensive commuter railroad network that includes 13 separate lines still holds a healthy share of the market to and from Chicago's Loop.

The development of the suburb from early resort towns such as Hyde Park was an abrupt process historically, spurred not only by faster and more powerful locomotives that caused commuting to be quicker, but also by changes in state law that made incorporation easy. The Chicago Fire of 1871

Although apartment buildings have been growing in number and popularity, the typical suburban residence consists of a single-family home and garage surrounded by a yard. Photo © Mark Segal/Index Stock Imagery

There are still some farms in the suburbs, such as this one near Grayslake, but most have been gobbled up by developers of new subdivisions. The land is worth more planted with bungalows, driveways, and lawns than it is with corn. Photo © Tom Dietrich/Index Stock Imagery

helped create the first major migration from the city. There were only about 10 suburbs in 1870. The planned western suburb of Riverside, designed in 1868 by landscape architect Frederick Law Olmsted, did not begin to grow significantly until the 1880s because at 11 miles from downtown Chicago it was considered too remote. By 1900,

when Chicago reported a population of 1,698,575, there were only 386,175 people living in the six counties that now comprise suburbia. By then there were 56 suburbs.

Chicago continued to grow faster than its suburbs until the 1920s. In fact, the collective population of suburbia didn't reach one million until 1930

Improved construction materials such as drywall, nail guns, and housewrap enable homes to be built in less than a month—even in winter. Photo © Tom Dietrich/Index Stock Imagery

Employing the use of prefabricated roof trusses is one of the ways builders have found to increase efficiency in the competitive home-building market. These trusses are currently a part of most homes being built in the city and suburbs. Photo © 2000 Mark Joseph/Stone

when Chicago was already more than three times that size.

The Great Depression and World War II put a damper on growth until the late 1940s, when the flight to the suburbs began in earnest. The 1970 census showed that the suburbs (collectively with 3.6 million residents) for the first time passed Chicago (with 3,369,367 residents) in population. By the end of the century, the suburbs were approaching five million residents and Chicago had fewer than three million.

Decentralization or Urban Sprawl

Sometime in the early twentieth century the phenomenon of suburbanization began to evolve into what can be politely called decentralization, although its detractors referred to it as urban sprawl. The phenomenon was not unique to Chicago but was occurring in cities all over the world, developed and underdeveloped, regardless of whether there was high auto ownership. The Northeastern Illinois

Planning Commission reported that in the two decades between 1970 and 1990 the developed land area of metropolitan Chicago grew by 46 to 65 percent but the population grew by only 4.1 percent. Virtually all the growth was suburban.

In the last decade of the twentieth century there was a trend toward recentralization as suburbs built apartment complexes in their downtown areas near the commuter train stations and high-intensity retail and office development concentrated around regional malls. However, the verdict is still out on the process. Subdivisions continue to be constructed on farmland 40 or more miles from the Loop in places such as Elburn and Grayslake, and three-car garages are becoming as common as four-bedroom houses.

Nothing illustrates the transformation of suburbia better than the evolution of the garage, that ubiquitous structure in which Americans store their automobiles. The carriage houses behind the larger Victorian homes in the 1890s became the perfect place to store the horseless carriages that began to increase in popularity after 1895. By the 1920s, when cars became affordable to middle-class families in more modest dwellings in the suburbs, homeowners constructed small outbuildings called garages (from the French word for storage) at the rear of their properties. New homes were designed with garages and driveways.

By 1935 cars had become such an important part of suburban life that architects were beginning to design garages attached to houses. Within three decades it was not uncommon for the attached garage to consist of 400 square feet—a third the size of the house—and have room for two cars as well as assorted tools, lawnmowers, and gardening equipment. By then the garage had moved from the back of the lot to the side or front of the house with its doors prominently facing the street.

In the final decades of the century the suburbs were requiring the developers of apartment buildings to include garages in their structures. To enable their central business districts to compete with the malls and their vast parking lots, many suburbs were building multi-story public parking garages downtown.

Chicago's suburbs were frequently criticized as exclusive enclaves for the middle and upper classes, but in the second half of the twentieth century they have become considerably more diversified as the grandchildren of immigrants were absorbed into mainstream society and sought the American dream of a cottage in the country made popular by nineteenth-century authors Catharine Beecher, Andrew Jackson Downing, and Calvert Vaux. By 1970 the cottage came with a lawn in front, garden in the rear, two-car garage, family room, four or five bedrooms, and two and a half baths.

The "Land Beyond O'Hare" as *Chicago Tribune* columnist Bob Greene once described the suburbs north and west of Chicago's airport, is dotted with Chinese, Greek, Italian, Bohemian, and Mexican eateries. Le Francais, a dining establishment consistently mentioned among world-class restaurants, is in northwest suburban Wheeling. Tall Grass, another highly rated restaurant, is southwest of the city in the old canal town of Lockport.

There is also a uniformity creeping through the suburbs, not just in housing but in retail buildings as well, as large national restaurant chains open more outlets, sometimes making it impossible for a person to tell whether he is in Skokie, Illinois; Des Moines, Iowa; or Spartanburg, South Carolina.

Facing page: Pumpkins on the porch and a sprinkling of leaves can only mean autumn at this Wheaton residence. Some homes are now elaborately decorated for the Halloween and Independence Day holidays as well as Christmas. Photo © Bruce Leighty/Index Stock Imagery

Fast food and the golden arches of McDonald's are now as much a part of life in suburbia as maple trees, shopping malls, and flower gardens. Photo © BENELUX PRESS BV/Index Stock Imagery

The railroads built the first suburbs beginning in the 1850s, but the expressways and tollways have abetted their sprawl almost uncontrollably since World War II. Photo © Mark Segal/Index Stock Imagery

Many of the local hardware stores have disappeared as the big home centers hit the scene, just as the small local department stores in suburban downtowns became victims of the national chains in and around the regional malls.

Automobile Changed Suburbia

At the end of World War II, each suburb had its own downtown business district with a variety of stores catering to the needs of local residents and built around the train station. That profile fit most suburbs for a century, so long as the railroad was the principal connection with the outside world.

The automobile changed everything. The food stores were among the first to leave, evolving into supermarkets built along highways on the edge of town where cheap land was available for big parking lots. Then the dry cleaners, auto dealers, and drug and variety stores joined them. The latter evolved into discount houses of 30,000 square feet or larger. The regional malls appeared in the 1960s and 1970s, usually built about 10 miles apart, followed by the giant discount stores (100,000 square feet and larger) in the 1980s constructed on ever more remote sites.

By then the central business districts of most suburbs were dying, dotted with vacant stores, hobby merchants open limited hours, second-hand bookstores, and resale shops. New residents of the sprawling residential subdivisions built on the edge of town found that as long as they had to hop in the car to get a loaf of bread, they might as well drive to the shopping center to buy it. The subdivisions built on farmland far from the established suburbs simply incorporated as new towns without any retail base of their own or a recognizable town center. Eventually the supermarket chains discovered them and built small shopping plazas to serve them.

In the last two decades of the twentieth century, the central business districts of some of the more progressive old suburbs began fighting back, throwing up apartment buildings near the train stations to give local stores a captive audience, providing tax breaks for merchants to refurbish their buildings, encouraging specialty stores to locate there, and trying to lure some of the big national retail chains out of the malls. They have also been encouraging new restaurants to draw people back to the center of town.

In fact, by the end of the century some of the postwar, auto-oriented suburbs were trying to create town centers emulating the older suburbs.

Chicago's landmark signature is its lakefront, but in the suburbs a vast trail system built on abandoned railroad rights of way, plank roads, and alongside canals and rivers in the last half of the twentieth century has emerged to rival the public gardens as a collective signature of disparate suburbia. The region was a pioneer in the concept of urban trails, although similar linear

parks trace their roots back to the famous river walk Paseo del Rio in San Antonio, Texas, in the 1920s and Natchez Trace Parkway in Mississippi and Tennessee a decade later.

The trails movement began in Chicagoland in 1963, when a group of suburban conservationists banded together to save the right of way of a recently abandoned electric interurban railroad from being sold for development. That became the Illinois Prairie Path, the prototype for an urban trail system that by the end of the century

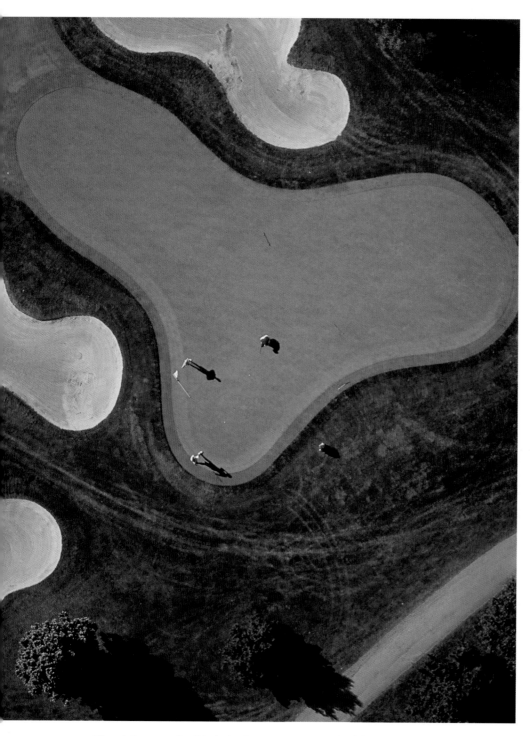

Although there are a few links in the city, most of the region's golf courses are concentrated in the suburbs where land historically has been cheaper. Some courses date from the 1890s. Photo © Jim Wark/Index Stock Imagery

try estates of wealthy industrialists who willed their land for public use. Many suburbs have discovered that formal public gardens and fountains enhance their downtowns. Arlington Heights converted an old schoolyard on the edge of its downtown into a garden.

Water-Powered Industry

Although the public perception is that Chicago's suburbs are much younger than the city itself, industrial development of the outlying areas began in the 1830s. It was about the same time as in the city, because water power was available to power machinery when industrial steam engines were in their infancy. Chicago's earliest industries were steam powered because the Chicago River was too sluggish, and, in fact, two of the city's earliest gristmills used windmills for power. Thus, when Cyrus McCormick built his mechanical reaper factory near the mouth of the Chicago River in 1847, he powered the nucleus of what would become the giant International Harvester Company with steam engines.

But more than a decade earlier and some 30 miles to the west pioneering entrepreneurs discovered that the Fox River and some smaller streams, if suitably dammed, could power water wheels. Carpentersville, settled in the 1830s, had a saw-, grist-, and woolen mill by 1851. The relatively small West Branch of the Du Page River about the same time got a saw- and gristmill in what would become Warrenville and Naperville, and the future site of River Forest on the Des Plaines River also had similar mills at about the same time. The gristmills for the most part ground wheat, the principal crop of local farms at the time, into flour for shipment in barrels. These were then carried by wagon east to Chicago. The booming city was also the biggest mar-

stretched for hundreds of miles through scores of municipalities and over the farmland of Northern Illinois. River walks also were built along various streams in the suburbs. The Illinois and Michigan Canal corridor not only has preserved sections of that 1848 waterway but has made them usable by canoeists as well as hikers.

The Chicago area also has a number of public gardens scattered through suburbia, many established from the coun-

ket for suburban lumber until the many local Wisconsin forests were exhausted.

The typical suburban mill of the time required a dam, or weir, to back up water in sufficient quantity to provide power. One side of the dam was a mill race—in effect a narrow canal through which the flow of the river was funneled. The rushing water would cascade over a water wheel that by means of axles and gears turned the machinery in the mill.

Agriculture dominated suburban industry for nearly a century, but by the early 1900s factory owners were looking at cheap land on which to build more modern facilities. The move to suburbia had been begun by the railroads in the 1800s as they searched for increasingly larger sites on which to build yards to handle growing traffic. The Galena & Chicago Union Railroad built its first yard along the Chicago River at Kinzie and Canal streets in 1848. As the yard became hemmed in by other development, it constructed progressively larger yards farther west until in 1903 its successor, the Chicago & North Western Railway, developed a gigantic classification yard in Proviso Township on the western border of Cook County. Other railroads joined in the trend, the Illinois Central moving from downtown Chicago to Homewood 20 miles to the south in 1926; the Chicago, Burlington & Quincy to Cicero; and the Chicago, Milwaukee, St. Paul & Pacific to Bensenville.

Other manufacturing companies took note. After the turn of the century, various automobiles were built in Argo, Joliet, and Kenosha, Wisconsin. Thomas B. Jeffrey and his son, Charles, manufactured Ramblers in Kenosha. In 1969, when the last of that model rolled off the production line by then owned by American Motors Corporation, more than 4.2 million had been produced.

Commonwealth Motors Corporation between 1917 and 1921 built 4,340 cars in Joliet before the company changed its name to Checker Motors Corporation, the taxicab maker, and moved to Kalamazoo, Michigan. Elgin Motor Car Corporation in Argo built 16,784 cars between 1916 and 1924.

The prototype of contemporary auto-oriented, "drive-in" suburban architecture in Chicagoland probably was the gas station designed in 1917 by Allan Jackson, the Standard Oil Company of Indiana regional manager in the Joliet area. It consisted of a small brick building on a paved lot with a canopy extended over the gas pumps.

By then, several southern suburbs surrounding Harvey had substantial manufacturing operations, as did some near-western ones. The origin of the retail architectural footprint that was to dominate the suburbs in the second half of the century also dates from the 1920s. Robert E. Woods, the Sears, Roebuck and Co. vice president in charge of factories and stores, concluded in 1925 from population trends that the future of his company was to build smaller suburban department stores rather than those in the Loop and to equip them with plenty of free parking.

Jewel Tea Company, a chain specializing in home delivery of prepared foods, built the prototypical suburban office campus in 1930 in northwest suburban Barrington. It later bought a distressed grocery chain and began building suburban supermarkets.

Although the regional retail mall—a collection of stores under one roof surrounded by a vast parking lot—can be traced to Kansas City in 1922, Chicagoland's first such facility developed almost by accident in 1949 when developer Philip M. Klutznick decided to include a small, 10-store retail center with plenty of parking in his planned far-south suburb of Park Forest. When a study the next year showed 74 percent of the stores' customers drove there by car, some from as far as 30 miles away, a succession of Loop department stores rushed to build outlets there. The completed center a decade later consisted of 60 stores containing 700,000 square feet of retail space and parking for 3,000 cars.

By the 1960s regional malls had evolved into enclosed developments containing two million square feet of retail space and parking for 8,000 cars. In the 1980s large national chains—the so-called "category killers" because they specialized in one type of merchandise, such as appliances or home improvement products—appeared. They were attracted by the traffic the malls generated and began building stores of 100,000 square feet or larger on outlying land around the malls. By 1992 the Fox Valley retail complex between Naperville and Aurora with four million square feet had more retail space than State Street in Chicago's Loop.

The Office Campus Arrives

The suburban office campus trend begun in 1930 picked up steam in the 1960s after the expressways and tollways were completed. Cheap land away from the congestion and high taxes of the Loop, not to mention the proximity of the golf courses and the houses of company executives, were the principal attraction of the suburbs. Ironically, some companies moved after they lost their Chicago buildings to expressway construction. W.W. Grainger, an industrial supply distributor, lost successive warehouse-office buildings to two expressways before moving to Skokie in 1962. Federal Signal Corporation, which manufactures municipal safety equipment, fire trucks, and street sweepers, lost its building in Chicago

and moved to suburban Blue Island in 1958. It next moved its corporate offices to an office tower along the East-West Tollway (Interstate Highway 88) in west suburban Oak Brook. Sanford Manufacturing Co., the pen and ink maker that rebuilt in Chicago after the Fire of 1871, lost its Chicago offices and factory in the path of a planned expressway and moved to west suburban Bellwood in 1947.

The outmigration of these and other industries, as well as the emergence of new companies in the computer and communications industries, meant that by the 1990s the suburbs could claim that collectively they were home to more corporate headquarters of major companies than was Chicago. One survey in early 2000 indicated that of the 20 largest companies in the metropolitan area in terms of market capitalization, 11 were in the suburbs. A 1996 computer study of the 919 Chicagoland public and private companies reporting annual sales of $100 million or more showed 266 (29 percent) were in downtown Chicago and 66 percent were scattered in the suburbs.

Telecommunications was big in the 'burbs with companies such as Motorola (Schaumburg), Andrew (Orland Park), and Tellabs (Lisle). Lucent Technologies' giant laboratories in Naperville worked on computer software, and Molex in nearby Lisle made electronic and fiber-optic connectors.

Tellabs, Lucent, and Molex are part of a science and technology corridor stretching along the East-West Tollway in Du Page and Kane counties, anchored on the east by Argonne National Laboratory in Lemont and on the west by Fermi National Accelerator Laboratory. Argonne, which dates from the World War II Manhattan Project that developed the atomic bomb, concentrates on scientific research for civil

Located in the Chicago suburb of Lombard, Corporate Travel Management Group's reservation center provides comprehensive travel management services to corporations and travelers throughout the world 24 hours a day, 365 days a year.

uses now that its onetime specialty, nuclear power, is in disfavor. Fermi, a research facility built beginning in the late 1960s in Batavia, concentrates on high-energy research with its giant accelerator.

Two big north suburban companies—Baxter International (Deerfield) and Abbott Laboratories (North Chicago) —specialize in health care products, including medicines. One of their neighbors is Walgreen, the Deerfield-based drugstore chain.

There are plenty of old-line manufacturers based in the suburbs as well. Illinois Tool Works in Glenview is a conglomerate making everything from custom-designed screws to packaging machinery. In transportation, United Airlines is based in Elk Grove Township

near O'Hare and the Wisconsin Central Railroad is on the other side of the airport in Rosemont. It is the sole survivor of a score of railroads that called the Chicago area home a century earlier.

Not only is suburbia dotted with the golden arches on scores of McDonald's fast-food outlets, but the "big arches" are there as well. McDonald's maintains its world corporate headquarters in Oak Brook in what may be the epitome of office campuses—a sprawling, 80-acre, wooded complex that includes a company hotel and "Hamburger U" where franchisees learn how to successfully operate their businesses.

Selling burgers is not exactly high technology, but McDonald's has adopted the game plans of many of its suburban industrial neighbors and gone

Many of the region's high-tech firms chose the suburbs to build their laboratories, and many older companies expanded into the suburbs because of the availability of large tracts of inexpensive land. Photo © Mark Segal/Index Stock Imagery

The professional work forces employed by high-tech businesses seem to have preferred the low-density suburbs to Chicago's dingy factory districts, but that is changing somewhat as auto congestion makes commuting a chore in the outlying areas where there is no alternative mass transit. Photo © Mark Segal/Index Stock Imagery

global. In fact, the ability of Chicago area companies to move into multinational markets has been an important ingredient in their success as well as their prosperity. Many of the region's old smokestack industries, like steel, suffered and shrank as a result of international competition.

In recent years, corporate financial officers are as likely to be concerned with such things as the exchange rate between the rupee and dollar or political unrest in Romania as they are the buying preferences of people in Denver. The talk in the suburban executive suites in the last decade of the twentieth century was not so much the geopolitical consequences of the fall of the Iron Curtain as the business opportunities it opened in Eastern Europe. East Africa is seen not so much as a great place to take a safari as a potential market for cellular phone technology because the cost of wiring such a place for traditional telephones is beyond the capacity of the local economies.

Colleges Join the Suburban Boom

For more than a century after they came into existence, Chicago's suburbs had only a handful of colleges, most of

them small, private schools with religious affiliations. But the dramatic growth of suburbia over the past 50 years acted as a magnet to attract all sorts of institutions of higher learning, some of them branches of major universities. In other cases, entire colleges moved from rural areas to the suburbs to capitalize on the boom.

The biggest and best-known institution of higher learning and research in suburbia is Northwestern University in Evanston 12 miles north of the Loop. It is the only private school in the Big Ten athletic conference and has a strong academic reputation in such fields as journalism, engineering, business management, music, speech, dentistry, medicine, and law. It also boasts one of the most beautiful campuses in the nation, sprawling as it does along the shore of Lake Michigan.

NU has nearly 12,000 students enrolled on its Evanston campus and another 1,800 full-time and 3,000 part-time students on its downtown Chicago campus that houses the law, medical, and dental schools.

The university began offering classes with 10 students and two faculty members in 1855 after its trustees acquired 379 acres of then-undeveloped lakeshore property. The town that grew up around the campus was named Evanston after John Evans, one of the university's founders.

The Chicago area's central location in the Midwest means that prospective students have a wide range of major public and private universities to choose from if they decide to attend school away from home, and industry has plenty of research and consulting facilities available within an easy drive. Purdue University in Lafayette, Indiana, famed for its engineering school; the University of Illinois in Champaign-Urbana, a research university; the

University of Iowa in Iowa City; the University of Wisconsin in Madison; Marquette University in Milwaukee; Notre Dame University in South Bend, Indiana; and both Michigan State University in East Lansing and the University of Michigan in Ann Arbor are all within a few hours' drive of Chicago.

Northern Illinois University in DeKalb—about 55 miles west of the Loop and just beyond the fringe of suburbia—is a major state school with 23,000 students, many of whom hail from the suburbs. NIU evolved from a state-subsidized teachers' college (Northern Illinois State Normal School) founded in 1895 to become a university with seven colleges granting 51 different undergraduate degrees, 70 graduate degrees, and 10 doctoral programs. The school name was changed in 1957 to reflect its academic growth.

The university is one of many to capitalize on the suburban boom by establishing satellite campuses there. NIU opened a branch in northwest suburban Hoffman Estates in 1992 to consolidate at one location nearly 200 courses it had offered at 21 different locations. Eight years later it opened another satellite campus in Naperville to consolidate classes it had offered part-time students at 63 locations around Du Page County.

Chicago's Loyola University was one of the first schools to move to suburbia when it began offering extension courses in 1918 at Mallinckrodt College in Wilmette on the North Shore. In 1998 the Loyola trustees agreed to buy that campus. In 1968 Loyola moved its Stritch School of Medicine and Medical Center, probably best known for its cardiology unit, to west suburban Maywood. The dental college joined it a year later.

DePaul University in Chicago beginning in the 1970s became one of the

The "campus" format—low office buildings surrounded by landscaped open space and huge parking lots—has been the standard for corporate development in the suburbs since about 1930. The Abbott Laboratories campus in the North Shore suburbs is one of the largest. Courtesy, Abbott Laboratories

Northwestern University is the largest and most prestigious of the suburban colleges and one of the oldest. Its main campus sits on the shore of Lake Michigan just north of Chicago. Photo © Mark Segal/Index Stock Imagery

The 54,000-square-foot building includes computer facilities, engineering labs, television studio classrooms, and an electronic library.

Roosevelt University, the private school founded in downtown Chicago to educate returning World War II veterans, jumped on the suburban bandwagon in a big way in 1996 by opening a campus for 3,000 students in Schaumburg. It includes 60 computer-ready classrooms, an electronic library, and plenty of parking.

National-Louis University, a suburban school founded in 1886 as the National College of Education, has also been expanding from its Evanston base and has 15,000 students at assorted facilities across the United States and in Europe. In the Chicago area it added a Loop campus in the 1970s, campuses in Wheaton and Elgin in 1993, and in Wheeling a year later. The institution also broadened its academic programs to include business and arts and sciences.

Perhaps the most dramatic example of the suburban migration was the move of two entire colleges to the north suburbs. Carthage College was founded under another name by the Lutheran Church in 1847 and was moved to several different locations before settling in 1870 in Carthage, Illinois, near the western border of the state. But in the 1950s the college suffered from declining enrollments because of its remote location, and its trustees in 1962 packed up and moved it to Kenosha, Wisconsin, at the end of the commuter railroad 52 miles north of the Loop. That started a period of continuous expansion, and Carthage by the end of the twentieth century had 1,500 full-time and 750 part-time students on its lakeshore campus.

The other institution to move its campus from rural Illinois to suburbia was tiny Shimer College, which began

most aggressive suburban migrants with no fewer than five suburban satellites. It opened its first in Des Plaines in 1973, then added mini-campuses in Westchester, which later moved to Naperville in 1996; Oak Forest (1993); Lake Forest (1998); and Rolling Meadows (2000).

The dearth of colleges in the south suburbs caused the state in 1971 to open Governors State University in a warehouse in the new suburb of Park Forest South, which promptly changed its name to University Park. By the end of the century the school, which moved into a permanent campus in 1973, enrolled more than 9,000 students, about two-thirds of them women and more than 80 percent attending college on a part-time basis. The institution has programs in business and public administration, criminal justice, education, and health care.

The Illinois Institute of Technology in Chicago began offering classes in temporary space in Glen Ellyn in 1986, and in 1991 opened a permanent satellite campus on 19 acres in adjacent Wheaton. The Rice campus, as it is known after the local land owners on whose estate it was built, is typical of higher education in the Electronic Age:

as a seminary in remote Mount Carroll, Illinois, and in the 1890s affiliated with the University of Chicago. The school was almost forced to close for financial reasons in 1973, but a fund-raising effort by faculty and students saved it. Six years later the school, best known for its emphasis on the reading of the "great books" and "Socratic colloquium" discussions in classrooms, abandoned Mount Carroll and moved to north suburban Waukegan. In the most recent academic year it had 109 students and 11 full-time faculty members.

Also dotting the suburbs are a number of small liberal arts colleges, most of them church affiliated, dating back to the 1900s. North Central College, a United Methodist institution in Naperville, originated in 1861; Lake Forest College in that north shore town

began in 1856 as a Presbyterian school; and Elmhurst College, founded in 1871, is affiliated with the United Church of Christ. Wheaton College, a strongly evangelical Christian institution without affiliation with any particular sect, traces its origins to 1854 when it was a hotbed of abolitionist sentiment; and independent Aurora University dates from 1893 in that suburb. Those colleges have enrollments of between 1,000 and 3,000 students.

The suburbs also have an extensive public community college system as well as scores of local colleges to serve not only working students who choose to commute to class but adults who want to sharpen their academic skills or to obtain additional education to further their careers. Continuing education for adults has become a big market

Although most major Chicago universities in recent years have opened branches in the suburbs, Northwestern got a hundred-year start on them in 1851 when it was founded in Evanston and later opened branches in Chicago. Photo © Mark Segal/Index Stock Imagery

for colleges. Community college districts blanket the region with systems in the south: Prairie State (Chicago Heights) and South Suburban (South Holland); southwest: Moraine Valley (Palos Hills) and Joliet; west: Morton (Cicero), Triton (River Grove), Du Page (Glen Ellyn), and Waubonsee (Sugar Grove); northwest: Oakton (Des Plaines), Harper (Palatine), Elgin, and McHenry County (Crystal Lake); and north: Lake County (Grayslake). All are local taxing districts providing subsidized education to residents.

Oakbrook Terrace is home to the corporate headquarters of a former trade school that has gone national with its programs and branched into business and computer education. DeVry Institutes was founded in 1931 as DeForest Training School to teach technical work in electronics, television, radio, and motion pictures. DeVry has three Illinois facilities, in Chicago, Tinley Park, and Addison; and its partner, Keller Graduate School of Management, has eight centers in Illinois.

From Rails to Trails

There are nearly 400 miles of major nature and recreational trails in Chicago and its suburbs—one of the largest and oldest concentrations of such linear parks in the United States. There also are another couple of hundred miles of smaller and isolated trails in various parks and forest preserves scattered around the region. The master plan by the Illinois Prairie Trail Authority calls for the development of a 475-mile loop of trails sometime in the next century by connecting the existing trails.

The origins of the trail system date back to 1963 when the *Chicago Tribune* printed a letter by May Theilgaard Watts, naturalist emeritus of the Morton Arboretum, urging that the

right of way of the recently defunct Chicago, Aurora & Elgin Railroad be converted into a nature trail and hiking path. The railroad had abandoned passenger service in 1957 after losing its right of way into the Loop over an elevated railway line demolished to make room for an expressway.

Gradually a group of dedicated naturalists and open-lands enthusiasts convinced an assortment of suburbs, counties, and utilities that owned or had easements on the right of way that a nature trail was a good idea. The Illinois Prairie Path—a 55-mile, three-pronged trail from Maywood on the Des Plaines River to Aurora, Batavia, and Elgin on the Fox River—finally came into official existence in 1966 although pedestrians had been hiking on it for years.

Beginning in the 1970s Kane County followed suit with a trail system of its own on an abandoned railroad on the banks of the Fox River and the new network was connected to the Prairie Path. Chicago was the nation's railroad capital with thousands of miles of lines, and as the lesser ones were abandoned the rails-to-trails movement gained momentum and converted as many of them as possible to linear parks. Lake and Cook counties turned much of the former Chicago, North Shore & Milwaukee Railroad right of way into bikeways and hikeways, and Du Page, DeKalb, and Kane counties grabbed the Chicago Great Western Railway right of way for a trail after it was abandoned following a 1968 merger.

The trail movement then turned to the waterways. Portions of the old towpath used by mules to pull barges along the Illinois and Michigan Canal in antebellum times were converted by local, state, and federal governments into trails. The longest extends for 60.5 miles from Channahon in Will

Biology, zoology, and comparative anatomy are among the many subjects taught on suburban college campuses. This student examines the skeleton of a cat. Photo © 2000 David Joel/Stone

County to La Salle nearly 100 miles west of the Loop, but there is a 2.5-mile section in Lockport and an 8.9-mile section near Willow Springs in Cook County. That county also has built trails along the North Branch of the Chicago River and the Des Plaines River, as well as a canoe trail down the Des Plaines along the old 1673 canoe portage route used by Louis Jolliet and Father Jacques Marquette, Chicago's first European visitors.

River walks also have become popular in recent years, especially along the West Du Page River in Naperville and the Fox River in Aurora. Naperville's brick walkway began in 1981 as a project to clean up a dingy riverbank in celebration of the city's 150th anniversary and proved so successful it was extended to 3.5 miles. Several other suburbs are considering building river walks, although in some areas the flood plains along rivers are being returned to nature as marshes to prevent their development.

Gardens Bloom in the Suburbs

What would suburbs be without the cottages and, especially, the gardens advocated by Catharine Beecher, Andrew Jackson Downing, and Calvert Vaux—the creators of the "American dream" in the nineteenth century? The idea that every house should have a garden ultimately led in the next century to some large public gardens that originally were part of the suburban estates of the wealthy.

Sam Insull, the utilities magnate and personal secretary to Thomas Edison, built his country estate and mansion near Libertyville in 1914, and in 1937 John Cuneo acquired it and renamed it Hawthorn-Mellody Farms. Today the Cuneo Museum and Gardens, as it is known, is a 75-acre formal public garden with classical statuary, lakes, fountains, topiary, and a conservatory housing exotic plants.

Likewise, the Wheaton estate of Robert R. McCormick, publisher of the *Chicago Tribune*, was transformed after

One major attraction of the suburbs is that their school systems are generally considered to be superior to those of Chicago. Computers are now ubiquitous, even in elementary and middle schools. Photo © 2000 Ian Shaw/Stone

Continuing education is one of the fastest-growing offerings of colleges. Trade schools, such as DeVry Institutes, have become a common way for older workers and young people who have full-time jobs to upgrade their skills and learn new technology. Courtesy, DeVry Institutes

his death into a museum and gardens. Cantigny Park, which was named after the World War I battle in which McCormick fought, contains 15 acres of formal gardens as well as a unique "Idea Garden" demonstrating projects that visitors can undertake in their own backyards. The 500-acre Cantigny also has an unusual "Youth Links" on which youngsters can learn to play golf on a scaled-down course.

George Fabyan was an eccentric millionaire who built his Riverbank Laboratories and estate along the Fox River south of Geneva. It contained a Dutch windmill, a zoo, a house designed by Frank Lloyd Wright, and a formal Japanese garden designed in 1914 by Taro Otusaka. The Kane County Forest Preserve District ultimately acquired 235 acres of the estate after Fabyan's widow's death and in 1971 restored the Japanese garden. The windmill still stands, and the mansion now serves as a museum.

A succession of families owned White Birch Estate and its adjacent greenhouse in Elmhurst until various city agencies cooperatively acquired it in 1919 and turned it into a public park. A conservatory was added to the greenhouse in 1923 and has since been expanded.

The grandest of Chicagoland's gardens was once the Thornhill estate of Joy Morton, the salt king and son of J. Sterling Morton, the man who established Arbor Day. Joy retained his father's interest in flora and in 1921 began transforming his estate near Lisle into an arboretum—an outdoor museum of woody plants. By the time of his death in 1934, the arboretum was already 734 acres in size.

Today the Morton Arboretum sprawls over 1,700 acres and contains more than 30,000 plants of 3,600 different types from around the world. Its research program develops new trees, saves endangered plants, and studies how trees cope with the urban environment. Perhaps the most unusual aspect of the arboretum, which includes several gardens, is the winding system of roads that permits visitors to tour the facility without ever leaving their cars.

If the arboretum is the region's largest facility devoted to flora, the most elaborate is the 385-acre Chicago Botanic Garden in Glencoe that draws three-quarters of a million visitors a year to see its collection of 1.7 million plants. The total includes 14,545 aquatic plants, 10,936 assorted vines, and 420 cacti, although the bulk of its collection consists of bulbs (619,633), perennials (903,461), and shrubs (45,525).

The complex has 23 separate gardens devoted to various types of plants and floral landscape styles. The Chicago Botanic Garden, which sits on Cook County Forest Preserve land, is managed by the 110-year-old Chicago Horticulture Society. The facility opened in 1972 as a permanent site for the society's flower shows, lectures, and research.

The nine-sided Baha'i House of Worship overlooking the lake in Wilmette is not only a unique structure with a filigree dome and unusual ornamentation, but it has nine gardens radiating outward, one from each side. The structure, which was the sect's first house of worship in the western world, was built in 1935. A few miles to the south, tucked away in a nook of Northwestern University's campus, the Evanston Garden Club maintains a 70- by 100-foot Tudor garden called the Shakespeare Garden. It is now on the National Register of Historic Places.

Zoos Large and Small

The suburbs are home not only to the

Chicago Zoological Society's 216-acre zoo in west suburban Brookfield, but to several smaller zoos scattered around the metropolitan area. Brookfield Zoo, as it is commonly known, is the largest such facility in the region and one with an international reputation for its collection of 2,900 animals and its breeding and conservation programs. About two million visitors a year enjoy its collections of lions and tigers, primates, bears, exotic hoofed animals, and pachyderms.

In Tropic World, visitors wander through three indoor rainforests inhabited by New World monkeys, Asian orangutans, and African gorillas. The zoo also has an indoor desert and 2,000-seat dolphin aquarium, as well as a swamp and African savanna. Its staff manages three worldwide programs to save endangered animals from extinction—the Humboldt penguin, African wild dog, and the okapi, a shy relative of the giraffe that was first discovered living in the rainforests of central Africa in 1901.

The zoo, which was originally proposed in 1919 when Edith Rockefeller McCormick, the daughter of millionaire John D. Rockefeller, offered the site for that use to the Cook County Forest Preserve District, took seven years to build. When it opened in 1934 it featured outdoor exhibits in which the animals were separated from the people by wide moats. In recent years the zoo has added large buildings to house indoor exhibits as a concession to Chicago's often brutal winters.

The smaller zoos in suburbia tend to exhibit domesticated animals and local wildlife instead of the exotic animals found at Brookfield. Most have exhibits in which children can pet animals.

The 2.65-acre Cosley Zoo in Wheaton opened in 1974 to display domestic farm animals but has since been enlarged to include a variety of local wildlife, including pheasants, foxes, coyotes, and various birds of prey. Cosley, which is operated by the park district in Wheaton, also has a duck pond.

Garfield Farm Museum, five miles west of Geneva, is a 281-acre farmstead and former stagecoach stop probably best known for its efforts to save from extinction the Black Java chicken. Once a popular domesticated breed, the Black Java fell out of favor as agribusiness developed meatier and more productive hybrids. By 1997 there were fewer than 500 Black Javas surviving.

Blackberry Farm-Pioneer Village

The unusual architecture of the nine-sided Baha'i House of Worship in Wilmette makes it one of the landmarks of the Chicago suburbs. Photo © Shmuel Thaler/Index Stock Imagery

west of Aurora is a 54-acre combination nineteenth-century farm, museum, garden, amusement park, and zoo with such domesticated animals as goats, chickens, and pigs. The center is run by the Fox Valley Park District.

The Cook County Forest Preserve District runs several mini-zoos in its extensive system of facilities. The Little Red Schoolhouse Nature Center near southwest suburban Palos Hills has some native wildlife as well as a small museum. The Tyrrell Trailside in River Forest since 1931 has functioned as a wildlife rehabilitation center for orphaned and injured animals, some of which are on display in cages. The Du Page County Forest Preserve District performs a similar function at its Willowbrook Wildlife Center in Glen Ellyn.

In the north suburbs, Lambs Farm in Libertyville has a petting zoo. This unusual facility had its origins in 1961 in a pet store in Chicago when the owners began hiring persons with mental disabilities to care for animals, and moved in 1965 to its present, 70-acre site.

Recreation: From Slot Machines to NASCAR Racing

While Chicago has all the region's major professional teams—the Kane County Cougars Minor League baseball team in Geneva and the Chicago Wolves International Hockey League team in Rosemont being exceptions—the suburbs have horse racing, gambling, amusement parks, and, most recently, auto-racing tracks. The suburbs also have a major college athletic program at Northwestern University, a member of the Big Ten conference, and Northern Illinois University plays in the Mid-America Conference. Five of the eight members of the College Conference of Illinois and Wisconsin, a league of smaller colleges, are located

Although forbidden in Chicago, suburban casino gambling boats ring the city from Hammond, Indiana, to Elgin. Illinois also allows betting on horse races and bingo games, and operates a statewide lottery. Photo © 2000 Andrea Pistolesi/ The Image Bank

in or near the suburbs.

State law does not allow casino gambling in Chicago, but the city is ringed with casinos in the suburbs of Gary, Indiana (Majestic Star and Trump Casino Indiana); Hammond, Indiana (Empress); East Chicago, Indiana (Showboat Mardi Gras); Joliet (Empress and Harrah's); Aurora (Hollywood); and Elgin (Grand Victoria). Combined, they have an estimated 9,000 slot machines. There are nine off-track betting parlors in the suburbs and two in Chicago in which fans can watch on television and bet on horse races around the nation.

Horse racing has been a fixture in Illinois for years, although the sport has been in decline in the last half of the twentieth century as competition for gambling dollars has increased with the inauguration of the state lottery, casino gambling, and off-track betting parlors. Arlington International Racecourse in northwest suburban Arlington Heights first opened its doors in 1927 offering thoroughbred racing. After a fire destroyed its grandstands in 1985 they were rebuilt and the track was reopened in 1989. A political dispute caused it to close again for a few years in the 1990s but it reopened in time for the new millennium.

Balmoral Park Race Track in far south suburban Crete has offered harness and thoroughbred racing since 1926, and Maywood Park in the western suburbs stages harness racing year-round. The granddaddy of horse tracks is Hawthorne Race Course just over the Chicago city limits in the suburb of Cicero, opened in 1891. Nearby is Sportsman's Park, built in 1932.

In 1998 Sportsman's teamed up with an auto-racing group to build the Chicago Motor Speedway inside the park—the second such dual-purpose facility in the nation. The one-mile oval NASCAR (National Association for

Stock Car Auto Racing) track, which was completed a year later, sits inside the seven-furlong horse track and has stands seating 67,000.

The region's second major auto track complex is near Joliet. The Route 66 Raceway opened in 1998 as a half-mile oval for drag racing and the following year its owners teamed up with the Indianapolis Motor Speedway Corporation to begin construction of the Chicagoland Speedway to feature

urban Gurnee about halfway between Chicago and Milwaukee.

The new park, designed by Hollywood director Randall Duell, was in the style of Disneyland in that it combined the traditional thrill and kiddie rides of an amusement park with live entertainment, restaurants, gift shops, theme displays, immaculately clean grounds inviting to families, and a single admission charge. (The older parks charged by the ride.) Great

Above: Stock car racing has gained in popularity in the Chicago area in recent years with new tracks opening in Cicero and Joliet. Photo © 2000 Garry Gay/The Image Bank

Left: Horse racing comes in a variety of forms at suburban tracks, like this one in south suburban Crete—thoroughbred, pacing, and trotting. Dog tracks are just over the border in Wisconsin. Photo © Ellen Skye/Index Stock Imagery

Indy-style racing on the same grounds. The 1.5-mile, D-shaped track has stands for 75,000 spectators. The Indianapolis group finally settled on the Joliet area after proposals to build the track at two other suburban sites met with objections from neighbors over the prospective noise and crowds.

The suburbs also have a number of amusement parks. In the first half of the century Chicagoland residents wanting to ride roller coasters or visit fun houses went to Chicago's White City on the South Side (1905-1934) or Riverview Park on the North Side (1904-1967). They were effectively replaced in 1975 by Six Flags Great America in north sub-

America, which has undergone continuous upgrading since its opening, in the year 2000 had 40 rides, including no fewer than five roller coasters.

On a smaller scale, Kiddieland in west suburban Melrose Park and the Three Worlds of Santa's Village in northwest suburban East Dundee offer rides. Kiddieland, which opened in 1929 as a pony ride concession, grew to offer 30 different rides, including roller coasters.

Museums Abound

Although Chicago is the center for world-class museums in the region, there are a number of unusual muse-

Six Flags Great America in far north suburban Gurnee serves both the Chicago and Milwaukee metropolitan areas. Its attractions include five roller coasters. Photo © Mark Segal/Index Stock Imagery

ums in suburbia in addition to a score of facilities featuring local history. One of the largest is the Illinois Railway Museum in the northwest corner of the metropolitan area, and one of the most unusual is the entire Village of Oak Park, where many Frank Lloyd Wright structures stand, some still in private hands. Naperville preservationists have recreated a nineteenth-century town-inside-a-town by moving older struc-

tures to a park called Naper Settlement. Nearby Wheaton has a military museum dedicated to the Army's First Infantry Division.

The Illinois Railway Museum began in 1941 with a single electric inter-urban car that had to be pressed into service on a railroad in Iowa during World War II, but in 1964 purchased 26 acres with an option on 20 more along the former right of way of the

Elgin & Belvidere railway in Union. By then the museum had 42 mainly electric cars and had decided to begin acquiring steam and diesel locomotives and mainline railway equipment.

The museum's collection includes an 1859 horse-drawn streetcar, a 4-4-0 "American style" locomotive typical of the middle 1800s, assorted electric streetcars and interurban cars from the early twentieth century, the *Nebraska*

Zephyr, an early diesel-powered passenger train, 23 steam engines, and the *Electroliner*, an electric-powered streamliner used between Chicago and Milwaukee. In warmer weather the museum offers rides on many of its antique trains.

Since its opening in 1966 the Fox River Trolley Museum in South Elgin has specialized in electric-powered trains, including interurban cars from the defunct Chicago, Aurora & Elgin Railroad, a local commuter line, and equipment donated by the Chicago Transit Authority. Rides are available on some of the antique trains on the museum's 3.5-mile line.

Although most suburban museums deal with artifacts and events from the past two centuries, the recently expanded Mary and Leigh Block Museum of Art at Northwestern University has a collection of prints dating from the medieval period in Europe. Its collection of 2,000 items also includes drawings from the Renaissance and Baroque periods, as well as a garden full of sculpture.

The Lizzadro Museum of Lapidary Art in Elmhurst is well known for its collections of rare stones, Italian mosaics, ivory, and gems. It has one of the largest collections of Chinese jade carvings in the nation, as well as a diamond collection and exhibits on how gems are formed geologically.

As Naperville grew from a small town into a major suburban center with more than 100,000 residents, conservationists there banded together to preserve and recreate what the Naper settlement was like in the 1830s when it was founded and was still in danger from Indian attack. The Naper settlement includes a replica of Pre-Emption House, the 1834 inn that served stagecoach passengers on their treks west from Chicago. The original was demolished in 1946 to make way for development. Other replicas are Fort Payne, a small, stockade-enclosed fortification built to protect settlers during the Black Hawk War of 1832, and a log cabin typical of the time.

The Isle a la Cache Museum in Romeoville features the colonial period (1672-1783) when the Chicago area was primarily a canoe portage, and the Illinois and Michigan Canal Visitor Center in nearby Lockport deals with the Canal Age (1848-1900) when the I-M Canal was second in importance as a waterway only to New York's famed Erie Canal. The Aurora Regional Fire Museum in that suburb maintains a small collection of antique fire equipment, and the First Infantry Division Museum in Wheaton has indoor exhibits of that unit from its inception in World War I through Vietnam. It also has an outdoor display of American battle tanks.

In the northern suburbs, the Cuneo Museum and Gardens in Vernon Hills displays art, tapestries, statuary, and European furnishings in an Italianate-style mansion. Nearby in Libertyville the unique Chicago Car Exchange is a combination antique and classic car museum and dealership. How many museums are there where visitors can buy the artifacts on display? The collection for sale includes everything from 1930s Packards to Ford Thunderbirds of more recent vintage.

Frank Lloyd Wright Country

Chicago is a Mecca for modern architecture, especially the skyscraper invented there, but its suburbs often have been belittled in popular literature as monotonous agglomerations of tract houses and strip centers, which some certainly are. "Ticky-tacky" was an adjective frequently (and often correctly) used in conjunction with the suburban residential subdivisions.

But many of the older suburbs along the North Shore and west of Chicago have magnificent neighborhoods of Victorian homes, interspersed with bungalows from the twenties, California-style ranch houses from the fifties, and the ubiquitous split-level. There also are plenty of surviving mansions.

The suburbs also feature the work of

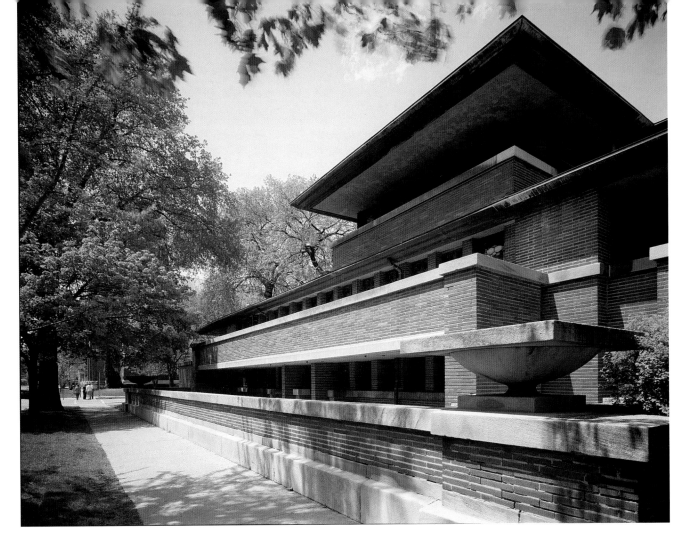

Frank Lloyd Wright (1869-1959), the founder of the Prairie School of architecture, and Frederick Law Olmsted (1822-1903), the landscape architect who designed entire suburbs. The influence of both men is still felt in the design of homes and villages across the landscape.

Oak Park has sometimes been described as a veritable open-air museum for Wright's work because it and neighboring River Forest are the site of 25 buildings he designed, as well as his home and studio. Most of his structures are homes of the Prairie Style— plenty of interior light and open space in low structures—but the Unity Temple (Unitarian Church) in downtown Oak Park is world famous. The Johnson Wax headquarters building about an hour's drive north of Chicago in Racine, Wisconsin, is a classic as well.

Riverside a few miles south and west of Oak Park has a couple of Wright houses, but its fame lies in the very design of the village itself—the blending of dispersed human settlement with a

sylvan environment in stark contrast to the rows of tenements then being built in Chicago. Olmsted designed New York's Central Park, then turned his attention to a commission to develop as a town 1,600 acres of land along the Des Plaines River near Chicago. It was the first of 16 planned suburbs Olmsted and his partner, Calvert Vaux, designed in Illinois, Maryland, Massachusetts, and New York.

In Riverside, Olmsted abandoned the familiar grid pattern and built tree-lined, curvilinear streets that wandered across the landscape, dotted the suburb with small parks and public greens, and built a small retail district around the new Chicago, Burlington & Quincy Railroad commuter station. The houses were built on relatively large (100- by 225-foot) lots and set back 30 feet from the street to increase the sense of openness. Almost every suburb built since Riverside owes at least some of its design to the ideas Olmsted put into effect in that village.

Frank Lloyd Wright was the most famous of the suburban architects—world famous, in fact. Most of his "Prairie Style" houses are located in the suburbs, but Wright's Robie House is on Chicago's South Side. Photo by Christopher Barrett/© Hedrich Blessing

CHAPTER SIX

Land of Lincoln and Soybeans

Left: Illinois has 76,000 farms averaging 368 acres in size. The state is in the center of the nation's Corn Belt and its second-largest crop is soybeans. Photo © 2000 Jamey Stillings/Stone

I f there is any single term that could accurately describe Illinois—a state that variously has been known officially as the "Prairie State," unofficially by the nickname "Sucker State," and most recently as "Home of the Flatlanders"—it would be "Crossroads of the Nation." (The term "sucker" may refer to the seasonal migrations of miners in the nineteenth century, much like the movements of spawning fish, not necessarily the gullibility of new immigrants.) Illinois is a place in which everything seems always on the move: Dodging trucks on the highways or waiting for long freight trains at crossings seem to be favorite sports. "Bumper-to-bumper" is no longer a term that refers solely to annual crops.

A substantial amount of the nation's commerce crosses Illinois' borders on barges, ships, trucks, trains, and airplanes. Its residents are constantly bombarded by ads from neighboring states extolling their scenic virtues to entice Illinoisians to spend elsewhere their dollars earned in factories and on farms.

A person cannot take a respite atop one of the idyllic palisades along the Mississippi River for very long without seeing a string of barges pushed by a towboat or the contrails of transcontinental jets crisscrossing the skies. Fifteen interstate highways intersect the state, and these do not include the urban expressways. More than 30,000 commercial vehicles a day cross the Illinois-Indiana state line on Interstate 80. The U.S. interstate highway system cut its teeth in the 1950s with a four-year national test near Ottawa on what is today I-80 to determine the standards to which the system was to be built.

There are few ski bums in Illinois, or surfers, but there are a fair number of river rats. That is the term sometimes applied to residents who live or make their living along Illinois' more than 1,000 miles of navigable rivers. There also are plenty of farmers, factory workers, and warehouse stock pickers.

It is sometimes said that Illinois is three states—Chicago, its suburbs, and everything else. Downstate is what "everything else" is called. It is the 96 counties of Northern, Western, Central, and Southern Illinois that are not part of Chicagoland.

Above: Downstate Illinois is known for its agriculture, not its scenery. The palisades along the Mississippi River are a notable exception. Photo © 2000 Steven W. Jones/FPG International LLC

Right: Soybeans, like this crop near St. Anne, account for a significant share of the state's overseas exports of about $4 billion annually. Photo © Mark Segal/Index Stock Imagery

It is also a misnomer: The driftless area in the northwest corner of Illinois was not flattened by the glacier that covered the state 10,000 years ago and has a greater affinity with Wisconsin than Peoria; and the people in the southern portion of the state, Little Egypt as it is called, speak with the same drawl as their neighbors in Kentucky, not the twang of Chicagoans. St. Clair and Madison counties are suburbs of St. Louis and root for professional baseball's Cardinals, not the Cubs or White Sox.

To the traveler passing through downstate on his or her way somewhere else, the ride can be boring. The region is for the most part flat; there is less than 1,000 feet difference between the highest (Jo Daviess County in the northwest corner) and lowest (Alexander County in the extreme south) points in the state. Downstate seems to be covered from horizon to horizon by farms growing corn, soybeans, cattle, and hogs. The skyline is sometimes punctuated by a gaggle of grain elevators patiently awaiting the frenetic fall harvest, but little else.

The scenery is somewhat illusory, however. Although Illinois' $9-billion annual farm industry ranks fifth in the nation in agricultural income, exceeded only by California, Texas, Iowa, and Nebraska, net farm income accounted for only about 5 percent of total income in the state's rural counties. Beneath those endless farm fields, especially in Southern Illinois, are gigantic seams of coal and lesser deposits of oil, and dotting the pastoral landscape are mid-size cities with factories making everything from bulldozers to booze. Caterpillar builds its familiar yellow bulldozers downstate and Deere makes its green farm tractors there as well. Industries and distribution centers, the new name for warehouses, have begun to spring up around nodes on the interstate highway system.

Downstate Illinois has had its share of problems over the years. The western section of the state along the Mississippi River felt so neglected that its residents nicknamed it "Forgottonia," and Southern Illinois fell on hard times as the demand for its high-sulfur coal declined. Cheap foreign oil doomed the local drilling industry.

East St. Louis had slums as abysmal as anything in Chicago, and abandoned railroad yards as well. Caterpillar has been vulnerable to swings in the world economy as well as the waxing and waning of the value of the dollar. The fortunes of the downstate farm economy were dependent on how much grain the state could export overseas, as well as the market price of pork or beef.

In some cases adversity became opportunity. The state for decades has aggressively sought foreign investment to boost the downstate economy, and one of its biggest successes was the construction in Normal in the 1980s of the Diamond Star Motors plant to build Chrysler and Mitsubishi cars as part of a joint venture between those companies. Illinois farmers convinced the federal and state governments to use corn-based ethanol as an ingredient in gasoline to cut pollution, creating a

Above: Galena, a bustling lead center in antebellum times before the mines played out, was almost a ghost town during the early twentieth century before it was rediscovered as a tourist destination. Photo © 2000 Peter Pearson/Stone

Facing page: Its preserved nineteenth-century architecture makes Galena a municipal museum, drawing tourists from around the Midwest. Its hilly environment in Northwest Illinois is one of the state's most scenic. Photo © Mark Segal/Index Stock Imagery

new market for their crop. Galena in the first half of the nineteenth century was a booming lead-mining center, but it declined into a backwater town when the mines played out. A century later Galena residents awoke to the fact that they were living in a municipal museum—a snapshot of the Mark Twain era when everything traveled by river. So they redeveloped the town as a tourist destination.

Other such projects have had mixed results. The state redeveloped the long-abandoned Illinois-Michigan and Hennepin canals as state parks, but they have not proven to be economic engines for tourism. Tiny Metropolis on the Ohio River on Illinois' southern

border was only partially successful in using its affinity with the Superman comic-book character to boost its fortunes, although the superhero lived in the fictional city of Metropolis, not a river hamlet of approximately 7,000 residents. So the town in the 1990s added a riverboat casino and drew gamblers from as far away as Nashville and Cincinnati.

Population and Politics

In the twentieth century the relative dispersal of Illinois' population between the Chicago area and downstate has resulted in a political system in which compromises were necessary to satisfy the urban constituency of the metropolitan area and the rural interests of the rest of the state. The factory worker in Chicago needed elevated trains to get to work, but the farmer needed good roads to get his crop to market. Before the mid-nineteenth century, when the population was split roughly 50-50 between city and downstate and the suburbs were still not much of a political factor, compromise was necessary to accomplish anything. When Chicago sought a branch of the University of Illinois, downstate agreed only if Southern Illinois University also received a new branch in the St. Louis suburban area. Both campuses were built.

The rapid growth of the suburbs after World War II changed the equation considerably. By 1970 the population was split roughly 1/3-1/3-1/3 between the city, its suburbs, and downstate—a factor that required a three-way compromise or two of the three jurisdictions joining to impose their will on the third. As a practical matter, the interests of the three areas often overlap: A jobless resident of East St. Louis, despite the fact that he is a suburbanite, often has more in common with someone in a similar plight in Chicago than with a farmer downstate. A factory worker still carries a lunch pail when he rides to work on the L in Chicago or drives from his farm to a factory in downstate Bloomington.

At the end of the twentieth century, about 4.3 million people lived in downstate Illinois, contrasted to roughly 2.8 million in Chicago and almost 5 million in Chicago's suburbs. (See Table 6-1). As a practical matter, downstate's population has been relatively stagnant since 1970 when it exceeded four million for the first time, and the population actually declined in the 1980s when the region was hard hit by a recession.

The population of downstate Illinois is relatively dispersed, although more than 540,000 persons live in the subur-

Table 6-1

Illinois and Chicago Metropolitan Census Data,1950-2000

YEAR	ILLINOIS	DOWNSTATE*	METROPOLITAN	CHICAGO	SUBURBS**
1950	8,712,176	3,534,576	5,177,600	3,620,962	1,556,638
1960	10,081,158	3,860,248	6,220,913	3,550,404	2,670,509
1970	11,110,285	4,133,018	6,977,267	3,369,367	3,607,900
1980	11,418,461	4,316,133	7,102,328	3,005,072	4,097,256
1990	11,432,602	4,169,426	7,180,235	2,783,726	4,477,450
2000	12,419,293	4,327,573	8,091,720	2,896,016	5,195,704

*96 counties outside the Chicago metropolitan area
** Includes that portion of Cook County outside of Chicago, and the entire counties of Du Page, Kane, Lake, McHenry, and Will
Source: U.S. Bureau of Census

Galena was once larger and more important than Chicago, which is why one of the state's first railroads was built there. Photo © Joseph Fire/Index Stock Imagery

ban St. Louis counties of St. Clair and Madison on the Illinois side of the Mississippi River. Downstate collectively has 800 communities, but only three (Rockford, Peoria, and Springfield) have populations exceeding 100,000. However, there are an additional four metropolitan areas of two or more cities with populations that size— Rock Island-Moline-East Moline, Bloomington-Normal, Champaign-Urbana, and Kankakee-Bourbonnais. The area around Decatur in Central Illinois also exceeds 100,000.

Rough and Tumble Politics

The politics of Illinois over the years have been rough and tumble, especially when compared to some of its neighboring states. Illinois has been a swing state in national elections, and is often credited with providing President John F. Kennedy with the boost over the top in his close election victory over Richard M. Nixon in 1960. Kennedy won the state by a few thousand votes, or less than one vote per precinct.

The state has also had its share of scandals involving some of its top politicians. State Auditor Orville Hodge in 1956 went to prison after embezzling

more than one million dollars in state funds using phony warrants, as well as misappropriating $500,000 by liquidating funds of closed banks, and padding expense accounts. Former Governor Otto Kerner (1961-1968) after he left office to accept a federal judgeship was convicted of his role in a bribery scheme involving the horse-racing industry while he was governor. His prosecutor was James R. Thompson, who used his crusade against corrupt politicians as a stepping stone to the governor's office.

After Illinois Secretary of State Paul Powell died in office in 1970, some $150,000 in cash was discovered in shoeboxes in his Springfield hotel room and another $650,000 in cash was found in his office. The source of the money was never identified, but it was widely assumed that it came from bribes paid to obtain state licenses.

Former Governor Dan Walker (1973-1977) was convicted of bank fraud several years after he left office after lending himself $1.4 million in federally insured funds from an Oak Brook savings and loan association he headed. Ironically, Walker had won election in 1972 as a reformer against the Democratic machine, and the case against him did not involve his administration. He was defeated for reelection by Thompson.

The scandals aside, Illinois politicians in the last half of the twentieth century collectively could be characterized as having increasingly professionalized state government over the old spoils system that had been in place for generations. As in other states, some of the progressive change was mandated by the federal government, which after mid-century had an increasing influence in what formerly had been strictly the prerogative of the states. For example, as a result of a federal court case, much

The circa 1857 Belvedere Mansion in Galena is one of that city's showcases. Similar architecture, though not as well known, occurs in Illinois towns up and down the Mississippi River. Photo © Joseph Fire/Index Stock Imagery

of the old patronage system was replaced by civil service and, because of the strings the federal government attached to its grants, competitive bidding became the method by which the state selected many of its vendors.

In other cases, the impetus for reform arose through the political process. The competitive two-party system in which office seekers tried to impress voters with their interest in good government was the impetus for some of the change; in other instances initiatives came from the grass-roots level. The state in the 1960s reformed its court system and in 1970 adopted a new constitution that permitted such things as a more progressive tax system, including an income tax, and subsidies to mass transit systems. The Granger-era constitution was 100 years old and showing its age.

Illinois elects six constitutional officers—governor, lieutenant governor, attorney general, secretary of state, comptroller, and treasurer—and voters historically have engaged in ticket splitting to ensure that opposing parties keep an eye on each other. As the twentieth century closed, four of those offices were held by Republicans and two (secretary of state and comptroller) were occupied by Democrats. In the legislative branch, the Illinois Senate had a Republican majority, but the Democrats were more numerous in the House of Representatives.

Despite the fact that Illinois is a swing state, the Republican Party in the last quarter of the twentieth century came to dominate the governor's office. Although the office was occupied by Republicans for 13 years and Democrats for 11 in the quarter-century after 1950, the Republicans held the office for 23 of the final 25 years of the century. Thompson was elected governor for a record four terms (14 years), followed by Jim Edgar for two terms and George H. Ryan for one.

For the most part, Illinois' governors

roots to Illinois was a transplanted Californian. Ronald Reagan grew up in Illinois but moved west to California, where he was eventually elected governor.

A National Crossroads

Illinois has 2,165 miles of interstate highways, some of which are toll roads, and the state is crossed by three of the nation's five transcontinental interstates (I-70, 80, and 90). Although those limited-access expressways account for less than 2 percent of the 139,000 miles of state and local roads in Illinois, they carry about a quarter of the more than 100 billion vehicle miles traveled annually in Illinois.

The state also has 8,900 miles of

Illinois native Ronald Reagan, shown speaking here in Decatur, was one of three U.S. presidents with strong ties to the state. The others were Abraham Lincoln and Ulysses S. Grant.
Photo © George Cassidy/Index Stock Imagery

have not gone on to higher office, although perhaps the most famous occupant in the office in the last half of the twentieth century, Adlai Stevenson II, ran unsuccessfully for president twice. But most governors simply returned to private industry or to their law practices after leaving office. None ran for the U.S. Senate. In fact, the only U.S. president in the twentieth century who could trace his

railroads—the second-highest total (after Texas) in the nation. Virtually every major railroad in the United States and Canada meets in Chicago, and most of them have routes to East St. Louis as well.

Amtrak also operates a sizable network of passenger trains on 10 different routes crossing Illinois to the corners of the nation. The state subsidizes local Amtrak routes across Illinois to cities including Carbondale, Champaign, Springfield, Quincy, and Milwaukee (jointly with Wisconsin). The state is also exploring the possibility of high-speed routes on which express trains travel in excess of 100 miles an hour between Chicago and such cities as Milwaukee, St. Louis, and Detroit.

For a state that is 1,000 miles from the nearest ocean, Illinois surprisingly accounts for more than 100 million tons a year in waterborne commerce. The bulk of this is on river barges although some moves on boats on the Great Lakes. The state has 1,119 miles of commercially navigable waters, the longest of which is the Mississippi River which runs the entire length of the state. The Illinois River crosses the state and connects Chicago with the Mississippi.

Illinois also has more than 130 public airports, most of them scattered across downstate. Although there are some commercial flights serving smaller Illinois cities, the bulk of the commercial aviation flights are from major metropolitan airports in Chicago and St. Louis.

Household Names in Industry

Downstate Illinois does not have the concentration of major corporations that typifies the Chicago area; indeed, only 28 of the 297 largest publicly traded corporations in Illinois are downstate, according to one 1998 study, but there are some major ones. The Big Five billion-dollar companies downstate are Caterpillar Corporation in Peoria, Deere & Company in Moline, State Farm Insurance in Bloomington, Newell Rubbermaid (formerly Newell Co.) in Freeport, and Archer Daniels Midland, the food-processing giant, in Decatur. Cat, Deere, Newell Rubbermaid, and ADM are publicly traded multinational giants with products known around the world.

At one time, "Cat" almost achieved the status of a common noun, a synonym for bulldozer, and the leaping deer of Deere is as familiar a logotype as exists on the globe. There are few homes in America that don't contain several products made by subsidiaries of Newell, a conglomerate that owns scores of smaller companies making low-technology consumer products, everything from window shades to plastic kitchen storage containers. State Farm is a mutual company owned by its policyholders.

The rest of the corporations with downstate headquarters are predominantly banks and manufacturing firms. According to the 1998 study, the 28 largest corporations there include 10 manufacturers, nine banks, two transportation firms, two utilities, two insurance companies, an agricultural processor, a supermarket chain, and a casino.

Deere is the oldest of the group, tracing its history back to 1837 and the conquest of the prairie by pioneers. John Deere, a blacksmith by trade, noticed the difficulty farmers had cutting the tough prairie soil with cast-iron plows made in the East, and developed from a mill saw blade a polished steel plow that scoured itself clean. The company's development is prototypical of many of the giants of American industry. What it couldn't develop in-house it obtained by acquisition of other companies. In 1911 Deere & Company bought out six other farm implement manufacturers to provide a full line of farm equipment, and in 1918 it bought a tractor maker.

John W. Daniels and George P. Archer ran their own linseed-crushing businesses in the late 1800s and, after combining their companies in 1902 and acquiring a competitor in 1923, became the world's largest firm in the industry. Over the years the company expanded

Governor George H. Ryan meets with Mexican President Vicente Fox. During his career in public office, Ryan has worked to forge stronger trade relations between Illinois and Mexico. Courtesy, Illinois Department of Central Management Services

Above: Cairo, at the southern tip of the state, was the Union army's main depot during the Civil War and still has important connections to the South by means of the highway bridges spanning the Ohio (shown) and Mississippi rivers. Photo © 2000 Tim Bieber/The Image Bank

Right: This Union Pacific train carrying coal from Wyoming to the cities of the Midwest is rumbling over the state's first successful railroad line. It was originally built beginning in 1848 to carry grain east to Great Lakes ships and pioneers westward. Photo © Lynn M. Stone/ Index Stock Imagery

into flaxseed, wheat milling, soybean processing, corn sweeteners, ethanol production, and peanut processing. Today the corporation operates a fleet of 13,000 railcars, 2,250 barges, and 900 trucks to move its products used by a variety of food, beverage, nutraceutical, industrial, and animal feed manufacturers worldwide. The ADM logo painted on the side of jumbo covered hoppers is a familiar sight on railroads in the Midwest.

Caterpillar traces its origins to the steam tractors built independently in the 1890s by Benjamin Holt and Daniel Best. Holt's caterpillar-style tracked vehicle received international notice during World War I when it was used by the Allies for off-road transportation. The company later built military tanks using its track system, but its biggest growth came by diversification into construction and mining equipment, including bulldozers and backhoes, and diesel engines. Like many of the nation's industrial giants, Caterpillar after World War II expanded globally to increase its markets.

Newell Manufacturing Company began modestly in 1902 as a curtain

rod manufacturer and a few years later acquired a subsidiary in Freeport, Illinois, where it eventually moved its headquarters. It wasn't until 1965 that then-president Daniel C. Ferguson led the firm on an expansion program by acquiring small consumer product companies that made everything from paint applicators to cookware and office supplies. In 1987 Newell purchased Anchor Hocking Corporation, the glassware maker, and doubled in size. In 1999 it acquired another housewares giant, Rubbermaid, nearly doubling once again.

State Farm began in 1922, when George J. Mecherle began selling auto insurance to farmers after his employer at another insurance company spurned some of his ideas. By the end of the twentieth century it had become the nation's biggest auto insurer with policies on a fifth of America's fleet as well as the largest insurer of homes. It also had become a financial institution, a non-traditional bank offering services, not through branch offices like most banks but through its 16,200 agents, the telephone, mail, and even the Internet. The company had more than 79,000 employees in the United States and Canada, about 11,000 of them at its corporate headquarters in Bloomington.

Not all of Illinois' elite companies escaped the mergers that swept the business world in the final decades of the century. The A.E. Staley Manufacturing Company in Decatur, one of the nation's largest corn-based starch, sweetener, and ethanol producers, was acquired by British sugar giant Tate & Lyle when the latter expanded into the United States beginning in the 1980s.

Corn, Soybeans, and Hogs

Staley and ADM are among the 950 companies in Illinois engaged in the manufacture and processing of food. With combined annual revenues of $13.4 billion annually, food processing is the largest single industry in the state, grinding out such products as soap, ink, fuel, paint, animal feed, paper, cosmetics, glues, clothing, and medicines. Some 274 million bushels of Illinois corn are transformed into ethanol each year.

Even before the state's inception early in the nineteenth century, agriculture was its major industry. Before they were ousted from North America at the end of the French and Indian War in 1763, the French conducted a trade for beaver furs in the northern tier of the state, and farms along the Mississippi River south of what is today St. Louis served as the breadbasket for the French colony of Louisiana. The American pioneers after 1783 generally settled along the rivers so they could get their crops to market, and Chicago after 1830 became the outlet for the state's agricultural production via Great Lakes ships. Food processing was largely a mom-and-pop operation on the farm or at small local mills before the building of the railroads and, after the Civil War, the development of refrigeration made mass production of food feasible.

The success of that industry was made possible not only by Illinois' central location and an extensive transportation system but by the proximity of crops. It was cheaper and more efficient to process food near the farms and ship the finished product to market than to ship the raw materials to factories on the East Coast and then return the processed food to the Midwest.

About 89 percent of the state sits on flat land with a rich cover of glacial loess that makes it prime farmland, and eight out of every 10 acres in the state is farmed. A variation of only 10 to 12 degrees Fahrenheit in temperature; cool,

Today the people who till fields such as this are not so much farmers as they are agribusinessmen. They use the Internet to monitor crop prices and hedge against the future with the commodities markets based in Chicago, where it is possible to sell a crop even before it is planted. Photo © Jack Novak/Index Stock Imagery

dry winters; and ample rainfall in the spring and summer are excellent for the grain cash crops and pastures for livestock. As is true in most agricultural states, there were fewer farms in Illinois at the end of the twentieth century than there were three decades earlier but they are much larger. The families who run them are not so much farmers anymore as agribusinessmen, keeping an eye on the Internet for fluctuations in crop prices, hedging against the future by selling portions of their crops on the commodities markets even before they are planted, and investing in expensive machinery and fertilizers to increase yields. Farmers who clung to the old "guess and hope" methods for the most part watched their farms disappear in liquidation sales; the survivors managed by expanding and adapting to new technologies. Deluxe tractors can cost $100,000 and up but they enable farmers to cultivate more acreage.

Owners of the surviving smaller farms generally make their living in factories or other businesses and consider farming a secondary occupation. Almost two out of every five Illinois farmers commute to work elsewhere and till their land at night and on weekends. The state also has a fair number of "hobby farms" owned by people who work elsewhere and farm a small plot, often breeding horses or livestock for recreation.

The 76,000 farms covering Illinois' 400-mile length at the end of the century were fewer than half of the 164,000 that existed in 1959, but at an average of 368 acres they were double in size. Typically 40 percent of their income came from corn, 33 percent from soybeans, and 23 percent from livestock, dairy products, and poultry. There are truck farms in Illinois, raising vegetables for the metropolitan areas, and farms devoted to specialty crops, such as ginseng for the Orient. There are also fish farms.

Although the numbers have fluctuated over the years, agriculture accounts for a large share of Illinois' overseas exports each year—about $4 billion worth of goods out of a total agricultural production of $9 billion. The state accounts for about 7 percent of all U.S. agricultural exports.

The importance of transportation and the state's central location affects other industries as well. The rivers and

Great Lakes were the principal avenues of commerce until the Civil War and were supplanted by railroads for the next 100 years. However, the second half of the twentieth century belonged to the highways and the trend toward development in Illinois has been along the major interstate highway corridors, including the 90 miles between Chicago and Milwaukee, the Interstate 88 tollway between Chicago and DeKalb, the Interstate 80 freeway across the northern tier of the state between Chicago's suburbs and the Illinois River Valley, and along the Interstate 55 freeway between Chicago

Oil production isn't as important as it once was, but the 42,600 wells in the central and southern portions of the state still pump 10 to 12 million barrels a year. Photo by Ted Schurter

undersold by foreign imports.

Coal mining also has been in decline because the nation's environmental needs and regulations make it more expensive to burn the type of high-sulfur coal found in abundance in Illinois. Utilities, which bought 90 percent of the coal mined in Illinois, found it cheaper to burn the low-sulfur coal mined in western states and shipped 1,000 miles by train than to retrofit power plants to clean Illinois coal. As a result, the state's coal-mining industry centered in Southern Illinois—which during World War II employed more than 29,000 persons in 159 mines to produce more than

and St. Louis. The I-55 corridor cuts a wide swath that includes not only Springfield and Bloomington alongside that highway but Champaign-Urbana and Peoria, which are 30 to 45 miles away but linked to it by other interstate roadways.

The Decline of Mining

What was buried beneath downstate Illinois' rich soil has also provided the raw materials for an important industry, mining, although it has been in decline in recent years. The state had been the nation's largest producer of fluorspar, a mineral used to make everything from hydrofluoric acid to toothpaste, but the last mine closed in 1995 after being

70 million tons annually—by the end of the century had only about 3,600 employees in 20 mines producing about 40 million tons. Fifteen of the mines were underground, or shaft, mines which historically have been more expensive to operate than the open-pit strip mines typical in the West.

Oil and gas production in Illinois, once one of the major producers of those fuels, also has been in decline. Oil wells in the state date back to the 1860s and at their peak after World War II produced 80 million barrels a year mostly from relatively shallow deposits. By the end of the century the state's 42,600

wells collectively were producing only 10 to 12 million barrels annually.

Illinois ranks among the top 20 states in the nation in the mining of non-fuel minerals primarily because of large sand, gravel, and limestone deposits and the proximity of construction markets using them in the Chicago and St. Louis metropolitan areas. Such materials are heavy and expensive to ship long distances except by water.

Tourism's Modest Impact

Tourism in downstate Illinois is not a particularly large industry and most of the tourist dollars spent there are by

With thousands of miles of rivers tributary to the Mississippi and scores of lakes, the Prairie State still has some good fishing holes. Photo © 2000 Tim Bieber/The Image Bank

The ancient Indian mounds at Cahokia just across the Mississippi River from St. Louis are a major tourist attraction. The city that surrounded the mounds was abandoned hundreds of years before Europeans arrived in the New World.
Photo by Ted Schurter

people passing through the state rather than those driving 2,000 miles to stop for a week and gaze at soybean fields. Tourism is a $21-billion industry in Illinois but much of it is concentrated in Chicagoland. Of the state's 1,256,000 overseas visitors in 1998, for example, Chicago lured 1,208,000. Of the 76.3 million visitors to the state in 1998, 33.7 million visited downstate, about two-thirds of them for leisure. Nevertheless, downstate Illinois does have some things worth seeing, and the state, which ignored the potential of tourist dollars for generations, in recent years has more actively promoted its sights not only to attract out-of-staters but to keep residents at home as well.

The problem is that Illinois does not have many spectacular sights and its most scenic sections are in Southern and Western Illinois, farther from the potential tourist dollars in metropolitan Chicago than resort areas in Michigan

and Wisconsin. Lake Geneva and Door County in Wisconsin and Southwestern Michigan are popular weekend resorts for Chicagoans. Except for Chicago and Nauvoo, which is a Mormon tourist Mecca, there are few places in Illinois that can be considered true tourist destinations in that people are willing to drive 1,000 miles to build a vacation around a visit. So downstate Illinois tourism depends upon keeping Illinoisians close to home and attracting residents from other states within a 300-mile radius.

Nevertheless, there are some largely undiscovered gems in Illinois. The ancient Indian mound city of Cahokia near St. Louis, while not nearly as well known to tourists as the spectacular cliff cities of Mesa Verde and Chaco Canyon in the West, is one of the most important pre-Columbian archaeological sites in the United States. Starved Rock near Utica in North-Central Illinois was the site of a seventeenth-century French fort and an infamous Indian massacre. The Great River Road along the western border of the state is a scenic drive that passes the antebellum town of Galena, various Mississippi River palisades, Nauvoo, Cahokia, and several former French colonial settlements.

Central Illinois is the "Land of Lincoln," one of the prime tourist destinations in the state as tourists come to see where Abraham Lincoln lived before he became president. President Ulysses S. Grant's home is in Galena and President Ronald Reagan's boyhood homes are in Tampico and Dixon. The Illinois-Michigan and Hennepin canals across North-Central Illinois are long-abandoned waterways that have been preserved as parks by the state and can be traversed by car, bicycle, and canoe.

Perhaps the most spectacular concentration of scenery in the state is in and around the Shawnee National Forest that spans almost 270,000 acres across Southern Illinois from the Ohio to the Mississippi rivers. Though not as famous as many national parks, the hilly region has its share of unusual rock formations, forests, and abundant wildlife spread across Gallatin, Johnson, Saline, Pope, Hardin, Union, and

Jackson counties. The region also is interspersed with state parks and preserves. The national forest has miles of hiking and horseback trails and is open to hunting, fishing, and camping. Possibly its most scenic section is called Garden of the Gods, southeast of Harrisburg. The forest is traversed by the infamous "Trail of Tears" over which the Cherokee Indians in 1829 were forced to migrate from their ancestral homelands in the Appalachian Mountains to reservations in

President Ulysses S. Grant was born in Ohio but lived in this modest brick house in Galena when he was elected president. Photo © Joseph Fire/Index Stock Imagery

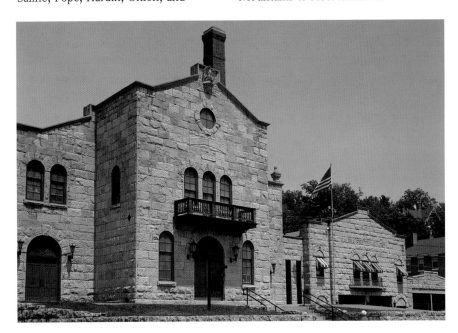

The huge limestone deposits beneath much of Northern Illinois were a ready source of building material in many communities. They still provide the state with an ample supply of stone for roads and structures. Photo © Joseph Fire/Index Stock Imagery

Wetlands in Illinois usually consist of grassy marshes, but there are a few swamps. These bald cypresses grow in a swamp in the southern part of the state. Photo © 2000 Tom Till/Stone

Oklahoma. Many Cherokees died from exposure, hunger, and exhaustion on the forced march.

State-operated parks and conservation areas near the Shawnee Forest include Heron Pond, a bald cypress swamp along the Cache River; Giant City, a 4,000-acre park of sandstone bluffs and forests near Makanda; and Cave-in-Rock, a state park and former river pirate hangout along the Ohio River in Hardin County.

The River Roads

The southern border of the state and portions of the Shawnee Forest are crossed by the 188-mile Ohio River Scenic Byway from New Harmony,

Indiana, to Cairo, the Civil War-era river town at the confluence of the Ohio and Mississippi rivers. Cairo was the western staging area and supply depot for the Union's invasion of the Confederacy. The byway is not a single road but an amalgamation of various highways in the region to provide a scenic route tourists can follow.

The Ohio Byway connects at Cairo with the 557-mile Great River Road that traverses the state from south to north along the banks of the Mississippi River. It, too, is a tourist route amalgamated from various highways. In many ways the Great River Road is a drive through history. It passes not only prehistoric Indian mounds dating from

A.D. 900 but French colonial settlements from the eighteenth century, the spot from which Lewis and Clark left on their expedition to explore the West at the dawn of the 1800s, and the 1966 St. Louis Gateway Arch built to commemorate the pioneers' westward migration. The 630-foot arch on the Missouri side of the river was designed by renowned architect Eero Saarinen.

The French colonial settlements of Prairie du Rocher, Kaskaskia, and Fort de Chartres are little known outside of Southern Illinois. Kaskaskia is the only section of Illinois west of the Mississippi River, and Fort de Chartres was the French capital in Illinois between 1720 and 1765, and the

British capital from then until 1772. Kaskaskia, which dates from 1703 as a French mission, was the original Illinois state capital but was inundated in the 1881 flood that changed the course of the great river.

Just eight miles east of downtown St. Louis but on the Illinois side of the river is the state's most ancient city— so old, in fact, that it was only a vague memory when European explorers arrived. The explorers and later settlers marveled at a giant hill on the site and wondered how it was formed. Archaeologists later proved it was an earthen temple mound with a base larger than the great pyramids of Egypt and was built by an Indian society in

prehistoric times (A.D. 900-1300) on the site now known as Cahokia.

Other remnants of that ancient society have been found as far north as Aztalan in Wisconsin and in the Illinois River Valley at Dickson Mounds near Lewistown, Illinois, where the state maintains an archaeological museum. The archaeological discoveries at Cahokia, which was neglected for years, caused the state in the 1970s to restore and upgrade that site. It is maintained by the Illinois Historic Preservation Agency.

The state maintains a park on the site of another important Indian settlement, Starved Rock near Utica on the Illinois River. It was on a bluff there sometime after 1769 during the raging Indian wars between the Illiniwek confederacy and their enemies that, according to tradition, members of the Peoria tribe of Illiniwek were besieged and starved almost to annihilation—hence the name Starved Rock. The battle was one of the last in the Indian wars that effectively destroyed the confederacy that gave the state its name.

The old Mormon capital of Nauvoo on the Mississippi River also has a

bloody history, including the assassination of Joseph Smith, the founder of the Church of Jesus Christ of Latter-day Saints (Mormons). The old Mormon settlement was largely abandoned after Brigham Young led the surviving Mormons on their long trek to Utah in 1846. Much of it has since been restored and the Mormon Church, which owns more than a third of the

Cave-in-Rock, now a state park in Hardin County, was where river pirates once hid to ambush flatboats sailing down the Ohio River. Photo by Ted Schurter

town, has been building a $25-million replica of its original temple there. The first one was destroyed by fire and tornado in 1848 after its abandonment. Nauvoo, despite its relative isolation, is one of the more popular attractions for tourists, many of them Mormon pilgrims, drawing an estimated 200,000 visitors a year.

Another snapshot of history is Galena, a town in the northwest corner of the state that looks today much as it did in the 1850s. Galena, a thriving city before its lead mines played out, bordered on being a ghost town until its residents discovered that tourism pays better than lead and fixed up its old buildings to appeal to shoppers and people on a weekend drive in the country. One of the main attractions is President Grant's home.

The Land of Lincoln

Undoubtedly downstate Illinois' biggest tourist attraction is in its center—the Land of Lincoln. The log cabin in which the future Great Emancipator lived with his family in 1830-1831 is near Decatur. New Salem, the small settlement in which he lived for six years after leaving home (1831-1837) and which has been restored to its original condition, is north of Springfield.

But it is Springfield, where Lincoln lived from 1837 until his election as president, that is the principal attraction. Popular tourist sites are his modest home, now a national shrine; his law office; and the old state capitol in which he conducted some of his business. Lincoln's Tomb is in Oak Ridge Cemetery in town. The city is also the site of the current state capitol and the Illinois State Museum.

Springfield for 10 days each year is also the site of the Illinois State Fair. Typical of such fairs in most western states, the Illinois Fair is an agricultural

extravaganza at which farm children have traditionally exhibited their prize chickens and cattle and their mothers have showed off the results of their favorite pie recipes and their latest quilt. Although the fair has been continually updated to reflect changing technology, it still maintains an agricultural orientation and managed during its run in 2000 to attract 1.1 million visitors.

The Abraham Lincoln Presidential Library and Museum will be the new home of the Illinois State Historical Library and its 46,000-item Lincoln

Above: A highlight of the Great River Road along the state's western boundary is the restored Mormon settlement at Nauvoo. It is from there that Brigham Young led his followers to Utah. Photo © Craig J. Brown/Index Stock Imagery

Top: Fort de Chartres along the Mississippi River in Randolph County is one of the few surviving remnants of French colonial rule in Illinois. Photo by Ted Schurter

Facing page: With the decline of the coal and oil industries, Southern Illinois has some of the most severe economic problems in the state but it is blessed with some of its most beautiful scenery. Photo © 2000 Terry Donnelly/Stone

350,000 photographs, and over 85,000 reels of newspapers on microfilm.

Visitors will learn about Lincoln's life and the monumental issues of the day, such as slavery, through life-like and innovative exhibits and presentations. Then they can complete their visit by viewing the Gettysburg Address, a signed copy of the Emancipation Proclamation, a portion of Lincoln's Second Inaugural Speech, personal items from the Lincoln family, and many other priceless original documents and artifacts that will be displayed in the new museum.

The Abraham Lincoln Presidential Library and Museum, being built in downtown Springfield, will be staffed and administered by the Illinois Historic Preservation Agency, an agency of state government.

Playing in Peoria

As might be expected in a moderately populated area bracketed by two major metropolitan centers—Chicago in the northeast and St. Louis in the southwest—downstate Illinois does not have a plethora of cultural institutions. The more than four million residents spread over 54,000 square miles of downstate Illinois can hop in their cars and drive to the two big cities to enjoy big league sports, symphony, ballet, opera, and museums.

Nevertheless, there are scores of cultural facilities scattered around downstate, many of them offering limited seasons and collections, to appeal to local tastes. The major university campuses often have museums, performing arts programs, and libraries. There are also hundreds of local historical museums and old buildings that have been preserved in various cities, towns, and hamlets downstate—so many that it would take a book just to list and describe them. Since the settlement of

Above: New Salem, a restored pioneer settlement north of Springfield, is where Lincoln lived for six years as a young man after leaving home. Photo by Ted Schurter

Top: The circa 1812 Rose Hotel in Elizabethtown in Hardin County is probably the oldest hostelry in Illinois. It is now operated by the state as a bed and breakfast inn. Photo by Ted Schurter

collection. The library portion of the complex will be completed in 2002, with the museum scheduled to open in 2003. The library will serve as a worldwide center for research on the life and times of Abraham Lincoln and the Civil War, plus it will continue to be the chief historical and genealogical research facility for all aspects of Illinois history. The museum building will feature exhibits about key periods in Lincoln's life. It will also include two theaters, a children's area, and a place to display some of the state's most precious Lincoln documents and artifacts.

The Illinois State Historical Library's Henry Horner Lincoln Collection will be the foundation of the Presidential Library and Museum. It includes the world's most complete collection of pre-presidential Abraham Lincoln material, including nearly 1,500 manuscripts written or signed by Lincoln, 10,000 books and pamphlets, 1,000 broadsides, and 1,000 prints and photographs. The historical library, founded in 1889, is also a valuable resource for scholars studying other aspects of Illinois history. Its collections currently include more than 174,000 books and pamphlets, 3,000 maps, 1,200 periodical series from colonial items to the present, 10.2 million manuscripts,

Illinois only dates from the 1700s, there aren't any Roman aqueducts or medieval castles, but there are plenty of log cabins and Victorian homes.

There also are a few estates reminiscent of the manors and chateaux of Europe. Robert Henry Allerton's 1,500-acre estate, formal garden, and mansion near Monticello was donated to the University of Illinois in 1946. The institution has used it as a conference center and public park since then. Allerton was the son of a Chicago millionaire who decided he would rather be a gentleman farmer than a business tycoon like his father. Bauhaus architect Mies van der Rohe's Farnsworth House is just outside Plano. There are buildings designed by Frank Lloyd Wright in six downstate cities.

In addition to the three world-famous zoos in Chicago and St. Louis, there are several more modest zoos downstate. The seven-acre Glen Oak Zoo in Peoria has 150 animals, including lions. The Henson Robinson Zoo in Springfield has more than 300 animals, including nine red-ruffed lemurs from Madagascar that are part of a program by zoos worldwide to save endangered species. There is also the Miller Park Zoo in Bloomington and the Scovill Children's Zoo in Decatur.

"How will it play in Peoria?" is an old saw from vaudeville days resurrected from time to time by political campaigns and by business analysts to describe the reaction of "Middle

America" to a candidate or product. Things do play in Peoria, including the Peoria Symphony Orchestra and assorted stage shows at the Madison Theater—a vaudeville and movie house that opened in 1920 and now stages live concerts with an occasional movie special. Peoria Players Theater, a community group that dates back to 1919, stages six plays a year. The Peoria Symphony traces its origins to 1897

The domed Illinois state capitol is in Springfield, although the state maintains extensive offices in Chicago as well. The capitol houses the offices of the governor and the General Assembly, as the legislature is called. Photo © 2000 Doris De Witt/Stone

and now performs seven concerts a year, including such challenging pieces as the Verdi *Requiem*.

It is one of a handful of part-time symphony orchestras in downstate Illinois. The University of Illinois Symphony in Champaign uses as a source of talent that institution's well-known music school. The Illinois Symphony Orchestra resulted from a consolidation of musical organizations in Springfield and the twin college towns of Bloomington-Normal. The allied Illinois Chamber Orchestra has played in both Chicago and New York's Carnegie Hall. Other downstate orchestras include the Knox-Galesburg Symphony, the Quincy Symphony, the Belleville Philharmonic, and the Rockford Symphony, as well as assorted youth groups.

Museums of Art, History, and Weapons

There are also a number of interesting museums scattered across downstate Illinois despite competition from the big museums in Chicago and St. Louis. The Rock Island Arsenal Museum on an island in the Mississippi houses a collection of 1,100 weapons, as well as exhibits on several wars and the Confederate Prison Camp that was there in 1863-1865. The arsenal surrounding the museum is an active military munitions factory—the army's last major base in Illinois.

The air force maintains Scott Air Base near St. Louis, and the navy has Great Lakes Naval Training Center north of Chicago. The former Chanute Air Force Base in Rantoul is now the home of an unusual museum displaying more than 30 aircraft and missiles, including replicas of Charles Lindbergh's *Spirit of St. Louis* and a World War I vintage Curtiss Jenny biplane. Jennies were in use when the base, named after Chicago glider pioneer Octave Chanute, a counselor to the Wright brothers, was founded in 1917. The base closed in 1993. The museum has the world's only surviving Boeing XB-47 Stratojet on display.

A few miles south in Champaign, the Krannert Museum on the U of I campus boasts it is the second-largest art museum in the state. It has a collection of more than 8,000 art objects, including pre-Columbian art as well as works from Asia, Africa, and the contemporary scene.

The Discovery Center Museum in Rockford specializes in hands-on science and art exhibits, Northern Illinois University in DeKalb has museums featuring art and the history of education, and Rock Island's Black Hawk State Historic Site features local Indian history. Just across the Mississippi River from Rock Island in LeClaire, Iowa, is the Buffalo Bill Museum featuring the life and times of Buffalo Bill Cody, a native of the town. There is an Amish museum in Arcola, and the Center for American Archaeology maintains a small museum in Kampsville.

Colleges Everywhere

Like most midwestern states, Illinois has a large system of public universities that came into existence as the result of a federal policy to grant large tracts of land for educational purposes after President Abraham Lincoln signed the Morrill Act in 1862. The act resulted in the founding of what became the University of Illinois, the state's major public research institution, in 1868. Most of the other state schools began somewhat later as teachers' colleges

and grew into major universities, some of them adding satellite and secondary campuses as they expanded.

Downstate Illinois is also home to a variety of private colleges. Bradley University in Peoria is probably the best known, although nearby Eureka College claims President Ronald Reagan among its alumni.

In fact, the state has nine public universities with 12 campuses, 48 community college districts, 103 independent colleges and universities, and 20 independent, for-profit proprietary institutions. Combined they enroll more than 728,000 students—192,000 at public institutions, 344,000 at community colleges, 175,000 at the independent schools, and more than 16,000 at the for-profit schools.

Although the University of Illinois over the years has added campuses in Chicago and Springfield, its main campus—with 26,000 undergraduates and 10,000 graduate and professional students—is in the twin cities of Urbana and Champaign, 136 miles almost due south of Chicago and 173 miles northeast of St. Louis. The institution, which has an international reputation for its engineering and agricultural colleges as well as medical, veterinary, architecture, and law schools, draws students from throughout the nation and around the world.

It counts 10 Nobel Prize laureates and 17 Pulitzer Prize winners among its alumni and annually ranks among the top five universities in the number of doctoral degrees granted. Its library is among the largest in the nation with 17 million items. The university was the first in the nation to retrofit its facilities to accommodate the disabled—decades before federal law required it.

On autumn and winter weekends Urbana-Champaign is where many Illinois residents go to watch big-time college sports. The U of I, like Northwestern, is a member of the Big Ten Conference. Its football stadium seats more than 70,000 and its basketball arena, which doubles as a convention center, seats 16,000.

The newest and smallest of three campuses of the University of Illinois system, the Springfield campus, formerly known as Sangamon State University, joined the University of Illinois system in 1995 and celebrated its 30th campus anniversary in 2000. Most of its 4,000 students are transfers

The frontier had passed Illinois long before the term "Wild West" became a cliché, but rodeos are still a popular attraction at county fairs. This cowboy is bringing down a calf at the 1999 National High School Finals Rodeo at the Illinois State Fairgrounds in Springfield. Photo by Ted Schurter

from community colleges and other institutions, with just a handful attending UIS in their freshman and sophomore years. The university is located on a 746-acre tract on the southeast side of Springfield near Lake Springfield.

Southern Illinois University in Carbondale more than 300 miles south of Chicago was chartered in 1869 as Southern Illinois Normal College, a teachers' college, but by 1947 had grown so large it was renamed. Two years later it began offering off-campus

courses in St. Louis' Illinois suburbs, which led to the development of its campus in Edwardsville and satellites in Alton and East St. Louis. SIU's medical school opened later in Springfield.

The Carbondale campus is known for its research into clean-coal technology at the Illinois Clean Coal Institute, reclamation and land use, science, aquaculture, groundwater quality, information management, early childhood education, rehabilitation, and health professions training.

SIU's schools of agriculture and forestry are highly respected, tackling subjects such as soybean research, wetlands restoration, and monitoring endangered species. Its College of Mass Communications and Media Arts operates television and radio stations and its student-run newspaper, the *Daily Egyptian,* is one of only a few in the nation with its own press.

As the twentieth century closed, SIU had become the preeminent university in Southern Illinois with an enrollment of 34,000 ranging from two-year technical programs to 27 different disciplines offering doctorates, including medicine and dentistry. It also operates a small campus in Nakajo, Japan, with an enrollment of 150 students.

The other major regional universities in the state include Northern Illinois in DeKalb; Eastern Illinois in Charleston, 183 miles south of Chicago; Western Illinois in Macomb, 230 miles southwest of Chicago; and Illinois State in Normal, 130 miles southwest of Chicago. Illinois State, founded in 1857 as a college to educate teachers, is the oldest of the public institutions of higher learning in Illinois. It now enrolls more than 20,000 students, 87 percent of them undergraduates.

Eastern Illinois, the smallest of the group with slightly more than 11,000 students at its 320-acre campus, is primarily an undergraduate institution. It is organized into four colleges: the College of Arts and Humanities, the Lumpkin College of Business and Applied Sciences, the College of Education and Professional Studies, and the College of Sciences. Western Illinois began in 1902 as a teachers' college, was converted to a university in 1957, and by the end of the century enrolled more than 12,000 students in 46 undergraduate and 36 graduate programs.

The Private Schools

Bradley University is the largest of the private institutions in downstate Illinois with an enrollment of nearly 6,000 students in its five colleges. The school was founded in 1897 and became a four-year college in 1920. A few miles to the east is Eureka College, a church-affiliated liberal arts school that boasts the 40th president of the United States, Ronald Reagan, as its most famous alumnus. He was a member of the class of 1932.

Eureka is typical of many of the small colleges in Illinois. For the most part they were founded between 1828 and 1860 by churches to provide higher education in a state that was in the process of being transformed from a wilderness by hardy pioneer families.

Knox College in Galesburg 180 miles west of Chicago also is small (fewer than 1,200 students) but is rich in tradition. On October 7, 1858, it was the site of one of the famous debates between Abraham Lincoln and Stephen A. Douglas—the one in which Lincoln denounced the immorality of slavery. Douglas won the race for U.S. Senate that year but lost to Lincoln in the presidential election two years later. Knox at the time was a hotbed of abolitionist sentiment: Hiram Revels, the first black elected to the U.S. Senate, studied there, as did Barnabas Root, the first black awarded a college degree in

Illinois (in 1870).

A few miles away to the east is Monmouth College, which enrolls 1,060 students and is known for its Scottish heritage, including a bagpipe band, and to the north in Rock Island is Augustana, a liberal arts school of about 2,000 students founded in 1860 by Swedish immigrants.

McKendree, a Methodist college founded in 1828 in Lebanon, claims to be the oldest in Illinois, but rival Illinois College, a Presbyterian- and United Church of Christ-affiliated school founded a year later in Jacksonville just west of Springfield, claims to be the earliest such institution in the state to have graduated a class. MacMurray College, which with 739 students is slightly smaller than its crosstown rival Illinois College (900 students), was founded by the Methodists in 1848.

Members of that denomination also founded Illinois Wesleyan University in Bloomington in 1850 and Greenville College (in the town of that name 45 miles east of St. Louis) in 1892. They had enrollments of 2,015 and 850, respectively, as the twentieth century closed. Illinois Wesleyan's most famous faculty member was perhaps John Wesley Powell, the explorer of the Grand Canyon and a founder of the National Geographic Society. The Presbyterian-affiliated Millikin University in Decatur 175 miles south of Chicago (enrollment 2,300) was founded in 1901, and Principia College (enrollment 550) is a Christian Science school founded in 1897.

Olivet Nazarene University (enrollment 2,400) is an evangelical institution in Bourbonnais 50 miles south of Chicago's Loop, and Quincy University (enrollment 1,175) in the Mississippi River town of that name is a Catholic school. Quincy was founded in 1860, and Olivet Nazarene in 1907.

Epilogue

Predicting the future of Illinois is as risky as predicting its rapidly changing weather. There is an old saw that says that if you don't like the weather in Chicago, wait 10 minutes. Weather prediction has improved considerably over the years, but not enough to bet the farm on.

The same is true of predicting the economy. The investors in the 1990s who bought on margin the hot "dot.com" stocks discovered as the new century dawned that the long-expected market correction was occurring—with their money. Illinois is not a center of the computer industry, but as investors there and everywhere else were hit with margin calls to cover their losses on the dot.coms, they hurriedly sold off "old economy" stocks, which also dragged down the prices of those Blue Chips. A number of those old economy companies, especially manufacturers, were based in Illinois.

So any analysis of the state's long-term future in the twenty-first century has to be confined to the basics—the underlying assets and deficits that make the state's economy what it is.

Illinois in the twenty-first century is likely to survive and prosper as it did in the first two centuries of its existence by constantly adapting to change and diversifying. Timber, meatpacking, steelmaking, and coal mining were all major industries in Illinois at one time. Their collective decline at different times, while it did cause pain, did not prove fatal to the state's economy. Illinois continued to grow and adapt during the second half of the twentieth century, though not at the rate of many Sunbelt states.

As the changes occurred, old industries died, and new ones sprang up to replace them, Illinois' economy became increasingly diversified. At least since the end of the fur trade that dominated the colonial economy, Illinois has not been a one-dish-diet state, dominated by one industry the way autos dominate Michigan and tourism runs Hawaii. As the economy continued to change in the last half of the twentieth century, diversification became an asset. No one industry could falter and bring down the economy.

Some Trends Favor Illinois

There also are a number of constants in Illinois' favor in the new century. It remains the nation's mid-continental hub—a factor determined by geography that cannot be changed by reprogramming computers. As the global population continues to increase, the world will have at least as great an interest in bites as it does in bytes, so agriculture will remain a core industry. The state also sits beside the greatest reservoir of fresh water on earth, the Great Lakes, at a time when development in sunnier but more arid states could become constrained by the overtaxed water supplies.

There were indications of a number of trends at work in Illinois at the end of the twentieth century. Although it was not possible to determine whether they were short-lived phenomena or the beginnings of long-term events that would have significant influence on the state, their appearance was the subject of some speculation.

For one thing, the process of decentralization, or urban sprawl, that character-

Facing page: The Merchandise Mart (turret in foreground) is Chicago's largest building in terms of floor area with four million square feet, and the John Hancock Center (background center with towers) at 1,127 feet is the city's third tallest. Photo © 2000 Mark Segal/Stone

ized the Chicago metropolitan area during the last half of the twentieth century seemed to be slowing as the twenty-first century dawned. Some urbanologists cited the reversal of Chicago's long population decline and a trend toward apartment construction in the downtown areas of many suburbs as early indications of a recentralization process.

Another event that occurred at the beginning of the new century was a sudden jump in energy prices. Although it wasn't entirely certain whether the increase was a temporary phenomenon mirroring a similar jolt that had occurred in the 1970s or the beginning of a long-term trend signaling an end to cheap energy in the United States, the latter scenario could raise transportation costs and slow the process of decentralization of both housing and industry. The metropolitan areas of Chicago and St. Louis—with their established mass transit systems—could survive somewhat better than cities with little or no transit infrastructure, and the state policy of subsidizing intercity rail service has resulted in continuing Amtrak passenger service to most of the largest Illinois cities.

Illinois' huge rail, highway, and waterway systems could leave it in a somewhat more advantageous position in the national economy than other states relying primarily on highways. Since the Chicago & Rock Island Railroad laid its tracks

Horses are no longer an important aspect of the state's economy, but they are a popular form of recreation in some areas, especially in Chicago's semi-rural exurbs. Photo © Mark Segal/Index Stock Imagery

adjacent to the Illinois and Michigan Canal in the 1850s, competition between the transportation modes has had the effect of keeping transportation costs lower in Illinois than they would have been under a transportation monopoly. The existence of a healthy barge system on the Mississippi River, for example, has forced the parallel railroads to adopt various measures to keep their rates as low as possible in the export grain trade between Illinois and the Gulf of Mexico.

The extensive highway system that includes three of the nation's transcontinental east-west interstate highways and two north-south interstates has been a bonus to downstate Illinois. Not only have many companies built new regional distribution centers along interstates downstate, but many communities that once languished as backwaters have become affordable housing markets for people who work in the sprawling suburbs and don't mind the long commutes on the interstates.

The transportation system is one of Illinois' many assets collectively known as "infrastructure." The state also had an extensive water and sewer system that didn't have to be built from scratch to support new development. Many Chicago suburbs now draw their water from Lake Michigan instead of continuing to rely on wells drilled deep in aquifers, a system that was vulnerable to depleted water tables that have plagued many areas of the country.

The Chicago skyline at night is an impressive sight. The Aon Center (background center), which originally was called the Standard Oil Building and later the Amoco Building, is the second tallest in the city at 1,136 feet. Photo by Phil Greer

The export of both agricultural products and the machinery to produce them has been an important part of the Illinois economy, albeit cyclic, since the 1840s. That is unlikely to change as the world population increases. More mouths to feed worldwide means a state with fertile soil, ample water supply, and favorable climate has a good long-term outlook.

The state has a skilled manpower pool, and its extensive college system continues to produce new graduates as well as retrain older ones in mid-career in the complexities of the computer age. The two national laboratories in Chicago's suburbs, as well as major universities including Northwestern, Chicago, and the University of Illinois, have acted as magnets for development in the new technologies and are likely to continue to do so.

Some Negatives Remain

Labor is another side of the equation. High labor costs have reduced Illinois' competitive position somewhat, especially during the postwar exodus to the Sunbelt and overseas after 1945, but a long period of relatively low inflation at the end of the twentieth century has mitigated that disadvantage somewhat. Increasing shipping costs resulting from the boost in energy prices at the turn of the century eventually could offset the state's labor costs and cause some companies to return their manufacturing operations to Illinois and neighboring states. Illinois' manufacturing industry learned the hard way during the recession in the early 1980s that it had to streamline not only the factory floor but the general office as well.

Except during wars, the state in the twentieth century has never been particularly dependent upon federal contracts to support its economy. In fact, Illinois is one of the nation's biggest net outflow states; it sent considerably more money in the form of taxes to Washington than it got back each year. That was considered a negative until the federal government began to shrink in the 1980s, especially the defense cutbacks that followed the end to the Cold War. Although the state lost Chanute Air Force Base, Glenview Naval Air Station, and Fort Sheridan in the cutbacks, their loss had a minimal impact on the economy. In the cases of Glenview and Sheridan, the sudden availability of large tracts of developable land was seen as a shot in the arm for those local communities.

The lack of any spectacular natural wonders and a climate infamous for long, cold winters means that Illinois will probably never be a major sightseeing tourist destination. The Chicago and St. Louis metropolitan areas have had their ups and downs over the years in the highly competitive convention business, primarily because of problems associated with controlling labor costs and keeping their meeting halls competitive with newer facilities being built in the Sunbelt. Both areas have continuously upgraded their convention centers and have the advantage of central locations and excellent transportation networks, but controlling costs has proved to be a never-ending struggle in which the cities have had some successes and some failures.

The Cities Adapt

Although there are some cities, such as Galena and Oak Park, that seem frozen in time, most of Illinois' municipalities have continually evolved and changed over time. Chicago, a town of wood houses before the Great Fire, became a city of brick and stone afterwards, and then a metropolis where skyscrapers dominated the skyline. The many neighborhoods of modest tenements on the West and South sides became huge slums after World War II as their white residents fled to the suburbs to be replaced by poor blacks, Appalachians, and Hispanics. Many neighborhoods were gutted by neglect, decay, fire during the race riots of the 1960s, and in some cases slumlords burning buildings for their insurance value.

But many of the modest neighborhoods, especially on the North Side, gentrified. Young, upwardly mobile singles and couples bought and rehabilitated the two and three flats. Middle-class blacks moved into many neighborhoods of single-family homes on the South Side and prevented their deterioration. The University of Chicago was able to stabilize the neighborhoods surrounding its South Side campus, and the University of Illinois' Chicago campus was able to accomplish the same on the West Side.

Madison Street just west of the Chicago River was once Chicago's worst neighborhood—a strip of cheap liquor stores, deteriorating buildings, and flophouses known as Skid Row. An aggressive building program by several government agencies and private enterprises, and a concerted effort on the part of the city, cleaned

Lippizaners, like this mare and her foal on a farm in north suburban Libertyville specializing in that breed, are famous for their skills in dressage exhibitions. Photo © Lynn M. Stone/Index Stock Imagery

up Skid Row and made it a place where sports fans, among others, could safely walk after a hockey or basketball game at the Chicago Stadium, or its replacement, the United Center.

The suburbs also saw considerable change, not just the growth of endless subdivisions of tract houses. Although places like Lake Forest and Hinsdale have remained enclaves of the wealthy since the nineteenth century, many older suburbs south and west of Chicago, such as Harvey and Maywood, became the home to blacks fleeing Chicago's slums. Other older, inner suburbs—"mature communities" was the euphemism sometimes used to describe them—suffered various stages of urban blight as their infrastructures began to deteriorate without a sufficient tax base to rebuild them.

Downstate Illinois, including the St. Louis metropolitan area, experienced the

Despite urban sprawl around Chicago and St. Louis, there are still plenty of places offering solitude in Illinois. This couple is watching the sunset from the banks of Carlyle Lake in South Central Illinois. Photo © Mark Segal/Index Stock Imagery

same range of changes that affected the big city and its suburbs but without the notoriety. One by one, individually and alone, towns all over the state suffered decline as their local industries—coal mining, for example—shut down. Some nearly disappeared; others survived on a smaller scale. Some were reborn and prospered. Rantoul lost Chanute Air Force Base and began to redevelop that site for housing and industry. Effingham, at the interchange of two major interstate highways, became a distribution center.

Galena, in the northwestern corner of the state, survived by running in the opposite direction. While the rest of Illinois scrambled to remain competitive in the twenty-first century, Galena returned to antebellum times. The town that nearly died after its lead mines played out in the nineteenth century redeveloped itself in the twentieth century as a historic tourist destination.

PART THREE

Illinois' Enterprises

by Irene Macauley

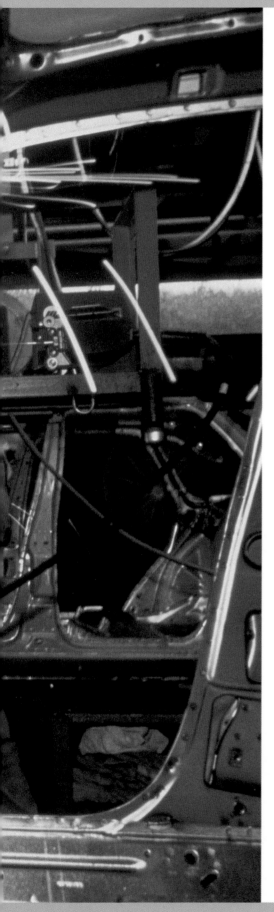

Manufacturing and High Technology

Illinois' central location and qualified work force attract global manufacturers and high-technology industries to the state.

Archer Daniels Midland **242-245**

Motorola, Inc. **246-249**

Deere & Company **250-251**

FMC Corporation **252-253**

Sara Lee Corporation **254-255**

A. M. Castle & Co. **256-257**

The Boeing Company **258**

Caterpillar Inc. **259**

Left: © 2000 Serge AEF.Attal/The Image Bank

G. Allen Andreas,
chairman of ADM.

"The Nature of What's to Come" aptly describes Archer Daniels Midland and its innovative efforts to feed the world. Though not apparent to average consumers, ADM products touch their lives every day. ADM—located in Decatur, Illinois, in the heart of the highest-yielding land in the country—is one of the world's leading grain trade and processing companies. It is an innovator in developing and providing value-added corn, soybean, and wheat processing for the food, feed, fuel, and pharmaceutical industries. ADM does not market products under its own name. However, its processed ingredients are found in thousands of brand-name products on supermarket shelves around the world.

ADM procures, transports, stores, processes, and merchandises agricultural products and, as such, it has a big appetite. For example, every minute of every day in the United States, ADM processes 44 acres of soybeans, 12 acres of wheat, and 8 acres of corn. It operates nearly 400 grain elevators, almost 40 percent of them overseas, and has part ownership of another 180. It owns 312 processing plants worldwide. All facilities are strategically located in grain-producing areas to be near the source of raw materials. ADM also owns 50 oil seed-crushing facilities throughout the Americas and Europe and its worldwide transportation network consists of 13,000 railcars, 2,250 barges, 900 trucks, and 78 towboats.

The origins of ADM date back to the 1800s when John W. Daniels and George P. Archer began their respective careers in the linseed-crushing business (linseed oil is produced by crushing the seed of the flax plant). The two combined their efforts in 1902, when they founded the Archer Daniels Linseed Company. They acquired a competitive linseed-crushing firm in 1923 and renamed their company Archer Daniels Midland. With nine mills and 334 presses, the new corporation would become the world's largest linseed oil producer.

The modern history of ADM is intimately tied to its former longtime chairman and now chairman emeritus, Dwayne Andreas. When he joined the company in 1966, ADM owned 40 processing plants and its work force was less than 3,000 strong. Andreas was elected chairman and chief executive officer in 1970. Over the next three decades ADM emerged from a modest farm supply company to a major multinational conglomerate. Today, under the leadership of current chairman G. Allen Andreas, ADM has over 300 plants around the world that process 11 grains and oilseeds into a multitude of products used by worldwide markets. It has more than 22,000 employees and has built a transportation network that spans the globe.

In every decade since it was founded, ADM has added a major profit center to its agribusiness operations: flaxseed, wheat milling, soybean processing, value-added products, transportation, corn sweeteners, ethanol, peanut processing, fermentation-based bioproducts, nutraceuticals (ingredients used in foods that promote health benefits), and functional ingredients.

ADM's strength is drawn from its relationship to the land and to agriculture. As a major link between farmer and food manufacturer, it provides farmers a market for their crops and, in turn, supplies feed ingredients for their animals. Its processing adds value to the farmer's corn, wheat, soybeans, and other grains, while its continued development of new products and processes increases the demand for those crops. At the same time, ADM has long been a champion of high-yield agriculture, and today, when every acre counts more than ever, it continues to believe this is critical to ensuring there is enough food to go around. High-yield farming employs such techniques as soil conservation, satellite positioning, and improved hybrids to produce more food without using more land.

ADM serves food processors and feed manufacturers by producing a wide range

of quality ingredients at low cost—enough to feed 130 million people every day. It works closely with its customers to tailor products to their specific needs, and to develop new products and applications that will satisfy the requirements of a changing and expanding marketplace. This is achieved by emphasizing quality and efficiency. For example, in many cases finished products from the processing of one commodity become the raw material for another product, while finished products from different commodities share the same storage and transportation facilities.

Research and development has long

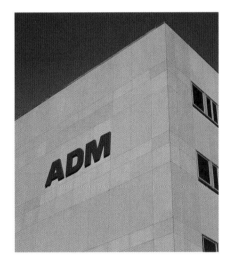

been a key to the company's success; over the years it has developed the use of textured vegetable protein, fuel ethanol, and 55 percent high-fructose corn syrup. ADM has been a pioneer in soybean processing, for example. Soybeans, a staple in China for 5,000 years, were brought to America in the early 1900s. American farmers eventually recognized the nutritional benefit of the bean and by 1920 they began to grow the crop in commercial quantities. ADM was there to buy and process the crop for them. It not only processed the crops beginning in 1929; it also marketed their nutritional value to the consumer. Today ADM soy products help improve nutrition in countries with a high risk of malnutrition and famine. Another exam-

ple is corn processing. Since 1971 ADM has been turning the basic elements of kernel corn into ingredients that help constitute common food and beverage products.

Every day ADM turns grain crops into everyday products: vegetable oil and lecithin from soybeans, high-fructose corn syrup and citric acid from corn, flour from wheat, cocoa powder and chocolate from cocoa beans. These natural ingredients are used by food processors in countless food and beverage items ranging from baked goods to dairy foods, from meats to confections, from soft drinks to sports drinks.

Its processed grains and beans—harvested from farmers' crops—are also returned to the farm in the form of animal feed. Worldwide producers, mixers, and millers use ADM feed ingredients to improve the protein quality, nutritional standards, and production efficiency of animal feeds. Livestock producers rely on ADM's feed ingredients to enhance animal diets. Today's genetically superior animals need advanced feeding programs. ADM's line of amino acids and vitamin pre-mixes are made specifically to help producers meet the nutritional demands of their animals and to ensure optimum animal health.

ADM is also committed to helping ensure optimum health for the world's peoples. It is at the forefront in developing

Above: The company's development of nutraceuticals, like Novasoy®, are continuing its enormous growth in the health and nutrition marketplace.

Left: ADM's headquarters is located in Decatur, Illinois.

Above: ADM produces ethanol, a corn-derived fuel that reduces air pollution.

Top: ADM has been an important pioneer in soybean processing.

Top right: Processed grains and beans are returned to the farm in the form of animal feed.

products with real health benefits; its all-natural product line contains countless items with real nutritional benefits, from soy protein to vegetable oil to vitamins and more. The company's focus on health and nutrition led to its use of nutraceuticals, or "functional foods," that are known to have specific medicinal or preventive health benefits. For example, there are nutraceuticals that help prevent heart disease, assist with brain and liver function, act as antioxidants, and help maintain healthy cholesterol. ADM's nutraceutical products are derived from corn and soybeans: vitamin E, vitamin C, tocotrienols, mixed tocopherols, phytosterols, and isoflavones. In fact, ADM is the world's largest user of isoflavones (natural plant phytonutrients similar in structure to human estrogen).

To meet ever-growing demand, ADM is constantly searching for new, more efficient ways of growing, producing, and transporting food. For instance, its research in biotechnology, the science of improving food at the genetic level, has resulted in new varieties of high-oil corn and high-protein soybeans. ADM is exploring partnerships with biotechnology companies in order to transform the results of this research into widely available food.

Another innovative effort to produce

food is taking place at the firm's Decatur headquarters. ADM researchers wanted to determine if fish could be raised in a greenhouse. The result of that research is the premier aquaculture facility in the Midwest. The primary stock is tilapia, a member of the perch family, which is fed a diet comprised primarily of lysine and soybean meal produced by ADM. Tilapia reproduce copiously and mature quickly, which gives them the potential to play a role in helping to alleviate world hunger. Even the nutrient-rich waters of the aquaculture facility are recycled to grow vegetables and herbs.

Developing alternate fuels is another area in which ADM has played a significant role, especially renewable fuels. Following the oil shortages of the early 1970s, the company built a $20-million plant to produce ethanol from corn; although ethanol proved expensive as a gasoline additive, it remains a viable alternate fuel and ADM continues to be a leader in its production. Ethanol-blended gasoline burns cleaner than traditional fuels, reducing carbon monoxide emissions up to 25 percent while maintaining vehicle performance. The company is now blending ethanol with diesel fuel to create oxy-diesel for use in the trucking industry. Since half of the vehicles on U.S. roads are

Left: The firm's efficient transportation network moves grain, food, feed, and fuel throughout the world.

Below: ADM raises tilapia in the firm's Decatur aquaculture facility.

trucks, oxydiesel can have a significant impact on reducing air pollution.

Its cogeneration program also demonstrates the firm's commitment to fuel efficiency and clean air. Its seven largest facilities in the United States and Europe are powered by cogeneration, which cuts electric purchases significantly and contributes to cleaner air. ADM's cogeneration plants burn cooler than traditional boilers, thus considerably reducing nitrogen oxide emissions. At its Decatur headquarters, the use of limestone in the process captures more than 90 percent of the sulfur dioxide (SO2) created. This reduces the problem of SO2 emissions and allows high-sulfur coal to be burned. The Decatur facility burns a mixture of 10 percent used tires along with coal; currently it burns about 11 million tires a year, more than the total discarded in Illinois.

ADM is very much an international business. Its worldwide network of plants and affiliates enables the company to effectively link farmers and food manufacturers throughout the world. In addition to facilities in 30 states, it has operations in 25 countries and that number is growing.

Operating facilities throughout the United States and around the world presents a challenge: how to transport raw materials and finished products from the crop field to the processing plant to the producer. To drive this movement—a vital link in its integrated approach to processing—ADM entered the transportation business in the 1960s. Trucks on their way to ADM's processing plants carry agricultural grain commodities from America's farms and elevators. Trucks leaving ADM plants carry value-added products— processed from grains and oilseeds—to food manufacturers and the export mar-

ket. Today that transportation network has grown significantly to service ADM's global marketplace. This network has long been the most efficient point-to-point supplier on earth, incorporating a system of barges, railcars, trucks, and ships to move grain, food, feed, and fuel all over the globe. However, changing times and markets make it necessary to stay in ever-constant motion. The company has recently invested in barge-towing operations in South America, renovated its shipyards, and made substantial additions to its fleet of railcars—all to serve its ever-expanding customer base.

Today ADM is a *Fortune* 500 company with 2000 revenues of $12.8 billion. The story of its growth is the story of twentieth-century business success: building a global network to serve a global marketplace. The future might well bring new methods of feeding the world. When it does, Archer Daniels Midland will be there to make sure that it happens. ■

ADM burns a mixture of 10 percent used tires along with coal, utilizing 11 million tires a year.

MANUFACTURING AND HIGH TECHNOLOGY ▪ **245**

Motorola founder Paul V. Galvin (1895-1959) served as the company's president until 1956, when he was elected chairman of the board of directors.

Galvin Manufacturing Company produced battery eliminators, car radios, and home radios at its first factory. The building was located at 847 West Harrison Street, Chicago.

*M*otorola, a $37.6-billion telecommunications company, has been in business for nearly 75 years. It was founded as the Galvin Manufacturing Corporation, a maker of radios for homes and automobiles. The second-generation Galvin to head Motorola led the firm into new technology with emphasis on semiconductors, pagers, and cell phones. Today the company is in the hands of a third-generation Galvin, who is focusing on communications solutions. His vision is the convergence of the Internet and wireless communications.

The history of Motorola is one of innovation and great success—and some missteps. It is also one of reinvention in order to constantly anticipate and participate in the development of leading-edge communications technology. The firm's mission is to provide the link between people's dreams and the promise of technology. This has been so since its founding in 1928.

Galvin and his brother, Joseph, started their manufacturing business with the purchase of the bankrupt Stewart Storage Battery Company in 1928. The enterprise was incorporated as the Galvin Manufacturing Company with five employees and a payroll of $63. Its assets were a cash reserve of $565, some $750 worth of tools, and a design for the firm's first product—a battery eliminator that allowed home radios to operate on ordinary household current. It was a short-lived product because battery-operated radios quickly became obsolete. There was still more work to be done.

Automobiles of the time were not equipped with radios. The Galvin auto radio, the first commercially practical and affordable radio for automobiles, was sold and installed as an accessory by independent auto dealers. The new product was named Motorola (from motor and Victrola) to indicate motion and radio. In 1930 net sales were nearly $300,000. Within a few years Motorola held a major portion of the U.S. auto radio market. A new line of home radios was announced

in 1937, the year Galvin Manufacturing moved to modern facilities on Chicago's West Side. And a new line of auto radios became the first to feature push-button tuning, a vibrator power supply, and fine-tuning and tone controls. The first national dealer to handle Motorola radios was the B.F. Goodrich Company.

Net sales approached $10 million in 1940 and the company employed 985 workers. Throughout most of the decade, Galvin concentrated on vehicular and portable two-way radios. It developed the first hand-held two-way AM radio for the U.S. Army Signal Corps; it was to become a World War II symbol known as the "handie-talkie." Another innovation also played a role in the war effort—the first portable FM two-way radio known as the "walkie-talkie."

Galvin Manufacturing, already trading as a public company, changed its name in 1947 to Motorola, Inc. That same year Motorola entered the television business with its "Golden View" model, the first television set to sell for less than $200. By now, autos had gained wide popularity among the public. People dreamed of getting news

and listening to music in their cars. The Motorola technology made that possible. The big automakers recognized the growing demand. By the end of the decade, Motorola was supplying auto radios to Ford and Chrysler and General Motors for installation in their cars. An auto radio-manufacturing facility was opened in Quincy, Illinois, the first Motorola plant outside Chicago. And in 1949 the company launched a research facility in Arizona to take advantage of the newly invented transistor. The work conducted there helped Motorola become one of the world's largest manufacturers of semiconductors. It remains the leading supplier of semiconductors to the auto industry.

The decade also ended with a failure. Motorola's automatic push-button gasoline car heater failed in the marketplace. From then on, Paul Galvin proclaimed, the company would "stick to electronics."

Sales in 1950 topped $177 million and there were now more than 9,000 Motorola employees. The company began production of a series of power transmitters and silicon rectifiers in 1952 and two years later introduced its first color television. The reins of leadership shifted in 1956 when a second-generation Galvin, Robert, was named president. Changes were ahead. An early decision was to bring to an end the company's initial attempt to market its color television; because of technical problems and a high price tag, it failed to gain commercial success. It was time to go back to the drawing board.

The firm incorporated transistors into its auto radios, making them more durable and energy efficient. Its first all-transistor pocket-size radio, the XII introduced in 1959, was considered the most reliable in the industry. Motorola also developed a new radio communications product, the pager; became a supplier of semiconductors for other manufacturers; and intro-

duced the highly successful "Motrac," the first two-way mobile radio to have a fully transistorized power supply and receiver.

The 1960s began with $300 million in sales, relocation to new headquarters in Franklin Park, Illinois, and the promise of new technology development. Motorola was the first to use the epitaxial method to mass produce semiconductors and, with its production of automobile alternators, took on a new role as a supplier of "under-the-hood" electronics.

The company also entered the space age. Motorola transponders were aboard *Mariner II* on its trip to Venus in 1962 and on the *Mariner IV* journey to Mars in 1964. Motorola also supplied transponders for the *Gemini* manned-space program. The first words from the moon uttered by astronaut Neil Armstrong in 1969 were relayed to Earth via a Motorola transponder. A Motorola FM receiver was used by the Lunar Roving Vehicle to provide a voice link between Earth and the moon in 1971. And five years later detailed color photos of the surface of Mars taken by *Viking 2* were relayed to Earth via Motorola equipment. Motorola equipment also accompanied *Voyager I* and *II* on their trips to Saturn, Uranus, and Neptune in the 1980s. And it supplied radio equipment for the Galileo, Magellan, and Hubble Space Telescope missions. Motorola's penchant for developing communications technology fit for use in outer space would lead to a pioneering effort in the early 1990s.

The 1960s were also years of important alliances. In a 1964 joint venture with National Video, Motorola developed the first rectangular picture tube for color

Above: Motorola introduced the world's first commercial portable cellular phone, the DynaTAC phone, in 1984. The company was the first to provide complete cellular infrastructure and subscriber product lines.

Above: Motorola developed the first commercially successful car radio in 1930. It was designed to be mass-produced, affordable, and easy to install: radio receiver (left), tuner (lower right), and speaker (upper right).

Above, left: Power transistors were the first commercial semiconductor devices offered by Motorola.

The TalkAbout T6000 two-way radio contained an FM stereo radio and headset, digital compass, thermometer, altimeter/barometer, and clock alarm and stopwatch. It was designed for consumer and recreational customers.

Right: Introduced in 1999, the Timeport model P8167 wireless phone contained a microbrowser for Internet access. It used both the code division multiple access (CDMA) transmission standard and the conventional analog standard.

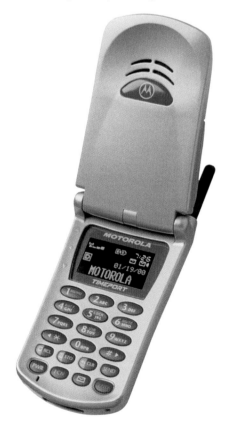

television, which quickly became the standard for the industry. The following year, in collaboration with Ford and RCA, Motorola designed and manufactured the first eight-track tape players for the automotive market.

Motorola's "Quasar" color receivers, introduced in 1967, were the first all-transistor color television sets in the country. Nevertheless, it sold its home television business in 1974 along with its Quincy facility to Matsushita. It was time to concentrate on new communications and semiconductor technologies. The company introduced its first microprocessors, the 6800 containing 4,000 transistors, and marketed them to the automotive, communications, industrial, and business-machines sectors.

Motorola moved to new international headquarters in 1976, to a 325-acre campus in the Chicago suburb of Schaumburg in Illinois. To further its strategy to become a leader in integrated computer circuitry, Motorola then embarked on acquisition. Codex Corporation, a leading manufacturer

of products and services for data communications networks, became a Motorola subsidiary and Universal Data Systems, a maker of moderately priced data communications equipment, was acquired in 1978.

The following year Motorola introduced its first 16-bit microprocessor, the 68000. It was capable of completing two million calculations per second and could be used to both run and write programs for scientific, data-processing, and business applications. Four-Phase Systems, a maker of networked computer systems, was acquired in 1982. In 1984 Motorola offered the first true 32-bit MC68020 microprocessor, which, with its 200,000 transistors, was capable of accessing up to four billion bytes of memory.

Motorola produced its last auto radio in 1987 and divested its display systems business and its automotive alternator and electromechanical meter product lines. The company went on to develop a low-cost secure telephone terminal to protect sensitive information relayed by voice and data telecommunications for government agencies and defense contractors. And in 1989 Motorola produced its "Micro-TAC" personal cellular phone, the smallest and lightest on the market. Motorola was now the world's leading provider of cell phones and systems.

The 1990s opened with another foray into space-age technology. In 1991 Motorola led a 19-member consortium to develop "Iridium," an early global satellite phone network based on an array of 66 small satellites in low-Earth orbit. Its architecture was based on a narrow-band, voice-only system. Shortly after its inception, the Internet swept the communications world and cellular standards for a global system for mobile communications changed significantly and more rapidly than could have been anticipated. Iridium essentially failed in the marketplace in the face of demand for broadband architecture and smaller and more streamlined cell phone designs.

Another technology advance had an

adverse impact on Motorola's position as the world's leading provider of cell phones. Nokia developed digital phones in 1994, and within four years had overtaken Motorola in market share. Motorola had ignored the importance of digital technology in favor of building smaller and faster voice phones.

The 1996 appointment of a third-generation Galvin, Christopher, to lead Motorola was a time of reassessment. The company's long tradition of linking people's dreams to technology's promise would remain its mission. But a commitment was made to move Motorola from a business that provides products to one that provides solutions. Extensive market research was conducted to assess what people wanted. The results revealed the public's demand for products that are smarter, simpler, safer, and more synchronized. Motorola listened. It reformed its strategy.

In April 2000 Chris Galvin outlined the company's new emphasis on technology solutions in a *BusinessWeek Online* interview. "Our strategies focus on three levels of the value chain," he explained. "On solutions on a chip, on

integrated embedded solutions—chips and circuit boards that power everything from automotive dashboards to toasters—and on end-to-end network solutions. We will deliver wireless, Internet, and broadband especially tailored for the individual, the work team, the home, and the car."

To assure its leadership in broadband technology and to solidify its broadband strategy, Motorola bought cable set top box maker General Instrument Corporation. That merger was completed in early 2000, making Motorola a leader in providing end-to-end solutions to the broadband access market. The company is also developing a new Internet protocol communications architecture in partnership with Cisco Systems and Sun Microsystems.

Motorola's vision of bringing the Internet to wireless is becoming reality. It is poised to fulfill the promise of bringing converged video, voice, and data networking into the home—and to be a leading architect of a world without wires … or limitations. ■

Far left: Motorola's V. Series phones included a microbrowser to enable Internet access and to exchange short e-mail messages, and contained an FM radio.

Left: The TalkAbout T900 personal interactive communicator enabled users to send and receive e-mail messages and download information from the Internet. To appeal to younger customers, it was available in four different colors.

The world headquarters of Deere & Company in Moline, Illinois, personifies both the midwestern "can-do" spirit and the beauty of the prairie landscape. The 1,000-acre world headquarters was one of the last designs of world-class architect Eero Saarinen. Saarinen wanted to express all that is functional, simple, and handsome without "chromium doodads or showiness." He achieved his goal. That architectural symbol of excellence reflects the commitment to high standards of quality throughout the long history of Deere & Company.

John Deere, a young blacksmith, left Vermont for Illinois in 1836, one of many who came west to improve their lot. Most were farmers (who comprised 90 percent of the U.S. population at that time) who brought with them their eastern cast-iron plows and other farm implements. Within

The Deere & Company administrative center in Moline, Illinois, serves as the firm's world headquarters and was designed by renowned architect Eero Saarinen.

two days of his arrival, John Deere had built a forge in the village of Grand Detour and was in business making and maintaining farm implements. And there was an immediate need to be met. The farmers' plows, appropriate for plowing the sandy soils of New England, were not designed for scouring the rich black soil of the midwestern prairies. The heavy soil stuck to the wood and iron moldboards and had to be scraped off every few steps. Frustrated, many farmers considered leaving the area to search for soil conditions better suited to their equipment.

Blacksmith Deere believed that it was

the equipment that needed changing. He was determined to find a solution to help farmers in their backbreaking work. He experimented with various shapes and materials for plow bottoms and, in 1837, solved the problem. He developed a plow that was made of steel—recycled from a discarded mill saw blade—that scoured itself clean. Demand for the new self-polishing plow soared; farmers called it the "singing plow."

John Deere moved his operations to Moline in 1847. That year, 1,000 plows were produced before orders were in, a revolutionary approach to manufacturing and selling in those early pioneer days. However, steel quality was inconsistent and supplies limited. Deere solved that problem by commissioning the first-ever cast plow steel to be rolled in the United States.

John Deere died in 1886. By now, his son Charles was president of Deere & Company (incorporated in 1868) and for most of the next century a descendant of John Deere headed the business. John Deere's lasting legacy was his insistence on high standards of quality. "I will never put my name on a plow," he said, "that does not have in it the best that is in me."

By the turn of the century Deere was making a wide range of steel plows, cultivators, corn and cotton planters, and other farm implements. The company then embarked upon a strategy of expansion through acquisition, making it a full-line manufacturer of farm equipment. Six acquisitions were made in 1911, including a developer and producer of corn planters, a company that had produced the first successful broadcast seeder and the grain drill, and a pioneer in hay tool development and manufacturing. In 1918 Deere entered the tractor business with the acquisition of the Waterloo Traction Engine Company, maker of the Waterloo Boy Tractor.

Over the next decades Deere & Company prospered. During the Depression, even as sales plunged, the firm refused to repossess equipment and

The first John Deere Tractor, the Model D, was introduced in 1923. Its economical and dependable two-cylinder design played a role in the transition of agriculture from animal to mechanical power. The Model D, a giant in its day, is dwarfed by today's huge 225-horsepower, four-wheel-drive tractors.

Far left: John Deere is the U.S. market leader in combines due in part to innovative, productive equipment such as the 9750 STS model.

other products from farmers unable to make payments, winning their unceasing loyalty. By the time of its centennial in 1937, Deere & Company sales had reached $100 million.

The 1940s and 1950s were decades of new product development. John Deere's self-propelled combine, combine headers for corn and wheat, and cotton picker were all introduced. In the late 1950s Deere began to make its mark as a multinational company with expansion into Mexico and Germany. Four- and six-cylinder tractors were introduced in 1960, marking the end of the famous two-cylinder "Johnny Poppers." Three years later John Deere entered the lawn- and grounds-care business and separately achieved status as the world's leading agricultural equipment company. In 1966 sales exceeded one billion dollars. The 1970s saw sales increased fivefold. During the severe agricultural recession of the 1980s, John Deere actually gained market share and was the only agricultural equipment company to survive or remain independent.

John Deere remains the world's premier producer of agricultural equipment and is a leader in the production of equipment for construction, forestry, and com-

mercial and consumer equipment. It is also a business leader in parts, engines, financial services, and special technologies. Deere has manufacturing facilities in Europe, Asia, and in North and South America, and markets its products in more than 160 countries.

Deere & Company aspires to double and double again the John Deere experience of Genuine Value for stakeholders, through innovative customer solutions and global customer coverage.

One major effort to incorporate core business functions with corporate branding is sponsorship of the John Deere Golf Classic and its new home course, the PGA Tour Tournament Players Club at Deere Run. John Deere's full line of construction and golf course maintenance equipment played a vital role in developing the club. In fact, John Deere equipment maintains all 25 PGA Tour-owned golf courses.

Deere & Company has grown and prospered through a long-standing partnership with those who work and shape the land. It continues to do so today. ∎

The John Deere Pavilion is rated as one of the world's most comprehensive agricultural exhibits. It features antique and state-of-the-art equipment as well as interactive computer displays and videos.

The history of the multinational FMC Corporation—and its ability to reinvent itself—spans nearly 120 years. John Bean, inventor and entrepreneur, left the Midwest for California in 1883. He purchased an almond orchard but quickly discovered that his trees were blighted with scale. To solve the problem, he developed a continuous-action pump for spraying insecticide. Demand for the new pump by neighboring fruit farmers grew rapidly and the Bean Spray Pump Company was in operation. From these beginnings emerged today's $4-billion FMC Corporation, one of the world's leading producers of chemicals and machinery for industry and agriculture.

In 1928 the John Bean Manufacturing Company purchased San Jose-based Anderson-Barngrove Manufacturing Company, a builder of canning machinery. The deal, consummated within 24 hours, made the combined firms the world's largest manufacturer of fruit machinery. A program of rapid acquisition significantly expanded the company's geographic and industrial base. With the 1929 acquisition of Sprague-Sells, a vegetable canning machinery company, the Bean company name was changed to the Food Machinery Corporation. That same year Food Machinery also acquired several fruit-handling machinery companies and began its foray into international markets—Australia, South Africa, and the Soviet Union.

The Depression years took their toll on sales. Particularly hard hit was the company's line of sprayers. Sales plummeted, wages were cut, and employees were furloughed. The hard times persisted until World War II. Nevertheless, in 1932 Food Machinery acquired the Peerless Pump Company, a manufacturer of deep-well turbines for irrigation, to help stabilize erratic sprayer sales and to diversify its pump line. It was a sound strategic move. Peerless Pump won a government bid to design and provide high-capacity pumps for an Arizona reclamation district. The project, completed in 1934, increased pump sales by more than 200 percent and Food Machinery was established as an industry leader.

The company's growth strategy—to identify and remedy weaknesses in existing businesses while opportunistically entering related new businesses—continued to shape its future over the coming decades. By 1940 Food Machinery was transformed into a diversified corporation supplying specialized machinery to satisfy nearly every need of the agricultural and food-processing industries.

World War II put Food Machinery on the front lines. The company entered the defense business developing and manufacturing a range of products and equipment including a series of amphibian vehicles for the Navy and Marine Corps. Its wartime output earned the company the coveted "E" award for outstanding production of war materiel. Food Machinery emerged from the war a stronger and more diversified venture.

Facing page, top left: FMC is taking a new, state-of-the-art biotech approach to its agricultural discovery efforts. The company is focusing on the genetic make-up of insects to identify target sites and develop pesticides to act on those sites.

Below: FMC FoodTech engineers have developed the largest oven in any USDA application—the GRYoCOMPACT oven that can cook more than 10,000 pounds per hour.

The postwar period began another series of acquisitions and introduction of new products, including a number for the food-processing industry. There was a push to expand Food Machinery's chemical business through acquisitions. With the purchase of Westvaco Chemical Corporation in 1948, the corporate name was changed to the Food Machinery and Chemical Company.

Food Machinery's commercial revenues topped $100 million for the first time in 1950; half were derived from chemicals. The 1950s saw a surge in defense business—the firm produced 730 armored infantry carriers for use in the Korean Conflict and by the end of the decade it was supplying high-energy rocket fuel to the U.S. Air Force and later to the space industry. This decade also saw another spate of acquisitions, this time into petroleum and oil field equipment, and expansion into overseas markets. Sales offices were opened in Europe, Mexico, Brazil, and Israel and operations were expanded in Australia, Japan, South Africa, and Canada. Revenues from overseas operations in 1957 were a record $30 million.

The company changed its name in the early 1960s from Food Machinery and Chemical Company to FMC Corporation and it was about to make its biggest acquisition to date. In 1963 it purchased American Viscose Corporation, a leading producer of cellulose fibers and films; this was seen as a natural fit with FMC's chemicals business. After a string of overall record earnings, in 1966 FMC revenues exceeded one billion dollars for the first time. *Forbes* called FMC a "supercompany."

The economic downturn of the 1970s put downward pressure on FMC earnings—reduced demand for textile fibers, plant overcapacity, strikes, excessive startup costs, even the core machinery business declined. New and aggressive direction was required to identify weaknesses and to set the company back on course.

Reorganization included development of management, raising capital expenditures, modernizing outdated facilities, increased research and development, and divesting unprofitable businesses. An early move was the relocation of FMC headquarters to Chicago. FMC's restructuring efforts bore fruit. Worldwide operations were streamlined. Revenues jumped to $2 billion in 1976. Investment in new technology increased significantly.

By the early 1980s FMC had built up substantial cash reserves. Its 1986 recapitalization plan via a public leveraged buyout helped it enhance shareholder value while also affording long-term strategic development. Today FMC operates nearly 100 plants and mines in 26 countries. It is organized into five divisions: energy systems, food and transportation systems, agricultural products, specialty chemicals, and industrial chemicals.

In another strategic move to optimize shareholder value and to maximize its growth potential, FMC is taking a bold step. It recently announced a restructuring plan, to be completed in late 2001, which will split FMC into two separate and independent companies—a machinery business and a chemicals business.

FMC chairman and chief executive officer Robert Burt puts this new move into perspective: "FMC has a long and proud history as a company able to reinvent itself to meet the needs of our customers and to provide value to our shareholders. This next step better focuses us on providing technology and providing solutions to customers that meet the needs of the marketplace." ∎

Above: FMC's facility in Bayport, Texas—the largest hydrogen peroxide facility in the world—incorporates new, low-cost technology that delivers greater operating and expansion efficiencies.

Below: FMC Energy Systems is a global leader in the design, manufacture, and supply of petroleum exploration, production, measurement, and transportation solutions. FMC production systems can be found within the Gulf of Mexico and North Sea, as well as off the coasts of West Africa and Brazil. FMC's transportation and measurement systems are found in all industrialized areas of the world.

In the United States and abroad, the products of Sara Lee Corporation can be found, not only in people's freezers, but in their dresser drawers and supply closets, too. From its famous *Sara Lee* cheesecake to *Hills Bros.* coffee, *Hanes* underwear, *L'eggs* hosiery, *Kiwi* shoe polish, and *Ambi Pur* combination air freshener and bowl cleaner, Sara Lee is in touch with consumers through innovative products they use virtually every day.

Chicago-based Sara Lee is a global manufacturer and marketer of high-quality, branded consumer packaged goods that have become household names around the world. Sara Lee's greatest strength is its skill at developing megabrands—representing products people everywhere know and trust.

Sara Lee builds these leadership brands in three areas: Food and Beverage, Intimates and Underwear, and Household Products. The company, which has annual revenues of approximately $20 billion, is known globally for its leading brands and market positions.

In fact, Sara Lee is the world's largest packaged meats company, with brands marketed in the United States, Mexico, and Europe; the number-one frozen baked goods company in the United States and Australia; and number three in roast and ground coffee worldwide.

Sara Lee's Intimates and Underwear business includes some of the most powerful brand names in the apparel industry. For example, of the top 10 brands in the U.S. intimate apparel marketplace, measured by consumer awareness, the Sara Lee portfolio is represented by *Playtex* (#1), *Wonderbra* (#3), *Hanes Her Way* (#4), *Just My Size* (#5), and *Bali* (#6).

The corporation's Household Products business markets branded packaged goods in more than 180 countries. Sara Lee is the world's number-one shoe care marketer, the leading company in the $5-billion European bath and shower market, and one of the world's most prominent producers of branded air fresheners and insecticides.

Focused on serving consumer needs, Sara Lee offers innovative new products in all of its markets. For example, because consumers today often prefer convenience foods that can be eaten on the go, Sara Lee created *Cheesecake Bites*. This line of indulgent bite-size snack cakes, which can be eaten right out of the freezer, revolutionized the frozen retail bakery business.

Product development in Sara Lee's Food and Beverage business focuses on offering products that are great tasting and easy to prepare to meet the needs of busy consumers who want convenience without sacrificing taste.

to communicate its consumer marketing orientation, as well as its commitment to high-quality, brand-name products. C. Steven McMillan was named chairman, president, and chief executive officer of the corporation in 2001.

Commitment to the community has forged a strong relationship between Sara Lee and Chicago. The Sara Lee Foundation, the philanthropic arm of the company, recently marked its 20th anniversary. Always actively seeking to serve the communities in which it operates, Sara Lee annually donates at least 2 percent of its U.S. pretax income in cash contributions and product donations to the nonprofit sector.

The company directs its grants in three areas: arts and culture, women's issues, and the needs of people who are living in disadvantaged circumstances.

Sara Lee supports many arts organizations, including the Goodman Theatre, the Joffrey Ballet, and The Art Institute of Chicago. Furthermore, from 1999 through 2001, Sara Lee dispersed 52 works from its renowned art collection to 40 museums around the world through an unprecedented Millennium Gift.

The vast majority of the company's consumers are women, and in fiscal 2000, 43 percent of the Foundation's funding of social service programs was directed to those committed to issues affecting women and girls.

Sara Lee also has been a longtime supporter of America's Second Harvest, the largest domestic hunger relief organization, which serves 26 million Americans each year, eight million of them children.

Sara Lee, a strong presence in Chicago for more than half a century, is committed to the community and its consumers. From this base, it has become a global leader in consumer packaged goods, serving both developed and developing markets around the world. ■

Responding to the increasing demand for more comfortable intimate apparel, Sara Lee developed *Barelythere* seamless bras and panties that have redefined the standards for product design in the intimate apparel category.

And when consumers wanted skin care that offered the right combination of moisture, nutrition, and protection, the company released its new *Sanex Facial Care* line.

Headquartered in Chicago, Sara Lee today has operations in 58 countries and employs approximately 166,500 people. But it began modestly in 1939, when Canadian Nathan Cummings acquired the C.D. Kenny Company. The firm was a small, Baltimore-based distributor of wholesale sugar, coffee, and tea, which Cummings moved to Chicago in 1942.

The company expanded rapidly, and by 1975, when recently retired chairman John H. Bryan was named CEO, it was earning nearly two-thirds of its profits from non-food businesses. The board of directors renamed the company Sara Lee Corporation in 1985

Three years before the World's Columbian Exposition opened in Chicago in 1893, a young Scotsman, with the aid of a horse and wagon, laid the foundation for what would become a thriving metals-distribution business. Today his company is the largest distributor of a wide range of highly engineered grades and alloys of metals in North America. It is also an industry leader in integrated supply and materials management.

Alfred M. Castle was a 24-year-old metals salesman in the 1880s. This was an auspicious time for metalworkers and building tradesmen in Chicago, which was still undergoing an extraordinary architectural metamorphosis in the wake of the

The original location of A. M. Castle & Co. and its dray horse wagon used to deliver iron and steel in the 1890s and early 1900s.

Fire of 1871. Alfred worked for a local iron and steel merchant where he developed valuable relationships with East Coast producers and shippers of steel. He soon recognized a need in the marketplace—some blacksmiths and wheelwrights were too small to buy directly from foundries hundreds of miles away. Their supply problems provided an opportunity to develop a niche market and Castle grabbed it. He left his job in 1890, rented quarters near the railroad docks, and began his rounds to collect and

deliver orders to small shops scattered throughout Chicago's downtown.

By 1900 Castle had an inventory of $50,000, offices in the Monadnock Building, and warehouse space. The company was earning a solid reputation and substantial accounts. Its fortunes were further improved in 1901 when William Simpson, a fellow Scotsman known as a "master steel salesman," joined the firm and invested $8,000. Three years later inventory was damaged in a fire. Castle's suppliers helped rebuild inventory and its customers exercised patience—a testimony to Castle's reputation for reliability and integrity. That same year, 1904, A. M. Castle & Co. incorporated with an initial capitalization of $100,000 and purchased its own building.

When Alfred Castle died in 1908, Simpson became company president. Offices and warehouse were moved to Castle-owned land on Goose Island in 1913, which served as headquarters for the next 44 years. Castle became a publicly traded company in 1928 with a capitalization of $3 million. Nevertheless, the firm remained a closely held one. Simpson kept the business on a conservative track even during boom times. It was a sound strategy. The company survived the 1929 stock market crash in an enviable position—no long-term debt, no outstanding bonds or stocks, large cash reserves, and land ownership. This conservative approach assured ongoing prosperity.

Over the next few decades the company expanded its business and holdings. The post-World War II boom and a growing appetite for home appliances drove the demand for more sophisticated manufacturing materials. Castle added new stainless steels, enameling sheets, and galvanized products to its older lines of structural shapes and bars. Gibb Steel, a major warehouser purchased in 1946, was an example of Castle's expansion strategy to acquire product sources in an era of scarce supplies. The strategy paid off. In both 1947 and 1948, net

Castle's landmark logo and one of the company's readily recognizable orange trucks.

earnings were $1.4 million.

In order to meet stiff competition, the company had to be the best-equipped and -supplied operation possible if it was to live up to its slogan, "Everything in Steel." It achieved that not merely by high-volume production, but by technological innovation, fine precision work, and streamlined services. Castle warehouses—renamed service centers—were kept busy servicing new industries.

There were 11 service centers in the Castle network by 1953. Meanwhile, the company was outgrowing its Goose Island quarters. In 1957 a 500,000-square-foot plant was built in Franklin Park, close to what is now O'Hare International Airport. This facility continues to serve as Castle's corporate headquarters, as well as its flagship distribution center.

In 1965 Castle made its largest acquisition to date. Pacific Metals, a West Coast distributor of nickel alloys and aerospace grades of stainless steel and aluminum, provided Castle with its first major access to the high-tech metals markets, which today constitutes 40 percent of the company's total sales. Fifteen years later, with ongoing acquisition and diversifying product lines, management set a new course that transformed the business into a distributor of specialty metals.

Starting in the late 1980s and continuing through the mid-1990s Castle embarked on a series of internal investments, acquisitions, and joint ventures designed to enhance its preeminent U.S. market position in the distribution of highly engineered materials and to expand its geographic reach. This resulted in new locations in Canada and England as well as a joint venture in Mexico. Other initiatives to further strengthen key products were the establishing of H-A Industries, a state-of-the-art bar processing facility in Hammond, Indiana; and the acquisition of Oliver Steel Plate Co. in Cleveland. Expansion into new products was also a priority during this period, as witnessed by the acquisition of Keystone Tube Co. in Riverdale, Illinois, and Total Plastics, Inc., a Michigan-based distributor of industrial plastics. Finally, Castle entered into three joint ventures designed to develop new channels to market. These included Kreher Steel Company, a bulk distributor based in Melrose Park, Illinois; Energy Alloys, an oil field equipment specialist in Houston, Texas; and Metal Express, a small-order specialist that has grown to 24 locations around the country in just three years.

Castle's reputation for leading-edge product innovation and processing technologies, and its long-held expertise in procurement efficiency and cost reduction, distinguish the company from other metals service centers. Not only is Castle a market leader in providing core metals products to major industrial manufacturers and thousand of smaller customers, it is the supplier of choice in its national and overseas markets.

With 1,800 employees and more than 40 locations, Castle has annual sales approaching three quarters of a billion dollars. Its tradition of building lasting value for both customers and shareholders is symbolized by the company's distinctive twin-towered Castle Metals logo. ■

The firm has built the world's most advanced capabilities for the machining of carbon, alloy, and stainless bars.

The story of the 86-year-old Boeing Company is intimately connected to that of aviation worldwide. From early pioneer in the age of flight through decades of achievements in air and space transport and communications, the firm today is the world's leading aerospace company and the country's largest exporter.

William Boeing, a shipbuilder and timber magnate, founded the business in 1916. The B&W—a two-person seaplane made of wood, wire, and linen built in

The Boeing world headquarters building is the newest addition to Chicago's prominent skyline.

1916—was the first in a long line of innovative products that would move the company from aviation pioneer to leading aircraft manufacturer.

Over the decades Boeing's innovative engineering earned it many development firsts, including the transoceanic mammoth 314 flying boat in 1939, large bomber aircraft for use in World War II, the pressurized airplane cabin, the jetliner (the four-engine 707) in 1958, and the world's first jet jumbo jet (the 747) in 1969. It is continuing to work on ever-more high-capacity aircraft.

In an effort to diversify after the war, Boeing built the world's first gas-turbine-powered truck in 1950. To further that strategy of diversification, the company

became an early contributor to the space age. It developed the first supersonic missile (Bomarc), which was launched from Cape Canaveral in 1952, began work on the Lunar Orbiter spaceship in 1963, built the first Lunar Roving Vehicle that landed on the moon in 1971, and for the past decade has been building the orbiting International Space Station.

The Boeing penchant for technical excellence and innovation has allowed it to continuously expand its product line. With the acquisition of McDonnell Douglas and North American Rockwell's aerospace and defense units in the late 1990s, Boeing is the largest manufacturer of satellites, commercial jetliners, and military aircraft, and is a global market leader in missile defense, human space flight, and launch services.

With ongoing growth and diversification came the need to be more centrally located to all operating units, customers, and the financial community. A strategic decision was made: separate headquarters from Boeing's major business units in Seattle. This was an integral element of Boeing's business strategy to further transform the company into a broad-based global corporation in order to continue to focus on long-term growth and value creation.

Boeing chose Chicago for its head offices because it is a culturally diverse city that offers ready access to global markets, provides a strong pro-business environment, and allows easy access to major Boeing operations and customers worldwide. The move was completed in September 2001. According to an accounting firm study, Boeing's move to Chicago will provide Illinois with a $4.5-billion economic benefit over the next 20 years.

With revenues of $58 billion, Boeing's global reach includes customers in 145 countries, over 179,000 employees in more than 60 countries, and operations in 26 states—quite an achievement for an aerospace giant that was built from a two-seater seaplane made of wood, wire, and linen. ■

CATERPILLAR INC.

For more than 75 years Caterpillar Inc. has been building the world's infrastructure and, in partnership with Cat dealers, is driving positive and sustainable change on every continent. Caterpillar is the world's leading manufacturer of construction and mining equipment, diesel and natural gas engines, and industrial gas turbines. The company is a technology leader in construction, transportation, mining, forestry, energy, logistics, financing, and electric power generation. Continued diversification, flexibility, and global reach are crucial elements of the company's strategy.

Since its beginnings Caterpillar has brought innovation to product development, the best quality to manufacturing, cost-effective solutions, and customer service to help the company remain an industry leader.

Two early pioneers in developing combine harvesters and tractors moved to California in the 1880s, an era of tremendous transformation in farming brought about by the invention of the combine harvester. Midwesterner Daniel Best and New Englander Benjamin Holt were both intimately involved in its early development. Each formed a company to develop and produce his own combine. Both experimented with track-type, steam-powered, and gas-powered tractors. Holt developed the first successful tracks to replace wheels; this track-type machine was trademarked Caterpillar.

In April 1925 the C.L. Best Tractor Co. and the Holt Manufacturing Co. merged to become Caterpillar Tractor Co. The headquarters was located in Peoria, Illinois, thus earning the city fame as the "earthmoving capital of the world."

Caterpillar has always been committed to continual quality improvement. To meet that goal, the company made a tremendous investment of resources in its quest for ultimate levels of quality, reliability, and cost-reduction. It adopted the 6 Sigma philosophy company-wide in January 2001. This means that all employees and dealers pursue a relentless quest for perfection through the disciplined use of data-based, fact-driven decision-making methodology. It is key to the firm's business strategy of growth through cost reduction and quality improvement.

Another aspect of Caterpillar's overall business strategy is its total commitment to sustainable development. It consistently meets or exceeds environmental regulations, develops solutions to environmental challenges, advocates free trade, and leads the business community on important policy issues. One example of technology leadership is ACERT®—Advanced Combustion Emissions Reduction Technology. When it reaches the marketplace in the fall of 2003, it will dramatically reduce engine emissions without sacrificing the reliability and durability that are Caterpillar hallmarks.

Other innovative, state-of-the-art technology is incorporated in Caterpillar prod-

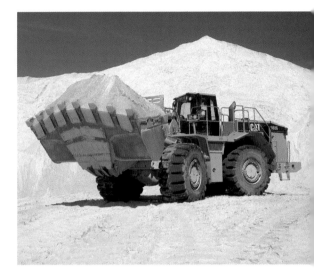

ucts. Diagnostic, prognostic, and satellite-based navigation systems are among recent innovations developed by Caterpillar people. Astonishingly, nearly 3,000 patents have been earned by Caterpillar employees since 1996.

Caterpillar, a *Fortune* 100 company, is the world's largest manufacturer of construction and mining equipment, diesel and natural gas engines, and industrial gas turbines. It also offers customers affordable financing and leasing options and provides them with integrated logistics solutions such as warehousing and distribution. In 2001 sales and revenues approached $20.5 billion. ∎

Above: Caterpillar builds a wide variety of products — including wheel loaders, track-type tractors, excavators, off highway trucks, articulated trucks, and integrated toolcarriers — to help customers turn their ideas into realities.

Middle: Caterpillar manufactures a complete line of wheel loaders, including the Cat 988G.

Top: Benjamin Holt merged his company, Holt Manufacturing Co., with the C.L. Best Tractor Co. to found Caterpillar in 1925.

CHAPTER EIGHT

Business and Finance

*B*usiness and financial institutions, accounting firms, and computer technology combine to put some impressive numbers on Illinois' ledgers.

Heller Financial, Inc. **262-263**

Bank One, N.A. **264-265**

Carr Futures **266-267**

CNA Financial Corporation **268**

Safeway Insurance Group **269**

Left: © 2000 Alan Klehr/Stone

On the old Main Street, products and services were not as exotic as they are today, but they were vital to American industrial growth. For example, World War I clearly demonstrated that it was practical to move large-scale motorized traffic—and therefore goods—by road.

In 1919 Walter Heller, who had tried and rejected a career in his family's sausage-casing factory, established W.E. Heller and Company in the heart of Chicago's financial district to finance auto-

mobiles and trucks. He founded his company with a $100,000 loan from his father, whom he had no doubt convinced that automobiles would drive forward America's heavy industry.

"Mr. Heller," as he was always called, branched out into financing taxicabs, home-improvement companies, and installment notes for business and commercial account receivables. From the beginning, Heller always did asset-based lending—loans backed by account receivables or other collateral.

During the Great Depression Heller sold its auto-financing business and diversified by lending to a wider variety of businesses—manufacturers of oil burners, radios, and commercial refrigerators. In 1932 the company launched the first factoring business in the Midwest. Heller factoring provided a kind of bridge loan to ease cash flow for furniture, lumber, shoe, textiles, and toy companies. In the 1950s

Heller diversified further by financing movie and television productions. Among the films it backed were *The African Queen, High Noon*, and *Never on Sunday*, and the original "Lassie" television series.

In 1956 the company went public. The next few years saw tremendous growth. Offices were opened around the country, overseas expansion began, new businesses were acquired, and there was a move into selling commercial paper and joint-venture participation.

During the 1970s, a period of higher interest rates, Heller considered more creative financing options; providing leveraged leases to airlines was one of these. But problems began to emerge, as competition from banks, business sectors, and a few costly mistakes put the business in jeopardy.

In 1982 Moody's and Standard & Poor's downgraded Heller's credit rating. Fortunately, The Fuji Bank Limited, one of the world's largest banks, purchased Heller in 1984, infusing cash into the business and putting a new management team in place. Heller Financial's traditional emphasis on diversity of product lines and services to protect it against volatility in the marketplace was reinforced. Its long-held commitment to small and medium-size businesses continued.

Today Heller Financial's approach to diversification is illustrated by its range of financial services: equipment and leasing, sales, collateral and cash flow, health care, and commercial real estate.

Even though Heller Financial works with high growth and higher leverage it is also very careful when it comes to credit and risk. It continues its diversification strategy to ensure that it is in the right place, and that it is not too exposed in any specific area—for example, it is no longer in the domestic factoring business. The company's overall strategy proved effective during the recent volatility on Wall Street in which Heller performed more strongly than did most of its competitors. In fact, the business has experienced record profits for the past eight years.

Right: Walter E. Heller during an interview with *Business Week* magazine, October 1958.

Below: Heller Financial headquarters in the heart of Chicago's financial district.

The celebration of Heller Financial's return to the New York Stock Exchange with an IPO that generated more than one billion dollars, May 1998.

The Heller approach produced another tremendous result. Heller Financial returned to the New York Stock Exchange in 1998 with the largest IPO in two years, generating one billion dollars for growth and expansion.

Despite its successes, Heller has not lost its straightforward midwestern values. As Richard J. Almeida, chairman and chief executive officer, has said: "The ability to be at home on both Main Street and Wall Street is one of Heller Financial's key competitive strengths. We've built our business serving small to mid-size Main Street companies, the backbone of the world's economies. Our employees embody Main Street values of hard work and a no-nonsense, roll-up-the-sleeves attitude. Yet we apply sophisticated financing expertise and use Wall Street's capital markets in the service of our clients everyday."

Heller Financial is also a good citizen. The success of its community services efforts is clearly demonstrated by one of its community programs that focuses on education in the inner city. Heller employees pledged 2,400 volunteer tutoring hours to the program in the year 2000.

Heller has earned a strong reputation in the financial marketplace despite its relatively small size—$19 billion in assets and 1,600 employees worldwide. This gives the organization a nimble edge. Heller's business strategy is summed up in its motto: "Straight talk. Smart deals." ■

Heller Financial
Straight talk. Smart deals. ℠

An earlier site of The First National Bank of Chicago's headquarters in downtown Chicago.

he story of Bank One, N.A. (a subsidiary of Bank One Corporation), is intimately tied to that of the life of Chicago. The story began in 1863, with the founding of The First National Bank of Chicago.

At the height of the Civil War, President Abraham Lincoln signed a bill to permit "national banks" to operate along with the more familiar state-chartered banks. This legislation provided an opportunity for a group of Chicago entrepreneurs led by banker Edmund Aiken. They raised $100,000, established The First National Bank of Chicago, and began operations in Aiken's office on Chicago's La Salle Street. The bank opened for business on July 1, 1863, the first day of the

President William McKinley's Cabinet.

First National quickly reoccupied its damaged headquarters and backed many Chicago businesses in the effort to rebuild the city. In 1882 the bank began declaring quarterly dividends, opened a women's banking department, and moved to a new building at Dearborn and Monroe streets. A year later the interiors were lighted by electricity.

The turn of the century brought with it a rapidly expanding economy and an unprecedented demand for credit. First National met this challenge by acquiring two Chicago banks and organizing the First Trust and Savings Bank in 1903. By the end of 1904 First Trust had more than

Right: The entrance to Bank One Plaza in Chicago.

Below: James Dimon, chairman and chief executive officer, Bank One Corporation.

Battle of Gettysburg.

Five years later, flush with success, First National completed its own building of iron, stone, and brick. However, the supposedly fireproof structure was soon to be tested by the Chicago Fire of 1871. Though the building was severely damaged, the bank's safes and vaults withstood the heat, and their contents survived intact. The young cashier—Lyman Gage—who discovered that the bank's cash and papers were safe would later become the bank's president and eventually secretary of the treasury in

10,000 depositors with balances totaling nearly $18 million. Growth was steady until the late 1920s, when the industry witnessed a steady stream of large withdrawals, particularly for the purchase of equities as the public began to speculate in stock issues with soaring market values.

Suddenly, the stock market crashed. During the Great Depression that followed, more than 11,000 U.S. banks failed. Yet First National continued to pay interest on savings deposits and to absorb the business of other banks. In 1938 the bank's assets reached one billion dollars.

They doubled within the next six years.

The bank's aggressive program to meet expanding credit needs gained momentum. Throughout the 1950s and 1960s First National undertook a program of overseas expansion and was the first U.S. bank to open a representative office in China. The year it moved into its new 60-story quarters, 1969, it formed a bank holding company—First Chicago Corporation. During the ensuing decade First National's assets nearly quadrupled. Also in the 1970s, the bank added regional offices and established new retail facilities to serve its customers' expanding needs.

First Chicago continued to make acquisitions throughout the 1970s and 1980s. However, by 1985 signs of problems with Third World lending began to emerge, resulting in losses. The bank's earnings suffered again in the early 1990s during the severe slump in real estate markets. Yet before long, the bank recovered under new leadership, and acquisitions continued apace. First Chicago merged with NBD Bancorp in July 1995. (NBD Bancorp had been established in 1933 as the National Bank of Detroit.) That union created First Chicago NBD, the seventh-largest bank holding company in the country.

Indeed, the 1990s saw active consolidation within the U.S. banking industry. Since mid-1997 the pace of mega-mergers among financial institutions has accelerated—notably among the banking giants. First Chicago NBD was no exception. In April 1998 First Chicago NBD merged with Banc One Corporation.

Banc One's roots went back to 1868, with the founding of Sessions & Company—later known as the City National Bank & Trust Company—in Columbus, Ohio. The company began operating as a bank holding company, First Banc Group of Ohio, in 1968. In the mid-1980s, then known as BANC ONE CORPORATION, it embarked on a series of acquisitions that expanded its reach throughout the country.

Today Bank One Corporation is the

fifth-largest U.S. bank, with assets exceeding $270 billion. In addition to offering a full range of financial services to consumers and to commercial and business customers, it is the largest issuer of Visa cards, the third-largest bank lender to small businesses, and one of the top 25 managers of mutual funds.

What's more, its economic impact on the 14 states in which it has retail is significant. In Illinois alone, Bank One employs nearly 17,000 people, serves more than 1.2 million retail households, and offers access to more than 1,000 ATMs and 200 banking centers. In addition, Bank One makes more than $8.5 billion in Community Reinvestment Act small-business, home, consumer, and community-development loans. Thousands of its employees—who collectively return $29 million in withholding taxes to Illinois' coffers—volunteer countless hours and make other substantial contributions to a host of community initiatives.

After the merger with First Chicago NBD, Banc One Corporation moved its headquarters to Chicago and began spelling "Bank" with a "k." With these changes came the retirement of the First Chicago name, which served as a symbol of Illinois banking for nearly 140 years.

In 2001, under new leadership, Bank One brings a new energy to its operations and a renewed commitment to offering exceptional customer service. It's likewise committed to serving customers consistently well, developing a meritocracy system for employees, using technology to improve services and money management, and achieving strong shareholder returns.

With its history stretching nearly a century and a half, Bank One remains as dedicated as ever to helping customers achieve their financial dreams. ■

The 60-story Bank One Corporation headquarters building soars above Chicago's Loop.

"The first futures and stock options exchanges were founded in Chicago and continue to operate here," states Didier Varlet, Carr Futures' chairman and chief executive officer. "This city plays an important role in the global marketplace, and it has played an important role in our corporate development."

Carr Futures is a subsidiary of Crédit Agricole Indosuez, which is wholly owned by Caisse Nationale de Crédit Agricole, one of the world's 10 largest banking institutions. Founded in 1987, the firm provides institutional customers with access to nearly all of the world's major futures, options, securities, and over-the-counter (OTC) markets. It is consistently among the leaders in customer volume on several of the world's exchanges, with a strong presence on three continents and offices in nine major financial centers.

Carr Futures' early ties to Chicago and the futures markets allowed the company to develop its present position as a global brokerage firm. But, it was the strategic acquisition of Dean Witter's institutional futures business in 1997 that enabled the group to extend its business beyond its traditional focus of financial futures. The result was increased market share and a more established global presence in the industry for Carr Futures.

Through the acquisition, Carr Futures added energy, metals, and soft commodities, as well as foreign exchange and OTC derivatives to its product line. While it remained committed to its existing customer base, Carr Futures used the acquisition to attract business from other domestic and international customers, and as a result earned a fifth-place ranking in the global futures marketplace. The following year, in a move to further enhance customer services, Carr Futures organized teams of brokerage professionals in multiple locations worldwide. The goal was to provide all clients with efficient access to the markets while keeping the central back-office in Chicago, ensuring fast and accurate transactions.

"Excellence in today's market environment requires a professional, knowledgeable staff," Varlet states. "We stake our reputation on providing the highest-quality service, and by selecting Carr Futures, our customers are assured that their financial transactions will be handled efficiently and effectively."

Carr Futures at a Glance

Carr Futures provides trade-execution and global-clearing services to 1,400 large institutions worldwide. Its staff of nearly 800 people is committed to the highest professional standards. In addition to its headquarters in Chicago, Carr Futures has brokerage offices in Frankfurt, Hong Kong, London, Madrid, New York, Paris, Singapore, and Tokyo.

With a long-standing presence in the brokerage business, Carr Futures also benefits from the backing of an AA rated* parent company (Crédit Agricole Indosuez). Recognized worldwide for its expertise and its strong commitment to high-quality service, Carr Futures' innovative technology and experienced staff have added to its unmatched reputation for meeting the special needs of institutional clients.

*As rated by Standard and Poors

Local Roots, Global Outlook

Chicago has proven incredibly beneficial to Carr Futures and its operations. For example, with all back-office processing centralized in Chicago, the sales force can take advantage of the fact that Chicago is situated in the last time zone of the global trading day. In addition, from its trading desks at the Chicago Board of Trade and at Chicago Mercantile Exchange Inc., Carr Futures can provide up-to-the-minute market surveillance and live market coverage of key products over the Internet. Indeed, the Internet is proving to be an innovative tool for both Carr Futures and its clients.

Electronic brokering and use of the Internet have changed the ways in which both futures trading and options trading are conducted around the world. Carr Futures has been able to maintain its position as a leader in global brokerage by embracing technology and researching innovative methods of customer-service management. As a result, Carr Futures has developed tools with which clients can electronically enter, transmit, and manage trades.

With CARR ONLINE, Carr Futures has developed a trade execution system that provides its clients with real-time, direct access to all major capital markets in a fast, reliable, and secure trading environment. Built-in risk-management controls greatly limit the chance of trading errors. The system also is flexible so that it can grow or change given a client's business needs.

On the clearing side of operations, Carr Futures also has developed a suite of Internet-based services to meet the specific needs of institutional customers.

Mission Statement

Carr Futures is dedicated to providing its institutional customers with efficient access to financial and commodities markets around the world. We deliver quality products and services in the field of risk transfer mechanisms, financing, and investment techniques to our customers. Carr Futures' teams maintain the highest professional standards and integrity in their relationships with customers. We are always mindful of the long-term perspective to ensure our ability to meet the needs of our customers, employees, and shareholders.

Through RTA-*net*, clearing customers can download account statements, confirm trades, review real-time positions, and perform many other back-office functions.

In addition, Carr Futures' Web site offers educational and analytical support, as well as some of the industry's highest-quality research.

Yet, despite all the electronic advancements that have made it easier to conduct business in other parts of the world, Carr Futures still has a very real physical and emotional tie to Chicago. "It's our home," Varlet says. "Chicago has a spirit unlike that of other cities, and we're proud to be a part of it." ■

The CNA Insurance Companies are headquartered in downtown Chicago. Employees like to refer to CNA Plaza as "Big Red."

Below and right: The CNA Foundation has been a national sponsor of the KaBOOM! LET US PLAY campaign since 1998, when it committed to fund and build playgrounds across the country where CNA has a business presence. At the end of 2000, CNA had built 40 playgrounds for children in underprivileged areas.

With assets of more than $62 billion,* CNA** is the second-largest commercial insurance writer in the United States. CNA offers a wide range of property/casualty and life products and insurance-related services that are marketed through independent retail and general agents, major brokerages, and managing general underwriters.

Long an icon in Chicago's business world, the company dates to 1897 when a group of Detroit's leading citizens formed the Continental Assurance Company of North America (CAC) to provide health and accident insurance. In 1900 CAC merged with Chicago's Metropolitan Accident Company and relocated to Chicago. The combined enterprise, the Continental Casualty Company of Chicago, included four insurance departments: railroad, factory, industrial, and health.

Premium income grew from $225,000 in 1901 to $13 million in 1928 due to expansion into other lines of insurance. CNA's history of innovation remains part of its business philosophy even today. For example, Continental Casualty was the first insurance company to mail renewal notices to policyholders, one of the first to insure women, and it helped to pioneer retirement annuities for seniors. In 1911 Continental Casualty formed a separate company, the Continental Assurance Company, through which it offered life insurance.

Over the next several decades

Continental Casualty pursued acquisitions, chartered insurance subsidiaries, and continued to expand its product lines. With the 1956 purchase of the National Fire Insurance Company of Hartford, Continental changed its name to the CN Group. In 1963 it purchased the American Casualty Company of Reading and changed its name to Continental National American, later shortened to CNA. The $1.1-billion acquisition of the Continental Insurance Company in 1995 allowed CNA to complement existing lines of business and enter new markets as well.

As CNA enters its second century of doing business in the insurance industry, the company is strategically poised to manage risks that face businesses today and in the future. Its vision is to be the premier provider of insurance and insurance-related services to commercial customers across the globe. CNA customers range from small businesses to *Fortune* 500 companies. CNA's ongoing commitment to

its shareholders, business partners, and customers is to remain financially strong and stable, which is part of its 100-year-old legacy.

CNA is headquartered in Chicago and has field offices across the United States and in many international locations. It employs approximately 18,000 employees worldwide. ∎

*as of December 31, 2000
**CNA is a registered service mark, trade name, and domain name of CNA Financial Corporation authorized for use by its affiliates.

A prestigious business publication describes the Safeway Insurance Group, headquartered near Chicago, as a company that provides protection "for things that go bump" in the night ... and day. Doing that well has earned the family-owned Safeway Insurance Group an "Excellent" rating from the country's leading independent insurance industry analyst, the A.M. Best Company.

William J. Parrillo, Sr., chairman of the board, founded the firm in 1962. A former auto insurance company executive, Parrillo believed there was need for better automobile coverage and more efficient ways of providing it. To test his hypothesis, he founded a small auto insurance company in 1959. He then established Safeway Insurance and added property and casualty insurance to its product line. Now, four decades later, the company has grown to a network of regional insurers operating primarily in the southern, southeastern, and western United States. It operates seven companies with 10 offices in nine states, maintains licenses to operate in 18 states, serves nearly 210,000 policy holders, and has sales approaching $300 million.

The offices of the subsidiary companies span the south and southeastern United States—Alabama, Florida, Georgia, Louisiana, Mississippi, and Texas. With offices in Arizona and California, Safeway is well on its way to expanding its presence on the West Coast. However, its growth strategy is not one of expansion for its own sake. One of the group's hallmarks is to grow its businesses organically rather than through mergers, takeovers, and acquisitions.

Safeway Insurance Group is committed to growing each of its insurance markets in the local communities that it serves. Its mission is to provide affordable insurance coverage and to service it in the promptest manner possible. This is how the group has earned its reputation for ease of doing business: competitive premium rates, quick handling of claims, and

efficient customer service.

Safeway Insurance Group, with corporate headquarters in Westmont, Illinois, continues to provide property and casualty insurance and to specialize in nonstandard automobile insurance. The company continues to be headed by William Parrillo, Sr., but now his son, William Jr., is a member of his corporate executive staff.

The firm's reputation for excellence is not its only achievement. Safeway Insurance Group has earned the ranking as the largest privately held automobile insurance company in the country. ■

Safeway Insurance Group's executive staff (from left to right): Michael Mulligan, vice president and corporate counsel; William J. Parrillo, chairman, president, and founder; William G. Parrillo, vice president; and Robert Bordeman, chief executive officer.

The firm's corporate headquarters is located in Westmont, Illinois.

CHAPTER NINE

Networks and Professions

An integral part of the state's infrastructure, the communications, transportation, and professional communities provide a wealth of vital services, expertise, and insight.

Graycor **272-273**

International Profit
Associates, Inc. **274-275**

Suburban Chicago
Newspapers **276-277**

Accenture **278**

Chicago Defender **279**

Daniel J. Edelman, Inc. **280**

Jordan Industries, Inc. **281**

Amtrak **282-283**

Left: © Michael Brinson/Index Stock Imagery

Melvin Gray, chairman and chief executive officer of Graycor.

Ford Motor Company's Chicago Assembly Plant.
Photo © Johns Bryne Photography

The nearly 80-year-old Graycor has grown strong on a diet of hard jobs. Over the decades it has evolved from providing concrete-blasting services to its current leadership position in the construction industry: It is on a number of lists of top U.S. contractors and design-build firms. Today the company has 1,500 employees, its 1999 revenues reached $325 million, and it remains a family-owned and -operated enterprise.

Edward Gray founded the Chicago Concrete Breaking Company (CCBC) in 1921. He brought to Chicago more than a decade of experience as head of Gray Brothers Cleaning Company in St. Louis, Missouri. Gray Brothers was founded in 1910 to clean building exteriors and windows; it soon expanded to include sandblasting with pneumatic tools. But Chicago provided better opportunities for growth—and more hard jobs.

Five years after its founding, the Chicago Concrete Breaking Company received a large contract to remove a retaining wall along the Illinois Central Railroad tracks in Chicago's Grant Park. The job was completed on time and without any interruption of train traffic. This impressive achievement earned CCBC national recognition and its slogan: "Wanted—a hard job." During the 1930s CCBC expanded into servicing the steel

industry when it pioneered the use of dynamite to remove salamanders from blast furnaces; it would later develop new machines to speed up steel extraction and, years later, a remote-controlled furnace-cleaning machine. Another highlight of the decade was demolishing the 628-foot Sky Ride Tower at the closing of the Chicago World's Fair in 1934.

In 1951 CCBC established offices and shop facilities in South Chicago, closer to its steelmaking customers, and added construction of industrial and commercial facilities to its list of services. In 1954 the company was organized under the name The Edward Gray Corporation. After the death of Edward Gray in 1962, the company expanded further and began offering full-scale industrial services. In 1971 Melvin Gray, Edward Gray's son, took control of the company. The Edward Gray Corporation's growth continued throughout the 1970s. Multimillion-dollar projects included construction of a railroad tank car-manufacturing plant and nuclear fuel-recovery facilities for several major power-generating plants.

By the end of the 1970s, the company had evolved into a full-scale construction and industrial services organization, initiated state-of-the-art computerized cost-control and planning systems, and successfully completed construction projects throughout the United States. It established long-term relationships with many customers in the steelmaking and automotive industries by adhering to the philosophy that fostering client relations by effectively meeting their needs is one of the most valuable assets a business can earn.

The Edward Gray Corporation acquired Inland Construction Company, a large commercial construction firm, in 1982. With the addition of Inland and the growth of its other businesses, Gray was organized as a holding company, Graycor, in 1984. Inland's commission to build the 65-story mixed retail and residential complex at 900 North Michigan on Chicago's

Magnificent Mile illustrates Graycor's growing leadership in the construction industry. Other milestone construction projects include Chicago's Water Tower Place, Steppenwolf Theatre, and the 333 Wacker Drive building. The company's work ranges from heavy industrial to manufacturing to commercial, and includes clients such as BP Amoco, Circuit City, ComEd, Ford Motor Company, LTV Steel, and U.S. Steel.

In 1992 Graycor relocated its headquarters to south suburban Homewood, Illinois. It was now firmly established as one of the country's largest general contractors. Graycor organized its diversified construction services into four operating units: Graycor Industrial Constructors Inc. to serve the general industrial, power, and metal markets; Graycor Construction Company Inc. to handle commercial, retail, and institutional markets; Graycor Blasting Company Inc. to provide demolition and specialty blasting services; and Graycor International Inc. to service clients in Canada and Mexico. During the company's celebrations to mark its 75th anniversary in July 1996, the four divisions were brought under one banner and name—Graycor.

Graycor's leadership in technology and networking provides a competitive edge in the industry. All work sites are linked to headquarters, allowing Graycor to maintain excellent communications and exceptional control, often meeting rigorous schedule and cost commitments. To achieve this goal, the corporation self-performs much of the trade work including concrete, carpentry, equipment installation, refractory, boiler work, steel erection, demolition, and specialty blasting. Graycor's commitment to quality has earned it ISO 9000 registration, which means it has been recognized by the International Organization for Standardization for its compliance to ISO 9000 criteria and for its commitment to continuous improvement. The company also earned Ford Motor Company's coveted Q1 Quality Award. Another priority is work-site safety. Clients, employees, and subcontractors are assured that their well-being is guaranteed. Graycor instituted a Zero Injuries Program that is now an industry standard—quite an accomplishment for a company that directly employs 2.5 million hours of craft every year.

The evolution of Graycor from the original concrete-breaking company is, and continues to be, based on its early tenet. Melvin Gray, chairman and CEO, underscored that underlying philosophy when he said: "Our business growth reflects the rock-solid belief that hard jobs make us stronger." ∎

Above: LTV Steel Company's H-4 blast furnace, East Chicago. Courtesy, LTV Steel Company Inc.

Top: 333 Wacker Drive, Chicago.
Photo © Hedrich Blessing, Ltd.

Ten years ago Chicago entrepreneur and former lawyer and trader John Burgess founded a company to help other entrepreneurs and their small businesses to achieve optimal profits through more efficient management and operational procedures. Today his company, the $140-million International Profit Associates (IPA) and its affiliate, Integrated Business Analysts (IBA), are among the leading management-consulting firms in North America.

It was a hardscrabble beginning in pure entrepreneurial style; yet, first year sales in 1991 reached $335,000. It was an auspicious start. Between 1992 and 1996 sales grew by an extraordinary 7,200 percent. IPA's fast-track success earned it an unusual accolade in 1996 and 1997 from *Inc.* magazine: For two years running it was ranked among the top 10 fastest-growing companies in the United States.

IPA and its affiliates provide consulting services and guidance to small and mid-size businesses. According to its founder and managing director, John Burgess, the company's rapid growth is the result of putting the client first, a strong and highly motivated management team and staff, quality consulting, and an aggressive marketing style.

IPA's headquarters is located in Buffalo Grove, Illinois, close to Chicago. Its 30,000-square-foot modern facility was completed in 1998 but already the company has outgrown its space.

From corporate headquarters and offices in Illinois to consultants and services staff in the field throughout North America, IPA's highly educated 1,700-member work force provides what has been described as preventive maintenance programs for a variety of clients—more than 100,000 of them since 1991. IPA's hands-on consulting services and other programs provide a cost-effective way for companies to gain insights into improving their business, to focus on enhancing operations, and to gain dramatic profitability. A significant investment in personnel, training, and technology has paid off not only for IPA but also for its clients.

IPA offers broad-based expertise in a wide range of areas and is divided into several service groups. Business Analysis examines business operations to determine weaknesses and to recommend improvement. Consulting Services works with clients to assess company strengths and challenges and to implement improved procedures and solutions tailored to the client company's business. Advisory and Intermediary Services evaluates and advises on strategic alliances, packages company offerings, and provides operational audits to establish third-party valuations of client companies. International Tax Associates performs in-depth reviews of clients' tax and financial situation, including succession planning; structures business operations; and keeps clients abreast of changing tax laws. Integrated Financial Services examines alternative investments and financial planning and advises clients on how to acquire operating and expansion capital. Professional Development Services provides executive coaching over the phone for a company's owners and managers to enhance their performance and competitiveness in a rapidly changing business environment.

IPA is a full-service consulting company with the expertise to address all aspects of a client's business in any industry. This requires a staff of highly specialized professionals with experience in a diverse mix of industries and disciplines. IPA applies a team concept to all of its assignments to

Chicago entrepreneur and former lawyer and trader John Burgess founded his company to help small business owners achieve optimal profits through more efficient management and operational procedures.

ensure that the development and implementation of recommendations are tailored to the specific needs unique to each client's business.

Researchers gather data and information to provide consultants with the most up-to-date background resources relating to current marketplace issues and specific industry challenges. Business analysts conduct diagnostic studies to make recommendations of methods, systems, controls, and incentives to improve business operations and profitability. Consultants then work on-site with the client's senior management and staff to implement solutions for particular problems. Based on research, analysis, and on-site interviews and investigation, IPA's experts show business owners how they can join the ranks of the best managed and most profitable companies in business today. Another resource is IPA's confidential client case histories. There are thousands of them in the IPA library to which consultants have access. Implementation of final recommendations is conducted with each client's employees as part of the team.

IPA consultants are among the brightest management minds in business. They are familiar with the best practices and all have practical, hands-on management experience. Regardless of what issue is raised during a client assignment, there is always an IPA consultant who is not only familiar with the issue but also has experience dealing with its resolution. Nothing is left to theory.

As a mark of its success, for the past four years IPA has been able to attract national government officials as keynote speakers for its annual "Celebration of Success." Former presidents George H. Bush and Gerald Ford and Senator Robert Dole have all addressed company functions. In December 1999 former President Bush declared that IPA provides "the kinds of innovative services and products we need to stay productive."

IPA intends to continue to do so. Its future growth strategy is to increase its depth of services to small and mid-size companies. Rather than expand into overseas markets it will continue to concentrate its business in North America, to offer additional services to its current clients, and to broaden its full-service concept to meet all the business development needs of its entrepreneurial clients. ∎

IPA's staff of highly specialized professionals offers the firm's clients expertise in a diverse mix of industries and disciplines.

O f the 102 counties in Illinois, seven cluster around Chicago in the northernmost part of the state. The counties of Cook, DeKalb, Du Page, Kane, Kendall, Lake, and Will house some of the fastest-growing and upwardly mobile communities in the state.

Over the past nine decades the newspapers serving the area have included Copley papers whose publishing empire actually began in Aurora. The Fox Valley Press, Inc., division of the Copley Press published 17 papers including four paid dailies (*Joliet Herald News*, *Aurora Beacon News*, *Waukegan News Sun*, and

Several of Suburban Chicago Newspapers' publications.

Elgin Courier News) and 14 free community weeklies. Each of the four award-winning dailies has been on the state landscape for more than a century.

Newspapers in Illinois date back to 1814, four years before it became a state. The first was the *Illinois Herald* published in Kaskaskia, later to become the state capital. By 1840 some 43 newspapers were published in Illinois. Some were dailies, others weeklies; some were printed two or three times a week. Before the Civil War newspapers virtually shaped public opinion. Would-be opinion-makers proselytized their special interests and the newspapers most often reflected the poli-

tics of their editors.

Between 1833 and 1848, 21 papers were established in Chicago alone. By 1880 there were more than 1,000 papers in the state. With the proliferation came fierce competition. Not surprisingly, ownership changed hands frequently. Many efforts failed; they either folded or were merged into other papers. This was true of larger cities and smaller towns alike.

The smaller communities of Northern Illinois were no exception.

Chicago's first newspaper, the weekly *Chicago Democrat*, was less than six years old when the first edition of the *Joliet Courier* rolled off the press on April 20, 1839. This was the beginning of the long history of Joliet's *Herald News*. The original *Courier* underwent a number of name changes and mergers with other papers before it emerged as the *Herald News* under the ownership of Colonel Ira Copley in 1915.

Aurora is also home to a rich tradition of newspapering. The roots of the *Aurora Beacon News* go back to 1846. It, too, underwent many iterations and name changes as it absorbed other Aurora newspapers. Copley bought the *Daily Beacon* in 1905; it was his first purchase and on it he was to build a newspaper empire. When Copley later acquired the *Aurora News*, he merged the two papers and began publishing the *Aurora Beacon News* on June 2, 1912.

The *Waukegan News Sun* began with Frank Just launching the weekly *Independent* in Libertyville in 1892. Just bought, sold, and merged other papers and finally created the *Waukegan News Sun* in 1930. The paper, which is the longest continuously published daily in Lake County, remained family owned until 1984, when it became part of the Copley Press.

The *Elgin Courier News* dates back to June 1876. By 1915 it was part of the growing Copley chain of newspapers.

In 1928 the Copley-owned papers in Northern Illinois, all separately operated,

were organized into a division of Copley Newspapers. In the early 1990s printing of the four Copley Northern Illinois papers moved to Fox Valley Press, a state-of-the-art production facility in Plainfield. The division was eventually renamed the Fox Valley Press, Inc.

In addition to publishing the four daily newspapers, Fox Valley Press also publishes the thrice-weekly *Naperville Sun*, a collection of 12 free community weeklies, and one shopper.

Fox Valley Press newspapers recently received a new parent and a new name. In late 2000 Copley Press sold its Fox Valley Press division to Hollinger International, the global newspaper publisher that owns worldwide publications including the *Chicago Sun-Times*, the *London Daily Telegraph*, and the *Jerusalem Post*. Hollinger also owns the *Daily Southtown* in Tinley Park, and *Pioneer Press*, a group of weeklies in 58 North Shore communities.

Under the new ownership, the group of papers has been renamed Suburban Chicago Newspapers. Each independently operated paper has been given more control over its content development and decision-making. Along with additional autonomy, the papers also have greater access to resources and volume penetration for regional advertisers.

The newspaper group also includes SCNmedia, which provides multimedia business-to-business and business-to-consumer marketing expertise. Its approach to marketing campaigns integrates newspaper advertising, Internet presence, direct mail, and database marketing.

Suburban Chicago Newspapers publishes both print and online editions on its award-winning Web site. Each edition of the four dailies combines regional coverage of their circulation area with presentation of important international and national news. However, the emphasis is on local issues. As with the best of community papers, Suburban Chicago Newspapers reflect their locale and its readership. Their aim is to make readers aware of their surroundings and how changes that are taking place affect their community.

Though national and world news can affect smaller communities—all too evident in the wake of the terrorist attacks of September 11, 2001—the main mission of Suburban Chicago Newspapers is to tell readers not only what they need to know but also what they want to know. In one form or another, the papers have been doing this for more than 100 years.

As part of Hollinger International, the commitment of each of the newspapers is to create an even better news product for its readers. ■

Suburban Chicago Newspapers' central printing facility is located in Plainfield, Illinois.

Right: Accenture offers its people the finest training and mentoring, helping them to achieve their individual goals. Photo by John Dolan

Accenture may span the globe, bringing innovations to improve the way the world works and lives, but for over a decade now its Chicago roots continue to remain strong. A leading provider of management and technology consulting services and solutions, Accenture employs over 65,000 people, with 5,500 people based throughout five locations in the Chicago metropolitan area.

This high-profile global organization began to reinvent itself in January 2001 to become a market maker, architect, and builder of the new economy. In reality, Accenture's people do more than consult. They develop new technologies and soft-

Informal team meetings are another way that Accenture's people share their expertise and understanding to craft client solutions. Photo by John Dolan

ware that help transform their clients' business. They create alliances with companies such as MicroSoft and Blue Martini to build custom solutions. They provide outsourcing of non-core business functions. And they have their own venture capital efforts to invest in new companies and technologies that, again, create opportunities for their clients.

This is best explained by Joe Forehand, Accenture's managing partner and CEO: "By now it should be clear why we are so proud of and enthusiastic about the changes at Accenture. As you can see, there is much more to Accenture than a new name that expresses our vision of the future. We are, fundamentally, a new firm

…Our strength lies in our people and our ability to bridge both the old and the new economies."

The key to Accenture's success? Client service is the heart of this organization. And what distinguishes Accenture from other consulting firms is its dynamic structure that brings the right people to the right project. Using an integrated approach, teams are formed by people with profound industry knowledge, such as communications or retailing, and extensive expertise in professional disciplines, such as customer relationship management or human performance.

Transcending the boundaries of traditional consulting, Accenture develops new ways to deliver value to its clients. For example, Avanade is a partnership between Accenture and MicroSoft, whereby the two companies can provide services and consulting for e-commerce and other technology systems. In addition, Accenture has Business Integration Centers for industry-specific long-range planning, Centers for Strategic Technology that transform research into results, and Solution Centers to speed delivery through ready-made solutions.

A large contributor to Chicago, Accenture is an equally active member in the community through a combination of community service and volunteer activities. Accenture's people participate yearly in a myriad of civic, economic development, education, arts, and social service organizations. This philanthropic focus is a combination of training, mentoring, funding, and even just helping to make Chicago a better place to work and live. ■

The most influential African-American newspaper of the twentieth century was launched in Chicago nearly a century ago. The four-page weekly, established on May 5, 1905, with an investment of 25 cents, is the *Chicago Defender*. Its founder, Robert Sengstacke Abbott, the son of freed slaves, compiled copy at a kitchen table, borrowed money to print 300 copies, and sold and distributed the papers himself. It was an inauspicious beginning for a paper that would revolutionize African-American journalism.

Through the use of sensational headlines, cartoons, and red ink, the paper grabbed attention. As a northern black paper, the *Defender* was free to attack racial injustices; and it did so with verve and combativeness. Although it used sensationalism to boost circulation, its mission had far-reaching effects. Editorials attacked white oppression and lynching and urged equal treatment of black soldiers. In 1915 the *Defender*, now a 32-page weekly with a national edition, was selling 230,000 copies. With the help of black Pullman porters and traveling entertainers, wide distribution throughout the South was ensured; and each copy of the paper was estimated to have been read by as many as five people.

During World War I the *Defender* launched its most aggressive campaign to support the Great Migration in which more than 1.25 million blacks moved from the South to northern cities between 1915 and 1925. The paper provided first-hand coverage of the Red Summer Riots of 1919. It campaigned for anti-lynching legislation and for integrated sports, and actively supported the candidacy of black politicians. The *Defender* was the first black paper to publish a health column and a full page of comic strips.

Abbott was succeeded as publisher by his nephew, John Sengstacke, in 1940. Sengstacke worked with President Franklin Roosevelt to create jobs for blacks in the U.S. Postal Service and his efforts to improve the status of black armed forces led President Harry Truman to name him to a commission to desegregate the U.S. armed forces.

Sengstacke turned the paper into a daily in 1956 and continued to crusade for equal rights for blacks. Contributors included novelist Willard Motley, W.E.B. du Bois, and Gwendolyn Brooks. Langston Hughes penned his "Simple" stories in a *Defender* column from 1942 until 1962.

Sengstacke enlarged the Sengstacke enterprises to include the *Michigan Chronicle*, the *New Pittsburgh Courier*, and the *Tri-State Defender*. In 1970 he was elected to the board of the American Society of Newspaper Editors, the first black editor to earn that honor.

The *Defender*, after the death of Sengstacke in 1997, continues to inform the black community and to provide a training ground for young black journalists. And, in the words of Robert Abbott, it continues to "mirror the needs, opinions, and aspirations of my race." ■

Above: President Harry Truman, John Sengstacke, and Mayor Richard Daley ride in the *Defender*'s Bud Billiken Parade in the late 1940s. The parade was started by Robert Sengstacke Abbott in 1929 as a way to give children an opportunity to be in the limelight.

Top: Robert Sengstacke Abbott, 1868-1940, founder and publisher of the *Chicago Defender*.

Left: The *Defender* has been headquartered at 2400 South Michigan Avenue, Chicago, since 1959.

*D*aniel J. Edelman, Inc., a leader in public relations since 1952, has a staff of 2,000 in 39 offices in the United States, Canada, Mexico, South America, Europe, and Asia-Pacific.

Daniel J. Edelman founded the company in Chicago and continues to play an active role in its global management as chairman. His son, Richard Edelman, became president and CEO in 1996.

The firm's $248 million in revenues in 2000 marked its 20th consecutive year of growth. More than 400 Chicago employees serve clients including Bayer, ConAgra, Kraft, KFC, Microsoft, Pharmacia, Procter & Gamble, and the Illinois Department of Commerce and Community Affairs.

Daniel J. Edelman, Inc., is a PR-centric organization comprised of five operating units:

- Edelman Public Relations Worldwide offers global capabilities in all facets of public relations.

- PR 21 specializes in technology, new media, health, and consumer public relations.

- StrategyOne offers market and opinion research and works closely with client account service teams to develop customized programs.

- Edelman Interactive Solutions delivers online communications, including Web site design and development, Internet monitoring, online crisis management, Web site audits and traffic analyses, online promotions, and e-commerce and wireless applications.

- Blue Worldwide provides creative advertising services for building brand identity and developing grass-roots support on public issues.

Edelman combines strategic counsel with tactical skills to help clients communicate and build relationships with stakeholders. The firm's professionals create and implement strategic communications programs that influence public opinion, promote clients' brands and initiatives, and provide issues management and crisis preparedness.

Edelman has adapted to a changing communications environment. The firm invests heavily in new technologies that enhance client services and enable it to remain an innovator in public relations. Edelman also invests in continuous learning opportunities to help employees enhance their professional skills, build more meaningful careers, and offer clients superior counsel.

Edelman Worldwide is the largest privately held, independent firm dedicated solely to public relations. In 2000 Edelman earned a PRSA Silver Anvil Award, a Golden World Award from the International PR Association, a Creativity in PR Award, and a Gold Quill Award from the International Association of Business Communicators—and one Edelman program was recognized by the United Nations for addressing issues of concern to the UN. In 1999 Dan Edelman was awarded the PRSA Gold Anvil, the highest individual honor in public relations.

Edelman has been a leader and innovator in developing public relations practices, standards, and ethics in the United States and internationally. With its heritage of creativity and dedication to client service, Daniel J. Edelman, Inc., is a pacesetter in public relations locally and globally. ■

Daniel J. Edelman founded the public relations firm that bears his name in Chicago in 1952.

Chicago-based Pam Talbot is chief operating officer of Edelman's U.S. operations.

JORDAN
INDUSTRIES, INC.

*J*ordan Industries, Inc. (JII), is just 14 years old but it has already earned an enviable reputation among the financial press and within the industries in which it operates. JII is a billion-dollar diversified private holding company that helps its constituent companies grow their businesses. It is the entrepreneurs' entrepreneur. JII acquires companies for their long-term growth potential, not for resale or short-term gains. It helps its companies grow by providing them expertise and capital to achieve and expand market opportunities, improve plants and facilities, and build greater distribution channels for their products.

JII was founded in 1988 by John Jordan and Thomas Quinn, former roommates at Notre Dame University. From the beginning their goal was to partner with entrepreneurial companies that have the vision and drive to pursue aggressive growth but are in need of proven resources. JII's unique approach combines the advantages of consolidation with those of decentralization—which means the management of individual companies remains in place. As part of a consolidated group, each company has an opportunity to access a broad array of resources including planning, financing, market research, legal, and business development. With these resources at hand individual companies can identify opportunities for future growth—for example, domestic expansion, access to international markets, acquisitions that fit their business, or new product development. JII provides the essential framework for achieving these and other goals.

Jordan currently owns 80 businesses divided into 10 industry groups: Business, Industrial, and Commercial; Staffing Consultants, LLC, through Lakeshore Staffing, Inc., a provider of niche staffing services; Signature Graphics, Inc., a provider of fleet graphics; Internet Services Management; SourceLink, Inc., which provides data-driven direct marketing solutions; The Sensory Design Group; Specialty Plastics; Automotive Aftermarket; Healthcare

Products; Specialty Printing and Packaging; and Kinetek, Inc., which manufactures motors, gears, and motion control systems. A former group, Jordan Telecommunications Products, was sold to Emerson Electric in early 2000. Collectively, JII companies employ 7,000 people with combined 2000 revenues of one billion dollars. More than half of its companies are located in small towns that count on jobs and taxes created by these businesses.

Jordan Industries seeks companies with revenues between $5 million and $150 million that fit one or more of the following profiles: high margins through proprietary products or services with excellent growth prospects; well-managed private companies with a track record of consistent sales and earnings growth; synergy with Jordan's current businesses or industry groups; and subsidiaries and divisions of larger corporate entities whose goals coincide with JII's strategic objectives.

An important component of the Jordan philosophy is to assure that each of its businesses has achieved quality management at all levels and that company executives and Jordan share an esprit de corps. In sum, Jordan's businesses are based on the fundamentals of good judgment and common sense, fiscal planning and discipline, experience, and good old hard work. These values are critical to success and they have served Jordan Industries and its constituent companies very well. ■

Moving people faster, safer, and more economically, while moving their company straight up the growth charts, has been the goal of brothers Javad (left) and Majid Rahimian since forming their business in 1987. A JII company since 1997, Motion Control has tapped JII's resources to double its facility and partnered with other JII Kinetek companies to open new markets and expand its product line.

Co-presidents John Johnson (left) and Scott Allen were early to recognize the need for *Fortune* 1000 companies to hire experienced professionals on a temporary basis. Lakeshore Staffing recently was ranked number six on *Inc.* magazine's list of the top 500 fastest-growing privately held companies in America. This achievement was made possible in part by JII's unique approach to partnering with entrepreneurs to provide resources to help them achieve exceptional growth.

*T*he equivalent of one in 12 U.S. citizens does it every year ... and that number is rising. Many believe it is the civilized way to go. What they are discovering is that traveling by Amtrak is becoming distinctly more convenient than flying the friendly skies. That it is eminently less stressful than seeing the USA in an automobile. And that it can be highly comfortable, especially in light of sharply improving service standards.

Since Amtrak unveiled its 150-mph Acela Express and several customer serv-

ice programs in 2000—Satisfaction Guarantee Promise, frequent traveler, rail passes, and other new benefits—ridership satisfaction is being assured, clearly demonstrated by the virtual lack of passenger complaints. Business travelers and leisure tourists alike are enjoying Amtrak's commitment to style and service.

Amtrak promises safe, comfortable, and enjoyable rides to destinations of choice— quaint coastal towns, historic cities, unspoiled wilderness, snow-capped mountains, sun-drenched beaches, cosmopolitan urban centers. Partnerships with United and Icelandic, Greyhound and Coach USA, and Hertz and Rail Canada facilitate travel to out-of-the-way places Amtrak does not yet serve. In addition, Amtrak is

the country's largest provider of contract-commuter services for state and regional transportation authorities; this portion of its business represents two-thirds of total ridership each year.

Amtrak, America's only intercity passenger rail service, operates more than 22,000 route miles of tracks that are mostly owned by freight railroads. It serves more than 500 stations in 46 states; nearly 40 of them are in Illinois alone—from Alton to Urbana. Chicago's renovated Union Station, built in 1925, is the hub of Amtrak's Midwest Corridor, one of 11 corridors throughout the country. Chicago is the busiest station after New York City, Philadelphia, and Washington, D.C.

However, Amtrak's mission to provide efficient U.S intercity rail passenger service is proving to be a challenge that is testing its operational and marketing skills. Investment in passenger rail is low. Since 1971 seven times more money has been invested into U.S aviation and highways than into rail infrastructure.

Amtrak, or the National Railroad Passenger Corporation, began service in 1971 after its creation by an act of Congress that dictated that the corporation take over the country's rail passenger services and that it become financially self-sufficient. Though officially a private company, the vast majority of its shares are owned by the government. It is, in effect, a for-profit, quasi-government entity with all the unwieldiness that that status conveys.

When Amtrak (the "American Track") was created, U.S passenger rail service had lost its allure to what were then more convenient air travel and highway automobile driving. Gone were the days of the romantic passenger trains—the old chiefs, Limiteds, and Zephyrs. Gone was the elegance of impeccable train services, comfortable surroundings, and fine dining aboard—all that unobtrusive attention to creature comfort. By the 1960s schedules on by-then run-down trains were erratic and service all but nonexistent. Travelers

opted for flying and driving.

But times are changing. Traveling by airline and highway is becoming less convenient. For every flight added by the airline industry between 1997 and 2000, there were one-and-a-half times as many cancellations and diversions. And as the average rate of vehicle miles traveled outpaces population growth, 70 percent of highway driving in metro areas is done under congested conditions.

Nevertheless, Amtrak is facing the toughest fight yet for its survival. Amtrak efforts are beginning to pay off in terms of public perception. Since the inauguration of faster trains, guaranteed service, and guest rewards, ridership is steadily climbing—by more than 40 percent on some routes since the late 1990s. And over the first two quarters of 2001, revenues had increased significantly from the previous year.

The Amtrak Reform Council, established in 1997 to assess the future viability of the corporation, met on December 14, 2001, to consider a number of restructuring plans; final recommendations were submitted to Congress in early February 2002. Regardless of the outcome, existing corridors already designated for the development of high-speed rail will remain in place. Those are the 11 regions covering 38 states that have been designated as high-speed rail corridors.

The Northeast Corridor, where the high-speed Acela Express is already in service between Washington, D.C., and Boston, is a prime example of successful state cooperation. Acela cuts travel time by up to 10 times on some routes and, along the Northeast Corridor, Amtrak carries the equivalent of more than 120 airline flights every day. Other regional corridors are working to duplicate that success. In the Midwest Corridor, for example, five states are collectively working on a high-speed network that will cover 3,000 miles of tracks to provide high-speed links to destinations in Illinois, Indiana, Michigan, Missouri, and Wisconsin.

Public response to a November 30, 2001, *Chicago Tribune* editorial critical of Amtrak was strongly in support of Amtrak service by six to one. Senator Robert Torricelli of New Jersey echoed that support. A frequent passenger of the high-speed train, he described the Acela "as good as the great trains of Europe." He noted that the "Acela is everything an American passenger has never been: clean, quiet, stable, and fast."

Former Massachusetts Governor Michael Dukakis, Amtrak vice chairman, also noted the significance of the train's success: " ... if you give people first-class, modern high-speed services," he said, "they will come by the thousands." ■

CHAPTER TEN

Labor Unions and Contractors' Associations

Historically the champions of workers' rights, the state's labor unions continue to help improve the quality of life and work for their members.

IBEW Local 134 and Electrical Contractors' Association **286-289**

Chicago Journeymen Plumbers' Local Union 130 UA **290-291**

Plumbing Contractors Association of Chicago and Cook County **292**

Plumbing Council of Chicagoland **293**

United Brotherhood of Carpenters and Joiners of America **294-295**

Chicago and Northeast Illinois District Council of Carpenters **296-297**

International Union of Operating Engineers, Local 399 **298-299**

Architectural and Ornamental Iron Workers Local 63 **300-301**

International Brotherhood of Teamsters Joint Council 25 **302-303**

United Union of Roofers, Waterproofers and Allied Workers Local 11 **304-305**

Painters' District Council #14 **306-307**

International Association of Heat and Frost Insulators and Asbestos Workers Union 17 and the Illinois Regional Contractors Association **308**

Left: © Chris Corrie/Index Stock Imagery

An early IBEW Local 134 electrician works on the wiring of Chicago's subway system circa 1940.

NECA Chicago/IBEW Local 134 electricians and contractors work in the Monadnock Building in the 1920s.

Chicago, considered the most American of American cities, ushered in an era of technological innovation in architecture and construction. During the late nineteenth century the city epitomized innovation and change in building design. With it came a change in the relationship between workers and contractors, and eventual jurisdictional issues about which workers would perform which tasks as skills shifted in the face of changing technology. Chicago's electrical union and electrical contractors led the way to successfully forging a strong partnership to meet these new and increasing challenges.

The Chicago Fire of October 1871 destroyed 18,000 buildings. Architects and craftsmen, contractors and their work crews flooded Chicago to help rebuild the city. It was a rare opportunity to build a new city in the age of the Industrial Revolution. Crews worked nonstop, their nighttime labor illuminated by torches. One innovation of the 1870s was the elevator, which allowed for tall buildings. Another technology was illumination.

Among the incoming workers were gas fitters whose job was to pipe natural gas to street lamps and into homes and

offices. Within a decade the gaslight era was essentially coming to an end with the invention of the incandescent electric lamp in 1879. Chicago Edison opened its first central station for incandescent lighting in August 1888—the first electric company to house a generating station and to use direct-current electricity. The following year the first electric railway system began in Chicago with the introduction of the electric-powered trolley car. Electricity as a force for illumination, for speedy train transportation, telephony, and for driving small machinery, elevators, and printing presses grabbed the imagination of the public. The World's Columbian Exposition of 1893, referred to as the White City, exhibited new household conveniences such as chafing dishes, coffee pots, and grills—all driven by electricity. The exposition was open to visitors during the night because thousands of electric lights had been installed.

Electricians were in demand. Chicago's city directory devoted less than a column to listing electrical industry outfits in 1880; in 1893 it published 13 columns of electricians and electric companies. During the 1893 exposition six electrical contractors formed a club that would later become the Electrical Contractors' Association of Chicago. The demand for electrical application in all areas of building and transportation at the turn of the twentieth century made electrical workers and contractors an integral part of the city's growth. But there was need for an organization to ensure fair pay and working conditions.

Electricians and others in the building trades typically worked 16-hour days for as little as 15 cents an hour. Working conditions were dangerous and the death rate was double that of the national average. On Wednesday, July 16, 1890, a group of electrical workers met in the front room of an old building on Washington Street to discuss the rights of workers. They called themselves the Brotherhood of Electrical Mechanics. Ten years later they received

their national charter and became known as the International Brotherhood of Electrical Workers, Local 134.

As electricity took over as the most viable source of light, one group of tradesmen saw a dramatic decline in their work: gas fitters. Before the advent of electricity, gas had dominated the industry; and now the threatened gas fitters were compelled to take a stand. An onslaught of jurisdictional disputes ensued as gas fitters claimed the right to install all-electrical conduit. They were originally awarded half of the work, but it was a short-lived victory; by 1902 electricians had won total jurisdiction over installation of conduit.

The first conduit to be installed by IBEW Local 134 was the Illinois Theater. This experience led members to the realization that there was a need for a strong, unified group of contractors to provide support and balance within the electrical industry. They called on the Electrical Contractors' Association, which quickly recognized the clear benefits of such a partnership. The two groups established a historic labor-management partnership. This team set unprecedented standards for quality workmanship and commitment to customer satisfaction, tenets that remain in place today. In fact, the partnership became a model for other such partnerships throughout the country.

Local 134 electricians and contractors at work in the 1950s.

The commitment of ECA Chicago and IBEW Local 134 to producing the most highly skilled electricians in the country was fulfilled in 1906 with the establishment of the Electrician Apprenticeship Training Program; and after World War I the Joint Apprenticeship Training Committee was formed to design and implement intensive training programs. JATC was a special interest of business manager Michael Boyle, who served as head of Local 134 for nearly 40 years; he worked tirelessly to improve working conditions and wages for electrical workers. One of Boyle's greatest achievements was his partnering with Daniel Burnham, the prominent architect who laid out the 1919 plan for Chicago's lakefront. As a result, IBEW Local 134 members worked on Navy Pier, the Field Museum, and buildings that lined the Magnificent Mile, among other projects.

Until the 1920s electricity in the home was seen as a mark of high status, but now it was becoming a way of life for the middle class. As the use of electricity became more widespread, building trade

NECA Chicago and IBEW Local 134 contractors and electricians wired Chicago's subway system circa 1940.

The quality craftsmanship of NECA/IBEW Local 134 contractors and electricians can be found throughout downtown Chicago.

The new 62- by 35-foot sign at NECA/IBEW Local 134's recently renovated training center in Alsip, Illinois.

unions were gaining strength and increasingly high wages. But a wage cutback was on the horizon. Construction employers were frustrated by high wages, and an onslaught of jurisdictional disputes exacerbated the situation. Contractors forced a lockout of several building trades. Eventually, both sides agreed to enter into arbitration to decide the price of labor in Chicago. The decision-maker was Judge Kenesaw Mountain Landis. His famous decision in 1921 cut wages for most of the building trades, and outlawed terms of many union contracts. While many trade unions refused to abide by the Landis Decision, IBEW Local 134 and ECA worked together to accommodate the new ruling. They also established the first Joint Arbitration Board and developed the legendary Principal Agreement of 1921 that included a no-strike, no-lockout rule. This strategy paid off. Landis was so impressed by this example of labor-management partnership that he awarded the electricians the highest wages in the building industry.

At the beginning of the next decade, IBEW Local 134 and ECA instituted the Electrical Insurance Trustees Plan, the first ever in a building trade, to provide members group insurance and health benefits. The plan continues to grow and to provide members with the best benefits available. To weather the Depression, the union-contractor partnership worked together to create support systems that made financial contributions to unemployed members including the payment of union dues. The hardships of the Depression in Chicago were alleviated by the opening of the city's second world's fair, the Century of Progress, in 1933.

Another boost for union morale came in 1935

with the passage of the National Labor Relations Act. The Wagner Act, as it was called, allowed workers to conduct union activities and required employers to bargain in good faith. During World War II union workers were doing 92 percent of all construction work. That record was placed in jeopardy with the passage of the Taft-Hartley Act in 1947. The act placed restrictions on organized labor activities and decreed that union membership would not be a condition of employment. Taft-Hartley included institution of the Welfare and Pension Funds and the creation of the Labor Management Cooperation Committee (LMCC). However, Taft-Hartley impeded the activities of unions by creating unfair labor practices, thus making it easier for employers to take action against unions.

Nevertheless, the electrical construction industry and its unions flourished in the 1950s with the advent of television, shopping centers, and advanced communications. IBEW Local 134's control over residential wiring in Chicago and Cook County made it the most extensively organized residential jurisdiction of the IBEW. During the 1960s many improvements were made in wages and fringe benefits, including the establishment of the Plan Two Pension Fund.

Chicago's downtown construction boom of the next two decades strengthened the health of IBEW Local 134 and ensured that electrical workers continued to play an integral role in developing the ever-changing Chicago skyline. As ever, IBEW Local 134 and the ECA worked together as a cohesive team to consistently build on their solid relationship between labor and management. There has never been an economic strike by electri-

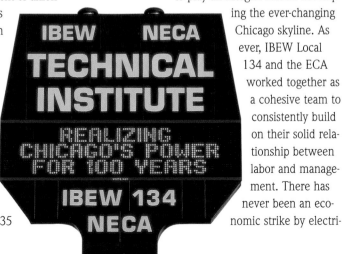

The photovoltaic array atop NECA/IBEW Local 134's training center is the first solar electricity training center in the state of Illinois.

cians in Chicago and Cook County and there has never been a lockout. If disagreements arise, the two partners manage to resolve issues.

IBEW Local 134 and ECA continue to boast one of the best training programs in the country with more than 2,500 apprentices enrolled. The program constantly breaks ground with cutting-edge training in new advanced technologies such as photovoltaics and telecommunications.

With new technologies, a big challenge is jurisdiction over who does what work and how that work is to be done. For example, as with the controversy between gas fitters and electricians in the 1890s about who should lay pipes, the current craft jurisdiction issue is playing out with photovoltaics, fiber-optic cabling, copper cabling, and data and communications work. These new state-of-the-art technologies bring about the need for even stronger education and training.

The training program is conducted in two complexes with a combined training area of approximately 140,000 square feet. An experienced staff of 40 full-time instructors teaches electronic and electrical systems to prepare apprentices for work in the industry. And that work is diverse—from residential lighting to outfitting radiology laboratories. The recent multimillion-dollar renovation of the training facilities speaks to the commitment to produce the most highly trained electricians in the industry. Each apprentice who completes the training program is assured of an opportunity to work in the electrical industry. And a significant effort is made to attract women and minorities to the industry.

There is also a concerted effort to promote a positive image of the union electrical construction industry. Working with the Labor Management Cooperation Committees of Chicago, which provides promotional support, the IBEW Local 134 and ECA fund scholarships, undertake safety programs, and sponsor charity events such as Habitat for Humanity and the Veterans' Stand Down. And the image-building program includes a full-scale marketing and advertising campaign—a variety of television, radio, and print ads—that have been key to enhancing the industry's positive image.

Today IBEW Local 134, one of the largest IBEW local unions in the country, serves approximately 18,000 member electricians in Chicago and Cook County. Nearly 1,200 electrical contractors are represented by the Electrical Contractors' Association of the City of Chicago, which is also the Chicago and Cook County chapter of the National Electrical Contractors' Association. Together, the two organizations continue the tradition of collaborating to meet industry challenges, training future electricians, undertaking collective bargaining, and ensuring the welfare of their members.

The more than 100-year-old partnership between Local Union #134 IBEW and ECA Chicago has achieved an impressive list of accomplishments: technological innovation, improved working conditions and benefits, safe and high-quality electrical work, the best-trained electricians in the country, and customer satisfaction. From installation of Chicago's early telephone system to wiring the city's historical landmarks and skyscrapers, to providing critical infrastructure support, IBEW Local 134 and ECA Chicago have played a vital role in the growth of Chicago and Cook County. They continue that tradition of serving as a reliable team for the benefit of the city of Chicago, Cook County, their residents, and their business customers. ∎

Mike Fitzgerald, business manager of IBEW Local 134, and Mark Nemshick, executive vice president of NECA Chicago, together throw the switch to officially open NECA/IBEW Local 134's 100th year anniversary dinner event held on July 15, 2000, at McCormick Place in Chicago.

CHICAGO JOURNEYMEN PLUMBERS' LOCAL UNION 130 UA

The organization of Chicago's plumbers had its beginnings more than 150 years ago. The first attempt took place in the late 1850s with the formation of the Worshipful Company of Plumbers. The Chicago Master Plumbers' Association was established in 1860. Both groups became inactive as their members went off to serve in the Civil War.

After the Chicago Fire of 1871, craftsmen flooded the city to help in its rebuilding. Within months, 14 plumbers formed a union to achieve a 10-hour workday for a minimum daily $2.50. And there were other concerns. Technology was one issue. The traditional role of the plumber as a maker of fixtures changed to that of installer. New technology brought with it the need for new skills. Illinois enacted licensing laws in 1881 to ensure that journeymen plumbers had reached a required skill level.

The Chicago Journeymen Plumbers' Local Union 130 UA has been headquartered on West Washington Boulevard since 1927.

Five years later plumbers reorganized as the Chicago Journeymen Plumbers' Benevolent and Protective Association. Its first achievement was an eight-hour day. The association joined the United Association of Journeymen and Apprentices of the Plumbing and Pipefitting Industry (UAJAPPI) in 1895. They were granted the charter number Local 130. Their stated goal: "A day's pay for a day's work." The next year Local 130 allied itself with the Master Plumbers' Association, which had reorganized in 1882. That alliance was based on an agreement of what constituted a day's work.

Local 130 prospered. It signed a historic pact with employing master plumbers in 1903—a 44-hour week for $24.75; in 1908 it negotiated a 65-cent hourly raise. Chicago's plumbers and their families were assured a predictable income. And there was plenty of work during the city's biggest building booms. An unheard-of $775 million worth of construction was completed between 1909 and 1916.

In 1918 plumbers' hourly wages rose to one dollar and, two years later, to $1.25. The Building Construction Employers' Association protested and fought to get wages cut back to one dollar—and they won. Local 130 fought back. Plumbers' wages rebounded to $55 a week in 1924, just as the city was embarking on its greatest building boom to date. Construction permits for $1.4 billion worth of work were issued between 1925 and 1929. One was for the new home of Local 130. The three-story headquarters, located on West Washington Boulevard, was dedicated in 1927. Plumbers' weekly wages were now $71.50.

Then came the Great Depression. Wages dropped, joblessness mounted, and new building activity virtually halted. It took World War II to reenergize the economy. By the end of the 1940s Local 130 was the sole owner of its headquarters building, which was valued at one million dollars. A new era of fringe benefits began in 1950 with the Welfare Fund for Plumbers Local 130. It had been negotiated the previous year when hourly wages reached $2.45 with an additional 7.5 cents—soon to be 15 cents—contribution for the Welfare Fund. Steve Bailey was named business manager in 1946, and plumbers were assured a minimum weekly wage of $94 for a 40-hour work week.

Steve Bailey would serve at the helm of Local 130 for 20 years; he had been brought on board in 1946 as the

THE PLUMBER PROTECTS THE HEALTH OF THE NATION

youngest-ever business manager for any building trades union. "Mr. Plumber," as Bailey was known, began the union's now-traditional sponsorship of Chicago's St. Patrick's Day parade. When he died in 1966, Local 130's membership was nearly 7,800—including the first female plumber, who had joined in 1959.

Stephen Lamb, an active member, succeeded Bailey. He had a special interest in the welfare and education of apprentices. A former head of training, he concentrated on innovation in plumbing and advancing job skills. He instituted an interest-bearing savings plan. By the end of his seven-year tenure, plumbers' weekly wages were close to $250.

After Lamb's death in 1973, Edward Brabec took over the leadership. He believed labor's interests were best served in a strong business environment. He was an early advocate of investing pension funds in new-home construction. Weekly wages topped $500.

During the leadership of the next business manager, James McCarthy, a major issue was achieving minority representation among union members. Local 130 set its goal at 30 percent, higher than recommended guidelines. In 1988 weekly wages broke the $1,000 barrier.

Current business manager Gerald Sullivan succeeded McCarthy in 1990. Under his decade-long leadership the image of plumbing trades has been greatly enhanced, recruitment of new members is growing through one of the most compre-

hensive organizing programs in UA history, and the union's charitable work has expanded. Innovation is also a priority led by a push into the world of computers.

Local 130's good-neighbor policy includes participation in extensive community projects. Among them is an annual Christmas party for hundreds of disadvantaged children. Much of its charitable work and educational outreach is conducted jointly with the Plumbing Contractors Association of Chicago and Cook County and the Plumbing Council of Chicagoland, and includes performing free plumbing services for senior citizens, donating labor and materials to build community centers, a public awareness marketing campaign, and improving educational opportunities to help prepare minority students to enter the plumbing trade.

Local 130 is the largest plumbers' union in North America. Its 5,200 members garner more than two-thirds of all plumbing projects in Cook and Will counties in Illinois, and that ratio is growing. It conducts the most aggressive union-organizing campaign on the continent—in the past few years it has added 500 new members to its roster.

Business manager Gerald Sullivan explains: "Our goal is to keep Local 130 a viable organization for plumbers and plumbing contractors. We want to continue to be strong so that current and future members and their families will enjoy the same standards of living as those who have preceded us." ■

"The Plumber Protects the Health of the Nation" is the theme of the mural inside the Local's headquarters building.

*T*he first recorded association of master plumbers was formed in Chicago in 1860. It lasted only a short time, as many of its members enlisted in the army at the outbreak of the Civil War in 1861.

There is no record of any attempt to form another organization until early in February 1882, out of which the Plumbing Contractors Association of Chicago and Cook County has grown. The first organization meeting was held in a hall at the northwest corner of La Salle and Randolph streets on February 24, 1882. At that meeting, the following resolution was adopted: "Whereas in consideration of furthering the interests of master plumbers and the want of closer business and social relations; the Master Plumbers of the City of Chicago, County of Cook, State of Illinois, do hereby organize and establish ourselves as an organization to be known as the Master Plumbers Organization of the City of Chicago."

Since its organization in 1882, the Plumbing Contractors Association (PCA) has taken the leading role in improving the individual standing of the master plumber and securing the protection of the entire plumbing industry. This exceptional unity and strength enabled the PCA to establish new trade conditions and institute groundbreaking reforms. Most recently, the PCA, working with the All Industry Committee and the Plumbing Council, successfully produced an industry-wide study measuring the hazards of lead exposure to the plumber, which OSHA has recognized. Quite simply, today's advanced sanitary and protective measures

are due largely in part to the energetic work of the officers and members of the Plumbing Contractors Association of Chicago and Cook County.

As the Plumbing Contractors Association enters its third century it looks to a very positive future. With membership rising from a low in the early 1990s of 53 to close to 200 members in 2001, more and more contractors are getting involved in their industry. These new members are bringing new ideas and energy to the association that is exciting for everyone.

Modern technology, the Internet, and the ever-changing business climate have changed the focus of the PCA. The organization's board of directors is strongly committed to increasing the resources of the association to expanded educational programs. Educating contractors on legal and business issues and PCA members' key people on safety, management, and current innovations in equipment and procedures will be PCA priorities in the coming years.

The PCA has also taken a much stronger stand on legislation that affects the plumbing industry as well as general business and public safety issues. Its participation in the legislative process is seen by the membership as a responsibility to use industry knowledge for the benefit of everyone.

A proud and historic past is the perfect bridge to a bright and prosperous future. ■

Above: John Delehant—Plumber—and his horse-drawn carriage, circa 1900.

Top right: An early plumbing shop in Chicago.

Below: PCA's 2000-2001 board of directors. Front row (left to right): Larry Juliano, Wally Brongiel, Pete Fazio, Bob Melko, and Al Gehrke. Back row (left to right): Owen Francis, Craig Campeglia, Lori Abbott, Jerry Roberts, Jerry Duever, Frank Kennedy, and Mike Giglio.

The Plumbing Council of Chicagoland was formed in 1968 to inform the public of the ongoing needs for plumbing standards, to help industry groups and civic agencies to advance plumbing standards, and to recommend highly skilled and reliable contractors to the public. Today the council promotes the interests of union plumbing contractors and their employees and works to enhance the image of plumbing as a highly skilled trade. It represents all members of Local 130 and the Plumbing Contractors Association (PCA). One of its former educational programs was the "Clean Water and Plumbing" exhibit at the Museum of Science and Industry. When launched in 1976, it was the first educational project designed to acquaint

by the Plumbing Council's own Bob Ryan as part of the Lou Manferdini show. The segment gives callers advice about household plumbing problems. The public relations campaign, which garnered the interest of major national media, is produced with the support of Gerber Fixture Corporation, an Illinois company.

The council also assists Local 130 and the PCA to ensure safety throughout the industry by supporting legislative efforts to bring about needed reforms. One example is the production of a recent study of the degree to which plumbers are affected by lead exposure. The PCA and the All Industry Committee undertook this study.

Much of the charitable work conducted within the industry is done in conjunction with Plumbing Council administrative sup-

Left: The Plumbing Council of Chicagoland completes 40 jobs a year for senior citizens in need under Mayor Daley's Plumbers for Seniors program.

the general public with a basic understanding of plumbing installations and water treatment.

In 1992 the council's marketing program took on new momentum when it joined with Local 130 in an effort to enhance the image of union plumbers, to provide useful information to Chicagoans, and to coordinate the charitable work conducted by Local 130. A half-million-dollar television campaign paid off. Prime time commercials appeared on all major local TV stations. The Plumbing Council produces a Saturday morning informational segment on WGN Radio's "Mr. Fix It Show" hosted

port. For example, the union and the council donated plumbing and labor to the Misericordia Heart of Mercy Home, Provident St. Mel's High School, the Family Inn to house families of kids undergoing organ transplants, and the Children's Advocacy Center. In 1995 Local 130 and the council launched Mayor Daley's Plumbers for Seniors program to cover plumbing emergencies of older citizens in need. Forty jobs a year are completed for seniors by teams of journeymen and apprentices. In the year 2000 the senior citizens program earned the Governor of Illinois' Unique Achievement Award. ∎

The United Brotherhood of Carpenters and Joiners of America, with half a million members in the United States and Canada, since 1881 has served the needs of carpenters, fought to improve their working conditions, and built solidarity among members in order to achieve common goals.

Today the international UBCJA is composed of 65 regional or district councils. Each of the councils is made up of local unions that work together to meet the special needs of regional construction markets and to continue to improve the quality of life for their members. One of those districts is the Chicago and Northeast Illinois District Council of Carpenters.

In the early days, journeymen carpenters worked under the artisan system. Employing master carpenters looked out

A residential construction carpenter cuts exterior trim.

for the long-term welfare of journeymen and apprentices. Apprentices could, in time, become journeymen. The economic interests of the three coincided. Until mass production began to emerge in the mid-1800s, employers respected carpenters' skills; until then, their economic interests dovetailed.

During the 1870s and 1880s Chicago, the immigrant metropolis, was the principal refuge for European immigrants who came with hopes for a better life and well-paying jobs. These semi-skilled workers

were hired at low wages. Many operated machines that mass-produced the doors, molding, and window frames once crafted by hand. Wages of journeymen carpenters plummeted to $2 a day.

Before the founding of UBCJA, carpenters, as did other tradesmen, took action to improve working conditions under the aegis of protective unions and benevolent societies. However, they lacked cohesion and were often ineffective in resolving issues of declining wages, long working days, and competition from inexperienced pieceworkers.

To help consolidate national efforts to improve working conditions, a 29-year-old carpenter, Peter J. McGuire, called for an organizing convention of carpenters. In August 1881, 36 delegates from 11 cities met in Chicago. Among them was Irish-born carpenter James Brennock, who had helped establish Chicago's first benevolent society for carpenters in 1878. The convention attendees passed resolutions demanding shorter workdays, higher wages for skilled labor, and abolition of piecework. The Brotherhood of Carpenters and Joiners of America was born (the word United was added to its name in 1888).

McGuire went on to become a well-known labor leader. He helped establish the American Federation of Labor with Samuel Gompers; suggested the 1882 parade to honor American workers, which was later declared the national annual Labor Day holiday; and led nationwide strikes for a shorter workday. More than 340,000 strikers marched on May 1, 1886 (the Chicago strike helped incite the Haymarket Riot two days later). In almost every city, carpenters led the marchers. These efforts paid off. Union carpenters won higher wages and/or shorter workdays in 53 cities.

The Brotherhood formed the United Carpenters Council of Chicago in 1887 with James "Dad" Brennock as its president. The UCC set up the multi-local system—including the formation of the

Chicago District Council—that divided the union into locals along ethnic and neighborhood lines. Over the next decades, the multi-local system represented 14 ethnic groups in Chicago. By the end of World War I, other trades had joined the Brotherhood including millmen and millwrights, shinglers, insulators, and pile drivers.

When McGuire retired as general secretary in 1902, his successors placed their emphasis on more efficient UBCJA administration, resolving jurisdictional conflicts, and battling open-shop competition. Despite the intensive efforts of open-shop employers, membership in the Brotherhood reached 200,000 by 1910. A union card was as important to a carpenter as a complete set of tools.

Nearly three-quarters of Chicago's carpenters and other construction workers were unemployed in early 1920 and there were emerging jurisdictional challenges in an era of new building technology—cheaper, longer-lasting, and less-combustible building materials were replacing wood. Building contractors called for massive wage reductions. The building unions rebelled. Contractors retaliated by forcing a lockout of building tradesmen from their job sites. Wages and work rules were submitted to binding arbitration. The so-called Landis Award—announced in September 1921—cut real wages for all trades in Chicago. Most tradesmen walked off their jobs. Lesser-skilled workers replaced them and thus the success of the open-shop movement was assured.

Conditions worsened during the Great Depression. Total construction nationwide amounted to $20.8 million in 1928; four years later it was just $6.6 million. UBCJA national membership dropped to a low of 242,000 in 1932 and 40 percent of members were unable to pay their dues. By the next year, less than 30 percent of the union's ranks were employed as carpenters. Local unions tried to bring relief—lowered dues, shorter workweeks, no

A residential construction carpenter frames a house in a Chicago suburb.

overtime, and job sharing. These efforts had little impact. There was no real relief until after World War II.

Wages of union carpenters rose 15 percent between 1945 and 1949, 30 percent through the 1950s, and 72 percent during the 1960s. UBCJA reached its peak membership of 850,000 in 1958 and again in 1973.

In response to the changing world of construction, the international Brotherhood undertook a number of initiatives in the 1980s to help district and local leaders deal with a number of emerging challenges. The goal was to organize more carpenters throughout North America and to strengthen standards of wages, benefits, and safety on every job site.

That is still the charge—to help improve the quality of life and work for its members ... and to maintain the union's hard-earned tradition of excellence, value, and quality work. ■

The counties of Cook, Lake, DuPage, McHenry, Kane, Kendall, Kankakee, Iroquois, Grundy, and Will in Illinois have something other than geography in common. Their carpenters are served by the Chicago and Northeast Illinois District Council of Carpenters. It is the largest labor organization in Northeast Illinois, and represents 35,000 skilled carpenters, journeymen, and apprentices and their 27 local unions throughout the 10 counties. It has been doing so for 120 years.

Historically, the District Council has always represented the most diverse membership based on race, language, ethnicity, and skills. And it remains a multi-cultural, multi-racial organization open to all men and women who want to work in the carpentry trade. As such it is a microcosm of Chicago's labor movement. It also provided impetus for what would become national programs.

For example, the District Council's leadership in apprenticeship education and training began in 1901 when it joined with contractors to establish what would become known as the "Chicago system" because it paid apprentices to attend public school for three months a year. The District Council urged the national Brotherhood to spearhead the fight for unemployment insurance in 1932 at the height of the Great Depression. And for many years—between 1957 and 1982— the District Council had the only single-wage rate in the country.

In the early 1970s the District Council began extending its jurisdiction beyond Cook County. Over the next years the multi-local system underwent a series of mergers. The last generation of ethnic carpenters had retired, giving way to younger, American-born journeymen. Life-styles were also changing from urban to suburban. To streamline operations, the number of locals was reduced significantly. And geographic outreach expanded. On January 1, 1984, 19 small locals merged into larger ones, and the District—now with jurisdiction in 10 counties—changed its name to the Chicago and Northeast Illinois District Council of Carpenters.

According to a dictionary definition, a carpenter is "a skilled worker who makes, finishes, and repairs wooden objects and structures." Actually, a carpenter is much more than that. Evolving technology and new building materials have drastically expanded the field of carpentry over the past several decades.

Carpenters work with more than wood; they also fabricate fixtures that use metals, plastics, and glass. They install acoustical ceilings, tile, windows, and insulation. They work with concrete, flooring materials, siding, and drywall. They build houses, erect skyscrapers, and construct bridges, tunnels, and highways. Today the carpentry trade even includes millwrights who install conveyor systems, escalators, giant electrical turbines, and generators. Carpenters are, in fact, the largest single group of skilled workers in the country. Developing young carpenters and maintaining journeymen skills is of paramount importance to the District Council.

In 1965 the District Council and the Employers Council created the Apprentice Program Fund to underwrite carpenter education at Chicago's Washburne Trade School. Growth of the apprentice program entailed a move to larger quarters in Elk Grove Village in 1988. The educational facilities have since been expanded into Elgin and Chicago.

Above: Commercial construction carpenters lay a plywood subfloor for a concrete deck.

Right and facing page: Commercial construction carpenters frame a concrete column on a Chicago high-rise.

Qualified applicants complete a pre-apprentice introduction course to learn what a carpenter actually does. At least 80 percent of the students are then admitted to a four-year program—the only certified carpentry apprenticeship program in the region that meets Department of Labor standards. Apprentices are employed and paid by participating contractors, where they gain on-the-job experience under the watchful eyes of journeymen carpenters. Approximately 3,800 students are enrolled in the apprenticeship program at any given time. In addition, journeymen carpenters are encouraged to attend continuing education courses held at the training facilities to help maintain the union's hard-earned and well-established reputation for excellence, value, and quality work. Members are kept informed about issues affecting their trade and jobs through a union newsletter and other District Council activities.

The Chicago District Council takes pride not only in the skill, experience, and hard work its carpenters bring to any building project, but also in the role carpenters play on the development team at each stage of a project—from zoning permits to ribbon cutting. Carpenters often join the development team before ground is broken to help with municipal approval and to assist in obtaining adequate financing for land development. One innovative program is helping to finance new construction, thereby ensuring union jobs. Both residential and commercial buildings built by 100 percent union labor are underwritten by loans backed by a small portion of the union's pension fund.

A District Council advertising and marketing campaign that underscores the value of union construction further supports these efforts. Public relations programs to educate consumers have been successful. Billboard advertising throughout Chicagoland emphasizes that union-built is quality-built. Television commercials (on the Saturday morning "New Home Showcase") and video productions rein-

force the value of a job well done by union carpenters. All these efforts have paid off. The majority of builders/developers in the District's 10-county area acknowledge that using union carpenters represents a 2 percent savings in overall costs.

The District Council's members also have a long record of volunteerism. Carpenters give of their time and resources to help young people, social services, and charity organizations in communities throughout the 10-county area.

More than 75 years ago the District Council dedicated its headquarters at 12 East Erie on Chicago's near North Side. Today it is located in a new state-of-the-art facility, which the District Council helped to develop. The work of earlier carpenters—walnut doors, paneling, and other interiors—will also move, a reminder of the true craftsmanship and fine quality work that are the hallmark of the union carpenter. ∎

Stationary engineers operate, maintain, and repair "stationary" equipment in industrial and commercial complexes: heating, air conditioning, ventilation, and electric- or steam-powered systems. To be accomplished in their discipline, stationary engineers must be proficient in chemistry, physics, applied electricity, and the reading of blueprints. This is a far cry from the days of early stationary workers, who operated steam boilers.

In Chicago in the late 1800s, much of that work involved large boilers that powered the city's breweries as well as its large industrial plants. The work was dangerous, the hours long, and the pay low. The work also entailed a high degree of skill and continuous training to work with

Local 399 engineers at work in an old engine room.

new techniques of the industrial age.

In an attempt to improve conditions, a group of stationary engineers met in Chicago on December 7, 1876, to form the National Union of Steam Engineers. Over the years other construction workers from across America and Canada—heavy equipment operators, mechanics, and surveyors—joined the union. Its name was changed to the International Union of Operating Engineers in 1928 to better reflect the make-up of the union.

In 2001 IUOE represented 400,000

men and women. Its network of 170 locals throughout North America includes Local 399, headquartered in Chicago. Local 399 represented 10,000 stationary engineers and skilled building maintenance workers throughout Illinois and Northern Indiana by year-end 2001. They handle virtually every aspect of facility operations at commercial, industrial, institutional, and government physical plants within the region.

The profession of stationary engineering, a highly technical field, demands not only arduous training, but also a deep commitment to life-long learning as new technologies come on line. As industrial technologies increased, stationary engineers were challenged to keep up to date with the new devices being introduced. Local 399 responded by offering continuing education to its members. This early, innovative approach to labor union management allowed Local 399 members to incorporate air-conditioning, refrigeration, and ventilation equipment into the growing list of equipment being operated, maintained, and repaired by its members. It also allowed for continued growth of the union, despite reductions in the number of boilers used by industry.

Local 399 offers more than 900 hours of continuous educational instruction for both trainees and journey-level members. During the year 2000, more than 2,300 students partook in classroom instruction, combined with on-the-job training. State-of-the-art training facilities throughout Illinois allow members to gain the educational tools necessary to meet the challenges of a changing workplace.

Local 399 also has a long tradition of leadership in the fight for workers' rights. From the fight for a 40-hour work week in the late 1800s to the modern-day struggle for global worker protections and equity, Local 399 and its leadership have consistently been at the center of the effort to promote workers' rights.

The exceptional leadership of Local 399 led the International Union of

Local 399 members marching in Chicago's 2001 St. Patrick's Day Parade.

Operating Engineers to consistently call upon Local 399 officers to serve in high-level positions with the International Union. One Local 399 leader served as the general president of the International Union; and six others served as general vice president.

During the 1960s the late Richard Wren served as president and business manager of Local 399 and led it through a period of growth and mergers, thus increasing its jurisdictional boundaries to six counties within the state of Illinois.

Throughout the 1980s, under the leadership of Lionel "Tiny" Gindorf, Local 399 exploded in growth, covering 102 counties, including 19 in Indiana. Membership within the Local rose dramatically from 4,000 in 1980 to more than 6,700 by 1992.

When Gindorf retired, the leadership of Local 399 was turned over to a younger generation who had new visions for organized labor and for the Local. John Phelan succeeded Gindorf and embarked on an even more aggressive course of growth. By the year 2000 Local 399 membership approached the 9,000 mark.

In recognition of this new style of labor leadership and the unprecedented success of his strategy for labor, Phelan was called upon for his advice and guidance by many organizations. At the time of his death at the early age of 56, he was a general vice president to the International Union, and held appointments on a number of boards representing several Chicago and Illinois port authorities and convention and tourism bureaus. And he was the first labor union representative on the Cook County Economic Development Advisory Committee.

In December 2000 Brian E. Hickey succeeded Phelan as president and business manager. He is one of the youngest ever appointed as general vice president. He also serves in other positions of national labor leadership and on city and state boards and committees.

Under Hickey's leadership, Local 399 has developed its most ambitious plan for growth. This new strategy includes developing and maintaining a highly educated workforce that is well prepared to meet the demands and challenges presented by new and sophisticated technologies and by global competition. The goal is to enhance the status of the American worker and to gain long overdue recognition of the services that they provide to America and its trade unions.

A great history has been written by Local 399, and an even greater history is in the making. ■

ARCHITECTURAL AND ORNAMENTAL IRON WORKERS LOCAL 63

Above: Local 63 members erecting glass curtain-wall panels on the Dearborn Center at Dearborn and Adams, Chicago.

Top: The Broadview, Illinois, headquarters of the Architectural and Ornamental Iron Workers Local 63 also houses state-of-the-art classroom and workroom facilities.

Right, bottom: Harold Washington Library, State and Congress, Chicago.

Iron workers—both structural and ornamental—have shaped most of Chicago's landmark buildings and its modern skyline. In the construction of big buildings, architectural and ornamental iron workers, also called finishers, follow behind structural iron workers—the cowboys of the sky—who form the skeleton of large structures such as bridges, towers, high-rises, and stadiums.

Ornamental iron workers erect the curtain walls and window wall systems that cover steel or concrete buildings. They build stairways, catwalks, gratings, railings, and fencing. It is they who give the cityscape its finished appearance.

Two places in the country train journeymen finishers for work as ornamental iron workers. One is in Broadview, Illinois, immediately west of Chicago. The apprenticeship program is held on-site at the headquarters of the Architectural and Ornamental Iron Workers Local 63. And the complex is about to get larger. The local is spending $1.6 million on the addition of 14,000 square feet of new state-of-the-art classrooms and workrooms. Here apprentices train to become part of a skilled work force of iron workers; here current journeymen finishers brush up on the latest technology.

The training program has long been rated one of the top in the country. Nearly 30 years ago it was selected by the Department of the Interior and the Federal Highway Administration to operate a special education program: the National Iron Workers Training Program for American Indians. Since 1972 more than 2,000 Native Americans have come to Local 63's Broadview complex for a 12-week course on the basics of iron working. After completing this preparatory course, the students are moved into regular apprenticeship programs throughout the country. The idea for training Native Americans was the brainchild of Raymond J. Robertson, a former Local 63 Apprenticeship Coordinator and author of the 100-year history of the International

Association of Bridge, Structural, Ornamental and Reinforcing Iron Workers.

Young apprentices and trainees earn while they learn. In a four-year comprehensive course that stresses safety first, they learn how to use different combinations of materials for erecting curtain walls and window wall systems, how to use a range of high-tech caulking, and how to work with a variety of materials such as steel, glass, bronze, aluminum, and composites. An important aspect of the program is earning welding certification for those who complete the rigorous course. As they prepare to enter into an age-old craft, apprentices also learn about the history of the union and the sacrifices made by early iron workers in their fight to gain a decent living.

And the craft is constantly changing, more so in ornamental iron work than in any other branch of iron working. Once most buildings were made of masonry, and stairs, railings, columns, and facades were made of cast iron. That all changed with the introduction of structural steel and the emergence of skyscrapers.

As newer technology changed building materials from masonry to structural steel, friction arose among different segments of iron workers. After coming through a dark decade of strikes, fighting for an eight-hour day, and the Haymarket Riot of 1886, a new breed of structural iron workers—former bridge builders—and traditional architectural iron workers vied

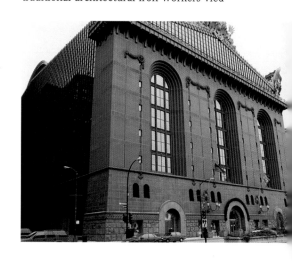

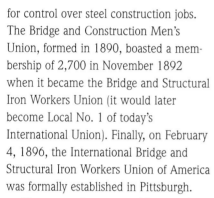

for control over steel construction jobs. The Bridge and Construction Men's Union, formed in 1890, boasted a membership of 2,700 in November 1892 when it became the Bridge and Structural Iron Workers Union (it would later become Local No. 1 of today's International Union). Finally, on February 4, 1896, the International Bridge and Structural Iron Workers Union of America was formally established in Pittsburgh.

The group of ornamental iron workers labored in shops and on the new skyscrapers. They had been active for some years but, when they officially organized as the Architectural Iron Workers on June 5, 1890, they were the lowest-paid mechanics in the city. The next year 1,500 architectural iron workers struck for higher wages and an eight-hour day. They went down in defeat in the face of better-organized employers. The union was nearly crushed. It was saved by the 1893 World's Columbian Exposition held in Chicago. The great need for architectural iron workers won the day; pay was increased and the eight-hour day was achieved.

In December 1900 the Architectural Iron Workers of Chicago became Local 14 of the United Metal Workers International, but not for long. Within three years they joined the International Bridge and Structural Iron Workers Union. It was chartered as Local No. 63 in October 1903. In 1914 the name of the parent union was changed to the International Association of Bridge, Structural and Ornamental Workers. Ornamental iron workers had arrived.

Today Local 63 serves 1,200 architectural and ornamental iron workers and fence installers throughout Lake and Cook counties and parts of Du Page and McHenry counties. Its intermediary role between members and contractor-employers assures top wages and comprehensive pension and health benefits that are among the best in Chicago's building trades. Amicable relations between union and contractors have resulted in no strike action since 1968.

After the Chicago Fire of 1871, the city teemed with skilled craftsmen who came from afar to construct a new metropolis. Among them were the fiercely independent ornamental iron workers. Their work helped imbue the city with its unique character. It continues to do so today. ■

Above: The Halo Corporation at Touhy and Lehigh in Niles, Illinois.

Top left: Chicago's Dearborn Center.

Left: 191 North Wacker Drive, Chicago.

Below: O'Hare International Airport.

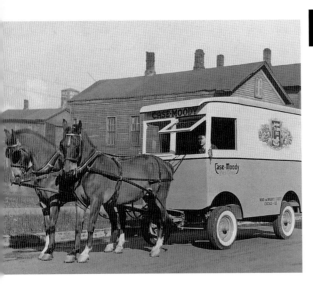

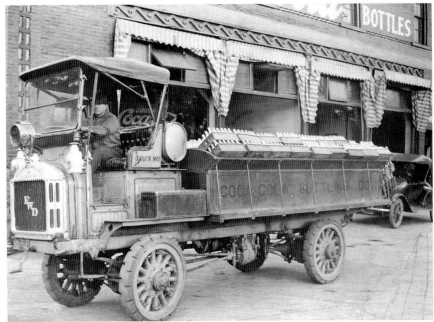

Above and facing page, top: Until the Teamsters Union was able to implement improved working conditions for its members, drivers typically worked more than 100 hours a week for as little as $10.

Top: In the early days of the teaming industry, drivers were responsible for feeding and grooming the horses that pulled the wagons.

The most diverse union in the United States and one of the largest in the world began with horses and wagons. Today it represents almost every job category from A to Z—airline pilots to zookeepers.

In the years surrounding the turn of the twentieth century, workers in the teaming, or hauling, industry toiled under oppressive conditions. Feeding and grooming horses, greasing and mending wagons, cleaning stalls and harnesses, these were a teamster's duties even before he began his long, back-breaking workday. Teamsters worked six and a half days every week loading their wagons and making deliveries. Some workers toiled even longer.

In Chicago, milk wagon drivers worked 100-hour weeks in all kinds of weather for as little as $10. The Fourth of July and Christmas Day were the only two annual holidays—and they were unpaid. Teamsters were considered unskilled laborers. Yet they were critical to the operation of commerce and industry in every community throughout the country.

In an effort to improve conditions, a group of teamsters, with the help of Samuel Gompers, established a national union—the Teamster Drivers International Union. Headquartered in Detroit, the TDIU was chartered by the AFL on January 27, 1899. Membership, 1,700 in its first year, grew rapidly; in 1902 TDIU boasted 13,800 members.

The most impressive TDIU local unions were those in Chicago. They were stronger, better organized, and more determined to improve the lot of the workingman. Chicago teamsters were the first to upgrade their status from unskilled laborers to craftsmen.

Nevertheless, the Chicago teamsters were not entirely satisfied with the TDIU. They wearied of what they considered to be an authoritarian attitude emanating from Detroit. The situation reached a critical point when the TDIU increased per capita fees by 400 percent—from 5 to 25 cents a month. Another bone of contention was the union's inclusion of employer-drivers who owned up to five teams. The Chicago locals believed this provision would allow employers to gain control of the locals. To exacerbate matters, the Chicago candidate for the office of delegate to the AFL convention was defeated.

In early 1902 Chicago split from the TDIU and formed the Teamsters National Union. Membership in the TNU was limited to teamsters and helpers. Those who owned and drove their own team were admitted only if they did not hire drivers.

The AFL urged reunification of the two unions. Thus encouraged, the groups held a joint convention in August 1903. It was a feisty and turbulent gathering. But the TDIU and the TNU did agree to merge. On August 22, 1903, the AFL chartered the International Brotherhood of Teamsters; national offices were in Indianapolis.

Monthly per capita fees were set at 15 cents and membership was restricted to owners of no more than one team of horses. The Chicago unions were the clear victors.

Chicago teamsters continued to dominate the international union. With about

half of the membership of the international, Chicago was where the future of the entire IBT was determined. The teamsters had a tremendous impact on the city's business activity. As one AFL leader said in 1903: "There is no industry today that can successfully carry on their business if the teamster lays down his reins." The Chicago penchant for using strong measures to gain their objectives was to be a hallmark of the international union over the next century.

To help streamline operations among local unions, joint councils were established in cities where there were at least three locals. Chicago's Joint Council—number 25—was chartered on March 24, 1911. As with other councils, its purpose is to serve as intermediary between locals and the international union. The IBT constitution gives them the authority to approve or veto work action being considered by locals, to evaluate wage scales, and to adjudicate jurisdictional disputes.

This system of oversight works well. It gives union members stronger representation and enhanced negotiating power. Collective clout at the bargaining table continues to ensure and sustain improved working conditions, top wages, and superior pensions and other benefits.

The joint councils were established in the face of changing technology. Horses and wagons were giving way to motor trucks that could move freight longer distances. Over the decades some freight-moving fields, such as coalmen, became obsolete.

In the early 1930s IBT began a push to organize the fast-growing long-distance trucking industry and related fields. By 1940 it was the largest private-sector U.S union. Today it serves 1.4 million members belonging to 550 local unions.

Joint Council 25 has jurisdiction over 22 local unions representing 115,000 members throughout Northern Illinois. In the Chicago tradition, Joint Council 25 wields significant clout; it is hard hitting and tough in its negotiating stance, but always fair.

Today the International Brotherhood of Teamsters, Chauffeurs, Warehousemen and Helpers of America represents everything that moves by truck, and then some. Union members have a tremendous impact on every aspect of daily living—delivering materials for building roads, bridges, and other infrastructure; hauling food, clothing, parcels, and magazines; transportation, conventions, and entertainment.

Everything, in fact, from A to Z. ■

Today the International Brotherhood of Teamsters represents 1.4 million members belonging to 550 local unions.

Horsepower!

UNITED STATES AIR FORCE
PLANT № 27
TOLEDO AIR PROCUREMENT OFFICE

Shelter from the elements. Protection against wind and rain. Ensuring dry and comfortable homes and businesses. These are the responsibilities of roofers and waterproofers. In Chicagoland, these skilled craftsmen are served by Local 11 of the United Union of Roofers, Waterproofers and Allied Workers.

Today Local 11 is the largest local roofers' union in the country with 10 percent of the international membership. It represents 2,200 members in 27 counties in Illinois and nine in Southern Wisconsin. It services nearly 200 contractors and oversees training of hundreds of apprentices and journeymen.

Local 11's training program is jointly administered with the Chicagoland Roofing Contractors Council. In fact, labor and management have jointly sponsored the Chicagoland training program since World War II. This is an unusual partnership. Now Local 11 is investing more than $2 million in a state-of-the-art training facility in Indian Head Park, Illinois.

The unusual union-contractor partnership is based on hard work and dedication. Building and maintaining good contractor relations has been a hallmark of Local 11 for many decades. However, as with other Chicagoland unions, this was not always the case.

In the early days, roofers had little protection from hard-scrabble living—low pay, long hard hours, unsafe working conditions, hazardous materials, and constant exposure to inclement weather.

The first formal roofers' organization to seek redress from unfair treatment was the International Slate and Tile Roofers Union of America, which was chartered in 1903. Three years later the International Brotherhood of Composition Roofers, Damp and Waterproof Workers was formally established. Both groups joined the AFL's Building and Trades Department in the early 1900s. This was another validation of their cooperative spirit and clearly demonstrated that the two independently operated roofers' unions were able to resolve some long-standing jurisdictional disputes.

After World War I the two unions merged to become the United Slate, Tile and Composition Roofers, Damp and Waterproof Workers. The new name, though clumsy, illustrated the desire to "maintain a more harmonious and amicable relation" with each other and to ensure the continuing independent status of the locals. The amalgamation of the two unions occurred just in time to battle the anti-union campaign of the 1920s. In the face of new building technology and jurisdictional disputes, contractors slashed wages. The building trades in Chicago went on strike. The courts upheld the employers' action in the so-called Landis Decision that reduced workers' wages by 25 percent and helped assure the open-shop movement. There were other battles over the next half-century. Despite the need for constant vigilance, the roofers' union prospered.

In 1978 the union underwent reorganization and its name was again changed to the one it bears today: the United Union of Roofers, Waterproofers and Allied Workers. Local 11 also prospered as it worked hard to maintain its solid working relations with contractors and to train highly qualified journeymen.

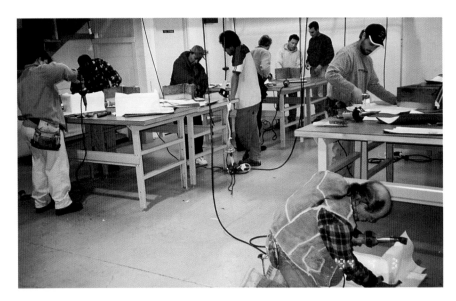

The forest of roofs, high and low, viewed from atop Sears Tower is testimony to the accomplishments of Chicagoland's roofers. Members of Local 11 also install waterproofing systems and materials to protect homes and businesses from the ravages of spring rains and winter snows, summer heat and autumn flooding. They help keep buildings dry, from basement foundation to rooftop.

The four-year apprentice training program consists of classroom instruction and 4,800 hours of hands-on work, under the tutelage of a journeyman. When course work is completed, apprentices earn the right to be journeymen roofers and waterproofers, fully qualified to work in the trade. The investment by the union and management ensures the consumer a quality product and installation of various roofing and waterproofing systems, on time, and within budget.

That it is hard and rigorous work—often in extreme weather—is illustrated by what is called "roofers' hours." To lessen wear and tear on both new and experienced roofers, the working day begins at 6 in the morning and knock-off time is 2 in the afternoon. This placement of the eight-hour day heightens productivity, helps prevent accidents, and serves the industry better for all—roofers, contractors, and consumers.

Safety is a major concern. The union uses the most comprehensive documentation on safety and health hazards ever developed for the roofing industry. These and other materials are an important part of apprentice training. In a highly rated health and safety program, Local 11 and the parent union have made increased awareness of job-related health hazards a focus of union activity. They have been doing so since 1978, the year the union got its current name. Since then, the union not only conforms to Department of Labor guidelines, it surpasses them.

Working with various roofing systems requires constant vigilance to avert exposure to hazardous materials—for both workers and consumers. The union works with the National Institute for Occupational Safety and health to evaluate job sites for risks of asbestos exposure and has developed an asbestos training program for apprentices and journeymen.

Providing lasting and safe shelter and protection for Chicagoland consumers remains the ultimate mission of Local 11 roofers and waterproofers. ■

In the early 1980s an event took place in Chicago that further ensured the health and safety of all employees in the state of Illinois. The venue on the near West Side of the city was the headquarters of the International Union of Painters and Allied Trades (IUPAT) District Council #14. Governor James R. Thompson signed into law the Toxic

Above: A family-owned painting business in the 1900s.

Right: Apprentice training in the 1950s.

Substances Disclosure to Employees Act, known as the Employee Right-to-Know Law, which became effective on January 1, 1984. The law requires employers to educate workers about the toxic hazards of materials with which they work.

The use of district council headquarters to publicize enactment of the law was most appropriate. IUPAT played a significant role in the passing of the Occupational Safety and Health Administration Act of 1970 and had waged a fight for the health and safety of their members for decades.

During the early 1900s most painting work, whether interior or exterior, was labor intensive—with the use of lead-based paints, calcimine, and wallpaper. The development of new paints and semi-gloss enamels brought about a reduction in labor needs.

In the spring of 1938 the Illinois Department of Public Health issued a report based on examination of more than 200 Chicago painters. That report clearly indicated the perilous conditions under which painters worked when it noted: "With the advent of fast-drying paints, the time for covering an area has been sharply reduced; in this increased rate of work lie several important health factors. First, fast-drying paints imply higher volatilizing solvents and dilutents, which in turn result in a more heavily contaminated working environment...Thus the painter today is subject to a greater hazard than formerly."

The speed-up system and inhalation of

ever more toxic fumes were taking their toll. IUPAT and Painters' District Council #14 redoubled efforts to fight for a healthy and safe workplace environment.

The Brotherhood of Painters and Decorators of America was organized in 1887 in Baltimore. Within a year the brotherhood had 7,000 members nationwide and more than 100 locals.

The oldest Chicago union is Painters and Tapers Local 147, whose charter was granted on April 1,1890. Among the Chicago organizers was James McKinney who, as head of the national union, would later lead the movement to break with the Baltimore faction and move headquarters to the Midwest. Another early local was chartered on October 14, 1892; 13 men

Painters join in at a labor rally in front of the state capitol in Springfield.

established Painters and Tapers Local 265 in order to organize opposition to George Pullman's onerous conditions of employment. Glaziers' Local 27 was established in May 1899. As with many other Chicago unions, the glaziers immediately became active in mobilizing against employers who hired cheaper non-union labor—thus producing shoddy work.

A painters' district council was founded in Chicago in 1891, Painters' District Council #3, but it was short-lived; the rank and file were dissatisfied with its performance. The present-day District Council #14 was formed on July 9, 1910.

The district council's fight to improve conditions in the industry became a hallmark of its accomplishments over the decades. Another major effort is its determination to ensure that contractors have access to the best-trained work force available.

Immediately after World War I, the painters' union apprenticeship program in Chicago took on renewed life when it and other unions entered into partnership with the city's public school system. The newly created Washburne Trade School became the center for training veterans for jobs in the trades. Among those trades were painting, decorating, and wallpapering. During World War II Painters' District Council #14 and the Painters' Contractors Association registered their own apprenticeship program with the government while continuing to teach courses at Washburne. Over the years other allied

trades were added to the curriculum. In 1962 the district council and the contractors formed a trust agreement to fund the Chicago-area Painting and Decorating Joint Apprenticeship and Training Committee (JATC). In 1995 the JATC training program left Washburne and moved into its own modern facility in Berkeley, Illinois.

JATC is dedicated to producing skilled, professional apprentices who provide contractors with a highly valued work force at reduced costs. The award-winning three-year training program (classroom instruction and on-the-job training) is recognized as one of the best painter apprenticeship programs in the country. It produces apprentices with a rounded education, highly competitive skills, and well-developed work ethics.

Today Painters' District Council #14 represents 16 local unions in Lake, Cook, Will, and Grundy counties, more than half of which have been around since before 1900. Among the union members it speaks for are painters, glaziers, drywall finishers, architectural metal and glass workers, wood finishers, tapers, and sign painters.

Painters' District #14 continues in its mission to organize workers—including minorities and women—educating members on safety and new technology in the workplace, and ensuring its record of winning for painters some of the highest wage rates and one of the most substantial benefits packages in the country. ∎

The state-of-the-art training facility for Painters' District Council # 14 is in Berkeley, Illinois.

INTERNATIONAL ASSOCIATION OF HEAT AND FROST INSULATORS AND ASBESTOS WORKERS UNION LOCAL 17 AND THE ILLINOIS REGIONAL CONTRACTORS ASSOCIATION

When steam power emerged as a technology in the late nineteenth century, a whole new industry was spawned. Pipe coverers were called upon to insulate new steam boilers and to convert old mechanical systems in order to conserve energy in homes and factories.

To improve working conditions within the insulation workplace and to ensure fair wages, delegates from locals in Cleveland, Pittsburgh, Boston, San Francisco, Detroit, and the four-year-old

A Local 17 skilled insulator applies pipe covering in a Chicago office building. Installing insulation will reduce the owner's energy costs.

Insulation work is performed on a reactor vessel at one of the many industrial job sites in Local 17's territory.

local union in Chicago convened in St. Louis for the first national convention in July 1903.

Chicago's Pipecoverers Union became Local 17 of the fledgling National (later International) Association of Heat and Frost Insulators and Asbestos Workers. The Chicago union has played a pivotal role in the history of the international union.

In 1913 Local 17 addressed its members' needs by reaching a two-year agreement that increased their pay to 65 cents an hour for the first year and up to 67.5 cents an hour the following year. In 1922 the union moved to 180 West Washington Street and Hugh E. Mulligan became the union's business agent. In 1937 John Quinn became a Local 17 apprentice. Rising through the ranks, Quinn was appointed by Mulligan to the position of

financial secretary. He served Mulligan and the membership with great loyalty and dedication.

In 1976, during the tenure of business manager Jack Keane, Local 17 purchased its current headquarters on Chicago's near South Side. The building houses the apprenticeship school, union hall, and the health and welfare, pension, and annuity funds office.

The mid-1980s saw the election of Terry Lynch as financial secretary and the election of Mike O'Neill as business manager in 1987. No Local 17 history would be complete without mentioning the union's own Father Gavin Quinn, O. Carm., son of the late John Quinn, chaplain to Local 17, the International, and the Chicago Building Trades.

The Illinois Regional Insulation Contractor's Association (IRIC), currently headed by Alec Rexroat, has worked with Local 17 for more than a half-century. Its goal is to promote union insulation contracting and to create an atmosphere in which Chicago and the Local 17 jurisdiction is a good place to conduct business for customers, contractors, and workers.

Local 17 and IRIC joined the national movement to help safeguard the health and welfare of both workers and citizens. Major concerns today continue to be life safety and energy efficiency. Current life safety efforts include the removal of asbestos from commercial and industrial job sites.

Under the careful guidance of its current administration—Terry Lynch, John Crinion, Brian Glynn, John Caddick, and Jack Shine—and the skilled craftsmanship of the Local 17 membership, Heat and Frost Insulators Local 17 covers 26 counties in Illinois and three in Northwest Indiana. Its 900-plus members provide insulation at refineries, steel mills, and factories, in commercial buildings, schools, hospitals, and industrial sites. However, the early principles remain the same: hard work and solidarity, public safety, and energy efficiency. ∎

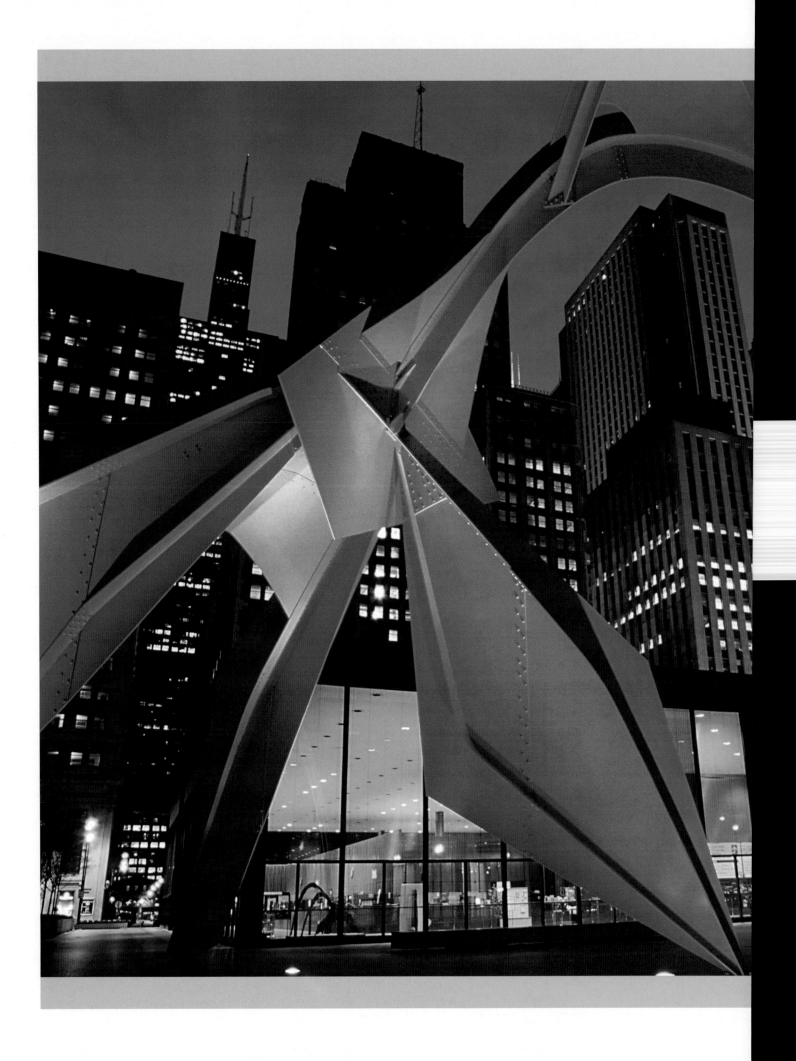

CHAPTER ELEVEN

Quality of Life

M edical and educational institutions contribute to the exceptional quality of life enjoyed by Illinois residents and visitors.

Abbott Laboratories **312-315**

Loyola University Chicago **316-317**

Illinois Institute of Technology **318-319**

Robert Morris College **320-321**

Blue Cross and Blue Shield
of Illinois **322-323**

DeVry Inc. **324-325**

Museums In the Park **326-330**

Hots Michels Enterprises
for Organ Donor Awareness **331**

Children's Memorial Hospital **332**

Left: © James Lemass/Index Stock Imagery

ABBOTT LABORATORIES

Abbott Laboratories' commitment to advancing the practice of medicine began with Dr. Wallace Abbott more than a century ago.

Right: Abbott Laboratories was a pioneer in the introduction of anesthetics and anti-infective medicines, including penicillin.

I t is one of Illinois' largest employers, one of the state's largest investors, and commits more capital to scientific research and development (nearly $7 billion in the past five years) than any other company in the state of Illinois.

It has consistently achieved medical breakthroughs that have advanced the practice of health care. It is a pioneer in the fight against AIDS. Its diversified line of products improves the health of the world's people. Each year it contributes millions of dollars to philanthropic causes throughout the state and around the world.

Industry Week has consistently named it one of the world's best-managed companies, and its strong financial performance earns it continuous listing in *The 100 Best Stocks in America*.

The company is the *Fortune 150* Abbott Laboratories, headquartered in North Chicago. The diversity of its health care business makes Abbott a strong and comprehensive presence in a growing number of medical markets throughout the world. The company's three major businesses—pharmaceuticals, nutritionals, and medical products—are all focused on the discovery, development, and marketing of products that address some of the world's most critical medical conditions.

Abbott's ongoing mission is to deliver breakthrough medical technologies that advance the practice of health care—from prevention and diagnosis to treatment and cure. To achieve this goal, the company combines the core strengths that characterize all of its diverse businesses: leading-edge science, extensive manufacturing expertise, well-developed distribution channels, and superior sales organizations.

Its medical breakthroughs include the development, in 1936, of the anesthetic Pentothal; early mass production of penicillin and development of other antibiotics; the introduction, in 1985, of the world's first diagnostic test for AIDS; the development, in 1996, of Norvir, one of the world's first protease inhibitors to fight HIV, the virus that causes AIDS; and the

launch, in 2000, of Kaletra, the company's next-generation HIV protease inihibitor that promises to further advance the practice of AIDS medicine.

Success is Rooted in Science

The source of Abbott's success over the past century is science. Abbott's tradition of innovation and scientific research began in the apartment of 30-year-old physician Dr. Wallace Calvin Abbott. In 1888 Dr. Abbott purchased a medical practice and drugstore in Chicago's Ravenswood neighborhood. From this operation, which he named the People's Drug Store, Dr. Abbott made house calls and sold the common medical treatments of the day. However, Dr. Abbott wasn't satisfied with the medicines available. Many consisted of alcoholic extracts or crude waters drawn from medicinal plants, which were hit and miss in their effectiveness.

Dr. Abbott advocated a new scientific theory of pharmacy based upon the alkaloid, or active ingredient, of a drug plant. This alkaloid could be compressed into a tiny granule or pill form and then taken orally. These, too, proved unsatisfactory, so, in search of a better alternative, he began producing his own.

Dr. Abbott's kitchen sink became the original production center for what he called the Abbott Alkaloidal Company.

Dr. Abbott, along with family members, worked around the clock forming the tiny granules. His new formulations were far more dependable than earlier preparations. Dosages were more accurate and uniform. Their ease of use helped his patients to comply with treatment regimens, resulting in better medical outcomes.

Dr. Abbott continued to research new alkaloidal treatments and remedies and created an arsenal of medicines for physicians to choose from. The early success of these medicines and the circulation of *The Alkaloidal Clinic*, a medical journal published by Dr. Abbott, firmly established the Abbott Alkaloidal Company as an innovative leader in the medical community.

By 1915 the market for alkaloidal remedies had peaked, with a number of competitors entering the market. Advances in chemistry and medicine led to a new pharmaceutical field—synthetic drugs. These medicines were made from synthetic chemicals rather than the alkaloids of plants. Recognizing this evolution, the Abbott Alkaloidal Company shifted its focus and became an early leader in synthetic treatments. In 1915 the firm changed its name to Abbott Laboratories, reflecting its emphasis on scientific research.

As a consequence of its new direction, Abbott doubled its revenues and created a need for larger production facilities. In 1920 construction began on a new manufacturing and headquarters facility in North Chicago. In 1921, just as the new headquarters of Abbott Laboratories neared completion, Dr. Abbott died. The business was 33 years old, growing robustly, and was firmly rooted in science. Its commitment to research and development would only grow in the years ahead.

Medical, Geographic Diversity Fuel Growth

An early focus of the company's research and development was anesthesia. Abbott has been a leader in this field since its creation of Nembutal in 1930. This orally administered sedative was widely used to ease childbirth, control convulsions, relieve insomnia, and alleviate disorders ranging from seasickness to delirium. Today Nembutal continues to be a part of Abbott's extensive portfolio of anesthesia products.

The success of Nembutal led Abbott scientists to a new formulation of the drug that could be used as an intravenous anesthetic. The drug, Pentothal, was introduced in 1936, and remains widely used today. Pentothal played a major role in saving lives in World War II by allowing wounded soldiers to be treated before they got to a hospital. For this important achievement its creators, Drs. Ernest Volwiler and Donalee Tabern, were inducted into the National Inventors' Hall of Fame in 1986.

Another treatment area in which Abbott has long specialized is anti-infective drugs. In 1941 Abbott became one of the first U.S. companies to commercially produce penicillin, contributing again to the U.S. effort in World War II. Abbott constructed a new facility in North Chicago to research and develop the best strain of penicillin possible. The company found the most effective mold strain on an overripe cantaloupe in a Peoria, Illinois, fruit stand and successfully mass-produced the antibiotic. This discovery would eventually lead to one of Abbott's most successful long-term franchises, anti-infective medicines, with widely used products such as PCE (erythromycin) and Biaxin (clarithromycin).

By the mid-1950s Abbott's sales surpassed $100 million and the firm had introduced hundreds of pharmaceuticals and health care products. While it had begun doing business outside the United States in 1931, Abbott now shifted to a true global, multinational focus and con-

Headquartered in north suburban Chicago, Abbott Laboratories is a *Fortune* 150 corporation and one of the world's largest health care manufacturers.

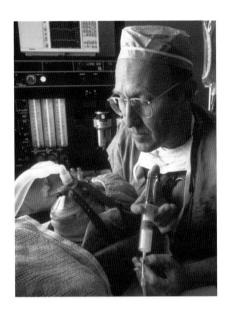

This page and facing page, bottom: Today Abbott Laboratories provides total, integrated solutions across the health care continuum through the discovery and development of pharmaceuticals, diagnostics, adult and infant nutritionals, and hospital products.

tinued to expand by offering its products throughout the world.

Today Abbott has 60 international affiliates, manufacturing sites in 24 countries, and markets its products in more than 130 countries. Worldwide, the company employs some 70,000 people. In Illinois there are more than 16,000 Abbott employees, making it one of the largest employers in the state.

Abbott has also grown through acquisitions that diversified its product line and strengthened its drive to improve the quality of health care—a strategy that continues today. The acquisition of M&R Dietetic Laboratories in 1964 was one of the company's largest and led to its long-term leadership position in nutritional products. This business, which became Abbott's Ross Products Division, allowed the company to expand its presence in the consumer market by offering products such as Similac, the best-selling infant formula in the United States, and Ensure, one of the world's leading brands of adult nutritional products.

To keep pace with its dynamic growth, Abbott purchased 420 acres of farmland in Lake County, Illinois, in 1961. Known as Abbott Park, this site would become Abbott Laboratories' world headquarters. Today it houses numerous research, manufacturing, and administrative facilities that involve all of the company's health care businesses.

In 1973 Abbott launched its diagnostics division, devoted to developing instruments and tests to detect diseases in their early stages and to prevent their spread. Abbott quickly became, and remains, the global leader in immunodiagnostics.

Abbott achieved a number of medical breakthroughs in the 1980s. In 1983 the company received approval to market Depakote, a new treatment for epilepsy that is also used to control bipolar disorder and to prevent migraine headaches. Two years later Abbott received approval from the U.S. Food and Drug Administration to produce the world's first blood test to detect the

AIDS virus. The test proved to be extremely accurate, and the company worked tirelessly to produce enough tests to quickly support the medical community's worldwide effort to fight this then-new disease.

Additional achievements by Abbott in the 1980s included the introduction of the ADD-Vantage intravenous drug delivery system, which allows potent drugs with short-term stability in solutions to be easily and efficiently mixed just before they are administered. In 1988 the company introduced its IMx immunoassay system, an automated instrument with a broad menu of diagnostic tests. It has become the world's leading immunoassay system and one of Abbott's best-selling products.

Through its own internal research and through the acquisition of complementary technologies and businesses, Abbott introduced many new products during the 1990s that target not only major diseases but also medical conditions such as ulcers and respiratory infections. By the end of the 1990s the company's catalog of products comprised some of the world's most important advances in medical technology and therapeutics: Norvir, an HIV protease inhibitor for the treatment of AIDS; Kaletra, an advanced-generation protease inhibitor; Biaxin, a potent anti-infective for treating serious infections, including those common in AIDS patients; Survanta and Synagis, two specialty pharmaceuticals for preventing serious respiratory conditions in infants; Ultane, a next-generation inhalation anesthetic; and AxSYM and ARCHITECT, advanced diagnostic systems for high-vol-

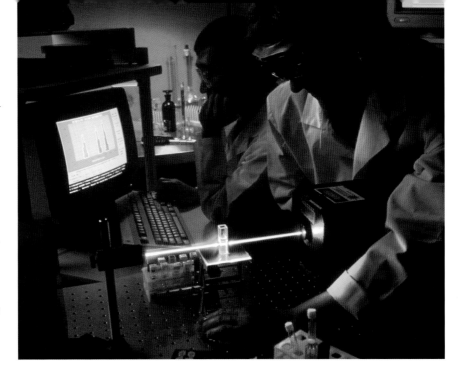

ume laboratory testing.

In the new millennium, Abbott has continued to strengthen its traditional businesses while expanding its business through new growth platforms. In 2000, Abbott acquired the pharmaceutical business of the German chemical manufacturer BASF A.G. Best known by the name of its largest component, Knoll Pharmaceuticals, the acquisition enhanced Abbott's portfolio of marketed drugs, with products such as Synthroid for thyroid disorders and Meridia for obesity. It also greatly increased Abbott's global scientific capabilities, significantly enhancing the company's research and development investment and bringing Abbott leadership in advanced scientific platforms such as monoclonal antibody research. This technology allows researchers to target specific proteins on human cells, leading to the rapid development of more effective treatments with fewer side effects.

Also in the first years of the twenty-first century, Abbott has leveraged its scientific and marketing expertise to build a multifaceted cardiovascular device franchise that includes products such as The Closer, a suture-based device that quickly closes arteries after vascular procedures; embolic protection devices that remove debris dislodged during cardiovascular procedures; catheters to treat chronic total occlusions that often result in by-pass surgery; and drug-coated stents that dramatically improve the long-term effectiveness of these devices used to reopen blocked blood vessels.

Success Reaps Dividends for the Community

As Abbott expands its worldwide presence, it remains firmly rooted in Chicago and the surrounding region, ensuring a vital place in Illinois' economy for years to come. As part of this commitment, the company plays an active role in supporting the communities in which its employees live and work. Abbott contributes millions of dollars annually to philanthropic organizations in Illinois and around the world, from educa-

tional initiatives, to cultural institutions, to human health and welfare organizations.

Among its greatest philanthropic contributions are the hundreds of thousands of dollars Abbott donates each year to many of Illinois' leading universities and medical and research institutions for research and development. Abbott supports the United Way and other health and human services organizations, and sponsors programs that enhance science education and promote environmental stewardship. While investing heavily in local communities near its major facilities, Abbott maintains an active involvement in worldwide relief efforts. Its annual donations of health care products to developing countries and to aid victims of natural and manmade disasters worldwide exceed $100 million. In 2000, Abbott launched Step Forward, a long-term global philanthropic initiative to improve the lives of AIDS orphans and vulnerable children in developing countries hardest hit by AIDS.

Abbott's diversified line of products—offering important therapeutics, diagnostic tests, nutritionals, and medical technologies—will continue to grow and advance to benefit the health of the world's people. In each of its businesses, the company is poised to introduce new products to prevent, detect, and treat many of the world's most urgent medical challenges. Through its innovative science and conscientious outreach efforts, Abbott Laboratories will continue to play an active role in improving the quality of life for people in the twenty-first century, around the world—and, always, at home in Illinois. ∎

Through world-class science, Abbott Laboratories focuses on developing breakthrough medical technologies that address the world's areas of greatest unmet medical need, including cancer, cardiovascular disease, AIDS, diabetes, obesity, and rheumatoid arthritis.

St. Ignatius Loyola established the educational principles that guide Loyola University Chicago in 1534, the year the Society of Jesus (S.J.) was formed by Ignatius. *Cura personalis*, "care for the individual," is at the core of the Jesuit philosophy that also strives to make each student a "person for others." Loyola University Chicago has adhered to this tenet since it was founded 130 years ago, when it emerged from a midwestern city mission. It has since grown into a world-class university providing education tempered with humanity.

The Reverend Arnold Damen, S.J., founded St. Ignatius College, located on Chicago's near Southwest Side, in 1870, next to Holy Family Parish, which Father Damen had inaugurated 13 years earlier. St. Ignatius College opened its doors with four professors, 37 male students, and a curriculum based on liberal arts and the sciences. The existence of this tiny college was sorely tested within the first year. The Chicago Fire of 1871 threatened both the single college building and the parish church, but in the end—after much prayer and supplication—both were spared. Emphasis on classical education in the Jesuit tradition took root. The first bachelor of arts degree was awarded in 1876. During its first decade, St. Ignatius' graduates included Carter H. Harrison, who would later serve five terms as Chicago's mayor. By 1895 the college's student body reached nearly 500.

The early decades of the 1900s were a period of rapid growth and expansion in academic programming. The first professional school, the School of Law, was established in 1908, and the School of Medicine was opened the following year. To better reflect its growing influence and purpose, in 1909 St. Ignatius

Right: Loyola University Chicago's Lake Shore campus stretches along Lake Michigan on Chicago's North Side. The university's Madonna della Strada Chapel is shown at lower left.

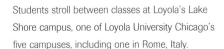

Students stroll between classes at Loyola's Lake Shore campus, one of Loyola University Chicago's five campuses, including one in Rome, Italy.

College changed its name to Loyola University. Academic programming made even greater strides in 1914: The School of Sociology opened; Loyola became the first Jesuit college or university to admit women; and a part-time division was established to provide education to working people. During the 1920s Loyola opened its School of Business Administration and its Graduate School. The School of Nursing was established in 1935, the first baccalaureate nursing program in Illinois. Six years later Loyola's Institute of Social and Industrial Relations opened. These and other efforts to enhance opportunities for professional education demonstrate the university's continuous commitment to play an active role in the life of the city. The evolution of its academic programming tells the story of its humanistic approach to education—law, medicine, sociology, business, and nursing.

Loyola's professional schools have brought it many distinctions. The School of Law exemplifies the Jesuit tradition by its commitment to social justice. Its Stritch School of Medicine and the Loyola University Medical Center have earned a worldwide reputation for excellence and innovation. The medical center is now nationally known for open-heart surgery

and, in 1988, opened the first cardiac care center in the country. Six years later the Loyola University Cancer Center opened as the only freestanding facility in Illinois entirely dedicated to cancer research, diagnosis, treatment, and prevention. Other areas of expertise include kidney transplants, microneurosurgery, care of burn victims, and neonatal care for high-risk infants.

Today Loyola offers 144 programs of study leading to 27 different academic degrees to a student body of more than 13,000 from 50 states and at least 74 foreign countries—an indication of its worldwide reputation. Nearly two-thirds of the students are women, one in four is a designated minority, and more than one in five is from a non-Christian tradition. Nearly all of Loyola's 1,100 full-time faculty (97 percent) hold a Ph.D. or equivalent. Its 120,000 alumni represent every U.S. state and 120 foreign countries. Alumni who work in the Chicago area provide an impressive range of services to the community, serving as many of the city's leading professionals—doctors, lawyers, school principals, social workers, and psychologists.

Loyola today boasts five campuses: Lake Shore on Chicago's far North Side; Water Tower on Chicago's Magnificent Mile; Mallinckrodt in Wilmette, Illinois; the Stritch School of Medicine and Medical Center in Maywood, Illinois; and the Rome Center of Liberal Arts in Italy.

Students are offered a wide range of programs for personal growth and professional enhancement, including study abroad. When Loyola opened its Rome Center of Liberal Arts in 1962, it was the first such center to be established in Rome by an American university; it remains the largest university study program in Western Europe. It is now part of the university's Office of International Affairs, which offers study-abroad programs in nearly 20 countries. Other personal-growth programs include The Center for Urban Research and Learning (CURL),

which has earned a national and international reputation for developing new models of teaching and research that center on the exchange of knowledge between the university and the community; CURL focuses on social and economic issues such as welfare reform and fair housing. This is just one of Loyola's many programs that allow students to obtain hands-on experience in community-based research projects that collaborate with local communities and social-services agencies.

Loyola was one of the first American Catholic universities to hire lay executives to handle administrative matters such as finances and development, to create a board of lay trustees, and to establish a women's board, thus giving women a strong voice in Loyola's governance. And today the Women's Studies Program, the first of its kind at a Jesuit university, is Loyola's largest interdisciplinary program.

Loyola University Chicago is nationally recognized for intellectual discourse and research, a commitment to community and social justice, and the premier education of students to be "people for others." For 130 years it has continued to provide education tempered with humanity. ■

Above: Loyola's downtown campus overlooks the historic Water Tower and Chicago's Magnificent Mile.

Top: Students study in the Cudahy Library at the Lake Shore campus. Loyola's top-ranked library system includes seven campus libraries.

Transforming lives. Inventing the future. Since 1890 Illinois Institute of Technology has been committed to this goal.

In late nineteenth-century Chicago, at the height of the Industrial Revolution, two men were convinced that a practical education was necessary for young people of slender means. To achieve that purpose, Philip Danforth Armour, a wealthy meat packer, and Allen Cleveland Lewis, a successful businessman, financed the establishment of two separate institutions of learning—Armour Institute in 1892 and Lewis Institute in 1890.

Armour was motivated by the famous "million dollar" sermon given by the Reverend Frank Wakely Gunsaulus in 1890 in which he said he wanted to found a school where students of all backgrounds could prepare for meaningful

S.R. Crown Hall is considered a masterwork of Mies van der Rohe, a leading architect of the twentieth century and former director of IIT's School of Architecture.

roles in a changing industrial society. The institute officially opened in 1893 with 700 students and Gunsaulus as president.

Gunsaulus bought the scientific displays of the World's Columbian Exposition held in Chicago in 1893 to help furnish Armour labs. He entered into an agreement with the Art Institute to jointly operate an architectural department known as the Chicago School of Architecture at Armour Institute. These ties to science

and technology, to architecture, and to Chicago's venerable institutions would help shape the future of IIT.

By the turn of the century, Armour Institute of Technology had earned a reputation of note for its scientific research work. (Lee DeForest, known as the father of radio, taught at Armour and at Lewis Institute and conducted his breakthrough research at Armour laboratories in 1907.)

The Research Foundation of Armour Institute of Technology (renamed IIT Research Institute in 1963) was established in 1936 to help industrialists find solutions to technological problems. One of the most dramatic projects during the foundation's early years was the design and construction of the Snow Cruiser, the large mobile laboratory to be used by Admiral Richard Byrd on his third Antarctic expedition in 1939. Just five years later Marvin Camras and his associates in research developed the first commercially practical magnetic recorders. This work resulted in more than 200 patents that earned him the title "father of magnetic recording."

At about this time Ludwig Mies van der Rohe, former director of Germany's Bauhaus, joined Armour as head of its school of architecture. Mies, who remained at IIT for 20 years, virtually defined high-rise architecture for the second half of the twentieth century. Another Bauhauser was already in Chicago. Laszlo Moholy-Nagy operated a school of design that would merge with IIT in 1949 as its Institute of Design.

In 1940 Lewis Institute, after decades of success in providing young men and women of diverse backgrounds with a sound practical and liberal arts education, merged with Armour Institute of Technology to become Illinois Institute of Technology.

The next decades were a period of expansion. The master plan created by Mies for the university's campus laid the groundwork. Between 1943 and 1968 campus expansion averaged almost two buildings a year. This extraordinary rate of

growth was made possible by a strong board of trustees who gave unstintingly of their time and money to make what *Architectural Forum* magazine then called "the best architectural expression of a technical college in the world."

Academic programs grew. A law school was added with the merger of Chicago-Kent College of Law in 1969. That same year the Stuart School of Business was established, named for Harold Leonard Stuart, a Chicago financier and an alumnus of Lewis Institute.

Today IIT is a Ph.D.-granting technological university that awards degrees in the sciences, mathematics, and engineering, as well as architecture, psychology, design, business, and law. More than 6,000 students were enrolled in 2000, representing every state in the union and 80 countries. At the turn of the new millennium, 1,500 degrees were awarded, including 75 Ph.D.s. IIT has developed an interprofessional, technology-based curriculum that prepares students for leadership in an increasingly complex and culturally diverse global workplace, while conducting a substantial program of applied and basic research that enhances human well-being.

The university has five campuses in metropolitan Chicago and one in India. In addition to its 120-acre Main Campus on Chicago's near South Side, there are two IIT complexes in downtown Chicago and one each—Rice and Moffett—in suburban Wheaton and Summit.

IIT and IIT Research Institute conduct $165 million of research each year for government and industry. For example, IIT's Moffett Campus is home to the National Center for Food Safety and Technology, a collaboration among the FDA, the food industry, and university-based food scientists.

Another area of leading-edge work is synchrotron radiation research at Argonne National Laboratory. Here, IIT research teams are working to design new drugs and diagnostic tools. In addition, an IIT-led consortium of five area universities is conducting research at the Fermi National Laboratory to create the next generation of accelerator technology. Finally, IIT is the leading Illinois university in the development of alternative energy sources from fuel cells and batteries.

IIT's board of trustees, among the city's business and civic leaders, assure the university's success by continuing a tradition of great generosity. In 1997 two long-serving trustees, Robert Galvin and Robert Pritzker, initiated a five-year campaign for campus renewal with a pledge to match $120 million in donations. The $250-million challenge was met in less than four years.

Today IIT remains true to its founding vision—to transform lives and invent the future. ■

Above: Main Building, the original Armour Institute site, is located on IIT's Main Campus, a 120-acre complex on Chicago's near South Side.

Left: The IIT campus in downtown Chicago, home of Chicago-Kent College of Law, Stuart Graduate School of Business, and Center for Law and Financial Markets.

The main campus of Robert Morris College is located in a recently renovated landmark building at State Street and Congress in downtown Chicago.

An extensive athletic program gives students the opportunity to participate in competitive sports with other colleges within Illinois and across the Midwest.

A recent addition to the educational and cultural corridor in Chicago's South Loop is a college with an attitude. It is the main campus for an educational institution that serves the needs of students throughout the state. Course work and teaching methods are geared to educating the whole student, to ensuring that each student's college experience is relevant and stimulating. It offers choices in its three-tiered academic system—professional diplomas, associate degrees, and bachelor degrees—so that students can opt for continuing their education or going to work, or both. The school is Robert Morris College and it is the fastest-growing private college in Illinois.

RMC is firmly rooted in old-fashioned midwestern principles and the value of hard work, but with a very modern twist. Its main focus is educating and preparing students for the world of work in today's rapidly changing corporate environment. Each of the college's four divisions—business administration, computer studies, health studies, and art and design—uses the most modern computer technology.

The main campus of Robert Morris College is located in a national historic landmark building that was erected in 1891. William Le Baron Jenney, a

renowned architect known as the "father of the skyscraper," designed the eight-story building.

In the early 1960s Carthage College, founded in 1847, decided to leave the city of Carthage in Illinois and move to Kenosha, Wisconsin. The community was left without an institution of higher learning. To fill the void, Robert Morris College was formed as a junior college on the site of the old Carthage College campus. The name of the new independent, not-for-profit institution was carefully chosen to symbolize commitment and creativity. Robert Morris, known as the "financier of the American Revolution," was a signatory to the Declaration of Independence, the U.S. Constitution, and the Articles of Confederation. He embodied the spirit of independence and personal resourcefulness, attributes that imbue an RMC education.

When chartered in 1965, RMC offered associate's degrees in liberal and vocational arts. A decade later it broadened its offerings to include business and allied health programs when it acquired the Moser School in Chicago and opened an RMC campus in the city's financial district. Moser School was established in 1913 to provide business education that helped students enhance their career opportunities, a mission that dovetailed with that of RMC. Today RMC offers bachelor's degrees in computer studies, graphic design, and business administration as well. It is also the state's leading provider of associate's degrees to minority students.

RMC undertook an aggressive pattern of expansion throughout the state in the 1990s: The Carthage campus moved to Springfield to better serve the needs of residents in Central Illinois. The Chicago, Springfield, Orland Park, Du Page, and O'Hare campuses, plus centers in Peoria, Oak Lawn, Lyons, and North Riverside, together form the Robert Morris College network of service to students in Illinois.

In addition to on-site learning, students

participate in classes offered elsewhere via distance learning. Each campus and extension facility is equipped with state-of-the-art video-conferencing technology. Acquisition of cutting-edge technology is imperative to providing real-world educational experiences that are relevant to the evolving workplace. In a move to upgrade facilities and to house a growing student body, the Chicago campus relocated to larger quarters in 1998.

The move from Lake and La Salle streets in downtown Chicago to new facilities at Congress and State provided a challenge. The landmark building, former home to Sears' flagship store, had to be converted from a retail and office environment into attractive, modern student space. It took great creativity and imagination, as well as $15 million, to transform the interiors. Now the building boasts classrooms equipped with uniquely designed multimedia podiums that permit access to a computer, VCR, document camera, and the Internet at the touch of a button. The 100,000-volume Thomas Jefferson Library, including computers, video monitors, and study areas, occupies two floors.

The boldly colorful facilities were designed to support the college's nontraditional approach to educating students from diverse backgrounds. Multicultural diversity and cultural enrichment to pro-

duce well-rounded students are hallmarks of an RMC education. It is a very student-centered place, as reflected by enrollment figures that have risen dramatically. Throughout the 1990s enrollment nearly tripled and it has grown by 31 percent since 1998, reaching more than 5,400 students in 2001.

Educational guidance often begins before college with efforts to reach and help prospective students through pre-college mentoring and tutoring. For example, RMC participates in a partnership with the Chicago public schools and city colleges in College Excel, a program that gives high school juniors and seniors the opportunity to enroll in college-level courses at RMC while earning college credit.

The RMC commitment to higher education in Illinois is threefold: to match curricula to the changing needs of employers; to nurture the educational aspirations of all students; to ensure relevance to life and work. Faculty and staff are committed to promoting student success by providing structure and guidance. RMC stresses to its students that success comes with meeting high standards for attendance, homework, and adherence to a dress code. Such standards do not, however, preclude participation in varsity sports and cultural events. RMC has an active varsity lineup and interactive cultural program.

Real-world education experience with a focused career foundation is why employers vie for RMC graduates. That is why 97 percent of RMC students find jobs upon graduation. ■

Left: All campuses of Robert Morris College have the latest in classroom technology.

The Robert Morris College administration works closely with corporations and industry leaders to provide curricula that are relative to the needs of the business world.

BLUE CROSS AND BLUE SHIELD OF ILLINOIS

The largest health insurance company in Illinois is also the oldest. For nearly 65 years Blue Cross and Blue Shield of Illinois has operated as a not-for-profit corporation whose mission is to improve the cost effectiveness and accessibility of health care. Its purpose is to allow its members to plan for the future without concern for how to pay health care costs for themselves and their families.

The early Illinois pre-payment plan to cover hospital costs was based on the 1929 Texas plan that guaranteed schoolteachers 21 days' hospital stay for just 50 cents a month. The teachers of Texas were enthusiastic; more than 1,300 enrolled on the first day and other workers throughout the state clamored to join them.

In Chicago, Taylor Strawn, head of the Elgin Watch Company and a trustee of Grant Hospital, and Charles Schweppe, president of the board of trustees at St. Luke's Hospital, believed the Texas program could provide a model for a low-cost hospital plan in Chicago. In 1935 Strawn and Schweppe raised more than $30,000 as an interest-free loan to help finance a plan. Meanwhile, the Illinois legislature passed the Hospital Service Corporation Act to permit the formation of a hospital care plan.

In October 1936 the Plan was incorporated as the not-for-profit Hospital Service Corporation. It was managed by a new organization, the Chicago Plan for Hospital Care. By year's end, the Plan signed its first employee group, Rand McNally and Company. The Elgin Watch Company followed suit, and so did the Women's Christian Temperance Union and the Modern Hospital Publishing Company. The Plan enrolled 32,000 members in its first six months of operations.

The Chicago Plan officially adopted the Blue Cross symbol in 1939. By the end of 1940 there were more than 100 employees serving 150,000 members. Financial solvency was clearly demonstrated by

repayment of the $30,000 start-up loan made by the Plan's founders. By early 1942 the Blue Cross Plan, as it was now called, had provided nearly $6 million in total benefits on 100,000 claims.

In 1947, at the height of the postwar baby boom, annual coverage under the Blue Cross Plan was increased from 21 days to 30 days. And it was growing across the state at a fast pace. The Peoria Blue Cross Plan and the Danville Plan merged with the Chicago Plan in 1947. Decatur followed suit the next year and, in 1951, members in Southern Illinois formerly served by the St. Louis Plan were signed up. The last stand-alone Illinois Plan, Rockford Blue Cross, merged in 1982.

The Blue Cross Plan continued to cover hospital care costs but, to fulfill its commitment to its members, began a move toward full health care coverage. The Plan proposed a prepayment policy to cover physicians' services. To serve that goal, Illinois mandated the formation of a not-for-profit medical/surgical prepayment plan. The Chicago Blue Shield system was inaugurated in November 1947 and Chicago Medical Service was incorporated to administer the Plan to cover doctors' fees. The Plan proved so popular with people around the state that CMS changed its name to Illinois Medical Service in 1950.

To further increase member services, Hospital Service Corporation established the Fort Dearborn Life Insurance Company in 1966. A few years later the Plan introduced the state's first Health Maintenance Organization.

Although Blue Cross and Blue Shield were operated under a single management, they were separate corporations with two separate boards. State law was revised in 1975 to permit Hospital Service Corporation and Illinois Medical Service to merge into one organization, Health Care Service Corporation (HCSC), and into one Plan, Blue Cross and Blue Shield of Illinois.

The Mandel-Lear Building overlooking the Michigan Avenue Bridge was home to Blue Cross and Blue Shield of Illinois from 1948 to 1968.

Facing page, top left: One of the CareVans sponsored by Blue Cross and Blue Shield of Illinois. These traveling immunization clinics help combat disease in Chicago's poorest neighborhoods and downstate Illinois.

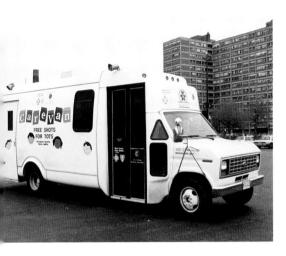

In the early 1990s HCSC garnered more customers and expanded member services with the acquisition of the Colorado Bankers Life Insurance Company. This was the beginning of a move to build a national presence. Meanwhile, services to the community at large were expanded. Part of an energetic corporate citizenship program is underwriting numerous community events and social programs throughout the state. One example is sponsorship of CareVans, traveling immunization clinics that help combat disease in Chicago's poorest neighborhoods and downstate Illinois.

In the late 1990s HCSC began to pursue a strategy of consolidation of not-for-profit Blues Plans. But first there was a move—the seventh within Chicago's downtown. The strength of the Illinois Blues Plan was symbolized by relocation to new corporate headquarters in October 1997 without disrupting services or increasing member premiums. The 30-story facility at 300 East Randolph was the first high-rise building in the country to be designed for vertical growth—it can be expanded to 54 floors.

On the last day of 1998, the Blue Cross and Blue Shield Plans of Illinois and Texas merged to generate economies through joint administrative operations under HCSC management. Together, the two Plans provide health coverage for nearly seven million people. In March 2000 HCSC announced its intention to acquire Blue Cross and Blue Shield of New Mexico. A few months later Blue Cross and Blue Shield of Illinois announced an affiliation of Blues Plans from six states to enhance the local focus on customers while providing a national scope to better control costs.

Blue Cross and Blue Shield of Illinois is well positioned to serve its members for another six decades, at least. ■

Above: The 30-story headquarters of Blue Cross and Blue Shield of Illinois is located at 300 East Randolph in Chicago. It was the first building in the country to be designed for vertical expansion—to an ultimate 54 stories.

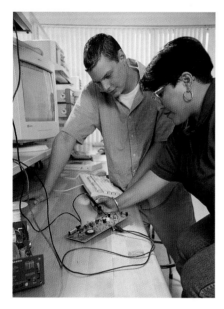

Above: DeVry's hands-on education builds the technology skills that are in demand by today's employers.

Top: Ronald L. Taylor (left), president and chief operating officer, and Dennis J. Keller (right), chairman and chief executive officer, of DeVry Inc.

*F*or the past seven decades, DeVry Inc. has provided career-oriented education to help its graduates gain employment and to meet the shifting work force needs of corporate America. Its history and achievements span the era of early radio to today's complex information age. Based in Illinois, it is now one of the largest publicly held education companies in the world.

Since its initial public offering in 1991, DeVry has achieved an enviable record of growth and financial performance. The company, headquartered in Oakbrook Terrace near Chicago, has earned respect not only for its solid investment returns but also for its promotion of socially responsible business practices. It has an outstanding reputation for producing a highly qualified pool of career-ready graduates who help enhance a community's ability to attract new economic development. In Illinois, it is one of the most important contributors to the state's growing technology sector.

DeVry Inc. is the holding company for DeVry University, which is comprised of DeVry Institutes and Keller Graduate School of Management. Combined, DeVry's degree-granting institutions serve more than 54,000 students in North America.

DeVry has a long tradition of providing lifelong learning and adult education. Its success in meeting the needs of students and employers has been rooted in its ability to respond to the challenges of a dynamic marketplace and changing technology. It has been doing so successfully since 1931.

In March 1931 Herman DeVry, an engineer and inventor of the first portable silent motion picture projector, founded the DeForest Training School in Chicago, named for Lee DeForest, considered the "father of radio." Its purpose was to train students for technical work in electricity, motion pictures, radio, and, eventually, television.

The school's name was changed to DeVry Technical Institute in 1953, and

two years later a DeVry Technical Institute was opened in Toronto. The school's first associate degree, in electronics engineering technology, was offered in 1957. Over the decades the curriculum expanded to meet the constantly changing needs of the marketplace for a well-trained, technology-savvy work force.

DeVry Technical Institute was acquired by Bell & Howell in 1966. The name was changed to DeVry Institute of Technology two years later and it began to offer its first baccalaureate degree, in electronics engineering technology, in 1969.

In 1987 the Keller Graduate School of Management acquired the assets of DeVry Institute of Technology and the parent company was incorporated as DeVry Inc. and went public in 1991.

Keller Graduate School was established in 1973 to offer evening programs in practical business management, and KGSM founders Dennis Keller and Ronald Taylor were former DeVry executives. It began offering MBA degrees in 1976. As it grew, Keller Graduate School added six master's degree programs to its curriculum for a total of seven. Practitioner-oriented programs are intended to bridge the gap between the typical academic experience and the everyday hands-on demands of business. Through its Center for Corporate Education, launched in 1994, Keller Graduate School helps companies enhance work force performance through its high-quality training programs in business and technology.

Today Keller Graduate School operates 42 centers in 14 states; eight of those centers are in Illinois. It also offers distance learning from its Online Education Center, which integrates interactive technology electronics, in technology and technology-based businesses with proven education methodologies.

DeVry Institutes offer eight bachelor's degree programs and an associate degree program in electronics. Full-time students can earn a bachelor's degree within three years, part-timers within five years. All

DeVry's Tinley Park campus is one of three in Illinois and 22 in North America. Keller Graduate School, also located at this site, has 42 education centers in the United States, including eight in Illinois.

programs include hands-on laboratory application as well as classroom theory. Students can also take the business administration degree program via the Internet through DeVry Online. Increasing proportions of the diverse student body are adults and multiracial; nearly half are over 25 and half are minorities. The needs of the working student population are served by offering flexible scheduling options. Evening, weekend, and year-round classes on campuses located in major centers of employment make it possible for anyone to learn new high-tech skills or to enhance existing capabilities.

DeVry operates 22 undergraduate campuses in the United States and Canada; three are in Illinois (Chicago in the old Riverview Park area, Addison, and Tinley Park). In an effort to increase access to its educational programs and to better serve working adults, DeVry Inc. has begun to offer both graduate and selected undergraduate degree programs at single locations, called DeVry University Centers, to benefit working adults. The first DeVry University Center, located at 225 West Washington in downtown Chicago, offers a bachelor's degree program in business administration and six master's degree programs in business, management, and technology.

In addition to its degree-granting institutions, DeVry Inc. owns Becker Conviser Professional Review, a leading provider of exam-preparation review courses. Becker Conviser has 40 years of experience in preparing students for the certified public accountant certification exam. It has recently expanded its courses to include the chartered financial analyst and certi-

Keller Graduate School of Management's practitioner-oriented faculty members bring their real-world experience to the classroom.

fied management accountant exams. Becker Conviser has a global presence, operating in more than 300 locations worldwide and serving 32,000 students each year.

DeVry graduates are reputed to be more technology savvy than are most other job candidates. And DeVry's success in meeting the high-tech needs of the marketplace is clearly demonstrated by the employment rates of its graduates. In Illinois, 93 percent of students who graduated from degree programs in the past year who actively pursued and obtained employment or who were already employed held jobs in their field of specialty within six months after graduation.

When companies relocate to Illinois, one of the major incentives is the availability of a well-trained work force of talented information technology and other professionals. DeVry graduates fit the bill. ■

There is a cultural consortium in Chicago that compares to any successful corporation in its positive economic impact on the region. It provides nearly 18,000 direct and indirect jobs for Illinoisians, attracts more tourists to Chicago than combined major sports events, plays host to more than nine million visitors each year, and pumps $450 million annually into the region's economy.

The Museums In the Park, a consortium of nine of Chicago's major museums located in lakefront parks, achieved that record in the year 2000.

Individually, each of the museums reflects the spirit of generosity bestowed on it by founders and benefactors; for example, 40 percent of visitors in 2000 were admitted with no fee. Collectively, they ensure that young people share in the spirit of exploration and discovery that has helped make Chicago a world-class city.

Combined, the nine institutions that comprise the Museums In the Park have given nearly 800 years of service to the citizens of Chicago. Eight of the nine museums are located in or near the parks that are a feature of Chicago's superb lakefront. Three are linked together into a tightly knit campus that was created by moving a stretch of Lake Shore Drive; the others are accessible through a network of transportation.

The museums, as with many of the city's cultural centers, were for the most part founded through the support of city fathers and merchant princes.

Chicago's first cultural institution, the Chicago Historical Society, was founded in 1856 by the city's leading entrepreneurs to help develop their brawling frontier town into a major urban center with proper regard for both local and national history. In spite of losing its priceless original collection in the Chicago Fire of 1871, today CHS houses more than 20 million objects, images, and documents, including books, manuscripts, paintings, sculptures, costumes, prints, photographs, news films, architectural drawings, and fragments.

Dynamic permanent and special exhibitions, educational programs, and research assistance to the collection are offered to the public at its museum at the corner of Clark and North streets in Chicago's Lincoln Park.

The Historical Society has long been involved in collaborative programs with Chicago-area schools and communities. Its History Explorers outreach program helps young students and their teachers integrate CHS resources into American history studies. Another works with neighborhoods to help communities create and maintain historical records and stories. Yet another is preparing minority college students to prepare for graduate studies in museum studies and careers.

The Peggy Notebaert Nature Museum, formerly known as the Chicago Academy of Sciences, was the first scientific museum in the West. The academy was organized to bring together the work of Robert Kennicott, whose studies of the birds, reptiles, and mammals of Illinois were the earliest efforts to document the state's fauna. In its early days the academy was the rallying spot for discussions of the mound builders in nearby Rockford, Davenport, and counties in Missouri. These archaeological discussions were indicative of the lively spirit of learning at the academy and underscore its continuing dedication to enhancing the scientific literacy of all citizens.

In 1999 the academy was expanded to become the Peggy Notebaert Nature Museum. It is the only museum to specialize in the ecology and natural history of the midwestern United States, from the Great Lakes to the prairies, examining the relationship between people and nature. Its interactive and permanent exhibits include the Judy Istock Butterfly Haven, the region's only year-round exhibit of international butterflies; a family water lab that explores urban river systems and water chemistry; computer-generated environmental crisis scenarios; and urban ecosystems. The Nature Museum's collab-

Chicago Historical Society west entrance, Clark Street at North Avenue, Chicago.

orative programs include classroom teacher training and support that brings hands-on science, math, and technology experiments to students; classes for teenagers in the museum setting; and workshops to increase young girls' interest in science and math.

Two large bronze lions guard the entrance steps to The Art Institute of Chicago at Michigan Avenue and Adams Street in Grant Park. Since the original Neo-Classical Beaux Arts-style building was completed in 1893, a number of additions have been built to house its growing world-class collections and the School of the Art Institute. The museum's extraordinary art collections include works by the French Impressionists and Post-Impressionists from Monet to Seurat; Italian, Spanish, Dutch, and Flemish Old Masters; and an extensive collection of American, European, and Asian art. It is also renowned for its collections of architecture, photography, and textiles; and one of the most important collections of modern and contemporary sculptures and paintings in the world.

The Art Institute offers schools 18 different topics for student tours, and the Teacher Resource Center provides innovative materials, workshops, and courses for educators throughout the year. A new year-long program provides Chicago public high school science teachers with strategies for relating their curriculum to principles of creating and conserving art.

The Field Museum, founded in 1893 during the World's Columbian Exposition,

was made possible by a million-dollar donation by merchant prince Marshall Field. It was housed in the exposition's former Palace of Fine Arts Building until 1921, when it moved to its current location in Burnham Park just south of Grant Park. Today its collections in anthropology, botany, geology, and zoology have earned it renown as one of the finest natu-

ral history museums in the world. The museum is filled with priceless collections of prehistoric and recent cultures, including Sue, the largest, best preserved, and most complete *Tyrannosaurus rex* ever found, and 1,400 rare artifacts and treasures of ancient Egyptian civilizations.

The John G. Shedd Aquarium, close to

Above: Egyptian mummy mask, Field Museum, 1400 South Lake Shore Drive, Chicago.

Left, top: The Art Institute of Chicago's west entrance, Michigan Avenue at Adams Street, Chicago.

Left, bottom: A youngster satisfies his "natural" curiosity at the Peggy Notebaert Nature Museum, 2430 North Cannon Drive, Chicago.

Above: The *Heart Exhibit* featuring a 16-foot-tall replica of the human heart, Museum of Science and Industry, 57th and Lake Shore Drive, Chicago.

Above: John G. Shedd Aquarium, aerial view, 1200 South Lake Shore Drive, Chicago.

Right: Adler Planetarium & Astronomy Museum, aerial view, 1300 South Lake Shore Drive, Chicago.

the Field Museum and Adler Planetarium in Burnham Park, was founded by John G. Shedd, a partner of Marshall Field. The aquarium, which opened in 1930, is one of the country's oldest institutions devoted to living specimens of aquatic life, and it is the world's largest indoor aquarium. It boasts a global collection of fishes, invertebrates, amphibians, reptiles, aquatic birds, and both freshwater and marine mammals. The Oceanarium, which opened in 1991, nearly doubled the size of the aquarium and gave visitors their first chance to see beluga whales and sea otters in Chicago. The aquarium offers an extensive mentoring program in the aquatic sciences for students in grades six through 12, including a high school marine biology course aboard its research vessel in the Bahamas.

State of the art in 1930 when it opened as the first planetarium in the Western Hemisphere, the Adler Planetarium & Astronomy Museum today remains on the cutting edge of technology. Now housing 11 galleries and two theaters, the Adler successfully blends the exhibits featuring modern space exploration with the history of astronomy. Foremost among these exciting new offerings is the world's first Star Rider™ Theater, a technologically advanced audience-interactive planetarium that transports visitors to the outer edges of the

universe on a virtual flight through the cosmos. In addition, the historic Sky Theater also offers unique sky shows that have delighted and entertained visitors for decades. Of special note is the Adler's collection of scientific instruments, rare books, photographs, early maps, charts, and star atlases. Considered one of the pre-eminent collections in the world, the Adler highlights these unique objects in the History of Astronomy Galleries.

The Museum of Science and Industry is known as one of the world's premier science learning centers, providing its visitors with unique and interactive experiences.

The museum was founded by one of America's leading philanthropists, Julius Rosenwald. After a visit with his son to the Deutches Museum in Munich in 1911, Rosenwald sought to build an institution that would spark America's "inven-

tive genius" by enabling visitors to learn through hands-on exhibits. Rosenwald restored and converted the historic Palace of Fine Arts, the last remaining major structure from the 1893 World's Fair, into the Museum of Science and Industry. In 1933 the museum opened its great brass doors to the public for the first time.

Since 1933 the Museum of Science and Industry has continued to inspire the inventive genius in everyone with educational and entertaining exhibits such as *The Farm* and *Time*, and classics such as the *Coal Mine* and the *U-505 Submarine*. The Museum of Science and Industry also continues to lead the way with groundbreaking exhibits including *NetWorld*, which takes visitors into the high-speed world of the Internet, and *Genetics: Decoding Life*, the nation's first permanent exhibit devoted to the fascinating science of genetics.

In 1961 a group of 11 artists and educators, including Margaret Burroughs and her husband Charles, set out to correct the apparent institutionalized omission of black history and culture in education by founding what is now known as the DuSable Museum of African American History. It is the oldest independent institution of its kind in the country dedicated to the collection, preservation, interpretation, and dissemination of African American history and culture.

The Ebony Museum of Negro History and Art was begun in the former South Side home (Quincy Club) of prominent contractor John Griffin. It was then the only institution of its kind in the country to grow out of the indigenous black community. In 1968 the museum was renamed after Jean Baptiste Pointe DuSable, a pioneer fur trader of African descent from Haiti and the first non-native permanent settler in Chicago.

In 1971 the Chicago Park District granted the museum's request to use a former Washington Park administration building that was designed by Burnham and built in 1910. The city officially made DuSable Museum the principal memorial to Jean Baptiste Pointe DuSable. In 1993 the museum opened a 28,000-square-foot addition named after the late Mayor Harold Washington featuring a 466-seat auditorium and additional galleries.

The DuSable Museum's diverse holdings include artifacts, rare books, photographs, recordings, costumes, personal papers of noted African Americans; original documents; civil rights memorabilia; nineteenth- and twentieth- century paintings, drawings, prints, and sculptures by prominent African American artists; and art from Africa. Exhibitions and programming reflect the museum's commitment to exploring the heritage and achievements of Africans in America and throughout the Diaspora.

The largest Mexican museum, and the first in the Midwest, is the Mexican Fine Arts Center Museum located in near Southwest Chicago's Pilsen/Little Village neighborhood, the largest Mexican community in the Midwest. It was founded in 1987 to celebrate Mexican culture through a range of exhibits, events, and classes covering the gamut of art, theater, music, and dance.

The nine museums that comprise the Museums In the Park consortium participate in a variety of special programs that provide invaluable education resources. They include development of teaching materials, distance learning opportunities, and virtual exhibits on the Internet.

The highly acclaimed educational partnership between the Museums In the Park and Chicago's public schools, referred to as MAPS—*Museums and*

Left: Baby photo of Ida Mae Cress in christening dress, DuSable Museum of African American History, 740 East 56th Place, Chicago.

Untitled, 1955, by Diego Rivera, Mexican Fine Arts Center Museum, 1852 West 19th Street, Chicago.

Public Schools: A New Direction for Teaching Chicago's Children—is proving to be a model program for school systems throughout the country. Museum educators and third- to sixth-grade public school teachers collaborate to design curricula that incorporate the vast resources of the museums into teaching language arts, math, social studies, and science.

MAPS entails a two-year commitment by participating school principals and teachers. They must attend professional development sessions, incorporate the MAPS teaching guides into the general curriculum, take field trips to the nine museums, and participate in other support activities. The goal is to create a sustained impact on teaching and learning by integrating museum resources into the educational process and providing authentic learning experiences for both students and teachers.

The Museums In the Park consortium also underwrites another innovative collaborative program, this one with the Chicago Park District. *Park Voyagers, Kids for Creative Exploration*, is a cultural outreach program that builds bridges among the parks, museums, and neighborhoods and allows young students to probe the excitement and wonder of learning about art, history, and science through the museum experience. It encourages them to develop creativity and critical thinking skills. In addition, the families of the students learn about the value of museums as places not only of learning, but also of fun.

The three-year, four-phase Park Voyagers program is designed for third- to seventh-graders and their parents. In the first phase, each enrolled student attends an after-school course three days a week for 12 weeks and each month visits a museum with his or her family. The courses are developed and taught by museum educational staff and park district administrators. In the second phase, the young students and their parents participate in a weekly family event in the parks and a weekend visit to the museums. In

the next phase, during a monthly family night at each of the museums, families receive single-use museum passes and begin receiving a monthly newsletter. Finally, participating families receive a year-long pass to special museum events and exhibitions and a "passport" to be stamped each time the family visits a museum.

The free Park Voyagers program is offered at 54 of the city's major parks. Courses, taught by educators from the museums as well as park district staff, offer a blend of materials and curricula from the various museums. Within its first four years the program has served more than 3,000 children and adults.

Another creative partnership is the one between the museums' consortium and the Chicago Public Library system. In a program that further enhances outreach to the city's residents, the network of more than 80 neighborhood public libraries has an additional learning and exploration tool in its collections—"Check Us Out!" passes to Museums In the Park. The passes, which are free to library cardholders, can be checked out just like books. They provide free admission to any of the nine museums on any day of the week. What's more, they cover admission for an entire family. And, because the leading distribution point is the local library, they are easily accessible in virtually every neighborhood in the city. Since its inauguration in 1995, the Check Us Out! program has allowed more than 215,000 families free access to the city's nine major museums.

It was on November 26, 1922, that Howard Carter peered into the tomb of King Tutankhamen newly discovered by him and the Earl of Caernovan in the Valley of the Kings near Luxor in Egypt. When breathlessly asked what he saw, Carter exclaimed, "Wonderful things!" This is the sense of wonder and discovery that the Museums In the Park consortium is imparting to people young and old, from Chicago and from around the world. ∎

HOTS MICHELS ENTERPRISES FOR ORGAN DONOR AWARENESS

*I*n memory of his mother, Bill Ellis, owner of Farley Food Company based in Chicago, instituted The Katherine Ellis Foundation in 1991. His philanthropy encompassed a broad spectrum and benefited numerous individuals and organizations.

In 1995 Ellis was diagnosed with incurable heart disease. He became one of the many in like circumstances who suffer the agony of waiting for an organ donor. Their lament—shared by their loved ones—is reduced to a common denominator: "Will I live long enough?"

In one of those moments of synergism, and just when Ellis' condition became critical, the parents of an 11-year-old accident victim donated their child's organs. Ellis became the recipient of a successful heart transplant. The magnitude of this gift of life touched him so deeply that he became an integral part of the donor family, both emotionally and monetarily.

It wasn't all that long ago that the first transplant of a human heart made headlines throughout the world. With the advent of anti-rejection drugs and advanced surgical procedures, the progression from heart transplants to the replacement of other organs was inevitable. What had been extraordinary became almost commonplace. It soon became apparent that the availability of donor organs lagged far behind the demand. It was time to begin an aggressive campaign to educate the public and enlist their participation.

Coincidentally, Hots Michels, a well-known Chicago entertainer and Ellis' friend, was named administrator of The Katherine Ellis Foundation. It was the perfect vehicle for Michels, who maintains close friendships with a veritable "who's who" of business and community leaders, elected officials, and "just plain folks." He has enjoyed a distinguished career as a radio broadcaster, newspaper columnist, and pianist. The success of Bill Ellis' heart surgery was the catalyst for Michels to establish a special arm of the foundation, calling it The Katherine Ellis Foundation

Hots Michels (left), administrator, and Bill Ellis, founder, at ceremonies marking the opening of The Katherine Ellis Foundation's Organ Donor Awareness exhibit at the Chicago Police Museum in 1999. The museum attracts more than 40,000 visitors a year.

for Organ Donor Awareness.

Ellis lived a healthy and productive life before succumbing to an unrelated illness in 2000. His demise meant the dissolution of The Katherine Ellis Foundation, but not the end of Michels' dedication. He now administers the Hots Michels Enterprises for Donor Awareness.

"I'm on a mission," explains Michels. "Organ donors are the ultimate care givers. Their caring gives life to countless numbers of children and adults whose very existence depends on their charity. Lives are being needlessly lost for lack of organ donors. Too many of us put off or ignore doing what is really quite simple: Sign up. The foundation offers this hotline number for information: 1-800-SHARE."

Aware of his dedication, Michels' many contacts were eager to cooperate in this worthy cause. As examples, a local grocery chain printed the message on 32 million grocery bags; an outdoor advertising firm donated signage on a major expressway reaching an audience of more than 80 million; cable network CNN broadcast the message as public service announcement to a worldwide audience. In one year alone an estimated 800 million people saw or heard the plea. And the work goes on. The need is great; the message is simple: "The Gift of Life Is to Save a Life." ■

A place where kids come first: That's Children's Memorial Hospital in the heart of Chicago's Lincoln Park neighborhood. It is consistently ranked as one of the 10 best pediatric hospitals in the country and the top-ranking one in Illinois.

Julia Porter founded the hospital in dedication to the memory of her 13-year-old son, Maurice, who had died of acute rheumatism. The Maurice Porter Memorial Hospital opened in 1882 as an eight-bed facility in a Lincoln Park cottage. Its sole

Above: Children's Memorial Hospital in Chicago's Lincoln Park is ranked as one of the 10 best pediatric hospitals in the country.

Right: Pediatric hematologist/oncologist Paul Haut, M.D., administers care to a stem cell transplant patient in the new Stem Cell Ambulatory Unit at Children's Memorial Hospital.

purpose: to provide free care and treatment for sick children. By 1890 the hospital, now in expanded facilities, had a professional staff of six caring for 68 patients. The hospital's name was changed to Children's Memorial Hospital in 1904; it moved to its current location a year later.

Today Children's Memorial Hospital invests millions of dollars annually for pediatric health care research, more than any other hospital in the state. Its Institute for Education and Research is the only Illinois institution dedicated solely to pediatric research and one of only five to do so in the United States. Current research in progress includes investigation of the development, growth, and aging of the human brain; enhanced understanding of birth defects; developing alternatives to powerful anti-rejection medication for organ transplant patients; investigation of

genetic events that trigger childhood cancers; the study of how the gene gun can shrink tumors without damaging surrounding tissue; and development of diagnostic tools for pediatric brain tumors. A recent breakthrough was the discovery of an alternative to radiation therapy for cancer patients, thus shortening chemotherapy treatments and sparing children long-term side effects.

The hospital's specialized centers provide for a variety of pediatric health care needs—heart treatments, organ transplants, brain tumors, epilepsy, cancer and blood diseases, spina bifida, asthma and allergies, pediatric surgery, cystic fibrosis, and infectious disease including HIV.

Each year more than 236,000 outpatient visits are made, 13,000 children are admitted, and nearly 11,000 surgeries are performed. Advocating for children's health and safety is a vital part of the hospital's mission, with Children's Memorial providing millions of dollars in care to those who lack financial resources.

A single-minded focus on caring only for children has brought the hospital an unparalleled level of skill in working with its patients and their families. Dedication to the health and well being of all children has been its purpose for more than a century. Children's Memorial has grown into a premier pediatric hospital with state-of-the-art technology and a highly renowned staff of thousands.

It is indeed a place where kids come first. ■

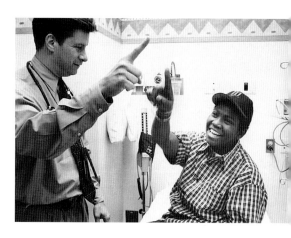

CHAPTER TWELVE

The Modern Marketplace

*T*he state's retail and dining establishments, service industries, products, and convention facilities offer an impressive variety of choices for Illinoisians and visitors alike.

Illinois Department of Commerce and Community Affairs **336-339**

Sears, Roebuck and Co. **340-343**

Ace Hardware Corporation **344-345**

Jewel-Osco **346**

Galileo International **347**

The Spiegel Group **348-349**

Chicago Convention and Tourism Bureau/ Metropolitan Pier and Exposition Authority **350-351**

Corporate Travel Management Group **352-353**

Cardwell and Randall Enterprises, LLC **354-355**

Gibsons Bar and Steakhouse **356**

J&B Signs **357**

Left: © 2000 Doris De Witt/Stone

Above: Breathtaking caverns can be found in Illinois' Shawnee National Forest.

Top: Illinois is a global leader in agri-technology.

New investment, new jobs, enhanced tourism opportunities, and renovated main streets are blazing a trail throughout Illinois from Rockford in the north to Pinckneyville in the south. The state's revitalized economic development agency, the Department of Commerce and Community Affairs (DCCA), has stepped up efforts to create new opportunities for economic development while working to enhance the quality of life for all Illinois citizens. Under the leadership of Governor George H. Ryan, DCCA is strengthening Illinois' competitive edge by providing technical and financial assistance to businesses, local governments, workers, and families. The agency works with the private sector to build upon the state's reputation as a center for business and industry.

DCCA was formed in 1979 by combining several existing agencies—the departments of Business and Economic Development, Local Government Affairs, and Human Development—into one umbrella agency. The purpose was to streamline and expand economic development efforts to help companies in the state increase market share and to improve the quality of life for all Illinois residents. After a budget crunch in tight economic times, DCCA programs took on new life in the late 1990s.

Today DCCA is structured into the bureaus of Business Development, Community Development, Tourism, Energy and Recycling, and Technology and Industrial Competitiveness. In addition, the agency encompasses the Office of Coal Development and Marketing, Illinois Trade Office, and Illinois Film Office.

DCCA believes that economic development begins at the local level and that efforts should be made to help Illinois companies focus on the bigger economic picture. This is achieved by administering scores of DCCA programs that affect every aspect of the Illinois business environment.

DCCA director Pam McDonough sums up the work of her agency: "DCCA is an advocate for companies and our first order of business is to take a lead role in coordinating the state's efforts to attract and retain business enterprises, to help new and existing companies operate successfully in our highly diversified economic environment, and to clear hurdles to help them grow in the convergence economy. At the same time, we are enhancing the quality of life to ensure Illinois is a great place in which to live."

Due in large part to the pro-business agenda of Governor Ryan and the support of the Illinois General Assembly, the state's success in economic development was dramatic in 1999 and 2000. Scores of DCCA programs to promote economic growth throughout the state, to create good-paying jobs for Illinois residents, and to help businesses and workers meet the challenges of a changing economy have paid off. The state, through the efforts of DCCA, helped secure billions of dollars in investment, resulting in the creation of 32,000 jobs and the retention of 30,000 other jobs in danger of moving to other states during that two-year period.

In the year 2000 Illinois was voted third among the best business climates in the United States by *Site Selection* magazine. What a difference a year makes. The position of Illinois in the 1999 poll was number 10. In addition, the magazine's survey of corporate real estate executives rated Illinois number three based on lack of red tape, depth of financial assistance, and cooperation of government officials.

Other kudos were earned in 2000. *Industry Week*'s survey of world-class manufacturing facilities found that more large manufacturing companies are located in Illinois than in any other state. *InfoWorld* magazine rated Illinois second best in its e-business survey. And *Site Selection* rated the DCCA's Web site as one of the best-designed and most informative in the country.

Through its Bureau of Business Development, DCCA works one on one with companies at both the state and local levels to develop customized support packages, not only to help companies grow businesses, but to induce companies to locate or remain in Illinois. Packages include expansion incentives, technology support, access to capital, and job training.

Small businesses are vital to the economy of the state and DCCA works hard to provide entrepreneurs with needed resources for success. Special emphasis is placed on nurturing high-tech start-ups and on helping minority and female small-business owners.

Efforts to help Illinois' 650,000 small businesses compete in a changing economy continue to expand. Support of regional Small Business Development Centers is on the rise.

DCCA's Small Business Division provides advocacy, business assistance, training, and information resources to help entrepreneurs and small companies enhance their competitiveness in a global economy. One example is the development of a universal certification system for minority and female businesses to reduce the red tape that can often slow down the process of procuring government contracts. These are services not readily available in the private sector.

Illinois offers a number of tax credits in addition to those for job creation and investment. Other areas include credits for R&D, training, Enterprise Zones, and the purchase of manufacturing machinery. DCCA also provides grants for industrial and job training, labor management, and welfare-to-work.

The Economic Development for a Growing Economy program for the State of Illinois, known as EDGE, was established in August 1999. In its first two years EDGE was credited with creating more than 7,000 new jobs in the state and adding $22 million in annual tax revenues for state coffers. EDGE heightens the state's competitive edge by providing tax credits based on the number of jobs a company creates in Illinois. To be eligible, companies must create at least 25 jobs and invest $5 million or more in Illinois. Companies that have qualified for the EDGE tax credit include Deere & Company, Matsushita Universal Media Services, and Molex.

Deere needed to build a new technical center and was considering doing so in Iowa. However, tax credits available through the EDGE program convinced Deere to invest $13.5 million to locate the center near company headquarters in Moline, Illinois, keeping 82 jobs in the state and creating hundreds of other construction and indirect jobs.

Matsushita and Panasonic created a partnership called MUMs that oversees the production of DVDs. Rather than locate new facilities out of state, which had been a consideration, MUMs decided to expand the existing Panasonic Disc Services facility in Pinckneyville, Illinois. By utilizing EDGE tax credits, the company invested nearly $20 million, retained 400 jobs, and created 200 new jobs. The project has provided a significant eco-

Chicago is consistently ranked as the number one global city for manufacturing.

Right: Work force development is a priority for Governor George H. Ryan.

Below: Illinois leads the country in the number of technology workers.

nomic boost to an area that had suffered from a declining coal industry.

EDGE also played a role in Molex's decision to expand two facilities in Lisle and Bolingbrook to the tune of a $45-million investment and more than 1,000 new jobs.

Other recent economic development projects include:

- The Boeing Company's decision to locate its world headquarters in Chicago, which will pump an estimated $4.5 billion into the Illinois economy over 20 years.

- The establishment of North America's largest intermodal rail hub at the site of the U.S. Army's former Joliet Arsenal. This project, which also includes the creation of a new business park, is expected to create up to 2,000 new jobs and is the largest military base conversion project in the country.

- Tellabs' expansion in Naperville will add as many as 2,300 jobs.

- Ford Motor Company's planned automotive supplier manufacturing campus on Chicago's Southeast Side will create 1,000 jobs and result in a $1.3-billion economic impact for the area. This is the only North American location for this new Ford business model of a supplier park.

- ABN-Amro announced plans to build a new high-tech office tower in Chicago's West Loop. The project will result in the creation of up to 500 new jobs and the retention of 1,500 other employees.

- Solo Cup is building a facility on Chicago's South Side, creating up to 1,000 jobs and transforming a former brownfield site for USX to a new manufacturing facility.

- ATA will create 2,500 new jobs at Chicago's Midway Airport through new flight training operations and expanded gates.

- Sprint PCS' customer service center in Bolingbrook is creating 1,200 high-tech jobs for that community.

Another major economic development initiative created by Governor Ryan is the Illinois FIRST (Fund for Infrastructure, Roads, Schools, and Transit) program. Illinois FIRST is a $12-billion, five-year investment in the state's infrastructure, transportation systems, mass-transit systems, schools, and communities. Illinois FIRST funds have been utilized to provide infrastructure support for many DCCA economic development projects, including Ford, Solo Cup, and MUMs.

The Bureau of Technology and Industrial Competitiveness places emphasis on the importance of preparing the state's work force and businesses for the new economy. It ensures that high-tech job training and development programs of DCCA are fully coordinated and integrated into all of Illinois' economic development efforts. The bureau administers programs to foster technological innovation such as the Technology Challenge Grant and Technology Enterprise Centers.

DCCA's Industrial Training Program is a flexible development program to help businesses train and develop employees. ITP funding played an important role in Quaker Oats' decision not only to keep open its Danville plant, but to also expand its facilities there. Since 1999 more than 43,000 jobs have been created or retained under ITP by providing companies with funding to teach workers new skills.

Illinois VentureTech, a five-year, $1.8-billion project, was unveiled in 2000. It invests state money in advanced R&D, information technology, biotechnology,

and health sciences. It also provides venture capital to help emerging technology companies gain a foothold to achieve eventual success. DCCA is charged with implementing VentureTech programs that help entrepreneurs take their innovations to the marketplace. The Technology Challenge Grant program is designed to fund science and technology projects, partnerships between universities and industry, high-tech commercialization projects, transfer projects, and infrastructure improvements. Illinois Technology Enterprise Centers (ITECs) provide operational support for regional centers to serve technology entrepreneurs, innovators, and small business and to provide investments to or on behalf of young or growing companies in cooperation with private-sector investments.

Building a vibrant economy includes ensuring strong communities and families. Through its Bureau of Community Development, DCCA coordinates federal, state, and local assistance for low-income residents, helping local governments with their management and infrastructure needs. DCCA community development programs have helped hundreds of small-town and rural areas throughout the state share in the good economic times. For example, since 1999 nine companies began businesses in Ottawa, creating 600 jobs and pumping revenues into local taxes. In Washburn, with a population of 1,110, residents received DCCA support to buy the town's only grocery store, the anchor of its block-long business district.

The Bureau of Energy and Recycling promotes the use of innovative energy, recycling, and waste-reduction technolo-gies. The Office of Coal Development and Marketing meanwhile works to promote efforts to maximize the use of this abundant natural resource in a manner that benefits the Illinois economy without hurting the environment by administering grants for clean coal technology development.

Tourism also comes under the aegis of DCCA, and for good reason. Each year the state's tourism industry pumps at least $22 billion into the Illinois economy. Through its Bureau of Tourism, DCCA works tirelessly to promote Illinois resources and attractions to the rest of the world. Although the lion's share of tourism dollars comes from Chicago, the entire Land of Lincoln offers much to be enjoyed by visitors from around the world. One of the most recent tourist attractions under development is the Abraham Lincoln Presidential Library and Museum in Springfield, slated to be completed in 2002.

Illinois business is global. It markets more than $34 billion worth of products throughout the world. In fact, one out of every eight jobs in Illinois depends on international trade. To support that demand, DCCA operates nine foreign trade offices outside the United States—Brussels, Budapest, Hong Kong, Johannesburg, Mexico City, Shanghai, Tokyo, Toronto, and Warsaw. Plans are in the works for other trade offices in Israel and South America.

DCCA's ability to help companies meet the challenges of work force and infrastructure demands, and thus to attract and retain businesses, has helped Illinois achieve a Gross State Product approaching a half-trillion dollars, which makes the state the world's 14th-largest economy. ∎

Above: Illinois' work force is among the most productive in the world.

Top: Recreational opportunities abound in Illinois.

*M*ore than a century ago, two young midwestern entrepreneurs combined their talents to create what would become one of America's premier retailing companies. Together, Richard Sears and Alvah Roebuck revolutionized America's shopping habits, defined "taste" among middle-class consumers, and identified price, convenience, and selection as critical components for attracting customers.

Today Sears, Roebuck and Co. is a $40-billion-plus retailer of apparel, home, and automotive products and services. The

40 ACRE HOME OF SEARS ROEBUCK & CO. THE LARGEST MERCANTILE PLANT IN THE WORLD

Above: Completed in 1906, Sears' West Side complex in Chicago served as the company's headquarters for the next 67 years.

Top: Railroad station agent Richard Sears founded the company that bears his name in 1886.

Right: Important to rural customers, the Sears catalog offered a wide variety of merchandise at reasonable prices.

company employs 300,000 associates, and serves consumers across the country through 860 full-line department stores, more than 2,100 specialized retail outlets, and a Web site offering many of the same items found in the stores, as well as merchandise specifically for Internet customers.

The contemporary Sears got its start back in 1886 when a Chicago jewelry company shipped gold-filled watches to a jeweler in Redwood Falls, Minnesota. When the local merchant was unable to accept the shipment, Richard Sears saw an opportunity.

Sears, a railway telegrapher/agent, purchased the watches and offered them to other station agents for resale up and down the line. The first venture being a success,

he ordered more watches; and within six months he realized a $5,000 profit.

In 1887 he moved his business, then called the R.W. Sears Watch Company, from Minneapolis to Chicago. His ad for a watchmaker in the *Chicago Daily News* was answered by Alvah Roebuck, of nearby Hammond, Indiana. Roebuck joined on for $3.50 a week plus room and board. Six years later one of America's most famous and trusted corporate names debuted when the young firm's name was changed to Sears, Roebuck and Co.

At that time, America was still predominantly rural. Farmers generally had no alternative to the inflated prices charged by nearby general stores. Sears catalogs, however, provided welcome relief from high prices and middlemen.

While the early selection was limited to watches and jewelry, Sears soon began publishing catalogs with more than 500 pages of shoes, clothing, wagons, fishing tackle, stoves, furniture, china, musical instruments, saddles, firearms, buggies, bicycles, and glassware.

Richard Sears was a marketing genius. A master of advertising and sales, he knew farmers and understood what they wanted. In 1893 sales topped $400,000 and nearly doubled in two years to $750,000. However, Richard Sears was

not a strong administrator. Employees sat on kitchen chairs and substituted dry goods boxes for desks. Office space was partitioned by chicken wire. Order fulfillment and accuracy, in turn, suffered.

Chicago clothier and philanthropist Julius Rosenwald came to the rescue when he bought into the company in 1895. The company was reorganized with Rosenwald serving as vice president and, later, treasurer. The company's business grew rapidly and the firm moved into a new six-story building the following year. By 1897 the catalog contained 786 pages and Richard Sears proclaimed "the best goods at lower prices than they can be had elsewhere." To the customer, the variety of merchandise was seemingly endless.

Each edition of the catalog unveiled additional lines of merchandise as well as an expanded range of traditional goods. Sears stressed its competitive advantages, which included economies of scale and no expensive salesmen or wholesalers. In turn, farmers and small-town residents preferred shopping Sears by mail to shopping locally. (Rural homes began receiving free mail delivery in the 1890s and parcel post was inaugurated in 1913.)

Sears had a wider selection of merchandise, the latest models and styles, home delivery and—best of all—lower prices. By 1900 Sears' mail-order sales approached $10 million. Sears' mail-order catalog, affectionately known as the "wish book," became the arbiter of taste in rural America.

The company's 1902 catalog featured 50 pages of yard goods with hundreds of different patterns and colors. Dining room chairs ranged from a 45-cent bentwood oak to a $2.95 model with a leather seat, "richly carved back," and "fine piano finish." Homebuilders could choose "fancy" front doors in six different designs. Customer response resulted in the distribution of more than a million spring catalogs the following year.

In 1906 Sears stock was sold publicly for the first time. That same year the company's newly constructed $5-million mail

order and office facility on Chicago's West Side opened as the world's largest business building. Despite all this success, however, operational difficulties still abounded. After much experimentation, an innovative time-scheduling system was introduced that allowed the company to handle 10 times more business. On the merchandise side, however, a policy difference between Richard Sears and Julius Rosenwald led to the founder's resignation in November 1908.

Further change encouraged new strategies for expanding market share. The growing popularity of automobiles was changing the demographic face of America. By 1920 the urban population outnumbered its rural counterpart for the first time. American cities were expanding, and Sears customers were abandoning their farms for jobs in factories. In light of this opportunity, Sears began establishing retail stores in 1925. The company added automobiles, as well as low-cost auto insurance through its subsidiary, Allstate Insurance Co.—named for Sears' tire brand. The transition to retailing was swift.

Within four years more than 300 stores were operating around the country. The pace of retail openings grew to an average of one every other business day. Meanwhile, a new approach to merchandising developed. Some mail-order merchandise was already marketed under

Above, left: The cost of the stately "Alhambra" model was kept reasonable by the customer furnishing his own exterior stucco. Today many of these Sears homes are being documented by owners who consider them a unique part of the American heritage.

Above: Typical of a Sears mail-order house sale during the 1908-1937 promotion, all a customer needed to provide in buying the 1919 "Langston" model was a lot and foundation.

Sears' Craftsman, Kenmore, and DieHard products remain top-selling brands today.

In 1999 Sears launched the world's largest appliance store on the Internet featuring more than 2,000 major appliances.

Sears' own trade name and this strategy was embraced within the stores. Here, Sears buyers developed exclusive items that resulted in the development of Craftsman, Kenmore, and DieHard products—which became top-selling brands and remain so today.

Sears' 1931 sales of more than $180 million were divided almost equally between catalog and retail. Stores continued to be opened throughout the Depression and expansion remained strong until World War II. Notwithstanding war shortages, Sears' revenues exceeded one billion dollars in 1945. With the postwar boom, expansion accelerated. By the end of 1947 there were 625 Sears retail stores across the country. Plants were modernized, scores of warehouses built, and a children's wear section was added to the catalog to accommodate the baby boom.

Other strategic moves throughout the 1930s and 1940s included implementation of a comprehensive code of retail operating techniques; the creation of a planning and display strategy that built stores around merchandise; the opening of local catalog sales desks and offices; and overseas expansion. In the 1950s an independent catalog merchant program was

inaugurated where merchants sold Sears merchandise in privately owned stores.

To coincide with its 75th anniversary in 1961, Sears undertook a new campaign to streamline its image. The company, known as the all-purpose purveyor to the middle class, decided to entice more affluent consumers through upscale products such as mink coats, diamonds, and fine art. While certain elements of the campaign were not successful over the long-term, Sears' fine jewelry departments remain a customer favorite.

In the late 1960s Sears announced plans to build new headquarters in downtown Chicago. The result was the 110-floor Sears Tower, the world's tallest building when it opened in 1973.

The 1970s brought recession, inflation, and an end to the baby boom. Sears' traditional markets felt the economic impact. In addition, new competition emerged in the form of expensive specialty stores and huge discounters. Again, Sears had to rethink its strategy and adapt to market conditions. It returned to its roots—serving middle-class Americans who continued rating Sears as one of the country's most solid and trusted corporations.

The 1980s was a decade of restructuring and expansion into the financial services industry. In 1981 the retail business was renamed the Sears Merchandise Group and the insurance business officially became the Allstate Insurance Group. That same year Sears acquired the Dean Witter Reynolds Organization and Coldwell Banker & Company. Its foray into financial services included introduction of the Discover Card in 1985.

Sears underwent another round of restructuring in the early 1990s. Although it divested itself of most of its financial services holdings, including the Discover Card, Sears today is the country's largest proprietary credit card issuer. Here, too, corporate headquarters relocated to a 200-acre campus in nearby Hoffman Estates, Illinois.

By the mid-1990s Sears' Internet presence became a cornerstone of its growth

strategy. Here, partnerships developed with GlobalNetXchange, America Online, and Sun Microsystems. In late 1999 Sears entered an agreement with CheckFree that allows its 60 million credit card customers to review and pay their Sears bills online in a safe, secure, and reliable manner. In February 2000 Sears co-founded GlobalNetXchange, the first online global exchange for the retail business-to-business marketplace. Meanwhile, the products and services of The Great Indoors—Sears' chain of upscale home remodeling stores—became available on the company's Web site.

The company's Internet presence led to *Information Week* ranking Sears 12th among the 500 leading technology business users in 1999. That same year Sears launched the world's largest appliance store on the Internet featuring more than 2,000 brand-name major appliances. Subsequently, Sears' online offering has expanded to include tools, lawn and garden equipment, home electronics, small appliances, cookware, computers, office equipment, baby products, and school uniforms.

For its Internet businesses, Sears has three clearly defined goals: being the premier "clicks-and-bricks" retailer, developing new home-related solutions, and leading the transformation to the con-

nected home. Building the ultimate customer-centric store will allow customers to interact with Sears anytime, anywhere, and in any manner they prefer.

Sears' responsibility to the customer extends to the customer's community, as well. In 1999 the Sears-Roebuck Foundation and Sears associates together contributed nearly $30 million in cash and merchandise to a large number of not-for-profit, family-focused agencies. That same year Sears' employees undertook a three-year pledge of one million hours of community service through the Sears Good Life Alliance.

Through a recent leadership transition, Sears underscored its continuing commitment to innovation and enhanced services to its customers and shareholders. In the fall of 2000 Alan Lacy took the helm of the company as chairman and chief executive officer. Says Lacy, "Sears will continue to be more than a retailer; instead growing as a unique, multi-faceted franchise operating multiple lines of business in multiple channels. We will continue to build on our strengths—bundling our products, credit, and services into solutions for consumers. And we will continue to work to create a diverse, high-performance culture with a total commitment to productivity and returns." ∎

Alan Lacy assumed leadership of the company as chairman and chief executive officer in the fall of 2000.

Top: Sears' corporate headquarters relocated to a 20-acre campus in Hoffman Estates, Illinois, in the 1990s.

Ace Hardware Corporation, a retailer-owned home-improvement cooperative, is marching into the twenty-first century with renewed vigor and energy. The firm's strategy for the new millennium is Vision 21. This strategic plan takes a more pro-active approach to ensuring ultimate customer satisfaction and increased profitability for its independent retailer-owned stores.

This is not a new concept for Ace. What is new is that Vision 21 pushes for more uniformity among store operations and layouts. It empowers retailer-owners, via leading-edge technology, to meet the challenges of increased competition and to make their stores more consistent in the eyes of the customer.

Ace Hardware began as a simple concept nearly 80 years ago: bring together independent hardware retailers as a buying group to purchase products in bulk, to cooperate in promotional efforts, and to provide customers satisfaction, service, and value.

In 1924 four Chicago-area retailers, headed by entrepreneur and local hard-

Ace retailers have access to more than 60,000 different home improvement-related products.

ware store owner Richard Hesse, embarked on a bold plan to help them achieve economies of scale. The first product they bought in bulk was a bale of Mediterranean sponges. They had cut out the middleman and shared in reduced costs. Just as important, they had sharpened their competitive edge in the marketplace. The privately owned cooperative incorporated as Ace Stores in 1928. A year later it opened its first warehouse.

By the end of the 1930s the cooperative, now known as Ace Hardware Corporation, had expanded to hundreds of retailers throughout the Midwest states. Growth continued at a sky-rocketing pace throughout the next two decades.

In the 1960s Ace adopted a computerized system for accounting and modernized the interiors and exteriors of all its stores. By the time of its 50th anniversary in 1974, Ace had expanded throughout the country and had established its current headquarters in Oak Brook, Illinois. By 1976 the privately held company was sold to its retailers and the transition to becoming a retailer-owned cooperative was completed.

By the end of the 1980s more than 4,000 Ace stores were located in all 50 states, providing consumers of all ages and economic backgrounds services and products needed to complete their everyday do-it-yourself home projects. To enhance distribution of hardware goods to retailers, Ace increased its retail support center network (former warehouses) from seven to 14.

Throughout the 1990s Ace initiated the "New Age of Ace," a strategic plan to help retailers continue their aggressive growth. In 1993 its first million-square-foot retail support center opened in Princeton, Illinois. By the end of 1998 Ace Hardware was one of the nation's largest co-ops and its focus on the end consumer was never sharper.

Ace is now heading into the new millennium with Vision 21, a strategy to position Ace member-retailers as part of a

Check Out

retail chain to help expand their business and attract more customers. Retailers are supported by a corps of retail business managers, programs, and services that target retailer profitability.

One of those services is Ace's customer loyalty program, the Helpful Hardware Club, in which more than one million customers across the country participate. Part of the program is a strategy to build awareness and loyalty among the younger generation and to reach out to more female shoppers.

Ace Hardware is a $3-billion-plus buying group that offers 60,000 different products to its retailers. Annual retail sales of all Ace member-retailers top $13 billion. Four thousand member-retailers operate 5,100 stores—nearly 500 of which are located in 68 countries outside the United States. Many of the U.S. retail stores have passed through two and three generations of ownership. This illustrates not only the confidence that hardware entrepreneurs have in the Ace brand; it also indicates enthusiasm for the business on the part of the younger generation.

The retail support team totals 5,100 and more than three-quarters work at

Ace's 17 North American retail support centers around the clock. They use the latest technology to provide optimum levels of service, hold down costs of distribution, and ensure order-fill accuracy.

Ace also operates corporate-owned stores that serve as a "laboratory" to develop and fine-tune best practices in retailing for the benefit of all Ace stores. For example, two prototypes are solutions concept stores that have been launched to cater to do-it-yourselfers.

David Hodnik, Ace president, chief executive officer, and 29-year veteran, aptly described the company's new evolution: "Ace is no longer a mere wholesale cooperative organization that supports our member-retailers. Through Vision 21 we are striving to achieve a single objective: to be a topnotch retailer that exceeds customer expectations day in, day out. Vision 21 represents a significant change for the better. It is a dramatic effort that will result in stronger-performing stores, more satisfied customers, and enhanced branding of our products and services." In other words, "Vision 21 allows us to reaffirm our pledge to be the very best 'helpful hardware folks.'" ■

Ace includes 5,100 stores in all 50 states and 68 countries worldwide.

JEWEL-OSCO

The Jewel man and his horse-drawn wagon became a familiar sight in Chicago in the early 1900s. He delivered freshly ground coffee, tea, and extracts to the homes of his customers.

Right: The first permanent location of the Jewel Tea Company was opened in Chicago in 1901.

The Jewel-Osco store in Bolingbrook, Illinois, 1996.

ewel food stores and Osco drug-stores share a similar history in the Midwest. Both were founded by entrepreneurs, both upheld high operating standards since their early days, and both emphasized an ongoing commitment to their communities.

Jewel's origins go back to 1899 when two brothers-in-law, Frank Skiff and Frank Ross, began selling tea and coffee from the back of horse-drawn wagons. Their commitment to bringing fresh products to their customers remains a fundamental tenet of Jewel's business to this day. The two Franks opened their first store in 1901, expanded their product line, and named the new enterprise the Jewel Tea Company.

The home-service industry faced a serious challenge in 1932. The village of Green River in Wyoming passed an ordinance to prohibit salesmen from making unsolicited house calls. The ordinance was passed by hundreds of municipalities across the country. To protect its business, Jewel purchased 81 self-service food stores in the Chicago area—and thus began the shift from home service to grocery stores.

The Osco story began in 1937 in Rochester, Minnesota, when L.L. Skaggs and Harold Finch founded the first self-service drugstores in the Midwest. Pay-Less Drug, as it was called, became Self-Service Drug with the purchase of another store in Iowa. In 1942 Self-Service Drug was succeeded by Owners Service Company, or Osco, and its offices were moved to Chicago.

Meanwhile, Jewel was expanding, literally. In the 1950s and 1960s the firm significantly increased the size of its stores to satisfy the demand for one-stop shopping and a wider selection of merchandise. Bigger stores led to extending the one-stop shopping concept.

Jewel approached Osco Drug Stores and the companies merged in 1961. Jewel-Osco developed a combination of side-by-side food and drug stores. To further this concept, the organization (known as Jewel Companies

since 1966) bought the Sav-On Drug Stores chain in 1980. Four years later American Stores Company acquired Jewel Companies.

In 1999 Jewel-Osco merged with Idaho-based Albertson's, Inc., and became part of the second-largest food and drug retailer in the United States. The merger increased the number of stores in Albertson's Midwest region to 191 Jewel/Jewel-Osco stores and 83 Osco stand-alone drugstores.

Also in 1999 Jewel celebrated its 100th anniversary. Jewel had become the number-one grocery store chain in Chicago, and Jewel-Osco employees pledged 100,000 hours of community service as part of the celebration.

Today Jewel-Osco provides one-stop shopping with food, drugs, on-site banking, a full-service bakery, prepared meals, flower shops, photo processing, and even a Web site.

Jewel is continuously retooling itself to adapt to changing times and customer expectations—from providing a home shopping service, to becoming a chain of small grocery and drugstores, to developing a network of dynamic supermarkets. Jewel-Osco's early efforts ensured the freshness and quality of its goods and services. "Keeping Customers First" has always been a primary operating tenet for the two companies.

Jewel-Osco is the largest private employer in Illinois with more than 40,000 employees serving customers throughout the state. Its commitment to the communities it serves is reflected in a number of achievements. For example, it is the largest single donor to the Greater Chicago Food Depository, a founding member of the Chicago Minority Business Development Council, an industry leader in recycling, and an active contributor to community health services including diabetes counseling and the United Way. ∎

Galileo International, a subsidiary of Cendant Corporation, is a global technology leader. Galileo is represented in 115 countries, providing travel agencies, corporate travel managers, and Internet users throughout the world with the ability to book travel via its computer reservation systems. Galileo's staff of approximately 2,000 professionals make customer service and satisfaction the company's highest priority.

With more than 30 years of experience, Galileo has the expertise that airlines, other travel suppliers, and travel agencies depend on. Galileo was founded by 11 major North American and European airlines, and in 1997 it became a publicly traded company through one of the largest technology initial public offerings in history.

Galileo's technology-related business focuses on three areas: its core global distribution services to the travel industry, its Internet e-enabling technologies, and its network/telecommunications capabilities, which deliver global Internet, virtual private network, and telecommunications network services to customers throughout the world.

Travel

Galileo handles approximately one-third of the world's travel reservations booked through computer reservation systems. The company is one of the world's leading providers of electronic global distribution services—connecting more than 44,000 travel agency locations to approximately 500 airlines, 40 car rental companies, 47,000 hotel properties, 370 tour operators, and all major cruise lines worldwide.

Galileo provides travel suppliers with cost-effective methods of distributing their products, services, and useful market data. The company also develops innovative product and service solutions that travel agencies can use to increase productivity and better serve customers, and tools that corporate travel managers can use to gain greater control over their companies' travel budgets. Galileo supplies information and systems support to travel agencies' computer terminals and to other Internet users, all of which are linked to the company's state-of-the-art data center, one of the world's largest commercial data-processing complexes, located outside Denver, Colorado.

Internet

Galileo e-enables the travel industry, providing industry-leading technology solutions such as an advanced suite of wireless applications and numerous Internet initiatives. The mobile business professional can access award-winning one-stop online travel services and technology solutions from Galileo. As an e-commerce enabler, Galileo allows travel suppliers to distribute their inventory on the Internet, helps brick-and-mortar travel agencies create an online presence and compete successfully on the Web, and provides the booking engine behind many popular Internet sites worldwide.

Galileo also is an end-to-end provider of Internet and Internet Protocol (IP) hosting for mission-critical e-business operations of mid-size to large companies. Galileo provides redundant, reliable, and sophisticated system and network solutions, ensuring optimal performance for customers' e-businesses now and in the future.

Telecommunications

Building one of the largest TCP/IP global networks, Galileo is providing advanced telecommunication services for a variety of customers both in the travel industry and beyond. The company currently is building an end-to-end private network on a standard TCP/IP and ATM platform to deliver global Internet, virtual private network (VPN), and telecommunications network services.

To learn more about Galileo International, visit **www.galileo.com**. ∎

GALILEO

Local people. Global technology. The ultimate choice.
www.galileo.com

We'll help you
manage
the world.

Above: Spiegel officially launched its mail-order business in 1905, offering home furnishings and credit services through the mail.

Top: In 1865 Joseph Spiegel established furniture retailer Spiegel & Company in a "wareroom" on Wabash Avenue in Chicago.

Right: A leading tri-channel retailer, Eddie Bauer offers men and women classically styled, casual apparel that combines comfort and versatility, and home furnishings for the bed and bath.

The Spiegel Group has been part of the fabric of American society since the end of the Civil War. It has weathered the difficulties and challenges of the Chicago Fire, two major depressions, and two world wars. Its early catalogs helped break down the isolation of rural America. And it has helped enhance the lives of modern working women by providing convenient shopping options.

Since 1905, when Spiegel entered the catalog business, the company has been an innovator in direct-marketing strategies. Today it is a multi-channel retailer—including stores, catalogs, and e-commerce—with a portfolio of powerful brands and sophisticated support operations. The Group offers unique apparel and home furnishings, but does so with a deep understanding of the lifestyle needs of its customers. This is an important concept in garnering market share and delivering outstanding customer service.

The Spiegel Group—whose businesses include Eddie Bauer, Spiegel, Newport News, and First Consumers National Bank—is a "lifestyle retailer." It focuses on fulfilling the needs of the consumer. This consumer-focused approach entails understanding and fulfilling customers' needs with trusted brands, quality products, and reliable services that cater to shifting lifestyle needs. It also means being where the consumer is at all times, providing around-the-clock access to products and services. It is this consumer-centric strategy that positions The Spiegel Group as a leading specialty retailer. The Group's record of customer service and of identifying marketplace opportunities has been a tradition for almost 140 years.

German immigrant Joseph Spiegel opened Spiegel & Company on Wabash Avenue in Chicago in 1865. From his "wareroom" he sold high-quality, top-of-the-line furniture to Chicago's emerging business class; his business was an important contribution to the city's burgeoning trade. The depression of the 1890s forced Spiegel to change its business. It added production line goods to compete with the low-cost merchants who had come to dominate the market. And it began to offer credit for the first time.

In 1905 Spiegel took a momentous change in direction, issuing its first catalog and filling orders through the mail. Over the next few years the Spiegel catalog set itself apart from the competition. It was the first catalog house to offer credit by mail, to use photos instead of illustrations in its catalogs, and to create a holiday edition. This penchant for innovation and customer service would serve the company well—even during the hard times of World War I, the Great Depression, and World War II. The company's resiliency pulled it through each crisis—and would continue to do so over the next decades.

By the mid-1970s, however, Spiegel had fallen on hard times. Management took another dramatic change in direction. It revamped its catalog, streamlined its merchandise to appeal to a more upscale market, and—most important—

THE SPIEGEL GROUP

LIFESTYLE RETAILERS®

Newport News, established in 1973 as Avon Fashions, is a leading direct marketer of moderately priced women's fashions and home décor through catalogs and an e-commerce site. To further its strategy of serving the moderately priced market, The Spiegel Group purchased Newport News in 1993. Since its acquisition, Newport News' sales have more than doubled, approaching the half-billion-dollar mark in 2000.

Spiegel, the group's namesake division, understands the way today's busy woman wants to dress and live, fulfilling her needs with tasteful, high-quality apparel, and home merchandise that uniquely combines function and style. A leading direct marketer through catalogs and e-commerce sites, Spiegel saw its sales exceed $800 million in 2000.

The Spiegel Group's brands receive valuable marketing support from First Consumers National Bank (FCNB), which joined the Group in 1990. FCNB serves a dual role in the Group, providing private-label credit card programs to the brands and third parties, and offering unique bankcard programs that target under-served market niches nationwide.

The Spiegel Group, headquartered in Downers Grove, Illinois, has about 12,000 employees and annual revenue of nearly $4 billion. Its top priorities are to keep merchandise offerings and marketing strategies in line with customer lifestyle needs and expectations, and to maximize the potential of its multi-channel marketing capabilities.

With its strong brand names, direct marketing expertise, convenient credit programs, and multiple marketing channels, The Spiegel Group is well positioned to serve the consumer marketplace far into the future. ■

Above: Spiegel Catalog understands today's woman and satisfies her lifestyle needs with an extensive array of fashionable apparel and home furnishings that are relevant, comfortable, and versatile.

Top left: Newport News addresses the modern woman's desire for fashionable merchandise that combines a youthful, feminine, spirited image with versatility, comfort, and affordability.

focused its marketing strategy on working women to bring more convenience and broader shopping choices to their increasingly busy lives. That strategy—along with continued hard work and innovation—has made Spiegel one of the nation's leading direct-marketing companies.

In 1982 Spiegel formed a relationship with Germany-based Otto Versand, the world's largest direct-marketing company. This relationship with Otto Versand has helped propel Spiegel to expand and diversify beyond a single retail division. Since then, the company has evolved into The Spiegel Group, a cohesive retail force that includes four distinct and powerful brands—Eddie Bauer, Spiegel, Newport News, and First Consumers National Bank.

The Eddie Bauer sporting goods business was founded in Seattle in 1920 to provide quality outdoor-living clothing and equipment. In 1945 it began distribution of mail-order catalogs. When Spiegel purchased Eddie Bauer and its 61 stores in 1988, sales were $250 million. Today Eddie Bauer is a leading tri-channel specialty retailer of casual apparel and home furnishings with more than 530 stores and sales of $1.8 billion in 2000.

CHICAGO CONVENTION AND TOURISM BUREAU

hicago is the leading convention and trade show city in the United States as well as one of the country's premier tourist destinations. And with good reason. The city and state have long invested precious resources to build and maintain Chicago's reputation as a world-class city.

The Chicago Convention and Tourism Bureau (CCTB), an independent nonprofit organization, brings conventions, trade shows, and business and leisure travelers to Chicago. It works closely with the Chicago Office of Tourism and the Illinois Bureau of Tourism to enhance the city as a popular visitor destination. In addition, CCTB is a partner with the Metropolitan Pier and Exposition Authority (MPEA) in its efforts to maintain Chicago's leadership as the convention and trade show capital in North America.

The City of Chicago was just 10 years old in 1847 when its first recorded convention was held. In May of that year, the River and Harbor Convention came together to discuss the St. Lawrence River and its role as a transportation route.

Among the 3,000 attending delegates were Abraham Lincoln and Horace Greeley. In 1860 Lincoln returned to Chicago to accept the presidential nomination of the newly formed Republican Party in the specially built Wigwam House at Lake and Market streets. All told, 25 national political conventions have been held in Chicago—more than in any other city. And, on four occasions, both political parties gathered in the city in the same year.

Chicago's popularity as a meeting place was apparent in 1907, when a broader effort was made by local business leaders to attract even more conventions to the city's growing downtown. The Century of Progress exposition held on the lakefront in 1933 and 1934 was widely successful and a precursor to Chicago establishing itself as a world-class meeting destination. A decade later the Chicago Convention and Visitors Bureau was founded as the marketing resource for attracting exhibitions of all sizes and types to the city. In 1970 the Bureau merged with the Tourism Council of Greater Chicago to form the Chicago Convention and Tourism Bureau.

McCormick Place, the nation's premier convention and trade show facility, attracts more than three million convention, trade show, and meeting visitors a year. Courtesy, Mike Gustafson

Meanwhile, the Metropolitan Fair and Exposition Authority (MFEA) was created in 1955 to operate a planned new exhibition hall on the lakefront. The original McCormick Place—named for its principal sponsor, *Chicago Tribune* publisher Colonel Robert McCormick—opened in 1960. Until then, trade shows were held at Navy Pier or other venues. After McCormick Place was destroyed by fire in 1967, a larger convention center was built on the same site. Two major expansions of McCormick Place were completed in 1986 and 1996. In 2001 the Illinois legislature authorized construction of another new building that will bring the total amount of exhibit space at McCormick Place to 2.8 million square feet.

The Hyatt Regency McCormick Place Conference Center also opened in 2001. The facility, which was designed to accommodate the increasing demand for meeting space, is owned by the MPEA and operated by the Hyatt.

After the East building re-opened in 1971, MFEA decided that the CCTB was best qualified to serve as the sales agent for McCormick Place to help it in its mission to sell and promote Chicago as the ideal destination for both business and leisure visitors. CCTB moved its offices to McCormick Place in 1980.

In 1989 the state legislature placed Navy Pier under the control of the recon-stituted Metropolitan Pier and Exposition Authority, an independent municipal corporation overseen by a board of directors appointed by the mayor of Chicago and the governor of Illinois. The state also provided an initial $150 million in funds to help redevelop Navy Pier into the unique urban entertainment and convention facility it is today.

The pier, an integral part of Daniel Burnham's "Chicago Plan," opened in 1916 as a shipping dock and as a place for public entertainment. During World War I and World War II the pier served as a military training site. Following World War II Navy Pier became the home for the University of Illinois' Chicago campus and remained so until 1964.

After its renovation, Navy Pier was rededicated in 1995 as a year-round entertainment and exhibition venue. It draws more than eight million tourists a year to enjoy its shops, restaurants, theaters, and recreational attractions, including its signature icon—the 150-foot-tall Navy Pier Ferris Wheel.

Through the combined efforts of CCTB and MPEA, the Chicago area hosted approximately 7.5 million group meeting travelers in 2000, bringing $6.3 billion in direct expenditures to the city. Overall, Chicago is a destination of choice for more than 30 million visitors from around the world. ■

Navy Pier is a world-class recreation and exposition center that offers space for small to mid-size conventions and meetings in Festival Hall. Other attractions at Navy Pier include the Chicago Shakespeare Theater, the 150-foot Ferris Wheel, an IMAX® Theater, Chicago Children's Museum, an indoor botanic garden, and a variety of restaurants and shops.
Courtesy, Mike Gustafson

As an innovator in the travel industry, Bonnie Lorefice has changed the face of corporate travel by offering services such as 24-hour-a-day, 365-day-a-year support to travelers worldwide.

Ensuring that every detail of a client's travel program is carefully managed, each member of CTMG's team, including the executive committee, is involved in the travel program.

*T*he year was 1976...Jimmy Carter beat Gerald Ford for the White House, and Steve Jobs founded Apple Computer in a garage. The first e-mail was only four years old, and the Internet was yet to be created. This was the year Bonnie Lorefice and three employees began business as Corporate Travel Consultants—now known as Corporate Travel Management Group (CTMG)—headquartered in Lombard near Chicago. CTMG's focus was, and still is, to provide superior customer-centered corporate travel management. It became one of the few success stories within the travel industry, recognized for its outstanding service and innovative technology.

Over the past 25 years, CTMG's staff has grown to nearly 200 to support its steadily increasing client base. It has also consistently ranked among the top 30 U.S. travel management firms in *Crain's* list of largest privately held companies in the Chicagoland area, and in its list of Chicago's top women-owned firms. Furthermore, CEO Bonnie Lorefice is frequently ranked in *Travel Agent* magazine's listing of top women in travel, and her agency has been recognized numerous times by *Working Woman* magazine as one of the leading women-owned corporations. Most recently, Lorefice received the Presidential Seal of Honor from the American Biographical Institute for her outstanding contributions in the travel industry.

From the beginning, CTMG has taken an aggressive stance in providing comprehensive travel management services. Lorefice was one of the first in the industry to recognize the need to customize services exclusively for the business traveler. Companies partner with CTMG to handle the time-consuming details of booking airline, car rental, and hotel reservations, as well as managing their travel dollars. The company's success has been dictated by its penchant for developing and retaining its client base. Rather than undertake a strategy of mergers and acquisitions, CTMG has relied on its own ability to provide strong customer service, and client access to its executive staff. It has also built strong relationships with its worldwide vendors—airlines, hotels, and car rental companies—which are leveraged to achieve exceptional benefits for its clients.

CTMG has also always offered round-the-clock access. It is, in fact, one of the few travel management firms that continues to do so. CTMG's unparalleled staff tenure, which averages seven years, remains the highest level in the travel industry. This staff commitment allows CTMG's consultants to understand the business goals of its clients, and to build for each company a travel program tailored to meet, and exceed, its needs. In other words, CTMG is both a partner and a consultant to each individual client, regardless of size. Each client demands first-rate travel programs managed by a team of experienced travel consultants who provide cost effective world-class service and performance. CTMG has demonstrated this, and in doing so, has achieved a reputation for excellence—earning many honors and awards from its clients and peers, including vendor of the year from GTE Directories/Verizon.

Throughout its 25 years, CTMG has opened offices in cities around the country

Left: From the moment a reservation begins, CTMG's innovative technology steps into place to manage every aspect of each traveler's itinerary through quality assurance audits, data capture, and by obtaining the lowest available fare.

including Dallas, New York, and downtown Chicago, as well as satellite offices located in various states. The company also established two divisions to broaden its scope of offerings: Oakbrook Travel and Corporate Motivations. Oakbrook Travel, CTMG's leisure division, provides travelers with exquisite vacation options to destinations throughout the world. CTMG's meeting and incentive division, Corporate Motivations, partners with companies to manage and organize every aspect of its events, conferences, and incentive travel programs.

Since its beginning, CTMG's goal has been to provide technology-based services that offer convenience to its clients. In 1987 CTMG pioneered the development of AutoCOP®, a PC-based software program that manages and compares policy compliance, lowest available fares, and traveler preference to the itinerary. Two years later it developed AutoTECH®, a PC-based management tool that provides clients with customizable reporting that details their travel spending.

In 1996 CTMG furthered its commitment to garnering state-of-the-art technology to enable it to provide the most sophisticated services in the travel industry. Among its accomplishments, CTMG became one of three launch partners with longtime supplier Sabre in introducing Sabre Business Travel Solutions (now Sabre BTS/GetThere). Sabre BTS/GetThere is a total integrated PC-based solution for travel booking, policy adherence, expense reporting, and travel management decision-making tools.

CTMG has since entered into relationships with other third-party software providers and now offers additional tools—for example, expense management, automated booking options, and E-track® for electronic ticket management.

Clients also benefit by having the ability to make reservations and access itineraries on-line and obtain up-to-date travel information at CTMG's Web site.

To further enhance the company's global presence and offerings to its clients, CTMG has developed partnerships with both Radius and First Travel Management. These alliances offer CTMG clients access to over 8,000 travel partners and negotiated rates and benefits at more than 6,900 hotels around the globe.

Travel management is key to any firm's ability to compete effectively in global markets; therefore, moving people from place to place efficiently and cost effectively is of utmost importance. Although each client has different requirements, CTMG strives to address individual needs and challenges. For 25 years its expertise and dedicated teamwork has allowed CTMG to tailor travel management services to meet every type of business travel requirement…worldwide. ■

Below: Dedicated service and attention coupled with continuous education is the force behind CTMG's success and one of the firm's many distinguishing features.

Below: With nearly 200 employees whose average tenure rate is more than seven years, CTMG provides its corporate clients with the personalized service and knowledge level that they have been missing from other travel management firms.

CARDWELL AND
RANDALL ENTERPRISES, LLC

Above: John S. Cardwell (seated) and James R. Randall.

Below: The Galleria Plaza.

Above: Village Town Homes.

Right: Park 101 Industrial Park.

*J*ohn Cardwell and James Randall have a vision that is to transform Central Illinois, and they are doing it one building and one business at a time. Their commitment to making Decatur and Macon County not only a vibrant residential and commercial environment, but also a destination of choice, is taking shape.

Cardwell Companies Incorporated was established in 1978 with interests in commercial development and realty, construction, travel, and restaurant services. Since then, Cardwell Companies has expanded its interests. In 1999, John Cardwell took on a partner, James R. Randall, the former president of Archer Daniels Midland Company. Together they formed Cardwell and Randall Enterprises to provide an umbrella organization for its hotels, restaurants, art gallery, and advertising agency. That same year Cardwell and Randall also founded Real Estate Developers of Decatur to handle commercial real estate investments.

The following year Cardwell and Randall purchased the Holiday Inn Select just west of Decatur. This property joined a growing portfolio of hotels owned by Cardwell and Randall Enterprises. Others are the Ramada Suites and the Country Inn and Suites, both in Decatur, and the Comfort Inn in South Jacksonville. Combined, the four hotels offer more than 600 rooms in the Central Illinois region. All include modern amenities to satisfy the needs of families and business travelers.

The Holiday Inn Select sits on a 23-acre complex dubbed the "Pride of the Prairie." It is among the largest hotel and conference centers in downstate Illinois. It features business and fitness centers; an Olympic-size swimming pool, whirlpool, and sauna; tennis courts; baseball diamond; and a lake. When purchased, it was one of the most inclusive Holiday Inns in the country. However, Cardwell and Randall are expanding facilities and renovating the property to further enhance its reputation throughout the Midwest. Rooms and suites have been

refurbished, the lobby and business center remodeled. With more than 65,000 square feet of meeting and conference space available in 27 rooms, and the new Crystal Ballroom, the Holiday Inn Select is the perfect trade show and convention location.

Plans for the Holiday Inn Select are to make it the premier resort and business destination in downstate Illinois. The nearly 400-room hotel is taking on an entirely new look. Nearly 25 percent of the rooms have been converted into one-bedroom suites and others upgraded. Existing restaurants have been renovated, as has the lobby; and a boutique mall with space for gift and apparel shops, art gallery, and beauty salon is planned.

In addition to renovation of the hotel, Cardwell and Randall is taking a bold step. The company purchased an additional 40 acres adjacent to the hotel. On this land, Cardwell and Randall is undertaking the multimillion-dollar Holiday Harbor development, a water and amusement park. The multipurpose park will include indoor and outdoor facilities, a lake for water sports, and miniature golf and go-cart courses.

The first phase of the project is under way. Indoor facilities comprise 40,000 square feet of space to house restaurants and lounges, game room and bowling alley, and water activities.

Second-phase development plans focus on the outdoor water park and beach area. This is where a Decatur landmark

will be created–the Holiday Harbor light-house. An amusement park will complete the ambitious three-phase development. When completed, Holiday Harbor water park will be one of the largest in Illinois and will transform Decatur into a popular destination. It will also bring to the town hundreds of new jobs and contribute millions of dollars to the city coffers.

Cardwell and Randall, together or individually, are more than hotel developers, however. The Commercial Realty One division is the largest real estate and development enterprise in Macon County. Inventory includes more than three million square feet of prime office, retail, and industrial space. Large retail centers to mini-malls provide shopping center space for national anchors and hometown merchants. The Fairview Park Plaza, a 340,000-square-foot center extensively renovated, is anchored by Kroger Foods. And the former 80,000-square-foot Fashion Mart is undergoing renovation and will operate as Merchants Value Mall. Zoned industrial development and ware-housing space are strategically located near major interstates and highways. Office space–350,000 square feet of it–is available in downtown Decatur.

In the city's historic West End, luxury apartments and townhouses are rising and serve the needs of new residents and business owners. Cardwell and Randall, together or individually, have developed or acquired service businesses to fit their life-styles. Nova Gallery of Fine Art features the works of renowned artists. Travel and vacation planning is provided by Carlson Wagonlit Travel; it has been in business for 50 years. Another acquisition is Nichols Advertising, a full-service marketing and public relations agency that has

been creating campaigns since 1958. Cardwell and Randall also owns and operates three restaurants in Decatur. The AllStar Diner, a fifties/sixties-themed restaurant, is an inexpensive family destination. Jimmy Ryan's is a moderately priced bistro offering aged steaks and premium wine. JR's Steakhouse is a five-star restaurant offering fine dining in an elegant candlelit atmosphere with a distinctive and original menu.

Cardwell and Randall has a vision and that is diversity. The company and its divisions are committed to developing Decatur and Central Illinois into a thriving metropolis and a major tourist attraction. That transformation is well under way. And it is being achieved one building and one business at a time. ■

Above: One Main Place.

Top left: Cardwell Centre.

Below: Holiday Inn Select.

Below right: Northland Shopping Center.

Chicago is a world-class city with an extraordinarily wide variety of restaurants. One of the most cosmopolitan is homegrown Gibsons Bar and Steakhouse, the power restaurant on Chicago's Rush Street. It is a meat-and-potatoes eatery that reflects the Midwest penchant for plain and hearty food. But it is much more than that. It is a restaurateur's restaurant operated under a sophisticated but simple strategy that ensures a seamless approach to food service, customer satisfaction, and staff retention.

The award-winning Gibsons is ranked as the 11th-largest independent U.S. restaurant by *Restaurants and Institutions* magazine; food and beverage sales amounted to $14.9 million in 2000. It has a staff of nearly 150 and its retention rate within the industry is enviable. Gibsons' success is based on old-fashioned values: insistence on fresh products, a hands-on buying strategy, controlled food preparation—everything on the menu is prepared in-house—unparalleled no-nonsense dining service, and value for money. It offers gargantuan portions of prime beef, chops, fish, and lobster tails. Sharing among diners is encouraged, which further enhances food value and the informal, friendly ambience.

Gibsons, named for the martini that comes with a pearl onion rather than an olive, is owned by a group of partners. Stephen Lombardo has nearly three decades in the restaurant business. He co-founded Gibsons in 1988 and the adjoining Hugo's Frog Bar nine years later. His former food and beverage operations include several landmark restaurants, among them BBC, Hotspurs, and Sweetwater, all in Chicago; and the Jubilation Bar and Restaurant in Las Vegas. His co-founding partner is European-born Hugo Ralli, for whom Hugo's Frog Bar is named. Ralli has spent almost four decades in the food and beverage industry, including serving as managing director of Tavern on the Green in New York City and director of food and beverage for Pan American World Airways. Other partners are members of Gibsons' senior staff—chief financial officer Lawrence Shane and executive chef Michael Clark.

Lombardo and Ralli believe in quality, value, and personal contact, and they practice what they preach; both owners are always on site. Lombardo explains: "We recognize that repeat business is of paramount importance. We have developed a clubby ambience where the whole staff knows the food and beverage preferences of each regular guest." Frequent diners include celebrities from the worlds of entertainment, sports, and politics—Chicago's Mayor Daley once hosted Bill Clinton at Gibsons. Other frequent celebrity diners include Liz Taylor, Jay Leno, Billy Joel, Michael Jordan, and Jack Nicholson—and photos of the famous who have dined at Gibsons adorn the walls.

The company's growth strategy has been deliberate. It opened Hugo's Frog Bar in 1997 and a Gibsons in Rosemont, Illinois, in 2000. Plans are on the drawing board for other venues. Wherever they are located, any new restaurants will adhere to the successful Gibsons model: Sell only the finest food and beverages, provide unequaled service to customers, never relax standards, and give a unique dining experience to all guests. ■

Above: Gibsons Bar and Steakhouse offers hearty portions of deliciously prepared food. Sharing among diners is encouraged.

Below: Gibsons offers unparalleled dining service, as well as a friendly atmosphere.

*B*illboard advertising is an art. It must be attention grabbing, sublimely succinct, exquisitely brief, and eminently "readable." Since the early days of highway billboards touting the benefits of Burma Shave, outdoor advertising has emerged as an important marketing support tool.

Among the billboards seen while riding the highways and expressways of Illinois are those produced by Chicago-based J&B Signs, Inc. Bob Hoelterhoff, an advertising and marketing executive, established his out-of-home company in 1981. His career included serving as regional marketing director for Ringling Brothers Barnum & Bailey and as national director of outdoor advertising for Post Keyes Gardner.

Founding Multi-marketing, Inc., in 1977 rounded out Hoelterhoff's skills in advertising. This small start-up venture of three individuals received an innovative contract awarded by R.J. Reynolds Tobacco to develop unique marketing strategies in resort markets targeting adults. The new company initiated events and elaborate "spring break" destinations such as Daytona Beach, Fort Lauderdale, Padre Island, and eventually every beach resort in the United States.

Under Hoelterhoff's leadership, the company grew to become the largest full-service marketing agency in Illinois, with departments employing research, creative, production, audiovisual, convention and event management, business trade programs, sales promotion, and a field force of thousands of managed young adults to execute the events and promotions.

J&B Signs has two divisions—Billboard Signs and Digital Broadcasting. J&B Signs' billboards are seen in more than 100 locations along Chicago's busiest expressways, highways, major routes, and surface streets. They also adorn the highways in other markets including Springfield, Illinois, and along I-75 between Toledo and Dayton in Ohio.

J&B's newest division is Digital Broadcasting Company, which uses the latest digital technology and patented software to reach the upscale, active life-style market. It produces digital advertisements sent electronically to display advertising in health clubs, tennis courts, ski facilities, golf clubs, museums, airports, and more. It is J&B's expertise in targeting and reaching a high concentration of active consumers that accounts, to a large extent, for the company's continued growth.

In addition to taking a commonsense approach to doing business, J&B believes in the personal touch. Its small, family-like atmosphere nurtures and strengthens existing client relationships as well as attracting and developing new customers. Each and every client has direct access to everyone in the company, and Hoelterhoff is proud of that. "No client call is transferred or bounced into voice mail," he says. "All calls are answered by a real human being and immediately directed to an appropriate staffer. We're proud of the fact that we not only have established ourselves with the oldest form of advertising through 'signage of all kinds,' but we're also positioned for what we believe to be the new growth area of advertising in the digital world." ■

Creative and effective outdoor advertising.

About Illinois Publishing Group

The use of advertising dates back to—
and before—the graffiti scratched
on walls to direct people to wine
shops and bakeries in ancient Greece
and Rome.

In the last half of the twentieth
century an extremely effective advertising tool, the specialty publication,
has emerged to aid city and state governments and chambers of commerce
in their necessary tasks of publicizing
their city or state and furthering their
economic development programs.

These elegant and influential books
typically feature well-written texts and
beautiful photographs to showcase
their subjects. Specialty publications
have also been used to great advantage
by universities and large associations.

Illinois Publishing Group, the
publisher of the State-sponsored *The
Illinois Story*, is the only company
of this kind headquartered in the
Midwest. The company boasts a staff
of professionals whose experience and
achievement are unequaled in this
field of publishing.

Don Toohey is the founder and
publisher of Illinois Publishing Group
and C. David Turner is director of
sales. Staff members include editorial
director Karen Story, design director
Ellen Ifrah, photo editor Doug O'Rourke,
and administrative assistant Kathy B.
Peyser. This talented team has collabo-
rated on more than 400 publications
over the past 20 years.

Writers and researchers who have
participated in *The Illinois Story*
project are Kenan Heise, a former
Chicago Tribune reporter who has
recently been inducted into the
Journalism Hall of Fame; William
Recktenwald, who retired from the

Chicago Tribune in 1999 and now
teaches in the School of Journalism
at Southern Illinois University at
Carbondale; David M. Young, a
reporter and editor for the *Chicago
Tribune* for nearly 40 years and the
author of several books on Chicago
history; and Irene Macauley, an
accomplished business writer who
has headed communications programs
for a number of Chicago's leading
institutions.

Top, from left to right: David M. Young,
co-author; C. David Turner, director of sales
(standing); Irene Macauley, corporate historian;
and Don Toohey, founder and publisher of
Illinois Publishing Group. Photo by Powell
Photography, Inc.

Above, left: William Recktenwald, co-author.

Above, right: Artist's rendering of a recent teaser
billboard promoting the publication of *The Illinois
Story.*

Notes on Sources

The following publications have been helpful in researching and writing this history of the state. The late Robert Howard's book, *Illinois, A History of the Prairie State*, stands out for its accuracy and thoroughness. Published in 1972, Howard's volume is the standard history of Illinois.

Allen, John W. *Legends and Lore of Southern Illinois.* Carbondale: Southern Illinois University Press, 1963.

Angle, Paul M., editor. *Illinois Guide and Gazetteer.* Chicago: Rand McNally & Company, 1969.

Armstrong, William. *Warrior for Two Camps: Ely Parker, Union General and Seneca Chief.* New York: Syracuse University Press, 1989.

Bartlett, Mabel Lane, and John E. Grinnell. *Illinois, Know Your State.* Carbondale: Southern Illinois University Press, 1961.

Bogue, Margaret Beattie. *Patterns from the Sod.* Springfield: Illinois State Historical Library, 1959.

Buisseret, David. *Historic Illinois From the Air.* Chicago: University of Chicago Press, 1990.

Carpenter, Allan. *Illinois, Land of Lincoln.* Chicago: Children's Press, 1968.

Deneal, Gary. *A Knight of Another Sort.* Carbondale: Southern Illinois University Press, 1998.

Derleth, August. *Vincennes: Portal to the West.* Englewood Cliffs, New Jersey: Prentice-Hall, Inc., 1968.

Federal Writers Project of the Work Projects Administration, Illinois, A Descriptive and Historical Guide. Chicago: A.C. McClurg & Co., 1939.

Gersbacher, Eva Oxford. *Hotel on the Ohio.* Carbondale: Egyptian Key Publishing, 1945.

Historical Committee for the Centennial. *History of Hardin County, Illinois.* Golconda, Illinois: Herald-Enterprise, 1939.

History of Knox County, Illinois. Chas. C. Chapman & Co., 1878.

Howard, Robert P. *Illinois: A History of the Prairie State.* Grand Rapids, Michigan: William B. Eerdmans Publishing Company, 1972.

Howard, Robert P. *Mostly Good and Competent Men,* second edition. Revised and updated by Peggy Boyer Long and Mike Lawrence. Springfield: University of Illinois at Springfield, 1999.

Jacobsen, James E. *The Illinois/Kentucky Ohio River Civil War Heritage Trail.* Illinois Historic Preservation Agency and the Kentucky Heritage Council, 1998.

Johnson, Charles B. *Growth of Cook County Volume 1.* Chicago: Board of Commissioners of Cook County, 1960.

Microsoft Encarta Online Encyclopedia, 2000.

Nelson, Ronald E., editor. *Illinois: Land and Life in the Prairie State.* Dubuque, Iowa: Illinois Geographical Society, Kendall/Hunt Publishing Co., 1978.

Osborne, Georgia, and Emma Scott. *Brief Biographies of the Figurines on display in the Illinois State Historical Library.* Springfield: State of Illinois, 1932.

Rothert, Otto A. *The Outlaws of Cave-in-Rock.* Carbondale: Southern Illinois University Press, 1996.

Acknowledgments

The publisher and the authors wish to thank the following individuals and organizations for their contributions:

Alpha Script
Sue Davis
Kathryn Harris
C.D. Hayden
Holden Color
Noel Hurford
Erin McAfee

Mary Michals
Eric Morgensen
John O'Dell
Gordon Pruett
Barbara Rumsey
Frank Lloyd Wright Preservation
   Trust Research Center

County Map of Illinois

Map of Illinois shows present
counties and county seats.

Number of counties: 102

Directory of Corporate Sponsors

Abbott Laboratories, 312-315
100 Abbott Park Road
Abbott Park, IL 60064
847/937-6100 • 847/938-6317 fax
www.abbott.com • Ticker symbol ABT

Accenture, 278
161 North Clark Street, Chicago, IL 60601
312/693-0161 • www.accenture.com

Ace Hardware Corporation, 344-345
2200 Kensington Court
Oak Brook, IL 60523
630/990-6744 • 630/990-3527 fax
www.acehardware.com

Amtrak, 282-283
525 West Van Buren
Chicago, IL 60607
www.amtrak.com

Archer Daniels Midland, 242-245
4666 Faries Parkway, Box 1470
Decatur, IL 62525
217/424-6182
www.admworld.com • Ticker symbol ADM

Architectural and Ornamental Iron Workers Local 63, 300-301
2525 Lexington, Broadview, IL 60155
708/344-7727 • 708/344-5577 fax
Ray Dean

Bank One, N.A., 264-265
1 Bank One Plaza
Public Affairs, Mail Code IL 1-0358
Chicago, IL 60670
312/732-4000
www.bankone.com • Ticker symbol ONE

Blue Cross and Blue Shield of Illinois, 322-323
300 East Randolph Street
Chicago, IL 60601-5099
Robert Kieckhefer,
Vice President Public Affairs
www.bcbsil.com

Boeing Company, The, 258
100 North Riverside Plaza
Chicago, IL 60606
www.boeing.com

brainScans
350 North Ogden, Chicago, IL 60607
312/733-8558, David Novacek
dave@brainscans.net • www.brainscans.net

Cardwell and Randall Enterprises, LLC, 354-355
One Main Place, 101 South Main Street
Decatur, IL 62523
217/233-6030 • 217/233-6043 fax

Carr Futures, 266-267
10 South Wacker Drive, Chicago, IL 60606
312/441-4304, Gregoire Faure, Sr.

Castle & Co., A. M., 256-257
3400 North Wolf Road
Franklin Park, IL 60131
847/455-2240 • www.amcastle.com

Caterpillar Inc., 259
100 Northeast Adams Street
Peoria, IL 61629

Chicago and Northeast Illinois District Council of Carpenters, 296-297
12 East Erie Street, Chicago, IL 60611
312/787-3076 • 312/951-1540 fax
Peter DiRaffaele
www.carpentersunion.org

Chicago Convention and Tourism Bureau, 350
2301 South Lake Shore Drive
Chicago, IL 60616
312/567-8500 • 312/567-8533 fax
James Reilly, President and CEO
www.choosechicago.com

Chicago Defender, 279
2400 South Michigan, Chicago, IL 60616
312/225-2400 • 312/225-6954 fax
Eugene Scott

Chicago Journeymen Plumbers' Local Union 130 UA, 290-291
1340 West Washington Boulevard
Chicago, IL 60607
312/421-1010, Gerald Sullivan

Children's Memorial Hospital, 332
2300 Children's Plaza, Box #4
Chicago, IL 60614-3394
800/KIDS-DOC
www.childrensmemorial.org

CNA Financial Corporation, 268
CNA Plaza, Chicago, IL 60685
312/822-4882 • 312/817-0775 fax
Pamela Lyons
www.cna.com • Ticker symbol CNA

Corporate Travel Management Group, 362-363
450 East 22nd Street, Lombard, IL 60148
866/545-6789 • 630/691-1088 fax
www.corptrav.com

Deere & Company, 250-251
One John Dear Place, Moline, IL 61965
309/765-8000 • www.johndeere.com

DeVry Inc., 324-325
One Tower Lane
Oakbrook Terrace, IL 60181
630/574-1982 • 630/571-0317 fax
www.devry.com • Ticker symbol DV

Edelman, Inc., Daniel J., 280
200 East Randolph Street, 63rd Floor
Chicago, IL 60601
312/240-3000 • 312/240-2900 fax
Robert Reincke

FMC Corporation, 252-253
Executive Offices, 200 East Randolph Drive
Chicago, IL 60601
312/861-6000
www.fmc.com • Ticker symbol FMC

Galileo International, 347
9700 West Higgins Road
Rosemont, IL 60018
847/518-4000, Beth Dempsey
www.galileo.com • Ticker symbol GLC

Gibsons Bar and Steakhouse, 356
1028 North Rush Street
Chicago, IL 60611
312/266-8999 • 312/787-5649 fax
Steve Lombardo
www.gibsonssteakhouse.com

Graycor, 272-273
One Graycor Drive, Homewood, IL 60430
708/206-3677 • 708/206-0505 fax
www.graycor.com

Heller Financial, Inc., 262-263
500 West Monroe Street
Chicago, IL 60661
312/441-7404 • 312/928-8794 fax
Gunnar Branson
www.hellerfinancial.com
Ticker symbol HF

IBEW Local 134 and Electrical Contractors' Association, 286-289
5 Westbrook Corporate Center, #940
Westchester, IL 60154
708/531-0550, Frank Peters
www.local134.com

Illinois Department of Commerce and Community Affairs, 336-339
620 East Adams Street
Springfield, IL 62701
www.commerce.state.il.us

Illinois Institute of Technology, 318-319
10 West 33rd Street
Chicago, IL 60616
312/567-3561 • 312/567-3004 fax
www.iit.edu

International Association of Heat and Frost Insulators and Asbestos Workers Union Local 17 and the Illinois Regional Contractors Association, 308
3850 South Racine Avenue
Chicago, IL 60609
773/247-8184 • 773/247-6724 fax
Terry Lynch
www.local17insulators.com

International Brotherhood of Teamsters Joint Council 25, 302-303
1645 West Jackson Boulevard, Room 600
Chicago, IL 60612
312/421-2600 • 312/421-1227 fax

International Profit Associates, Inc., 274-275
1250 Barclay Boulevard
Buffalo Grove, IL 60089
800/531-7100 • 847/808-5599 fax
John R. Burgess
www.ipa-iba.com

International Union of Operating Engineers, Local 399, 298-299
763 West Jackson Boulevard
Chicago, IL 60661
312/372-9870 • 312/372-9430 fax
www.iuoe399.org

J&B Signs, 357
642 North Dearborn Street, 4th Floor
Chicago, IL 60610
312/640-8181 • 312/640-9120 fax
Bob Hoelterhoff

Jewel-Osco, 346
1955 West North Avenue
Melrose Park, IL 60160
www.jewelosco.com • Ticker symbol ABS

Jordan Industries, Inc., 281
1751 Lake Cook Road
ArborLake Centre, Suite 550
Deerfield, IL 60015
847/945-5591 • 847/945-5698 fax
Thomas Caffery
www.jordanindustries.com

Loyola University Chicago, 316-317
820 North Michigan Avenue
Chicago, IL 60611
312/915-6459 • 312/915-6215 fax
www.luc.edu

Metropolitan Pier and Exposition Authority, 351
301 East Cermak Road, Chicago, IL 60616

Michels Enterprises for Organ Donor Awareness, Hots, 331
57 Erie Street, Chicago, IL 60610
312/951-8450, Hots Michels

Motorola, Inc., 246-249
1303 East Algonquin Road
Schaumburg, IL 60196
847/435-5320 • 847/576-7653 fax
Jennifer Weyrauch
www.mot.com • Ticker symbol MOT

Museums In the Park, 326-330
104 South Michigan Avenue, Suite 521
Chicago, IL 60603

Painters' District Council #14, 306-307
1456 West Adams Street
Chicago, IL 60607
Gerald C. Harms

Plumbing Contractors Association of Chicago and Cook County, 292
1400 West Washington Boulevard
Chicago, IL 60607
312/563-9526 • 312/563-9870 fax
Dan McLaughlin

Plumbing Council of Chicagoland, 293
1400 West Washington Boulevard
Chicago, IL 60607
312/263-6612 • 312/421-6982 fax
Bob Ryan
www.plumbingcouncil.com

Robert Morris College, 320-321
401 South State Street
Chicago, IL 60605
312/935-6800 or 800/225-1520
www.rmcil.edu

Safeway Insurance Group, 269
790 Pasquinelli
Westmont, IL 60559
630/850-3811 • 630/887-9101 fax
William Parrillo

Sara Lee Corporation, 254-255
Three First National Plaza
Chicago, IL 60602
312/726-2600
www.saralee.com • Ticker symbol SLE

Sears, Roebuck and Co., 340-343
3333 Beverly Road
Hoffman Estates, IL 60179
Ron Culp, Senior Vice President Public Relations and Communications
www.sears.com • Ticker symbol S

Spiegel Group, The, 348-349
3500 Lacey Road, Downers Grove, IL 60515
630/986-8800

Suburban Chicago Newspapers, 276-277
3101 North, Route 30
Plainfield, IL 60544
815/439-5300 • 815/439-4360 fax
Jerry Strader

United Brotherhood of Carpenters and Joiners of America, 294-295
12 East Erie Street, Chicago, IL 60611
312/787-3076 • 312/951-1540 fax
Peter DiRaffaele
www.carpentersunion.org

United Union of Roofers, Waterproofers and Allied Workers Local 11, 304-305
9839 West Roosevelt Road
Westchester, IL 60154
708/345-0970
Joseph Sullivan

Warling Studios
350 North Ogden, Chicago, IL 60607
312/733-5646, Brian Warling
brian@warlingstudios.com
www.warlingstudios.com

Index

Italicized numbers indicate illustrations.

Abbott Laboratories, 181
Abolitionists, 30
Addams, Jane, 75-76, 83
Adler, Dankmar, 72, 155; Auditorium build-
    ing, 72, 153. *See also* Sullivan, Louis
Adler Planetarium, 143, *145*
African Americans, 103, 235, 236;
    civil rights activists, 78; indentured ser-
    vants, 30; musicians, 86; politicians, 49
Agriculture, 103, *196-197*, 208-210, *211-213*;
    crops, *199*, *209*, 210; downstate, 198;
    number of farms, 210; suburban, 178-179
Airports, 43-44, 123, 142, 205. *See also spe-
    cific airports*
Altgeld, John Peter, 44, *46*, 75, 79, 97
American Revolution, 19, 20, 21, 58
Amoco, 136; building, 156
Andrew, 180
Angle, Paul, 108
Anker archaeological site, mask found at, *54*
Aon Corporation, 136
Archer, George P., 205
Archer Daniels Midland (ADM), 205-206, 208
Architects, 71-72, 122. *See also specific archi-
    tects*; Architecture
Architecture, 10, 121-122; Chicago, 71-73,
    155-157; Chicago School, 72; drive-in sub-
    urban, 179; suburban, 194-195; suburban
    office campus, 180-182. *See also specific
    architects*
Argonne National Laboratory, 180
Arlington International Racecourse, 190
Armour, Philip D., 65, 66, 80, 158
Armour Company, 136
Armour Institute, 66, 158
Armstrong, Louis "Satchmo," *86*
Art, public, 157, *160-161*. *See also specific
    artists*
Art museums: The Art Institute of Chicago,
    143, *146*, *147*; Chicago Academy of Fine
    Arts, 143; Chicago Museum of
    Contemporary Art, 143, 147; David and
    Alfred Smart Museum of Art, 147;
    Lizzardo Museum of Lapidary Art, 194;
    Mary and Leigh Block Museum of Art,
    194; Mexican Fine Arts Center Museum,
    147; Smith Museum of Stained Glass
    Windows, 138; Terra Museum of
    American Art, 147
Atomic power, beginnings of, 10, 120, 157-
    158, 180-181
Aviation, 43-44, 45, 120; Flying schools, 43.
    See also specific airports and aviators

Badgley, Daniel, 22
Baha'i House of Worship, 188
Bainbridge's Tavern, 24
Balmoral Park Race Track, 190
Barenboim, Daniel, 150-151
Baxter International, 181
Beaubien, Mark, 59

Best, Daniel, 206
Bettendorf, W.J., 104
Bickerdyke, Mary Ann, *101*, 102
Birger gang, *43*
Bishop Hill, 103, 104
Black Hawk, 92, *93*, 94
Black Hawk War, 92-94, 194
Black Watch, 20
Boher, Florence Fifer, *102*
Bond, Shadrach, *22*, 24, 26, *92*;
    swearing in, *22*
Bonfield, John, 74
Bookseller's Row, *65*
Borden, Gail, 106
Bourbonnais, Francois, 106
British settlement, 20-21
Brown, George W., 104
Browne, Ellen, 81
Browne, Maurice, 81
Burnham, Daniel, 72, 128, 155; Orchestra
    Hall, 151; Rookery, 72
Burris, Roland W., 49
Business and industry, 60, 62, 64-67, 69, 128,
    136-139, 230; communications, 180; com-
    puters, 180; downstate, 198, 205-206,
    208; farm equipment manufacturing, 10;
    food processing, 206, 208; health care
    products, 181; heavy-equipment manufac-
    turers, 10; lumber, 55, 63; meatpacking,
    65; mergers and acquisitions, 136-137; sub-
    urban, 178-182; suburban office compa-
    nies, 180-182; water-powered, 178. *See
    also names of specific businesses and
    types of businesses and industries*;
    Suburbs, Chicago

Cabrini, Francis Xavier, *70*
Cabrini Homes, 70
Cahokia Mounds, 16-17, *216*, 219
Calder, Alexander: Chicago public sculpture,
    157, *160-161*
Camp Grant, 48
Canals and waterways, 113-114, 123, 205,
    232; Calumet Sag Channel, 114, 124;
    Hennepin Canal, 217; Illinois and Michigan
    Canal, 56, 62, 63, 96, 107, 113, 178, 186,
    217, 233; Illinois Waterway, 113; Sanitary
    and Ship Canal, 56, 80, 114, 124
Capone, "Big Al," *84*, 115, 120
Carlin, Thomas, 94, *96*
Carson, Pirie, Scott & Co., 72, 155-156, 166
Caterpillar Corporation, 198, *199*, 206
Century of Progress World's Fair, *85*, 86
Cermak, Anton: assassination, 84, 113
Chagall, Marc: Chicago public mosaic, 157
Chanute, Octave, 43, 44, 227
Chanute Field, 48, 235, 237; Army Air Corps
    mechanics training, *44*; flying school, 43
Checker Motors Corporation, 179
Chicago, 10, 31, 32, 39, 42, 43, 48, 49, 92,
    102, 106, 107, 108, 109, 112, 113, 114,
    119, 184, 186, 194, 195, 197, 201, 205,
    208, 211, 216, 226, 230, 231, 235; aerial

view, *134-135*; cityhood, 60-61; Civil War-
    era, 64-65; corruption, 80, 81; Dearborn
    Street drawbridge, *58*; disasters, 81, 83,
    115, 120; ethnic neighborhoods, 123, 165-
    167; European exploration, 57-58; fire
    department, 83; geological history, 54-55;
    German population, 48; harbor/port, 60,
    62, 123, 142; lakefront, *72-73*, 124, 128,
    138, 177; land speculation, 60; Loop, 123,
    138, 147, 155, 164, 166, 167, 171; neigh-
    borhoods, 156, 161, 165-167, 235; nick-
    name, 120; 1980s recession, 137; 1919
    race riot, 83; Paleo-Indians, 56-57; police
    department, *80*; population diversity, 122-
    123; population figures, 61, 62, 71, 119-
    120, 172, 201; portage, 51-52, 53, 57, 89;
    prehistory, 54-55; retail district, 166; St.
    Patrick's Day parade, *127*; Skid Row, 235-
    236; village of, 52-53, 60. *See also*
    Chicagoland
Chicago Bears, 119, 143, 153, 155
Chicago Blackhawks, 153
Chicago Board of Trade, 62
Chicago Bulls, 153
Chicago Cubs, 153, 198
Chicago Cultural Center, 147, 150
Chicago Fire, 62, 67-69, 102, 120, 122, 161,
    171-172, 180, 235; aftermath, 69-71; fight-
    ing, *68*; museum exhibit, 147
Chicago Fire (soccer team), 155
Chicago Horticultural Society, 188
Chicagoland, 119, 136, 177, 179, 197;
    tourism, 216. *See also* Chicago; Suburbs,
    Chicago
Chicagoland Speedway, 191
Chicago Motor Speedway, 190
Chicago Municipal Airport, 43. *See also*
    Midway Airport
Chicago Plan of 1909, 128
Chicago Stadium, 235
Chicago Stock Exchange, *120*
Chicago Transit Authority, 194
Chicago White Sox, 153, 198
Chicago Wolves International Hockey League,
    190
Chicago Zoological Society, 189
City Cemetery, 69
Civilian Conservation Corps (CCC), 46, 49;
    Camp Cadiz, 49; Camp Saline, *47*
Cities and towns: Addison, 186; Alton, 27, 34,
    95, 228; Arcola, 227; Argo, 179; Arlington
    Heights, 178, 190; Aurora, 106, 180, 186,
    187, 190; Barrington, 179; Batavia, 181,
    186; Belleville, 43, 48, 49; Bellwood, 180;
    Bensenville, 179; Bloomington, 32, 102,
    113, 201, 202, 205, 214, 225, 226; Blue
    Island, 54, 180; Bourbonnais, 202, 229;
    Brookfield, 189; Cahokia, 17, 19, 21, 216,
    217, 221; Cairo, 28, 31, 32, 36, *206*, 218;
    Carbondale, 32, 33, 34, 49, 205, 228;
    Carpentersville, 178; Carthage, 96, 184;
    Centralia, 25, 32, 49; Champaign, 32, 44,
    202, 205, 214, 227; Channahon, 186;

Charleston, 34, 228; Cherry, 39, 41; Chicago Heights, 186; Cicero, 179, 186, 190; Crete, 190; Crystal Lake, 186; Decatur, 202, 204, 205, 208, 223, 225, 229; Deerfield, 138, 181; DeKalb, 107, 183, 211, 227, 228; De Soto, 38-39; Des Plaines, 184, 186; Dixon, 110, 217; Downers Grove, 102, 107, 109; Du Quoin, 38; East Alton, 49; East Dundee, 191; East Moline, 104, 202; East St. Louis, 17, 41, 201, 228; Edwardsville, 27; Effingham, 32, 237; Elburn, 175; Eldorado, 46; Elgin, 106, 184, 186, 190; Elizabethtown, 22, 23, 25, 37; Elmhurst, 188, 194; Evanston, 102, 109, 113, 155, 157, 182, 184; Fairfield, 41; Freeport, 34, 205, 208; Galena, 16, 31, 32, 36, 38, 54, 92, 99, 100, 107, 109, *200, 201, 202, 203, 217,* 223, 235, 237; Galesburg, 32, 34, 101, 104, 108, 229; Geneva, 188, 189, 190; Glencoe, 188; Glen Ellyn, 184, 186, 190; Glenview, 181; Golconda, 22, 27, 31; Goshen, 29; Grand de Tour, 94, 95; Grayslake, 175, 186; Greenville, 108, 229; Harrisburg, 217; Harvey, 179, 236; Herrin, 39, 42; Hinsdale, 236; Hoffman Estates, 183; Homewood, 179; Jacksonville, 31, 33, 229; Joliet, 106-107, 179, 190, 191; Jonesboro, 34; Kampsville, 227; Kankakee, 106, 202; Karnak, 29; Kewanee, 91, 109; Lake Forest, 184, 236; La Salle, 187; Lawrenceville, 49; Lebanon, 229; Lemont, 180; Lewistown, 108, 221; Libertyville, 187, 190, 194; Lisle, 180; Lockport, 175, 187, 194; McLeansboro, 27, 114; Macomb, 98, 228; Makanda, 218; Marion, 23, 24, 108; Massac, 22; Mattoon, 15, 32; Maywood, 183, 186, 236; Melrose Park, 191; Mendota, 32; Meredosia, 31; Metropolis, 200; Moline, 95, 104, 202, 205; Monticello, 225; Mound City, 37; Mount Carroll, 185; Naperville, 169, 178, 180, 183, 185, 187, 192, 194; Nauvoo, 95, 96, 216, 217, 221, *223*; New Salem, 29, 223; Normal, 96, 199, 202, 226, 228; North Chicago, 181; Oak Brook, 169, 180, 181, 202; Oakbrook Terrace, 186; Oak Forest, 184; Oak Park, 73, 195, 235; Orland Park, 180; Palatine, 186; Palos Hills, 186, 190; Park Forest, 179; Park Forest South, 184; Peoria, 15, 19, 23, 41, 100, 104, 106, 108, 198, 202, 205, 214, 224, 225; Petersburg, 107; Plano, 225; Quincy, 34, 95, 205, 229; Rantoul, 32, 43, 48, 226, 237; River Forest, 178, 190, 195; River Grove, 186; Riverside, 172, 195; Robinson, 108; Rockford, 32, 48, 92, 107, 111, 202, 227; Rock Island, 93, 103, 104, 202, 227; Rolling Meadows, 184; Romeoville, 194; Rosemont, 181, 190; Salem, 49; Schaumburg, 164, 169, 180, 184; Shawneetown, 22, *23,* 24, 26-28, 108; Skokie, 180; South Elgin, 193; South Holland, 186; Springfield, 28, 29, 31, 37, 38, 39, 99, 115, 202, 205, 214, 223,

224, 225, 228, 229; Sugar Grove, 186; Summit, 54, 56; Tampico, 110, 217; Thebes, 29; Thornhill, 188; Tinley Park, 186; Union, 193; University Park, 184; Urbana, 183, 202, 214; Utica, 216, 221; Vandalia, 27, 28, 29; Vernon Hills, 194; Vincennes, 27; Warrenville, 178; Waukegan, 185; Westchester, 184; Wheaton, 184, 187, 189, 192, 194; Wheeling, 175; Willow Springs, 187; Wilmette, 183, 188; Winnetka, 114. *See also* Chicago; Kaskaskia (village)
Civil War, 28, 35-38, 72, 99-100, 104, 211, 224; Camp Butler, 37; Camp Douglas, 65; casualties, 64; Chicago and, 64-65; Company A of 29th Infantry, 37; Copperheads, 36; District of Cairo, 38, 99, 101; 82nd Illinois, 36; newspaper coverage, 71; 13th Illinois, 36; 21st Illinois, 38, 99; USS *Neosho, 37;* women in, 101-102
Clark, George Rogers, *18, 19,* 20, 21, 23, 28
Clark, William, 19
Clybourn, Archibald, 62
CNA Financial Corporation, 136
Coal, 54, 198
Coal mining, 38-39, 41; fires, 39; safety reform, 39
Coatsworth, Stella, 102
Colleges and universities, 96-98, 157-158, 160-161, 164-165, 234; Armour Institute, 66; Aurora University, 184; Bradley University, 227, 229; Carbondale College, 34; Carthage College, 184; Chicago State University, 96, 165; Chicago Teachers College, 96; City Colleges of Chicago, 164; Columbia College, 164-165; Community college systems, 186; DePaul University, 155, 157, 161, 184; downstate, 227-229; Eastern Illinois University, 98, 228-229; Elmhurst College, 184; Eureka College, 227, 229; Governors State University, 184; Greenville College, 229; Illinois College (Jacksonville), 32, 33, 96, 229; Illinois Institute of Technology, 66, 150, 156, 157, 158, 160, 184; Illinois Normal College French Club, *32;* Illinois State University, 96, 228; Illinois Wesleyan University, 96; Knox College, 104, 108, 229; Lake Forest College, 98, 184; land grant colleges, 33, 96; Lewis Institute, 158; Loyola University (Chicago), 155, 157, 161, 183; McKendree College, 229; MacMurray College, 229; Mallinckrodt College, 183; Millikin University, 229; Monmouth College, 229; National College of Education, 184; National-Louis University, 184; North Central College, 184; North Park University, 157, 165; Northeastern Illinois University, 165; Northern Illinois State Normal School, 183; Northern Illinois University, *97,* 98, 107, 183, 190, 228; Northwestern Female College, 101, 102; Northwestern University, 96, 97, 98, 102, 108, 113, 155, 157, 182, 188, 190, 194, 234; Olivet Nazarene University, 229; Principia College, 229; Quincy University,

229; Roosevelt University, 164, 184; Rush Medical College, 62; Sangamon State University, 228; Shimer College, 184; Southern Illinois Normal College (Carbondale), *33,* 34, 228; Southern Illinois University, 26, 49, 200, 228; St. Ignatius College, 159; University of Chicago, 77, 84, 98, 147, 150, 157-158, *164, 165,* 184, 234, 235; University of Illinois (main campus), 97, 98, 102, 155, 157, 164, 225, 227, 234, 235; University of Illinois (Champaign-Urbana), 33, 96, 183, 227-228; University of Illinois (Springfield), 228; Wesleyan University, 229; Western Illinois Normal College, 98, 229; Western Illinois University, *98,* 228; Wheaton College, 184
Columbus Hospital, 70
Comiskey Park, 153, *155*
Commonwealth Motors Corporation, 179
Consolidated Foods Corporation, 138
Continental Bank, 136
Convention and tourism industry, 62, 138-139, 235. *See also* Hotel industry; Restaurant industry
Cook, Daniel Pope, 26, 91, *92,* 94
Cook County Forest Preserve, 188, 189, 190
Cornell, Paul, 171
Couch, Ira, *65*
Couch, James, 65
Coughlin, "Bathhouse" John, 80, *81,* 120
Counties: Alexander, 49, 198; Bureau, 39; Cook, 26, 44, 46, 49, 95, 114, 179, 186, 187; Calhoun, 15; DeKalb, 186; Du Page, 109, 180, 183, 186; Franklin, 41, 49; Fulton, 108; Gallatin, 16, 17, 27, 49, 217; Grundy, 39; Hardin, 16, 37, 218; Iroquois, 18; Jackson, 38, 217; Jo Daviess, 15, 19, 198; Johnson, 217; Kane, 180, 186; Kankakee, 18; Knox, 39, 104; Lake, 186; Macoupin, 18; Madison, 198; Menard, 107; Montgomery, 41; Peoria, 18; Pulaski, 37; Randolph, 16, 21; Rock Island, 39; Saline, 217; St. Clair, 21, 198; Stark, 39; Wabash, 18; Wayne, 41; Whiteside, 110; Will, 186-187; Williamson, 39, 41, 42, 49; Winnebago, 18
Court reform, 203
Crime, 21-22; Birger gang, *43;* gangsters, 83-84; Prohibition and, 83; Shelton-Birger gang war, 41
Crosby Opera House, Chicago fire destruction of, 69
Crystal Gardens, 138
Cuneo, John, 187

Daniels, John W., 205
D'Aquino, Iva Ikuko Toguri, 87
Darrow, Clarence, 46, 83, *84*
Davis, Jefferson, 60, 93, *94*
Dawes, Charles Gates, *109,* 113
Debs, Eugene V., 79, 83
Deere, John, 94, *95,* 205
Deere & Company, 95, 198, 205; factories, 103
Deere Foundation, 94, 95
DeForest Training School, 186
De la Forest, Francois, 104

Depression, Great, 46, 48-49, 110, 113, 152, 153, 173
Depression of 1893, 77
De Tonti, Henri, 90, 91, 104
DeVry Institutes, 186
Dewey, John, 81, 157
Diamond Star Motors plant, 199
Dickson Mounds, 221
Dix, Dorothea, 33, 35
Douglas, Stephen A., 28, 31-32, *34*, 35, 64, 65, 96
Downstate Illinois, 197-198, 200, 236-237; cultural facilities, 224-226; large communities, 202; metropolitan areas, 202; politics, 202-204; population figures, 200-202; problems, 199
Draper, Andrew S., 97
Duncan, Matthew, 26
Du Page County Forest Preserve District, 190
DuSable family: Catherine, 51; farm, 58; Jean, 51; Jean Baptiste Pointe, 51, 52, 53, 58; Suzanne, 51; trading post, 58

Economics, Chicago School of, 157
Edgar, Jim, 204
Education, 32-33, 157; first public high school, 33; free public, 10; public school tax, 33; school for the blind, 33. *See also* Colleges and universities
Edwards, Ninian, 33, *96*
Elgin Motor Car Corporation, 179
Ellsworth, Elmer, *62*, 64
Emancipation Proclamation, 28, 37, 224
Entertainment: movie theaters, 139; nightclubs, 139. *See also* Performing arts; Sports
European explorers, 18-19. *See also* French inhabitants
Evans, John, 182
Evanston Garden Club, 188
Evanston Historical Society, 109, 113

Fabyan, George, 188
Farmers. *See* Agriculture; Farming
Farmers Club, 41
Farming: hobby, 210; secondary occupation, 210
Farwell and Co., John V., 66
Federal Signal Corporation, 180
Ferguson, Daniel C., 208
Fermi, Enrico, 157, 158
Fermi National Accelerator Laboratory, 180, 181
Ferrell, Charles M., 37
Ferrell, John, 37
Field, Leiter & Co. department store, *64*, 65, 66, 70; Chicago fire destruction, 69. *See also* Marshall Field & Co.
Field, Marshall, 64, 66, 77, 80, 81, 142
Fifer, Gertrude, *102*
Fifer, Joseph, 102
Fitch, Leroy, 37
Flower, Lucy, 102
Ford, James, 22
Fort Dearborn Reservation, 63
Forts: Armstrong, 93, 103; Crevecoerur, 90; Dearborn, 51-52, *56*, 58-60; de Chartres,

19, 20, 219, *223*; Kaskaskia, 19, 20, 21; Massac, 18, 19, 20, 22, 23; Pimitoui, 91; Sackville, 19, 21; Sheridan, 20, *44*, 48, 235
Fox, Carol, 152
Fox Valley Park District, 190
Fox, Vicente, *205*
French and Indian War, 19-20
French inhabitants, 19-20, 218-219. *See also* Fur traders; *Voyageurs*
Friedman, Milton, 157
Fujita, Tetsuya "Ted," 157
Fur trade, 22-23, 51, 208, 230
Fur traders, 22-23, 51, 52, 56, 58, 59

Gale, George Washington, 104
Gangsters. *See* Crime
Garden, Mary, 87
Gardens, 187-188; Baha'i gardens, 188; Cantigny Park, 188; Chicago Botanic Garden, 188; Cuneo Museum and Gardens, 187; Japanese Garden, 188; McCormick estate, 187-188; Morton Arboretum, 186, 188; Shakespeare Garden, 188; White Birch Estate, 188. *See also* Parks
Gasoline tax, 42
Geisert, Arthur, 109
George Field, 49
Giant City State Park lodge, 49
Glenview Naval Air Station, 235
Glidden, Joseph, 98, 107
Goodman, Benny, 84
Government and politics, 120, 202-204; constitutional officers, 203; Democratic National Convention, *120-121*; 1968 Democratic Convention, 120; Republican Conventions, 63-64, 100, 120; scandals, 202
Grainger, W.W., 180
Grant, Ulysses S., 35, 36, 37, *38*, 72, 98, 99-100, 113
Great Lakes Naval Training Station, 45, 46, *47*, 48, 226
Great Lakes schooners, 60
Green, Dwight, *115*
Greene, Bob, 175
Greyhound bus lines, 136

Haish, Jacob, 107
Hancock Building, John, 156, 157
Harrison, Carter, 74
Harpe, Micajah, 22
Harpe, Wiley, 22
Harper, William Rainey, 77, 157
Hawthorne-Mellody Farms, 187
Hawthorne Race Course, 190
Haymarket Riot, 44, 46, 74-75; defendants, *75*; trial, 71, 75
Haynie, I.N., 36
Heron Pond, 218
Historic houses and estates: R.H. Allerton estate, 225; Belvedere Mansion, *203*; C.G. Dawes home, *109*, 113; J. Deere home, *95*; DuSable residence, *52, 56*; Farnsworth House, 225; U.S. Grant home, *217*, 223; Kinzie residence, *56*; A. Lincoln home, 29, 223, *225*; McCormick estate, 187-188; Palmer mansion, *66*, 67; R. Reagan boy-

hood homes, 217; White Birch Estate, 188
Hodge, Orville, 202
Holabird, William, 72
Holt, Benjamin, 206
Hopewellian culture, 16
Hopkins, John, 79
Horner, Henry, *46*, 49, 114
Hotels and hotel industry, 139; Briggs House, 67; Drake, 67; Grand Pacific, 67; Palmer House, 67, 69, 70; Rose, 26, *224*; Sauganash, 55, *59*; Sherman House, 67; Tremont House, 65, 67
Hubbard, Gordon S., 59, 62
Huck, Winnifred Mason, 102, *114*
Huff, George, 97-98
Hulett, Alta, 74
Hull, Charles J., 75
Hull House, 75, *76*
Hurlbut, Stephen, 35-36
Hutchins, Robert Maynard, 84, 158
Hyde Park resort, 171

IC Industries, 136
Illiniwek, 17, 56, 221; Cahokia, 17; Kaskaskia, 17, 89; Michigamea, 17; Moingwena, 17; Peoria, 17, 89, 221; Tamoroa, 17
Illinois: first Americans in, 20-21; geological history, 16; labor issues, 234; population figures, 22, 201; prehistoric inhabitants, 16-17, 26; prehistory, 15-16; state bird, 112; state flag, 112; state flower, 112; statehood, 26, 91; state nickname, 197; state song, 112; state tree, 112; U.S. vice presidents from, 112-113
Illinois, County of, 21
Illinois Confederation, 17
Illinois Constitution: first, 26, 92; 1970, 203; second, 31, 96
Illinois General Assembly, 102, 110
Illinois Glacier, 15
Illinois Historic Preservation Agency, 17, 19, 26, 221, 224
Illinois National Guard, 110
Illinois Prairie Path, 177-178, 186
Illinois Prairie Trail Authority, 186
Illinois River Valley, 15, 211, 221
Illinois State Capitol, 28, 29-30, 223, *226*
Illinois State Fair, 115, 223
Illinois State Hospital for the Insane (Jacksonville), 33, 35
Illinois Territory, 22, 23-24, 26, 91
Illinois Tool Works, 181
Indians. *See* Illiniwek; Native Americans
Industrial Workers of the World, 83
Ingersoll, Robert G., 100-101, 108
Inland Steel, 136; plant, *138*
Insull, Samuel, 152, 187
International Harvester, 136, 178

Jackson, Allan, 179
Jahn, Helmut, 156
James, Edmund, 97
Jansson, Erik, 103
Jenney, William Le Baron, 72, 155; Home Insurance Building, 72, 155

Jewel Tea Company, 179
Johnson, Adam R., 37
Johnson Wax headquarters building, 195
Jones, James, 108
Joliet Prison, Old, 35, 107
Jolliet, Louis, 18-19, *55*, 57, 89, 103, 106, 187
Jordan, Michael, 153; statue, *157*
Juvenile courts, first, 10

Kane County Cougars, 190
Kane County Forest Preserve District, 188
Kansan Glacier, 15
Kaskaskia (village), 18, 19, 22, 23, 26, 27, 28, 89, 92, 219
Kelly, Edward J., *113*, 114
Kenna, Michael "Hinky Dink," 80, 81, 120
Kerner, Otto, 202
Kiddieland, 191
Kinzie family: John, 58; John H., 59
Klutznick, Philip M., 179-180
Krainik, Ardis, 152
Ku Klux Klan, 39, 41

Labor laws, 44, 46; child, 44, 46; eight-hour work day, 44; occupational disease laws, 10; state civil service code, 46, 203; Sweatshop Act, 44; workplace safety, 44
Labor unions, 39, 41; AFL, 41; CIO, 41; United Mine Workers of American, 41
Labor unrest, 39, 41, 71, 74, *110-111*; Anarchists and, 74; Herrin Massacre, 42; Socialists and, 74; UMW strike (1922), 39
Lake Chicago, 54
Lake Michigan, 15, 16, 18, 21, 44, 51, 52, 53, 54, 55, 57, 60, 63, 69, 80, 89, 90, 91, 92, 114, 124, *126-127*, 143, 169, 171, 182
Lake Peoria, 18, 104
Lake Springfield, 228
La Lime, Jean, 58
Land Grant College Act, 33, 96
Land Ordinance of 1785, 25
La Salle, René-Robert Cavelier, sieur de, 18, 58, 90, 91, 106
Lawler, Michael, 36
Lead, 54; discovery, 92; mining, 200
Leiter, Levi Z., *64*, 66, 67
Leopold, Nathan, 84
Lewis, John L., *41*
Lewis and Clark, 19, 219
Libraries, 150; Chicago Public, 150; Harold Washington Library Center, 150; John Crerar (University of Chicago), 150; Illinois State Historical, 223-224; Lincoln Presidential, 223-224; Newberry, 150. *See also* Museums
Lillard, Joseph, 22
Limestone, 54
Lincoln, Abraham, 10, *28, 29*, 34, 35, 37, 63-64, 71, 93, 96, 98-99, 108, 113, 217, 223-224, 227; assassination, 38, 39, 65; funeral train, 38, *39*, 65; Illinois assemblyman, 28, 29-30; U.S. Congressman, 30
Lincoln-Douglas debates, 28, 34-35, 104, 229
Literature, 10, 81, 108; Chicago-area, 52. *See also* Writers, authors, poets
Little Theater Movement, 81

Loeb, Richard, 84
Logan, John A., *36*
Lord, Hugh, 20
Lovejoy, Elijah, 27, 30, 95, 108
Lowden, Frank, *106*, 110, 112
Lucent Technologies, 180

McCarty, Joseph, 106
McCarty, Samuel, 106
McClernand, John A., *36*
McCormick, Cyrus, 62, 136, 178; reapers, 62, 65
McCormick, Edith Rockefeller, 189
McCormick, Robert R., 111, *115*, 187-188
McCormick Place, 138, 143
McCormick Reaper Works, 74, 178
McDonald's, *175*, 181-182; world headquarters, 181
McDowell, Mary, 80
McFarlan, Elizabeth, 20, 25
McFarlan, James P., 20, 25
Mamet, David, 151
Marquette, Jacques, 18-19, 55, 57, 89, *90*, 103, 187
Marshall, John, 27
Marshall Field & Co., 66, 67, 166
Mason, Samuel, 21-22
Mason, William E., 102, *103*, 114
Maywood Park, 190
Mecherle, George J., 208
Medill, Joseph, 71
Medill, William, 64
Memorial Day, creation of, 36
Merchandising/retail, 65-66, 166-167. *See also specific stores*; Shopping
Metropolitan Water Reclamation District of Greater Chicago, 127
Mexican-American War, 31, 98-99, 100
Midway Airport, 43, 123, 142
Miles, Stephen, 23
Miles Trace, 23
Military Tract, 91, 98, 104
Mining, decline of, 214-215; coal, 214-215; fluorspar, 214
Mission of the Holy Family, 19
Mission of the Immaculate Conception of the Blessed Virgin, 89
Mississippian culture, 16, 17
Modoc site, 16
Molex, 180
Monks Mound, 17
Montgomery Ward and Co., 81, 128
Mormon Legion, 95
Mormons, 95-96, 103, 221, 223; Temple of Nauvoo, 95; tourist site, 216
Mormon War, 96
Morrill Act, 227
Morton, J. Sterling, 188
Morton, Joy, 188
Motorola, 180
Museum Campus (Chicago), 143
Museums, 121; American Police Center and Museum, 150; Amish, 227; Army's First Infantry Division, 192; Astronomy, 143; Aurora Regional Fire, 194; Black Hawk

State Historic Site, 227; Center for American Archaeology, 227; Chanute Air Force Base museum, 226-227; Chicago Academy of Science, 150; Chicago Car Exchange, 194; Chicago Children's, 138, 147, 150; Chicago Historical Society, 147; Chicago's, 142-150; Cuneo Museum and Gardens, 194; Discovery Center, 227; downstate, 226-227; Du Sable Museum of African-American History, 147; Field Museum of Natural History, 121, 142-*143*; First Infantry Division, 194; Fox River Trolley, 193-194; Hellenic Museum and Cultural Center, 147; Illinois and Michigan Canal Visitor Center, 194; Illinois Railway, 192-193; Illinois State, 223; Isle a la Cache, 194; Krannert, 227; Lincoln Presidential Library and Museum, 223-224, *225*; Museum of Broadcast Communications, 147, 150; Museum of Science and Industry, 142; Naper Settlement, 192, 194; Northern Illinois University, 227; Oriental Institute (University of Chicago), 147; Ridge Historical Society, 147; Rock Island Arsenal, 226; Spertus Museum, 147; suburban, 191-194; Village of Oak Park, 192. *See also* Art museums

Nash, Patrick, 113, 114
National Association for the Advancement of Colored People (NAACP), 78
National River and Harbor Convention, 138
National Road, 28
Native Americans, 17-18, 25, 52, 55, 56, 61; Algonquian, 17; as indentured servants, 30; Black Hawk, 92, *93*, 94; Cherokee, 31, 217-218; Chippewa, 17; Fox, 17, 92, 93; Illinois, 56; Kickapoo, 17, 58; Miami, 17, 58; Ottawa, 17, 20, 58; Plankashaw, 17; Pontiac, 20; Potawatomi, 58, 90; Sauk, 17, 92, 93, 94; Shawnee, 17, 25; Winnebago, 17. *See also* Illiniwek; Trail of Tears
Navistar, 136
Navy Pier, 138, *140-141*, 147; IMAX® Theater, 138; Skyline stage, 138
Nebraskan Glacier, 15
Negro Fellowship League, 78
Netsch, Dawn Clark, 113
Newberry, Walter Loomis, 150
Newell Manufacturing Company, 206, 208
Newell Rubbermaid, 205, 208
Newspapers: *Alarm, The*, 75; *Alton Observer*, 27, 30; *Chicago Daily News*, 83; *Chicago Daily Tribune*, 37; *Chicago Defender*, 112; *Chicago Legal News*, 74; *Chicago Sun-Times* building, *139*; *Chicago Tribune*, 46, 64, 69, 70, 71, 111, 115, 136, 175, 186, 187; *Illinois Herald*, 26; *Illinois Intelligencer*, 26; *Socialist, The*, 75; Tribune Tower, *139*
North Chicago Street Railway System, 81
Northeastern Illinois Planning Commission, 173, 175
Northern Illinois, 10, 55, 57, 61, 91-92, 178; small towns, 107-109. *See also specific*

cities; Quad Cities
Northwest Ordinance, 21
Northwest Territory, 21, 22, 52, 58

Oak Ridge Cemetery, 38; Lincoln's Tomb, 223
Ogden, William B., 61, 62
Oglesby, Richard J., *100*
O'Hare, Edward "Butch," 44
O'Hare International Airport, 43-44, 123, 124,
    129, *130-131*, 142, 143
Oil and gas production, 16, 49, 198, 214;
    decline of, 215
Oldenburg, Claes: Chicago public sculpture, 157
O'Leary, Kate, 69
Oliver, Joe "King," 86
Olmsted, Frederick Law, 172, 195
O'Neill, Lottie, 102, *107*
Orchard Place, 43

Paleo-Indians, 16-17, 56-57
Panic of 1837, 61
Palmer family: Bertha, 66, *67*; John M., *36*,
    100; Potter, 64, 66, 67
Parker, Ely S., *98*, *99*, 100
Parks and conservation areas, 122; Cave-in-
    Rock, 218, *221*; Giant City, 218; Grant, 63,
    128, *137*, 143, *151*, 157, *162-163*;
    Lincoln, 65, 69, *125*, *148-149*, 150, 167,
    238; Matteson State Park, *220*; Starved
    Rock State, 90, 91, 221; state-operated,
    218. *See also* Gardens
Parsons, Albert, *75*
Pennington, Lulu Shelton, 41
Performing arts, 84, 86, 87, 150-153;
    Auditorium Theater, 143, 151, 153;
    Belleville Philharmonic, 226; Chicago Blues
    Festival, *151*; Chicago Civic Opera, 151-
    152; Chicago Opera Association, 87;
    Chicago Opera Theater, 152; Chicago
    Shakespeare Theater, 138; Chicago
    Symphony Orchestra, 84, 119, 120-121,
    143, 150, 151; Chicago Theater, 152; Civic
    Opera House, 151; Civic Theater, 152;
    Ford Center for the Performing Arts, 153;
    Goodman Theater, 153; Grant Park Music
    Festival, 152; Hubbard Street Dance, 152;
    Illinois Chamber Orchestra, 226; Joffrey
    Ballet of Chicago, 152; Knox-Galesburg
    Symphony, 226; legitimate theater, 139,
    151; Lyric Opera of Chicago, 151, 152;
    Madison Theater, 225; Majestic Theater,
    153; Old Town School of Folk Music, 152;
    Orchestra Hall, 143, 151; Oriental Theater,
    153; Peoria Players Theater, 225; Peoria
    Symphony Orchestra, 225-226; Quincy
    Symphony, 226; Rockford Symphony, 226;
    Second City, 151, *153*; Shubert Theater,
    153; Steppenwolf Theatre Company, 153;
    University of Illinois Symphony
    (Champaign), 226. *See also* Entertainment
Picasso, Pablo: Chicago public sculpture, 157,
    160
Pierce, Bessie Louise, 63
Poetry: A Magazine of Verse, 10, 81
Pontiac (Ottawa chief), 20
Pope, Nathaniel, *21*, 26, 35

Pounds Hollow Lake, 49
Powell, John Wesley, 229
Powell, Paul, 202
Prairie du Rocher village, 19, 219
Prentiss, Benjamin, *35*, 36
Prohibition, crime and, 83
Pullman, George, 79, 80
Pullman (rail car manufacturer), 136, 137
Pullman Strike, 77, 79

Quad Cities, 103-104
Quaker Oats, 136

Racial unrest, 41-42
Railroads, 10, 31-32, 61, 62, 142, 204, 211,
    232; Amtrak, 142, 204-205; Burlington,
    104, 106; Burlington Santa Fe, 91, 104;
    Chicago, Aurora & Elgin, 186, 194;
    Chicago, Burlington & Quincy, 179, 195;
    Chicago, Milwaukee, St. Paul & Pacific,
    179; Chicago, North Shore & Milwaukee,
    186; Chicago and Northwestern, 179;
    Chicago & Rock Island Railroad, 232;
    Chicago Great Western Railway, 186; city
    growth and, 32; Elgin & Belvidere, 193;
    Galena and Chicago Union, 60, 62, 106,
    179; Illinois and Michigan Central depot,
    61; Illinois Central, 31-32, 39, *63*, 106,
    171, 179; Illinois Central construction, *30-
    31*; Military Tract, 91; Northern Cross, 31;
    Pioneer, The, 62; Rock Island, 107; Santa
    Fe, 136; Wisconsin Central, 181
Rand, Sally, *86*
Ray, Charles, 71
Raymond, B.W., 106
Reagan, Ronald, 110, *204*, 229
Reconstruction, 100
Recreation, 190-191; amusement parks, 191;
    gambling casinos, 190; horse racing, 190,
    191. *See also* Entertainment; Performing
    arts; Sports
Reiner, Fritz, 150
Religion: Baptists, 22; Catholic missionaries,
    19, 89-90, 91; Methodists, 22; Protestant
    clergy, 22. *See also* Mormons
Restaurants and restaurant industry, 139,
    166-167; Gibsons, *128*; Le Francais, 175;
    suburban, 175; Tall Grass, 175
Revels, Hiram, 229
Reynolds, John, 93
Rim Rock, 17
Riverbank Laboratories, 188
"River rats," 197
River roads, 218-223; Great River Road, 43,
    217, 218-219; Ohio River Scenic Byway,
    43, 218. *See also* River walks
Rivers: Chicago, 51, 52, 53, 55, 56, *57*, 58,
    59, 60, 62, 80, 115, 120, 123, 124, 127-
    128, 138, 178, 179, 187, 235; Cache,
    218; Calumet, 124; Cumberland, 37; Des
    Plaines, 51, 56, 57, 62, 80, 89, 106, 107,
    178, 186, 187, 195; Du Page, 178; Fox,
    18-19, 106, 178, 186, 187, 188; Illinois,
    10, 15, 16, 17, 18, 43, 51, 54, 57, 59, 62,
    80, 89, 90, 91, 92, 104, 107, 205, 221;
    Kankakee, 106; Mississippi, 15, 16, 18, 19,

21, 22, 28, 38, 43, 51, 54, 55, 57, 59,
    61, 89, 90, 91, 92, 93, 94, 95, 103, 104,
    110, 114, 123, 124, 197, 199, 202, 205,
    208, 217, 218, 219, 221, 226, 233; Ohio,
    15, 16, 18, 19, 20, 21, 22, 23, 24, 25,
    26, 27, 28, 31, 37, 43, 200, 217, 218;
    Rock, 93, 94, 95, 103, 104, 107; Saline,
    16, 27; Tennessee, 18, 19, 37; Wabash,
    16, 26; West Du Page, 187; Wisconsin, 19
Riverview (amusement) Park, 191
River walks, 178, 187
Roads and highways, 27, 42-43, 142, 197,
    204, 211, 214, 232, 233; Cumberland,
    28; East-West Tollway, 180; Highway 14,
    42; Highway 9, 42; Highway 1, 42;
    Highway 13, 42; Highway 30, 28;
    Highway 34, 23; Highway 3, 42;
    Highway 2, 42; I-80, 197, 204, 211;
    I-88, 211; I-55, 56, 211, 214; I-57, 106;
    I-90, 204; I-70, 28, 204; National Road,
    28; plank roads, 62; Tri-State Tollway, 54;
    U.S. 66, 42
Roche, Martin, 72
Rocheblave, Philippe de, 20
Rock Island Arsenal, 103, *104-105*
Root, Barnabas, 229
Root, John Wellborn, 72, 155; Rookery, 72
Root & Cady, 65
Rose, Sara, 25
Rosenwald, Julius, 83, 142
Route 66 Raceway, 191
Ryan, George H., 204, *205*

St. Clair, Arthur, 21
Salford, Mary, 102
Salt, 26-27
Sanford Manufacturing Co., 180
Sara Lee, 136, 137-138
Scammon, J. Young, *60*
Scott, Dred, 103
Scott Air Force Base, 45, 226
Scott Field, 48, 49; Army Air Corps troops,
    48; flying school, 43
Sears, Richard, 83
Sears, Roebuck and Co., 81, 83, 86, 136, 142,
    179; mail-order homes, 109
Sears Tower, 156, 157, *159*
Shawnee Hills, 15
Shawnee National Forest, 217, 218;
    Garden of the Gods, 217, *221*. *See also*
    Trail of Tears
Shedd Aquarium, John G., 143, *144-145*
Shelton family, 41
Sherman, William T., 101
Shopping: discount houses, 176; Fox
    Valley retail complex, 179; giant discount
    stores, 176; regional malls, 175, 176,
    179-180; supermarkets, 176; Water Tower
    Place, 167. *See also specific stores*;
    Merchandising/retail
Simon, Paul, 108
Six Flags Great America, 191; rollercoaster,
    192-193
Skyscrapers, 121, *122*, 155, 156, 194; first,
    72; Home Insurance Building, 72, 155;
    Monadnock Building, 155

Slavery, 34; movement to outlaw, 30
Small, Len, 42, 114
Smith, Joseph, 95, 221
Smith, Julia Holmes, 102
Snyder, Francis, 108
Soldier Field, 143, 155
Solti, Georg, 150, 151
Southern Illinois, 10, 28, 29, 39, 41, 43, 49, 198, 214
Spertus Institute of Jewish Studies, 147
Sports, 153-155, 190-191; auto-racing, 190-191; baseball, 153, 190; basketball, 153, 155; football, 153, 155; hockey, 153, 190; soccer, 155. *See also names of specific sports teams and venues*
Sportsman's Park, 190
Stagecoaches, 27, 43
Stagg, Amos Alonzo, 158
Staley Manufacturing Company, A.E., 208
Starr, Ellen Gates, 75, 76
Starved Rock, 104, 216-217
State Farm Insurance, 205, 208
Stateville Penitentiary, 107
Stead, William T., 80
Stelle, John, 114
Stevenson II, Adlai Ewing, *108*, 113, 114, 115, 204
Stewart, Marjabelle Young, 108-109
Stillman, Isaiah, 93
Stirling, Thomas, 20
Stone Container Building, *158*
Stony Island, 55
Suburbs, Chicago, 169, 197, 235, 236; autos and, 176-178; colleges and universities, 182-186; cornfield, 169; corporate head-quarters in, 180; drive-in architecture, 179; expressway, 169; first, 171; growth, 201; housing, 169-170; industrial, 169; mall towns, 169; mansions, 170; office companies, 180-182; old railroad, 169, 171; population figures, 172-173, 201; science and technology corridor, 180-181; slums, 170; telecommunications industry, 180; tract houses, 170; uniformity, 175-176; water supply, 233. *See also* Cities and towns
Sullivan, Louis, 72, 155; Auditorium, 72, 153, 155; Carson Pirie Scott and Company store, 72, 155-156, 166; Chicago Stock Exchange, 72, 155; Columbian Exposition Transportation Building, 72, *78*; Garrick Theatre, 72
Sullivan, William Leo, *83*
Swearingen, James S., *52*
Swift, Gustavus F., 65

Taft, Lorado: Chicago public statues and foun-tains, 157
Taylor, Zachary, 93, *94*, 99
Technical/trade schools, 186
Technoburb, 169. *See also* Suburbs, Chicago
Tecumseh, *25*
Telephone and Data Systems Inc., 136
Tellabs, 180
Temperance movement, 102
Thompson, James, 60, 202, 204

Thompson, William "Big Bill," 83
Three Worlds of Santa's Village, 191
Todd, John, 21
"Tokyo Rose." *See* D'Aquino, Iva Ikuko Toguri
Tourism, 215-218. *See also* Museums; Parks; Recreation
Township and range system, 24-25
Trail of Tears, 31, 217-218
Trails movement/system, 177-178, 186-187; origins, 186
Transportation, 210-211, 214, 232-233, 235; Chicago, 62-63, 81, 123-128; Chicago pub-lic, 123; freight train, *207*; "L" train, *132-133*; water taxi, *136*. *See also specific forms of transportation*
Treaties: of Chicago, 61, 94; of Fontainebleau, 20; of Greenville, 58; of Paris, 58
Turner, Jonathan Baldwin, *32*, 33

U.S. Constitution: 19th Amendment, 10; 17th Amendment, 34; 13th Amendment, 10, 38
U.S. land offices, 24-25; Kaskaskia, 24; Shawneetown, 27; Vincennes, 24
Underground Railroad, Galesburg and, 104
Union Station (Chicago), 142
Union Stock Yards, 63, 65
United Airlines, 181
United Center, 157, 236
Unity Temple (Unitarian Church), 195
University of Chicago Settlement House, 80
Urban sprawl, 173-176, 230-231

Valpariso Moraine, 54, 55
Van Osdel, John, 71
Vaux, Calvert, 195
Voyageurs, 57; American Fur Company, 59. *See also* Fur trade; Fur traders

Walgreen, 181
Walker, Dan, 49, 202
Ward, Aaron Montgomery, 128
War of 1812, 25-26, 51, 91, 93, 103-104
Washburne, Elihu, 99
Water Tower, *11*
Watts, May T., 186
Wells, William, 58
Wells-Barnett, Ida B., *78*
Western Cartridge plant, 49
West Jacksonville School District, 33
White City (amusement park), 191
Willard, Frances Elizabeth, *101*, 102
Wisconsin Glacier, 15, 16, 54, 198
Wisconsin Steel, 136
Wolf Point Tavern, 56, *57*
Woman's Christian Temperance Union, 101, 102
Woman's Crusade Against Alcoholism, 102
Women: business, 74; in Civil War, 101-102; politicians, 102; temperance activists, 102; writers, 10, 81, 84
Women's rights, beginnings of, 10
Wood, Robert E., 86, 179
Workmen's compensation insurance, first, 10, 39
Works Progress Administration (WPA), 49;

murals, 157
World's Columbian Exposition, 76-77, 79, 85, 102, 142; Chicago Day, 76; first Ferris wheel, 138; first U.S. Commemorative coin, *78*; location, 77; Transportation Building, 72, *78*
World War I, 43, 45, 48, 67, 83, 104, 106, 109, 110-112, 113, 188; Camp Grant, 111; Camp Zachary Taylor, 111; casualties, 111; Illinois casualties, 48; 33rd (Prairie) Division, 48, 111; training center, 48
World War II, 44, 48, 49, 86-87, 108, 114, 115, 124, 136, 152, 164, 173, 176, 184, 192, 200, 206, 214-215; Chicago's contri-bution, 86; Manhattan Project, 180-181; 33rd Division, 49
Wright, Frank Lloyd, 72, *73*, 122, 156, 188, 195, 225; Prairie School, 73, 122, 156, 195; Robie House, 156, *195*; structures, 192
Wright brothers, 10, 43, 44, 227
Wrigley Field, 153, *154*
Writers, authors, and poets, 10, 81; Margaret Anderson, 81; Sherwood Anderson, 81; Margaret Ayer Barnes, 84; Frank Baum, 52; Saul Bellow, 10; Gwendolyn Brooks, 10, *112*; Edgar Rice Burroughs, 81; Willa Cather, 81, 84; Chicago-area, 52; Robert Cromie, 70; Theodore Dreiser, 52, 79, 81; Finley Peter Dunne, 81; Janet Ayer Fairbanks, 84; Edna Ferber, 84; Henry B. Fuller, 52; Hamlin Garland, 81; Ben Hecht, 81; Ernest Hemingway, 10; Ring Lardner, 81; Vachel Lindsay, 10, 46, 81; Owen Lovejoy, 108; Edgar Lee Masters, 10, 81, 107-108; Mike Royko, 10; Carl Sandburg, 10, 72, *73*, 81, *83*, 84, 104, 108, 119; Studs Terkel, 10

Yerkes, Charles T., 80, 81
Young, Brigham, 95, 221
Young, S. Glenn, 39

Zinc, 54
Zoos and wildlife preserves, 188-190: Blackberry Farm-Pioneer Village, 189-190; Brookfield, 150, 189; Cosley, 189; down-state, 225; Garfield Farm Museum, 189; Glen Oak, 225; Henson Robinson, 225; Lambs Farm, 190; Lincoln Park, *150*; Little Red Schoolhouse Nature Center, 190; Miller Park, 225; Scovill Children's, 225; Tyrrell Trailside, 190; Willowbrook Wildlife Center, 190